THE WARTIME PRESIDENT

Terry M. Moe

CHICAGO SERIES ON INTERNATIONAL AND
DOMESTIC INSTITUTIONS
*Edited by William G. Howell
and Jon Pevehouse*

OTHER BOOKS IN THE SERIES

*The Judicial Power of the Purse: How
Courts Fund National Defense in
Times of Crisis*
by Nancy C. Staudt (2011)

*Securing Approval: Domestic Politics
and Multilateral Authorization for War*
by Terrence L. Chapman (2011)

After the Rubicon: Congress, Presidents, and the Politics of Waging War
by Douglas L. Kriner (2010)

THE **WARTIME** PRESIDENT

Executive Influence and the Nationalizing Politics of Threat

William G. Howell,

Saul P. Jackman,

and

Jon C. Rogowski

THE UNIVERSITY OF CHICAGO PRESS
Chicago and London

William G. Howell is the Sydney Stein Professor in American Politics at the Harris School of Public Policy Studies and professor of political science in the College at the University of Chicago. He is the author or coauthor of several books, including, most recently, *While Dangers Gather: Congressional Checks on Presidential War Powers.* **Saul P. Jackman** is a postdoctoral fellow in the Center for the Study of Democratic Institutions at Vanderbilt University. **Jon C. Rogowski** is assistant professor in the Department of Political Science at Washington University in St. Louis.

The University of Chicago Press, Chicago 60637
The University of Chicago Press, Ltd., London
© 2013 by The University of Chicago
All rights reserved. Published 2013.
Printed in the United States of America

22 21 20 19 18 17 16 15 14 13   1 2 3 4 5

ISBN-13: 978-0-226-04825-3   (cloth)
ISBN-13: 978-0-226-04839-0   (paper)
ISBN-13: 978-0-226-04842-0   (e-book)

Library of Congress Cataloging-in-Publication Data

Howell, William G.
    The wartime president : executive influence and the nationalizing politics of threat / William G. Howell, Saul P. Jackman and Jon C. Rogowski.
        pages ; cm — (Chicago series on international and domestic institutions)
    Includes bibliographical references and index.
    ISBN 978-0-226-04825-3 (cloth : alkaline paper) — ISBN 978-0-226-04839-0 (paperback : alkaline paper) — ISBN 978-0-226-04842-0 (e-book)   1. War and emergency powers.   2. War and emergency powers — United States — History — 20th century.   3. Executive power — United States.   4. Politics and war.   I. Jackman, Saul P.   II. Rogowski, Jon C.   III. Title.   IV. Series: Chicago series on international and domestic institutions.
    JF256.H69 2013
    342.73'062 — dc23
                                                                            2012051427

For our parents

CONTENTS

PART V: APPENDIXES

TABLES AND FIGURES

FIGURES

PREFACE

This is a book about the wartime power that presidents wield at home. It examines how presidents manage to enact domestic and foreign policy during war that would be unattainable during peace. And it investigates what it is about war that makes this happen.

The issue of presidential war powers once stood at the very center of political science. Indeed, the conventional wisdom about the topic was forged in the 1940s and 1950s by an assembly of American politics scholars who recognized the deep and lasting effects of war on the American presidency. As Clinton Rossiter argued, it is no less than an "axiom of political science" that "great emergencies in the life of a constitutional state bring an increase in executive power and prestige, always at least temporarily, more often than not permanently."[1]

Since Rossiter penned these words, however, progress has largely stalled. Scholars have tended to assume a relationship (and a powerful one at that) between war and presidential power, despite significant changes in how the nation wages war abroad, in the relative balance of power (during peace and war) between the various branches of government, and the absence of any quantitative evidence that supports causal inferences. War, as such, has become something of an afterthought to presidency scholars; and among scholars of interbranch relations, it makes nary an appearance.[2] Consequently, we know very little about how—or indeed if—wars alter the balance of powers across the various branches of government—that is, whether wars genuinely do exalt presidential power. No existing theory explains why, for instance members of Congress would vote with the

1. Rossiter 1956, 64–65.
2. The issue of war, to be sure, has not been entirely neglected by scholars of American politics. Indeed, in the last several decades they have devoted ample attention to the ways in which war reconstitutes states and state building activities (Bensel 1990; Saldin 2011; Tilly 1975, 1992); to the impact of war on domestic public opinion (Berinsky 2009); and to the domestic politics that inform decisions about whether and when the United States wages war abroad (Howell and Pevehouse 2007; Kriner 2010).

president in war when in peace they would vote against him. Empirically, we lack any systematic evidence that, as a matter of course, they do.

This book addresses both of these deficiencies. It develops theory that clarifies the capacity of wars to augment presidential influence over public policy, and it presents the results from a wide range of empirical tests, each explicitly designed to cohere with the theory and to overcome standard identification problems. What we find does not corroborate the claims of any single scholar who has reflected on war's contributions to presidential power. Some wars, we show, do in fact exalt presidential power. But others do not. Importantly, then, our theory offers a basis for understanding why this is so.

For a host of reasons, presidential power may expand during war. Wars may ignite the unilateral powers of the presidency. During war, Congress may grant bureaucratic agencies, staffed by employees of the president's choosing, more autonomy to conduct the country's business. Judges may be more willing to uphold presidential actions or policies that would not pass constitutional muster during peacetime. The Senate may be more willing to confirm a president's judicial nominees. Congress as a whole, meanwhile, may enact (indeed, has enacted, and by the hundreds) emergency laws that trigger new presidential powers during times of war. And during war the House and Senate may fully indulge their habit of delegating new responsibilities, and with them new powers, to the executive branch.

We do not rule out any such possibilities. Indeed, we fully expect that wars may enhance many sources of presidential influence. Rather than canvass all potential sources, we probe deeply into one. In particular, we focus on the propensity of members of Congress to vote in ways that more closely approximate presidential preferences in war than during peace. If Hamilton is correct that "it is the nature of war to increase the executive at the expense of the legislative authority,"[3] then we ought to observe members of Congress more closely adhering to the president's policy wishes in war than in peace. In this book, we theorize about the relevance of war for congressional voting behavior. Then, empirically, we investigate changes in members' voting behavior between periods of war and peace.

Bear in mind the stakes of this enterprise. Should neither our theory nor our empirical tests yield compelling reasons to believe that presiden-

---

3. Rossiter 1999 [1961], 36.

tial influence increases during war, we cannot dismiss Rossiter, Hamilton, and their intellectual brethren out of hand. The true origins of presidential influence during war may simply lie in other domains of public policy making. The lack of corroborative evidence of one source of presidential influence, after all, does not rule out the possibility of other sources. On the other hand, if we do find that members of Congress cast votes that more closely reflect presidential preferences during war than they do during peace, we may have identified a feature of American politics with far-reaching consequences. After all, the potential source of presidential influence that we investigate is particularly exacting. In other areas of research, scholars have posited the existence of policy influence without offering any reasons to believe that members of Congress actually change their voting behavior.[4] Observing wartime changes in congressional voting behavior, therefore, should only heighten our expectations of other kinds of political adjustments that favor the president.

By now, it should be clear that this is not a book about the president's ability to wage war. It does not explore the plainly obvious contention that during wars presidents do things that they do not do during times of peace—namely, they commit troops to battle, renegotiate relations with allies and adversaries abroad, and eventually broker the terms of peace. This is well known and requires no further exposition here. Instead, this book critically examines the proposition that during wars presidents can exercise a measure of influence over goings-on at home that eludes them during peace—that is, that presidents can leverage wars to advance policies that have more to do with the lives of everyday citizens than the mobilization of troops on the battlefront. Hence, we go to some lengths to demonstrate that presidential wartime powers extend to policy processes governed primarily by Congress (e.g., the appropriations process) and policy domains that only tangentially relate to the war (e.g., domestic policy). Though our basic conclusions are unlikely to surprise, the breadth of our evidence of wartime influence may. During periods of war, members of Congress regularly vote with the president, and they do so on policies that involve both foreign and domestic issues.

This book unfolds in four main sections. After considering what three of the most famous twentieth-century presidency scholars—Clinton

---

4. As just one example, consider the ongoing debate about the sources of interest group influence. Most scholars concede that interest group activities do not induce changes in actual congressional votes, but rather increase the odds that different interests receive an actual hearing.

Rossiter, Edward Corwin, and Arthur Schlesinger Jr.—had to say about war's contributions to presidential power, Chapter 1 reflects briefly on contemporary conceptions of presidential war powers. The chapter then takes stock of the arguments and evidence in support of their contentions. After clarifying points of agreement and disagreement, Chapter 1 goes on to survey the existing empirical and theoretical bases for the central argument that wars augment presidential power. Both, it turns out, are wanting. Empirical support for the contention comes almost entirely from extended narratives of wartime activities at home. To date, no one has offered a proper theory that identifies why presidents should exert this influence over domestic and foreign policy during war that eludes them during peace.

Beginning in Part II, this book makes its own contributions. In Chapter 2, we develop precisely the kind of theory that the existing literature on presidential war powers—which simultaneously paints with extraordinarily broad brushstrokes and eschews theoretical rigor for historical detail—neglects. This theory suggests reasons why members of Congress cast votes that more closely approximate presidential preferences during war than during peace. It does so, however, without explicitly referencing war. Cast in general terms, the Policy Priority Model examines the interactions between a president and a representative member of Congress, both of whom have well-defined preferences over policy outcomes but also lack information about how policies translate into outcomes. Unlike the existing class of bargaining models, ours also admits the possibility that one policy can translate into multiple outcomes, and, moreover, that the relevance of these outcomes differs for presidents and members of Congress. After demonstrating the existence of a closed form solution to the model, we recover its key comparative statics: members of Congress are more likely to support the president when they attach greater importance to national outcomes; they are less likely to do so when they care more about local outcomes.

Chapter 3 links the Policy Priority Model to the empirical tests that follow. It specifies how key theoretic parameters relate to war. It offers a definition of war that focuses on U.S. involvement in the largest military conflicts since World War II. The bulk of the chapter then distinguishes among these wars. In particular, it argues that two wars—World War II and Afghanistan—radically altered the importance that members of Congress assigned to local and national outcomes, whereas the other wars that we consider—Korea, Vietnam, and the Persian Gulf—had a more modest impact on the evaluative criteria that members of Congress relied on when deciding how to vote. Hence, we expect to find the largest and most consistent evidence of a more expansive wartime presidency during World War II and Afghanistan, and more modest effects for the other wars. The chapter concludes with a discussion of how our theory's predictions differ from other accounts of the relationship between war and presidential power.

With Part III, and the book's fourth chapter, we begin the empirical testing. In this chapter, we focus on appropriations, which offer the clearest fidelity to the Policy Priority Model while also addressing a host of identification problems that have plagued previous research on presidential power. To be sure, each empirical model offers only partial solutions to these problems; hence, no single test in this chapter, or anywhere in this book, should be considered dispositive. In the main, however, we find that final appropriations more closely approximate presidential proposals (and by extension, though not without complication, presidential preferences) during war than during peace. Moreover, we find the largest effects in World War II and Afghanistan, just as the Policy Priority Model predicts. These effects do not appear to be an artifact of any particular characterization of the dependent variable, any single model specification, or strategic proposal making by the president. Additionally, we find evidence of a wartime effect on both domestic and foreign policy appropriations.

Chapter 5 turns to roll call votes. Rather than examine the subset of bills on which presidents have chosen to take a public position, as most previous scholars have done, we study the universe of roll call votes in those congresses during which our wars either began or ended. More specifically, we track changes in individual members' voting behavior when the nation either entered or exited war. At the outset of the war in Afghanistan, when a Republican president held office, members voted significantly more conservatively than they did before; at the outset of World War II, when a Democrat held office, members voted more liberally. In the other wars, we did not find consistent evidence that members shifted in the ideological direction of the president, but at the termination of all these wars members routinely shifted away from the president.

In Chapters 6 and 7 we present a batch of case studies that reveal the channels through which foreign wars can affect domestic policy debates. Those that appear in Chapter 6, in the main, conform to the primary arguments and evidence that preceded them. Hence, in Wilson and Roosevelt's broad and radical domestic policy achievements during World Wars I and II, and in George W. Bush's efforts to strengthen border security, we find presidents exerting influence in war that assuredly would elude them in peace. The cases in Chapter 7, meanwhile, issue various challenges—some minor, others more substantial—to the basic story we want to tell. We see the federal government finally gaining entry into education policy at the moment the issue was framed in terms of national security rather than local concerns about race, housing, and religion—this moment, though, came during peace rather than war. We see Johnson's efforts to cautiously escalate in Vietnam in order to safeguard, rather than extend, his peacetime policy achievements. And, finally, we see Bush misgauging the extent to which ongoing wars abroad would allow him to recast a debate at home about the future of Social Security.

Our final chapter concludes our discussion. After summarizing our main findings and outlining areas for continued research, we reflect upon the core theoretical and empirical lessons of this book for a war on terror, the prosecution of two wars simultaneously, and changes in congressional voting behavior over the course of any single war. We end by reiterating the single most important lesson of this book: when politics focuses on national outcomes, as it so often does during war, presidential power expands portentously; when politics becomes intensely local, as it sometimes does, presidential influence reliably diminishes; and in between are the familiar politics in which presidents make do as best they can.

Finally, for the truly tireless reader, we offer a series of appendixes that include more technical treatments of the theory and numerous supplementary analyses to the main empirical chapters.

ACKNOWLEDGMENTS

This is not the book we intended to write. Not even close. We set out to write a short book that challenged the conventional view about war and presidential power, one that empirically demonstrated that our views about the stimulating effects of military action on executive influence were grossly inflated. We then planned to decry the utter lack of theory within the conventional view, theory that might explain why checks on presidential power at home might slacken during times of war. The resulting book would have been a useful corrective to the predominant arguments about the linkages between war and presidential power that, in our estimation, were overwrought, unsubstantiated, and undertheorized. This should be simple enough, we presumed.

The data, however, proved uncooperative. Indeed, the closer we looked, the more convinced we became that the empirical evidence from the last eighty years of American history confirmed neither the conventional view nor our skepticism of it. It became clear that at least some wars had the potential to augment the president's influence over both foreign and domestic policy. We soon recognized that just as the conventional view lacked a theory for why all major wars would augment the president's power, we lacked a theory for why a subset of wars would. Thus, an altogether new front to this book project opened up, and we began thinking about the plausible mechanisms through which wars might alter policy negotiations between Congress and the president.

In the ensuing years, a model of interbranch negotiations emerged that conformed with the empirical regularities that we already had uncovered, and suggested new avenues for continued empirical research. The culmination of these labors is a much longer book, one that makes a very different argument than we expected to produce, and presents an unanticipated set of empirical findings. But for the discoveries made along the way, and for the professional partnerships formed, this has been an immensely more rewarding book to write than we ever anticipated.

Writing this book, we have accrued some rather substantial debts—debts that are owed to colleagues, foundations, and friends alike. Over the last several years, chapters from this book were presented at workshops held at Duke University, Harvard University, the Massachusetts Institute of Technology, New York University, Northwestern University, Stanford University, Texas A&M, the University of California at Berkeley and San Diego, the University of Chicago, the University of Notre Dame, the University of Texas, Vanderbilt University, Washington University, and Yale University, as well as the annual meetings of the Midwest Political Science Association and the American Political Science Association. For especially helpful feedback, we thank Scott Ashworth, Adam Berinsky, Chris Berry, Ethan Bueno de Mesquita, George Edwards, Linda Fowler, Dan Galvin, Simon Jackman, Ruth Krucheli, Terry Moe, Eric Oliver, Eric Schickler, Betsy Sinclair, Sean Theriault, and Rob Van Houweling. Chuck Cameron, Doug Kriner, and Paul Peterson read early drafts of the book and provided extraordinarily helpful comments. Chris Berry clarified a great deal about the empirical tests of budgetary politics. In March 2011, this book was the subject of a one-day workshop at the University of Chicago. At this event, Steve Callander, Chuck Cameron, Brandice Canes-Wrone, Keith Krehbiel, and Nolan McCarty offered still more outstanding suggestions on how the manuscript might be improved. At the University of Chicago Press, much is owed to John Trynesti and John Donohue for their steady guidance and great support.

For able research assistance, we thank Faisal Ahmed, Alex Bass, David Brent, Hannah Cook, Colleen Dolan, Amir Fairdosi, Levi Foster, Robert Gulotty, Molly Jackman, Tana Johnson, Chad Levinson, Ari Shaw, Mateusz Tomkowiak, Thomas Wood, and Anton Zeitsman. Jim Golby provided extensive help in the research and early drafting of the first two case studies in Chapter 7. Saul Jackman and Jon Rogowski started out as research assistants on this project, but both made such foundational contributions that they were brought on as full coauthors.

For financial assistance, we thank the National Science Foundation (award number SES-1022764), the Bradley Foundation, the Program on Political Institutions at the University of Chicago, and the Sydney Stein family. This book was conceived, drafted, abandoned, and then reconceived at the Center for Advanced Study in the Behavioral Sciences at Stanford University, where Howell was on leave during the 2009–2010 academic year. A special thanks is given to the public library in Woodward, Oklahoma, where significant portions of this book were written.

Portions of this manuscript previously appeared in the following articles: William G. Howell, 2011, "Presidential Power in War," *Annual Review of Political Science* 14:89–105; William G. Howell and Tana Johnson, 2009, "War's Contributions to Presidential Power," in George C. Edwards III and William G. Howell, eds., *Handbook of the American Presidency*, Oxford University Press; William G. Howell and Jon C. Rogowski, 2013, "War, the Presidency, and Legislative Voting Behavior," *American Journal of Political Science* 57:150–66; William G. Howell, Saul P. Jackman, and Jon C. Rogowski, 2012, "The Wartime President: Insights, Lessons, and Opportunities for Continued Investigation," *Presidential Studies Quarterly* 42:791–810; and William G. Howell and Saul P. Jackman, forthcoming, "Inter-Branch Bargaining over Policy with Multiple Outcomes," *American Journal of Political Science*.

Finally, this book is dedicated to our parents, Susan Howell, David Howell, Mary Jackman, and, in memoriam, Robert Jackman and Jean and John Rogowski.

PART I

Background

CHAPTER 1

War and the American Presidency

Wars contribute mightily to presidential power, so statesmen and scholars have told us for centuries. The microfoundations for such claims are not always clear, and systematic evidence that wars, all wars, necessarily exalt presidential power remains in short supply. But before clarifying the theory and empirically evaluating the claims, we would do well to survey the existing intellectual landscape, to trace the broad contours of an argument that has stood at the very center of American political debate for the better part of two centuries.

Among the Founders, such arguments established a primary justification for vesting Congress, rather than the president, with the power to wage war—lest the nation quickly devolve back into monarchical rule. The exigencies of the nation's greatest wars—one civil, two world—encouraged subsequent presidents to articulate ever more expansive readings of their Article II powers. For scholars in the mid-twentieth century, the relationship between war and presidential power had become so self-evident that it warranted the status of "law" or axiom. With the threats of terrorism and state failure shaking the nation's conscience, some advocates of a unitary theory of the executive branch now insist that national security threats are so endemic and so pervasive that divisions between peacetime and wartime powers and domestic and foreign policy influence no longer make sense. With greater knowledge of foreign policy threats and the singular capacity to address them, presidents, it seems to some, demand continual deference during war.

Ideas about war and presidential power did not progress neatly, with each engaging and, where necessary, building off the insights of those that had preceded it. Disagreements regularly surfaced about a wide range of particulars—about the relevant constitutional justifications for wartime powers, assessments of the precedential value of specific wartime acts, definitions of judicial and congressional deference, and the like. Moreover, few writers bothered to hone the logic or build the evidentiary basis for the claim that presidents can, as a matter of course, accomplish things in war that would necessarily stymie them in peace. Consequently, contemporary arguments about war and presidential power are no more complete and no more exact than those offered centuries ago.

In the main, however, the arguments have been consistent. They can be reduced to the following claim: wars exalt presidential power. Or, more exactly, when the nation is at war, the president can (some would also say must) advance policy initiatives at home that during peace would surely fail. Over the last 250 years, this message has constituted much more than conventional wisdom—conventional wisdom, after all, typically presumes the possibility of contending (albeit inferior) schools of thought. On the matter of war and presidential power, however, all the greatest commentators on the American system of governance have converged upon a single view.

Going back to the nation's founding, political scientists have worried that through war presidents would find the means to exalt their power more generally. As Alexander Hamilton recognized in *Federalist* No. 8, "it is the nature of war to increase the executive at the expense of legislative authority."[1] Echoing these sentiments, in his fourth Helvidius pamphlet Madison argued, "war is in fact the true nurse of executive aggrandizement." To justify the conclusion, Madison noted:

> In war, a physical force is to be created; and it is the executive will, which is to direct it. In war, the public treasures are to be unlocked; and it is the executive hand that is to dispense them. In war, the honours and emoluments of office are to be multiplied; and it is the executive patronage under which they are to be enjoyed. It is in war, finally, that laurels are to be gathered; and it is the executive brow they are to encircle.[2]

Hamilton and Madison, of course, disagreed about the merits of a powerful presidency. But on their particular assessment of war's contribution to presidential power, the two adversaries stood together. On the basis of such judgment, they opted to vest Congress with the authority to declare war.

Those who opposed the Constitution at the time, of course, took such arguments even further. For them, the assignment of almost any war powers to the presidency inexorably led not merely to the expansion of executive power, but to the unraveling of a republic into tyranny. The *Anti-Federalist*

1. Rossiter 1999 [1961], 36.
2. Frisch 2007, 87.

Papers bristle with condemnation against an "elective king" whose war powers permit and even encourage the concentration of virtually all government authority. Writing under the pseudonym Cato, George Clinton recognized the president as "the generalissimo of the nation, [who] of course has the command and control of the army, navy and militia; he is the general conservator of the peace of the union." By taking the nation to war, Clinton insisted, the president would brandish powers that no government of a free people should retain. "Will not the exercise of these powers therefore tend either to the establishment of a vile and arbitrary aristocracy or monarchy?"[3]

Primary among the Anti-Federalists' fears was the possibility that the president, as commander in chief, would use the army as an instrument of his own empowerment. Many of the controversies surrounding the existence of a standing army and the subservience of state militias to a federal militia stemmed from abiding concerns that a federal military would become the arm of the president's dominion. Though Congress might ostensibly have the authority to declare war, who had the power to stop a president intent on using the military as he saw fit? Speaking before the Virginia ratifying convention, Patrick Henry intoned:

> Away with your President, we shall have a King: the army will salute him Monarch; your militia will leave you and assist in making him King, and fight against you: and what have you to oppose this force? What will then become of you and your rights? Will not absolute despotism ensue?[4]

With the military and through war, Henry and his fellow Anti-Federalists warned, presidents would trample upon every individual right that the Constitution ostensibly protected.

Anti-Federalists and Federalists, of course, interpreted the Constitution very differently, and they held wildly divergent views about the consequences of ratification. Anti-Federalists expected that presidents would exploit their narrowly defined powers, and therefore the states ought to reject the Constitution. Federalists pointed out that the Constitution granted the all-important decisions about war to Congress, and hence it deserved to be ratified. However, the two sides fundamentally agreed about the dangers of vesting excessive war powers in a single man, and they were deeply preoccupied by the possibility that through war a president might eventually become, for all intents and purposes, a king.

3. Storing 1981, 116.
4. Ketcham 2003, 214.

Nearly every subsequent generation of scholars has revisited the Founders' concerns that wars would exalt presidential power not merely on the battlefield but at home as well. Alexis de Tocqueville argued that the "first axiom of science" dictates:

> War does not always give over democratic communities to military government, but it must invariably and immeasurably increase the powers of civil government; it must almost compulsorily concentrate the direction of all men and the management of all things in the hands of the administration.[5]

Writing a half century later, James Bryce put it as follows:

> [Though] the direct domestic authority of the president is in time of peace very small ... [in war] it expands with portentous speed. Both as commander in chief of the army and navy, and as charged with the "faithful execution of the laws," the president is likely to assume all the powers which the emergency requires.[6]

In the words of Edward Corwin, whose views we examine in greater depth later in this chapter, the nation's greatest wars offer a clear lesson:

> The President's power as Commander-in-Chief has been transformed from a simple power of military command to a vast reservoir of indeterminate powers in time of emergency.[7]

According to the constitutional law experts Eric Posner and Adrian Vermeule:

> Because the executive is the only organ of government with the resources, power, and flexibility to respond to threats to national security, it is natural, inevitable, and desirable for power to flow to this branch of government. Congress rationally acquiesces; courts rationally defer.[8]

Says the contemporary champion of the unitary theory of the executive, John Yoo:

5. Tocqueville 1963 [1840], 2:268–269.
6. Bryce 1995 [1888], 1:48–49.
7. Corwin 1957 [1945], 261.
8. Posner and Vermeule 2007, 4. For a more general treatment of their views about presidential power, see Posner and Vermeule 2011.

War acts on executive power as an accelerant, causing it to burn hotter, brighter, and swifter.[9]

And on and on.

Within political science, the relationship between war and presidential power received its most careful attention in the mid-twentieth century. And no wonder. The devastation wrought by two world wars separated by little more than two decades demanded explanation. And so political scientists launched entirely new research agendas on security studies, international relations, and the domestic politics of war. Within this latter camp resided some extraordinarily influential scholars who argued that wars, particularly total wars, had utterly transformed the American presidency.

1.1 A Notion Expressed

For three of the most famous twentieth-century presidency scholars, Edward Corwin, Clinton Rossiter, and Arthur Schlesinger Jr., war stood at the very center of the American presidency. Individually, each of these three titans wrote prodigiously on the impact of war on our system of separated powers generally, and more particularly on the willingness of adjoining branches of government to actively promote presidential power during times of crisis.

Corwin devoted a significant portion of his masterwork *The President: Office and Powers* to the issue of presidential power during times of war, which he then followed up with a series of University of Michigan lectures published as *Total War and the Constitution*. Reflecting on the nation's three largest wars—the Civil War and the two world wars—Corwin saw the president's constitutional authority as being at its apex. Abraham Lincoln, Woodrow Wilson, and Franklin D. Roosevelt all flexed their Article II powers, and Congress and the courts steadfastly refused to stand in their way. Indeed, Corwin observed, Congress during these wars actively supplemented the president's constitutional powers with new statutory authority over a wide range of policy domains; and at least as long as troops remained in the field, the courts refused to interfere. Based on his reading of the historical record, Corwin concluded "the principal canons of

9. Yoo 2010, vii.

constitutional interpretation are in wartime set aside so far as concerns both the scope of national power and the capacity of the President to gather unto himself all constitutionally available powers in order the more effectively to focus them upon the task of the hour."[10] A wartime jurisprudence, one that looks considerably more kindly upon exercises of presidential power, supplants a peacetime jurisprudence for at least as long as American troops are fighting and dying.

Over the course of his career, Corwin appears to have been conflicted over whether presidential power promptly reverts to its prewar status when fighting at last ceases. Writing just a few months after the U.S. intervention into World War I, Corwin suggested that "in the heat of war the powers it confers are capable of expanding tremendously, but upon the restoration of normal conditions they shrink with equal rapidity."[11] If true, then those who worry about the state of the Constitution during war need only hasten the return of peace. Yet later in life, Corwin recognized that powers exercised during war may spill over into times of peace: "constitutional practices of wartime have molded the Constitution to a greater or less extent for peacetime as well."[12] Corwin further suggested that when presidents confront altogether new crises, they benefit from the powers claimed during past ones. "In each successive crisis the constitutional results of earlier crises reappear cumulatively and in magnified form."[13] New peaks of presidential power are reached with every successive presidency, as today's wartime president draws upon all the precedents of past wars, and tomorrow's president will add to that stockpile the actions and arguments asserted by today's.

The resulting increase in wartime presidential power may be steady, but it need not be precedent-setting. The precedent-setting value of some wars has been markedly greater than others. In this regard, Corwin distinguishes the Civil War from World Wars I and II. From Corwin's perspective, the Civil War, defined by Lincoln's fleeting incursions into the domestic polity and his continual homages to constitutional limits on presidential power, did not fundamentally alter the office of the presidency. But the two world wars, with their development of massive wartime administrations, sweeping claims of presidential power, and emergency delegations of authority, plainly did.

10. Corwin 1957 [1940], 262.
11. Corwin 1917, 153.
12. Corwin 1957 [1940], 262.
13. Ibid.

In even less qualified terms, Clinton Rossiter developed many of the same arguments. Trying to account for the astronomical rise of presidential power during the nation's first 175 years of history, Rossiter observed, "In such time, 'when the blast of war blows in our ears,' the President's power to command the forces swells out of all proportion to his other powers."[14] This influence, however, was hardly confined to the conduct of war. By Rossiter's account, it permeated policy domains that are only tangentially related to the war effort:

> As proof of this point, we need only think of the sudden expansion in power that the Presidency experienced under Lincoln as he faced the rebellion, under Wilson as he led us into a world war, or under Franklin Roosevelt as he called upon Congress to extend him "broad Executive power to wage war" against depression. Each of these men left the Presidency a stronger instrument, an office with more customary and statutory powers, than it had been before the crisis.[15]

This expansion, moreover, is not the exclusive province of great presidents in great wars. Rossiter admonishes:

> Nor should we forget lesser Presidents in lesser crises, for these men, too, left their mark on the office. When Hayes dispatched troops to restore peace in the railroad strike of 1877, when McKinley sent 5,000 soldiers and marines to China during the Boxer uprising, and when Harry Truman acted on a dozen occasions to save entire states from the ravages of storm or fire or flood, the Presidency moved to a higher level of authority and prestige—principally because the people had now been taught to expect more of it.[16]

According to Rossiter, presidents can claim new influence over the doings of government even without launching a massive war or keeping troops in the field for excessive periods of time. The equivalent of a battalion or two will often suffice, and the effects may be felt almost immediately.

In his doctoral dissertation "Constitutional Dictatorship: Crisis Government in the Modern Democracies," Rossiter was especially emphatic about the necessity of resurrecting an all-powerful executive for the duration of wars. Unless power is concentrated in the presidency, government

---

14. Rossiter 1956, 12.
15. Ibid., 64–65.
16. Ibid., 65.

policy reaches beyond its typical bounds, and the executive branch is liberated from constitutional proscriptions—the three criteria of Rossiter's "constitutional dictator"—a state's ability to survive is unnecessarily imperiled. While recognizing that an expansion of presidential power during war does not, of itself, ensure the state's survival, Rossiter argued that, other things being equal, "a great emergency in the life of a constitutional democracy will be more easily mastered by the government if dictatorial forms are to some degree substituted for democratic, and if the executive branch is empowered to take strong action without an excess of deliberation and compromise."[17] Should they renounce constitutional dictatorship, governments conspire in their own demise.

This leads to another distinction between Rossiter's and Corwin's treatments of the subject. Rossiter saw the aggrandizement of a wartime executive in much more universalistic terms than did Corwin. Having surveyed the wartime histories of ancient Rome and early twentieth-century Britain, France, and the United States, Rossiter insisted that "the universal significance of constitutional dictatorship should need no further demonstration."[18] Though the foundations and manifestations of constitutional dictators may vary somewhat across different systems of government, "it is always the executive branch in the government which possesses and wields the extraordinary powers of self-preservation of any democratic, constitutional state."[19] Corwin's gaze, by contrast, never left domestic shores.

Like Corwin, though, Rossiter recognized the dangers that accompany a more expansive wartime presidency. State survival may require the adoption of a constitutional dictator, but our lasting form of government and the civil liberties of average citizens will pay some cost in doing so. "The general principle and the particular institutions of constitutional dictatorship are political and social dynamite," Rossiter admitted. "No democracy ever went through a period of thoroughgoing constitutional dictatorship without some permanent and often unfavorable alteration in its governmental scheme, and in more than one instance an institution of constitutional dictatorship has been turned against the order it was established to defend."[20] The people and the legislative and judicial branches of government must doggedly guard against the exercise of powers of consti-

17. Rossiter 2005 [1948], 288.
18. Ibid.
19. Ibid., 12.
20. Ibid., 13.

tutional dictatorship in periods of actual peace or in the service of objectives that have little to do with state survival. But while admitting such "formidable dangers" and "knotty problems," Rossiter also reaffirmed the basic importance of an unfettered wartime executive. The challenge, Rossiter argued, was not to abandon constitutional dictatorship. It was to recognize its true form and to renounce any imitations.[21]

If World War II produced a distinctively "modern" presidency, as many presidency scholars have suggested, future wars yielded still more opportunities for presidents to augment their power. With the Korean and Vietnam wars in particular, members of Congress would appear to have abdicated what remained of their constitutional war powers,[22] and in assuming primary control over the conduct of war, presidents managed to expand their power more generally. By Richard Nixon's second term, presidents had so distorted the constitutional order that the nation's very system of governance appeared to be in crisis. In 1973, Arthur Schlesinger Jr. summarized the views of many constitutional law scholars and historians by heralding the emergence of an "imperial presidency."

Schlesinger's core argument rests on the premise that presidential power ebbs and flows during times of peace and war. For Schlesinger, presidential power was "resurgent" in World War II, "ascendant" in the Korean War, and "rampant" in the Vietnam War. In each of these wars, presidents further encroached on Congress's constitutional war powers, such that by the Vietnam War the practice of war appeared altogether out of sync with the principles laid out in Articles I and II. These facts had consequences that went well beyond decisions about military matters. Indeed, Schlesinger recognized that with war power firmly in their grasp modern presidents could lay claim to all sorts of foreign and domestic policies. The translation of war power into general power appeared entirely self-evident. Schlesinger asked, "If the President were conceded these life-and-death decisions abroad, how could he be restrained from gathering unto himself the less fateful powers of the national policy?"[23]

In two ways, Schlesinger's argument differs from Corwin's and Rossiter's. First, Schlesinger saw a direct connection between the size of a war and the amount of power accrued by the president. Whereas Rossiter suggested that most any war will redound to the benefit of the presidency,

21. For eleven criteria by which to identify and then evaluate constitutional dictatorships, see ibid., 297–306.

22. See, for example, Fisher 2000, 2004.

23. Schlesinger 1973, ix.

Schlesinger primarily feared large-scale and long-standing military enterprises. "The more acute the crisis," he insisted, "the more power flows to the president."[24]

Second, whereas Corwin and Rossiter saw successive wars steadily contributing to presidential power, Schlesinger argued that periods of executive expansion and decline coincided with periods of war and peace. "While war increased presidential power," Schlesinger noted, "peace brought a reaction against executive excess."[25] For Schlesinger, whether presidents were weak or strong crucially depended on whether the nation was at war. It was precisely for this reason that Schlesinger late in life saw an interminable and pervasive "war against terror" as a threat to the nation's system of governance. Lacking temporal and physical boundaries, Schlesinger warned, a war against terror might irreparably distort the balance of powers among the executive, legislative, and judicial branches of government.

Still, the Founders' basic concerns and Corwin's and Rossiter's observations resonated with Schlesinger. Wars, all of these men saw, concentrated the powers of the government in the presidency. With the nation's troops engaged in battle, presidents wielded unprecedented influence over all sorts of domestic and policy initiatives. Relief from such a state of affairs, if relief was possible, ultimately depended on the return of peace.

The discussions about war's contributions to presidential power did not end with Corwin, Rossiter, and Schlesinger. Indeed, they carry on to this day. Any bookstore will provide a healthy supply of popular titles intermittently decrying the abuses of presidential power aided and abetted by war, or less commonly insisting that presidents justifiably exercise altogether new powers in war that appropriately elude them during peace.[26] Meanwhile, legal scholars engage in lively debates about the proper boundaries of presidential power generally and in times of emergency more specifically.[27] Although in the past the debates about presidential power pitted reformers arguing for the wholesale reconstruction of political structures to meet contemporary challenges (e.g., the Progressives) against conservatives insisting upon strict adherence to first principles (e.g., originalists),

24. Schlesinger 2004, 46.
25. Ibid., 52.
26. See, for example, Crenson and Ginsberg 2007; Irons 2005; Posner and Vermeule 2011; Savage 2007; Schlesinger 2004; Schwarz and Huq 2007; Yoo 2010.
27. A sampling of recent publications includes Ackerman 2006; Fatovic 2009; Fisher 2008; Fletcher 2002; Gross 2003; Matheson 2009; Posner and Vermeule 2007; Posner 2006; Pushaw 2004; Wells 2004.

this time both sides of the debate invoke the Constitution.[28] At the heart of this debate are a set of concerns about how best to interpret vague Article II provisions about "the executive power" and the status of "commander in chief," different interpretations of the Founders' intent, and competing claims about what, if anything, can be read into constitutional silence.

In Corwin, Rossiter, and Schlesinger, we find all the central arguments about war and presidential power that still animate contemporary debate. In the writings of these presidency scholars, we find the most prominent and sweeping claims about the ways in which wars augment presidential power, sometimes through congressional and judicial abdication, but more often through the bold initiative of presidents themselves. We also find long historical narratives about notably egregious displays of presidential war powers, thoughtful reflections about the constitutional bases for the president's wartime powers, and competing assessments of whether a powerful wartime presidency serves the larger public welfare. The arguments by Corwin, Rossiter, and Schlesinger nearly perfectly encapsulate the conventional wisdom about war and presidential power. It is worth considering whether they were right.

1.2 *A Notion Evaluated*

The original architects of our system of government and the scholars who subsequently studied it presumed that, among stimulants to presidential power, war would know no equal. The Founders worried that through war a presidency might morph into a monarchy. While troops engaged in battle, successive presidents laid claim to ever more influence at home. In the mid-twentieth century, political scientists credited wars for the emergence of a modern presidency wholly distinct from its predecessor. By Nixon's time, according to what we will call the standard view, wars had catapulted the presidency out of the modern and into the imperial realm. And lest anyone doubt such claims   and few of prominence have   George W. Bush and Barack Obama's stewardship through wars in Afghanistan and Iraq and a clandestine global war on terror would appear ironclad proof that wars invariably lead to the aggrandizement of executive authority.

Viewed from another perspective, however, the standard view is not nearly so persuasive. The immense importance of Corwin, Rossiter, and

---

28. For more on how contemporary debates about presidential power fit into a longer historical narrative, see Skowronek 2009.

Schlesinger notwithstanding, the evidentiary basis for claims about war and presidential power remains underwhelming. The historical narratives on offer have a number of important flaws, not least of which is their inattention to the variable costs of waging war. Modern political scientists, meanwhile, have unearthed precious little quantitative evidence that presidential power expands during times of war. Many analyses reveal no relationship between war and presidential power, and some actually uncover a negative one.

The standard view, moreover, is almost entirely atheoretical. Presidential power, it stipulates, expands and contracts naturally, reflexively, as the nation moves into and out of war. Seeing a need during war, presidents seize new powers and the adjoining branches of government confer still more; when peace is restored, all is set right again. But none of the adherents of the standard view offer a theory of Congress or the courts that supports this contention. None, that is, embed in their narratives a clear explanation for why a member of Congress or judge would permit a presidential action during war that they would oppose during peace. Though adamantly argued and almost universally acclaimed, the claim that wars exalt presidential power remains woefully underdeveloped.

1.3 *Sifting through the Claims*

The widely held view—and, for some, concern—that wars consolidate power in the hands of the president belies considerable disagreement about why this is so. Here, we pay particular attention to the origins of these claims, seeking what it is about wartime politics at home that expands the president's reach over congressional and judicial affairs during wartime. Furthermore, and equally important, the standard view is altogether silent on a number of aspects related to war and presidential power. All wars are not the same. Nevertheless, it remains unclear whether claims about presidential power and war should be modified to account for the distinguishing features of various wars. Moreover, the standard view does not distinguish the president's ability to wield influence over war-related activities from other policy areas. Of greatest concern, the standard view does not implicate any specific feature of war in the expansion of presidential power. Relying upon weak—and often competing—claims about war and presidential power, the standard view says little about the conditions under which war increases presidential power, to what extent, and why.

LINGERING DISAGREEMENTS

There exists overwhelming consensus—expressed with ever more conviction—that wars are a boon to presidential power. We should not lose sight, though, of important disagreements among those who advance this claim. For starters, adherents of the standard view read particular constitutional provisions differently and assume altogether different postures with respect to the document itself. For some, the document requires preservation, and occasional wartime departures are only justified when the life of the nation (and with it, the Constitution) is imperiled. For others, the Constitution is very much a living document, and successive generations of presidents have an obligation to interpret it in ways that enable them to meet the challenges of their day.

For our purposes, the key points of disagreement relate to positive claims about the relationship between war and presidential power. On this score, two disputes are worth highlighting. The first concerns the relative importance of transitions from peace to war and from war to peace. The former, all agree, yields a more powerful president. But the effect of a peace settlement on domestic politics generally, and on presidential power in particular, remains contested. For Schlesinger, a restoration of peace entails a diminution of presidential power, as the adjoining branches of government retract emergency powers and scrutinize new exercises of presidential power. But for others—notably Rossiter and Corwin—the relevance of an armistice is not nearly so clear. Though Congress may suspend some emergency delegations, and the courts may feel free to overturn especially egregious exercises of presidential power, the conduct of presidents during wartime may yield lasting effects on the office and our system of government.

Substantial disagreements similarly arise when contemplating the different sizes of wars. Crises that imperil the life of the nation, all agree, do the most to augment presidential power. Furthermore, the advent of total war establishes a principled basis upon which presidents can seize new powers on the home front. But what of smaller engagements? Do the Korean, Vietnam, and Afghanistan wars do just as much for presidential power? And if not, how should we think about the nature of the relationship between a war's magnitude and the expansion of presidential power? With each battalion of troops sent abroad, does presidential power expand by some fixed quantity? Or does presidential power remain constant until some critical, but still unspecified, threshold is crossed?

Adherents to the standard view offer different answers to such questions. Corwin fixes his attention on the three great American wars, suggesting a belief that only great crises unleash presidential power. Conversely, for Rossiter, smaller military engagements also hold out the possibility of expanding presidential power. For Schlesinger, meanwhile, middling engagements in Korea and Vietnam were ultimately responsible for the emergence of an imperial presidency. War may augment presidential power, but the standard view offers widely different predictions about which wars will bestow presidents with newfound influence on the home front.

QUESTIONS UNANSWERED AND TYPICALLY UNASKED

An astounding amount of scholarship on war and presidential power has been amassed over the last several centuries. Here, we have summarized just a sliver of what has been written on the topic. For all that has been written, however, certain aspects about the relationship between war and executive power remain entirely overlooked.

To begin, no one has paid much attention to the possibility that presidential power expands and contracts during the course of a single war. Rather, the discussion tends to suppose that wars deliver a fixed dosage of influence, which the president retains as long as troops remain fighting abroad. But this seems unlikely. In the immediate aftermath of Pearl Harbor and 9/11, were Roosevelt and George W. Bush exercising the same amount of power as they were when the fight against the Axis powers appeared to have reached a stalemate in the spring of 1944 and the scandals at the Iraqi prison Abu Ghraib came to light in 2004? Or what about the supposed powers conferred by World War II and the post-9/11 wars when, at last, victory appeared within reach in Europe in late 1944 and violence in Baghdad at last subsided in 2007?

These questions prompt others, which have received equally scant attention. Do wars enable presidents, in equal measure, to censure seditious speech and revise health care? Adherents to the standard view would certainly say no. Yet on the basis of their published work, it is difficult to discern a standard that allows one to generate clear predictions about war's variable impacts on presidential power across different policy areas.

Based on conventional accounts, moreover, it is virtually impossible to discern whether certain features of war might actually constrain a president's ability to exercise power on the home front. The costs of war, political and otherwise, remain altogether missing from the discussion.

From Corwin, Rossiter, and Schlesinger, it is difficult to make sense of a Korean War that drove Truman's approval ratings into the low 20s, a Vietnam War that, just as it began to escalate, derailed Johnson's presidency, or an Iraq War that hung like an albatross around the neck of George W. Bush during his second term in office. Smaller wars, such as those in Lebanon and Somalia, yielded costs of their own—diverting resources away from other policy initiatives, requiring justification at home and abroad, and causing substantial embarrassment to the president himself. How do these variable costs figure into Rossiter's axiom that presidential power necessarily expands during war?

Nor is the standard view especially clear about the defining feature of war that does so much to stimulate presidential power. At its periphery, the standard view recognizes that the rules of politics necessarily change when the life of the nation is at risk, and that the rules change in ways that favor the individual charged with protecting the nation. This may go some distance toward explaining events around the Civil War and, perhaps, World War II. But the life of the nation decidedly was not imperiled in World War I, nor in the more limited conflicts of the second half of the twentieth century. What was it about these conflicts that spawned an imperial presidency? To be sure, the outcomes of these wars had important implications for national economic and security interests, but such interests are often at stake regardless of whether the nation's military is engaged in battle. A failure to peacefully resolve differences between nations does not present a unique moment wherein national interests are quite suddenly imperiled. Such interests are continually negotiated, and for at least the last half-century presidents have remained the chief defender of such interests in international relations.

So again, what is it about war per se that propels presidential power to new heights? Answers to such questions surely exist. Moreover, that the standard view itself does not offer clear answers is not evidence that its core claims about war and presidential power are somehow wrong. Rather, it simply indicates that the standard view, for all its opulence, remains underdeveloped.

PRESIDENTIAL IMPERIALISM

Rossiter, Corwin, and Schlesinger document, and sometimes celebrate, the presidents who have exercised newfound influence over policy domains that either were the province of congressional activity or were entirely neglected previously. These scholars argue that, largely because of presidential ambition, congressional power transfers laterally just as executive power grows independently.

But therein lies the key weakness in the standard view. Just because presidents want power, whether in war or peace, does not mean that the adjoining branches of government will grant it. It will not do to simply assume that power naturally follows ambition. We need to explain exactly how ambition yields power. To do this, we must clarify how war influences those political actors who must choose between contesting and conceding to presidential ambitions.

Given an institutional setting in which powers are separated and shared between and among the three branches, we must reflect upon how wars figure into congressional voting behavior and judicial decision making. It is in Congress and the courts, after all, that the president's powers may be checked and his legislative initiatives obstructed.[29] Consequently, theories of war and presidential power require ancillary theories of political institutions. Only by engaging the broader discipline and building off the insights of scholars of Congress and the courts will we deepen our understanding of what happens at the nexus of war, presidential power, and public policy making.

This move—which Corwin, Rossiter, and Schlesinger seldom take, preferring to fix their gaze on the president—has empirical justification as well. The reason is this: we cannot view presidential influence directly; like quarks, we can only see its traces. Hence, we must look to the adjoining branches of government, whose actions bear upon it—namely, to judges and members of Congress who respond to a wide variety of initiatives supported by the president. By calculating whether the courts are more likely to uphold policies supported by the president when the nation is at war, and whether members of Congress are more likely to vote in ways that reflect presidential preferences and priorities, we can obtain estimates of war's impact on presidential power. But to fully understand the stakes involved in these tests, of course, we need theory.

---

29. Of course, wars may disrupt domestic politics in other ways that affect, if indirectly, the president's capacity to advance a policy agenda. Wars, for instance, may enfranchise new voters and reshape the networks of interest groups operating in Washington, D.C. (Krebs 2009). When facing war, presidents may independently reconsider a variety of policy positions that they previously had held. In the chapters that follow, we will remain sensitive to such possibilities. Our theory and empirical tests, however, are meant to elucidate how another branch of government—Congress, possessing war powers of its own accord—responds to the president during times of peace and war.

THEORY NEGLECTED

Though gallons of ink have been spilled on the proposition that wars aug-ment presidential power, most work on the subject has taken the form of a simple assertion made over and over again, rather than a well-developed and empirically corroborated theory whose microfoundations are specified with increasing clarity. As Stephen Skowronek points out, "the politics behind the imperial presidency thesis was never very fully articulated; what there is could be summarized in a single sentence: imperial ambitions breed imperial powers."[30] Without theory, the standard view does not, indeed cannot, identify which elements of presidential power are likely to expand, and the precise conditions under which they will do so.

Periodically, one can detect only the glimmers of a theory. For Rossiter, wars lead to the expansion of presidential power "principally because the people had now been taught to expect more of it."[31] The public, for Rossiter, is the key channel through which wartime presidents augment their influ-ence. There is something unsatisfying, though, about an argument taking the basic form: presidential power expands; witnessing such expansion, the public expects more of the president, and therefore presidential power expands even further. Schlesinger, meanwhile, offers a more conditional argument, admitting that different wars affect presidential power in dif-ferent ways, and stipulating that while transitions from peace to war lead to expansions of presidential power, transitions from war to peace lead to contractions. The theoretical foundations to such claims, however, are al-together missing. With a compelling historical narrative about the ascen-dance of an imperial presidency as backdrop, Schlesinger advances these propositions not on the basis of well-defined first principles, but instead on their self-evident nature.

Rossiter and Schlesinger each offer the seeds of a theory, but no more. As a consequence, we lack answers to foundational questions. If wars con-stitute a boon to presidential power, for instance, what is the precise cause of the phenomenon? Does an expansion of presidential power result from the voting habits of a deferential Congress? Or does it reflect the propen-sity of an impressionable public to rally behind its president? Could the rulings of a judiciary lacking the powers of either the purse or sword be to blame? Each of these possibilities teaches us very different lessons about

30. Skowronek 2008, 151.
31. Rossiter 1956, 65.

the workings of our system of governance, and each rests upon very different assumptions about the behavior of our elected or unelected leaders.

Take, for instance, the possibility that congressional checks on presidential power slacken during times of war. Scholars have shown that in waging the war itself, Congress often appears perfectly willing to defer to the president—especially when the war is popular and successful. It is less clear, though, why a popular, successful war ought to encourage individual members of Congress to side with the president on altogether separate issues. What theory of congressional behavior predicts that a Democratic member of Congress would oppose a Republican president's tax cuts during times of peace but support them during times of war? Similarly, why would a Republican member of Congress oppose a Democratic president's welfare initiative in peace but support it in war? In either instance, the precise qualities of war and the foundations of congressional behavior that might evince such an about-face remain entirely mysterious.

Lacking a theory, we also cannot discern which dormant elements of a president's agenda might revive when the nation turns to war. The right barometer may concern a policy initiative's proximity to the war effort: those policies that most immediately concern war (e.g., funding for defense systems) may be most affected; those that are tangentially related to war (e.g., civil liberty protections) may be partially affected; and those that are unrelated to war (e.g., social welfare policies) may be completely unaffected. Alternatively, the extent of peacetime opposition to a bill might be the critical indicator: that is, those bills that require just a handful of new supporters may find their way into the law books during times of war, while those that require many more continue to languish in congressional committees. Yet another alternative is that war may not have any impact on actual voting behavior, but instead may modify the agenda that Congress considers. Wars, by this account, do not alter roll call votes; rather, they change the types of bills that come before a legislative body. The standard view does not even delineate, much less discriminate among, such options.

EVIDENTIARY STANDARDS

The standard view derives almost entirely from scholars' selective readings of a handful of wars. Evidence, in these instances, typically consists of long narratives of wartime presidential actions. As readers, we are asked to bear witness to presidents seizing industries, imprisoning citizens, monitoring communications, and fixing prices and wages, among other acts. The sheer audacity of these actions is offered as prima facie evidence of newfound power expressed by presidents and dutifully honored by Congress and the courts.

Unfortunately, these accounts do not offer a clear basis for comparison, whether by reference to actions presidents take during peace or to actions that presidents contemplated taking but ultimately abandoned during war. To see this, let us consider each possibility in turn. Undoubtedly, presidents have done extraordinary things in war, many of which, like the internment of Japanese Americans, are inconceivable during peace. But so too have peacetime presidents done extraordinary things. Most of the major civil rights advancements that built upon Roosevelt's wartime actions occurred during times of peace—the 1948 desegregation of the military, the 1957 Civil Rights Act, and the 1964 Civil Rights Act. The wartime administrative agencies of Wilson and Roosevelt were either modified or replaced by literally hundreds of administrative agencies created during times of peace.[32] Through a variety of executive orders issued during peacetime years, presidents extended their influence over the construction and implementation of the regulatory state.[33] It is not clear that these peacetime actions equaled the wartime records of Lincoln, Wilson, or Roosevelt, but that is just the point. Demonstrating the exertion of power during war does not, in itself, establish a case that wars per se are responsible for an expansion of executive authority, particularly when we see peacetime administrations exercising considerable amounts of power themselves.

The standard view also fails to account for actions that presidents contemplated but ultimately forsook in war. From the standard view, we are left to imagine those elements of a president's domestic and foreign policy agendas that remained shelved for a war's duration. This will not do. To assess the various trade-offs and concessions that presidents are forced to make, whether during peace or war, we need some indication of the policy preferences that underlay these actions. Without this information, it is nearly impossible to trace the limits of claims about war and presidential power. It makes a great deal of difference, after all, whether wartime presidents realize every element of their policy agenda during war, or whether they achieve but a small fraction of their policy objectives. The standard view, unfortunately, does not allow us to distinguish between these two conditions.

Lacking a basis for either type of comparison, we cannot evaluate the magnitude of influence that wars purportedly confer upon presidents. It

32. Howell and Lewis 2002.
33. Howell 2003; Lewis 2003; Moe and Howell 1999.

is not enough to simply list the many things that presidents have done at home while the nation has fought wars abroad. We also must account for the things they can readily accomplish during peace, and the things they would like to achieve but cannot during war.

1.4 *Quantitative Studies on War and Presidential Power*

Over the past several decades, a modest amount of quantitative research has examined the relationship between war and presidential power. These studies generally examine presidential success rates in Congress or the courts. And so doing, this research productively expands the scope of inquiry beyond the standard view's nearly exclusive focus on presidential wartime actions.

One would hope that this research might fill in the evidentiary gaps that were previously outlined, but unfortunately it does not. The theoretical contributions are negligible: few posit a behavioral theory of congressional voting or judicial decision making from which predictions about the effects of war on presidential power can be generated. The empirical results of these studies are similarly weak. Their proffered findings, for the most part, do not support the contention that wars lead to an expansion of presidential power. Congress does not automatically fall in line behind the commander in chief when the nation stands on a war footing. Moreover, the studies themselves have important limitations of their own, making it virtually impossible to assess the standard view articulated by Corwin, Rossiter, Schlesinger, and others.[34]

STUDIES ON CONGRESS

Though they have scrutinized almost every imaginable correlate of congressional voting behavior, political scientists have paid less attention to the precise relationship between war and presidential power. The findings that do exist, however, yield little support for the contention that wars necessarily augment presidential power. Andrew Rudalevige, for instance, tracked the fate of presidential initiatives put before Congress during the post–World War II era.[35] He found that "critical external events" prompted

34. Here, we briefly canvass those studies that speak directly to the relationships between war and presidential power. We thus exclude the voluminous literature on war and public opinion, which only tangentially relates to executive power. For a more thorough discussion of this and other literatures, see Howell and Johnson 2009.

35. Rudalevige 2002.

an increase of 18 percentage points in the probability that Congress would enact a bill in line with presidential preferences. Unfortunately, the analysis does not test the effect of war per se; war is merely one of several scenarios that are coded as critical external events. Other studies that explicitly controlled for war have offered more tempered assessments of its influence on presidential power. Jeffrey Cohen, for instance, investigated presidential legislative success during three time periods: 1861–1896, 1897–1932, and 1933–1972.[36] In his quantitative analysis, war's effect is positive and statistically significant in the earliest era, but not in either of the two latter periods. Cohen concluded that "wars are less able now to build congressional support for the president."[37]

By expanding the definition of war to include not only "hot" wars like Korea and Vietnam but also the Cold War between the United States and the Soviet Union, and by further restricting the analysis to foreign policy initiatives, some scholars have unearthed evidence of a relationship between war and presidential influence in Congress. Examining roll call votes taken between 1947 and 1988, James Meernik found that hot and cold wars encourage congressional support for the president's foreign policy and defense proposals.[38] According to Meernik, presidents enjoyed greater levels of support in both the House and Senate during the first half of the Cold War, and greater levels of support in the Senate during the Korean and Vietnam wars.

Other scholars have reached similar conclusions but coded for altogether different periods of the Cold War. Jeffrey Peake examined presidents' ability to convince members of Congress to vote for the executive's preferred foreign policy bills from 1947 to 1998.[39] Identifying the entire Cold War period between 1947 and 1990, he found a positive and significant effect. Brandon Prins and Bryan Marshall examined foreign, defense, and domestic policies introduced between 1953 and 1998.[40] Identifying the first half of the Cold War between 1953 and 1973, they found a significant positive effect for foreign and defense policies, but not for domestic policies. Eugene Wittkopf and James McCormick took a different approach, investigating whether the demise of the Cold War eroded congressional support for presidents' foreign

36. Cohen 1982.
37. Ibid., 528.
38. Meernik 1993.
39. Peake 2002.
40. Prins and Marshall 2001.

policy initiatives.[41] Wittkopf and McCormick examined initiatives introduced between 1983 and 1996 and coded for three stages during this time frame: Cold War (1983–1988), transitional period (1989–1990), and post–Cold War (1991–1996). Wittkopf and McCormick concluded that conflict between Congress and the president has risen in the post–Cold War era. Given the authors' varying approaches to coding the Cold War years, it is difficult to know how to interpret these collective findings, but it is worth noting that whatever influence the Cold War bestowed upon the president, it did so only in foreign policy.

To be sure, ascertaining presidential power on the basis of roll call votes on presidential initiatives is extraordinarily difficult. Presidents do not randomly select elements from their policy agenda to put before Congress. Rather, presidents carefully choose those policies that they think stand a decent chance of passage and set aside the rest. If such selectivity is a function of war—and there are ample reasons to believe that it is—then systematic biases are introduced that may obscure war's genuine effects on presidential power. Thus, some of the best quantitative work on presidential power within Congress has considered budgets, for in this area presidents do not have the luxury of selecting when to express a preference about an issue publicly and when to stay silent. Each year presidents must submit to Congress a detailed budget proposal on every facet of the government's operations—a fact that alleviates, though certainly does not eliminate, concerns about selection bias.

If wars expand presidential influence over the appropriations process, we can expect to observe two kinds of evidence: first, that presidents during times of war request higher amounts of funding for their preferred programs; and second, that Congress appropriates amounts that better reflect presidential priorities. The existing literature does not satisfy either expectation.

Roderick Kiewiet and Mathew McCubbins speak to the first point.[42] Examining submitted budgets for thirty-seven federal agencies from fiscal years 1948 to 1979, Kiewiet and McCubbins uncovered a statistically significant negative relationship between war and presidential funding requests. A follow-up study of sixty-three nondefense agencies during fiscal years 1948 to 1985 further showed that Truman cut his domestic appropri-

41. Wittkopf and McCormick 1998.
42. Kiewiet and McCubbins 1985.

ations proposals during the Korean War.[43] Kiewiet and McCubbins also found some evidence that Johnson and Nixon scaled back their budgetary requests during the Vietnam War, though the effect was much weaker.

Unfortunately, Kiewiet and McCubbins do not distinguish which programs the presidents supported or opposed, making it difficult to ascertain whether presidential power actually weakens during times of war. It is possible that during war presidents requested cutbacks on domestic policies that they opposed, and peacetime equivalent funding for programs that they supported. If true, then presidential power does not appear diminished. We can rule out the possibility, however, that presidents requested peacetime equivalent funds for programs that they opposed and increases for programs that they supported. And nowhere is there any evidence that wars systematically encouraged presidents to solicit higher levels of spending for domestic programs as a whole.

Brandice Canes-Wrone, David Lewis, and William Howell have investigated the conditions under which congressional appropriations better align with presidential priorities.[44] Analyzing appropriations data from fiscal years 1969 to 2000, they showed that foreign policy appropriations better reflect presidential requests than do domestic policy appropriations—a finding that is consistent with the "two-presidencies" hypothesis first articulated by Aaron Wildavsky.[45] The authors uncovered very little evidence, however, that wars systematically augmented presidential power. When the Vietnam War is considered in isolation, it looks as though congressional appropriations more closely matched presidential proposals; when the definition of war is expanded to include other military conflicts during the period, the observed relationship vanishes.

ISOLATING THE EFFECTS OF WAR

Systematic evidence that presidential power reliably expands during times of war is hard to come by. Many quantitative analyses have yielded null findings. Any wartime gains to presidential power that are observed, meanwhile, tend to be short lived.

Truth be told, though, the existing quantitative literature contributes very little to empirical evaluations of the standard view. Two limitations of this literature stand out, the first of which centers on how to define war.

43. Kiewiet and McCubbins 1991.
44. Canes-Wrone et al. 2008.
45. Wildavsky 1966.

Many studies identify only those periods in which the United States was involved in hot wars, such as Korea, Vietnam, and the two Persian Gulf wars.[46] Other scholars opt to cast a wider net, recognizing such smaller deployments as those that occurred in the 1980s and 1990s in Panama, Somalia, Haiti, Bosnia, and Kosovo. Still other scholars focus on the Cold War between the United States and the Soviet Union, and various periods therein. Over time, defining wars in different ways may make a great deal of sense. It is quite possible—even probable—that different wars affect presidential power in different ways, and scholars would do well to account for their distinguishing characteristics. It seems perfectly reasonable to expect that a war's size, popularity, duration, and ultimate success may crucially define its contributions to presidential power. In the short run, however, the existence of multiple definitions of war makes it difficult to compare results across studies.

Without an agreed-upon definition of war, it is difficult to ascertain the varying influences that long-standing military commitments in a single country or region can have on presidential power. During the course of one war, changes in the number of troops deployed, revelations about security lapses or battlefield victories, and evolving sentiments about the venture's contribution to the national interest may further adjust the influence of war on presidential power. The Vietnam War, for instance, started out as a series of small deployments of military advisers, steadily escalated into a fully fledged war under a Democratic president, and then morphed into a seemingly intractable campaign under a Republican president. There is no reason to expect that the nation's involvement in Vietnam in the mid-1960s had the same impact on presidential power as its involvement in the early 1970s. The existing literature on war and presidential power aims to uncover the average effect of war and tends to ignore its variance.

The second problem is more troubling still. Virtually all the existing empirical work on presidential power treats war as a control variable rather than as the key explanatory variable of interest. As a result, scholars have evaluated war's effect on presidential power only indirectly at best. Tellingly, few scholars have provided a detailed theoretical rationale for including a control for war or even cite other researchers who have established the importance of this variable. By relegating war to the status

---

46. Unfortunately—yet not surprisingly, due to the challenges of obtaining decades-old data—these analyses often exclude the two world wars, which provided much of the initial inspiration for Corwin, Rossiter, Schlesinger, and others who warned of imperial presidents.

of background control, this literature does not confront the extraordinary selection biases that complicate any effort to evaluate the impact of war. Because wars are not randomly assigned across history, and because all political actors, very much including presidents, continually adjust to new political developments, it can be extremely difficult to discern from trends in presidential actions and congressional and judicial responses the variable allotments of executive power. The existing quantitative literature, taken as a whole, simply does not establish an evidentiary record that either supports or negates the possibility that wars cause an expansion of presidential power.

1.5 *Moving Forward*

David Mayhew has called upon scholars to pay more attention to events when developing causal stories about institutional change. Among all possible events, Mayhew highlights the overriding importance of wars. "Wars," he writes, "seem to be capable of generating whole new political universes." Unfortunately, the exact features of these universes, and the opportunities for different political actors to advance their policy agendas within them, remain largely unexplored. According to Mayhew, "political scientists who study American domestic politics have underappreciated [war's] effects," preferring instead to read from a "peacetime script."[47]

Mayhew documents how five major U.S. wars supported the enactment of sweeping policy changes, the emergence of new issue regimes, alterations in electoral coalitions, and redefinitions of the two major parties. It stands to reason that wars also disrupt the fundamental balance of powers with the federal government. Indeed, we have inherited a long tradition of scholarship that argues precisely this point. If wars are to play a more central role in the work of political scientists generally, they certainly warrant greater attention from presidency scholars.

It will not do, however, to continue reiterating the basic assertion that war and presidential power go hand in hand. If progress is to be made, scholars must not presume such comity but instead initiate the harder work of scrutinizing it. In addition, scholars must do more than include war as one among many background controls in standard regression models. Instead, they must design tests that directly evaluate war's variable contributions to presidential power.

47. Mayhew 2005, 473.

The standard view is not so much wrong as it is in need of refinement. Before strong conclusions can be drawn about any of its claims, we need to develop tests that squarely examine the proposition that presidential power expands during times of war. Such tests, moreover, must address a wide variety of ancillary issues—about differences between the transitions from peace to war and war to peace, differences between the total wars of the first half of the twentieth century and the smaller engagements of the second, and the different policy domains in which presidential power can be expressed. Most importantly, these tests must be grounded in theory. And so it is to theory that we now turn.

PART II

Theorizing
about
Interbranch
Bargaining during
War

CHAPTER 2

The Policy Priority Model

For all that has been written on war and presidential power, we still do not have a clear theory that explains *why* presidents should enjoy a greater measure of influence over public policy making during war than during peace. No one has posited a theory of presidential influence that has clear microfoundations; that sorts out the key protagonists, their resources, and associations; that deduces predictions about the conditions under which members of Congress will vote with the president, and when they will, instead, oppose him; and, crucially, that is falsifiable. When it comes to theory building, we really are working from scratch.

To make headway, we abstract away from the historical details—that is, the personalities, contingencies, and cultural norms—that define particular wartime episodes in American history. In fact, in this chapter, we abstract away from war almost completely, and focus first on constructing a general theory of interbranch relations. Given our substantive interest in assessing the level of success presidents experience when negotiating with Congress over policies, we develop a theory that identifies the parameters of the political environment that lead Congress to enact policies that more closely resemble the president's preferred policies. In the subsequent chapter, we demonstrate how war changes the values of these parameters, thus establishing a set of predictions about the impact of war on presidential influence.

Our theory draws from the formal literature on interbranch and intrabranch bargaining, which captures many of the nuances of negotiations between governing units that may or may not have similar preferences over outcomes. These bargaining models, however, need to be enriched to capture central features of executive-legislative negotiations—features, as we shall soon see, that help explain a great deal about wartime politics at home. In particular, these models need to account for differences in the constituents served by presidents and members of Congress. Whereas members of Congress serve districts or states, presidents serve the entire country. This basic fact has crucially important consequences for the deliberations that occur across branches of government. Presidents focus on the national implications of public policies while members of Congress monitor the effects of public policy on both the nation as a whole and their local constituencies—and, crucially, often these emphases are in conflict with one another. In two ways, therefore, we refine the general bargaining models found in the literature: first, by allowing for the possibility that a single policy generates two outcomes (one felt at the national level, and another at the local level); and second, by recognizing the differential weights that presidents and members of Congress place on each of these outcomes. In so doing, we demonstrate that policy outcomes more closely approximate the president's preferences when members of Congress become more concerned with the national outcomes of policies.

Nothing about our theory expressly distinguishes periods of war and peace. Consequently, the next chapter clarifies our model's insights into how war might change congressional voting patterns. Suffice it to say here that a defining feature of war is the promotion of national concerns and the suppression of local ones. Most immediately, the exaltation of national concerns stems from security considerations. The merits of policy innovations that once were gauged by their contributions to local economies instead are assessed on the basis of their ability to meet the challenges presented by an enemy from abroad. Whereas members of Congress during peace may evaluate the value of a proposed weapons system in terms of its implications for local employment and investment, during war members of Congress worry more about the effectiveness of these weapons in actually deterring foreign threats. And war's reach extends farther still, for during war questions about training programs, grants-in-aid, infrastructure, regulation, labor–management relations, and myriad other concerns become linked, perhaps for the first time, to issues of national security.

More generally, wars reinforce citizens' (and by extension congressional representatives') common identity as Americans. In war, we recognize ourselves less as atomistic individuals or even residents of a community or state and more as citizens of a sovereign state who share a common history and collective fate. The flag is flown nearly everywhere. National anthems are sung at sporting events, just as gatherings of children and adults pledge their allegiance to their country. Politicians' speeches are infused with themes of unity, patriotism, and self-sacrifice. In war, we are told, we must set aside our private, parochial concerns and do what is right for the nation as a whole, just as our ancestors did in their own times of peril. Hence, the evaluative criteria brought to bear in policy debates abruptly shifts from the local to the national.

As much as possible, we have tried to make our discussion broadly accessible without sacrificing its specificity. We are well aware that many of the scholars who have worked on presidential power and war have had little training in game theory. Thus, for the reader who has absolutely no interest in the formal mechanisms that drive our model but wants to understand its central intuitions, we offer a nontechnical summary at the end of the chapter. Before readers skip ahead, however, we would like to encourage them to work through at least the first several sections of this chapter, where we outline the key motivations behind the theory and the model's basic setup. The core predictions of the model can be found in the sections on comparative statics. For those readers who are interested in the internal workings of the model, we also offer sections that explain the conditions under which specific equilibria hold, for which the mathematical proofs can be found in Appendix A.

2.1 *Theoretical Building Blocks: Policies, Outcomes, and Interbranch Bargaining*

When politicians evaluate the content of legislative initiatives, their primary concerns lie not in the words contained within the initiatives but in how their words spur government action and, by extension, change the material world. The stakes of most policy debates—and virtually all the most significant policy debates—are defined not over the elements of legislation unto themselves but over the elements of legislation as they relate to alterations in the real world. As Keith Krehbiel elaborates, legislators often care more about outcomes than policies per se. "Passage of a given policy has no bearing on a legislator's utility apart from the outcome associated with that policy."[1] Politics, viewed this way, is not an expression of abstract, disassociated national priorities, values, principles, and commitments; rather, it is a debate about the exercise of state power in the service of real-world objectives that help some people and possibly hurt others. When deciding how to vote on a policy initiative, members of Congress and the president try to forecast the identity of these winners and losers,

1. Krehbiel 1992, 66.

the particular gains and losses they experience, and how these facts translate into an objective utility function.[2]

Notice, though, that politicians cannot always shape the world as they would like. They cannot dictate that inflation will stabilize or that unemployment rates will drop. Rather, politicians must design policies that they hope will induce the desired effects. Hence, they must learn how specific policy instruments (over which voting occurs) are connected to specific policy outcomes (over which a politician's utility is defined). And the mapping of policies into outcomes, it bears emphasizing, can be remarkably complex.

Political disagreements persist, at least in part, because the acquisition of information about how policies translate into outcomes is costly—sometimes prohibitively so. To discern how increases in the minimum wage, heightened oversight of financial industries, and deeper investments in human capital manifest in local and national outcomes, members of Congress and presidents require information. The required information is not freely available, and expertise comes at a cost. A great deal of politics generally, and the design of political institutions in particular, thus involves creating incentives for politicians to pay these costs, collect reliable information about the likely outcomes of different policy initiatives, and then communicate this information to others.

MAPPING POLICIES ONTO OUTCOMES

To make sense of political debates over public policy, we need to think critically about who has information about the effects of public policy, when they will exploit this information, and how others are likely to respond. A substantial body of game theory is devoted to precisely these issues. This work attempts to specify the conditions under which individuals will invest in the development of expertise and then use this expertise to their advantage in communications with individuals who may not share their interests. Building off the core insights of Vincent Crawford and Joel

2. In the real world, of course, exceptions exist. Some policy domains are sufficiently charged as to become intrinsically meaningful. Members of Congress may avoid supporting any bills that increase taxes, support the administration of abortions, or reduce teacher salaries not because of the direct impacts of these policy changes on the world but because these issues are laden with symbolic value. The mere possibility of appearing to be associated with tax increases (no matter how small), abortions (no matter how few), or reductions in teacher salaries (no matter how scant) may be enough to convince some politicians to persistently vote against such initiatives.

Sobel,[3] political scientists have investigated these communications within a wide range of strategic political environments, including committee-floor relations within Congress,[4] congressional-agency relations across the legislative and executive branches of government,[5] the design of the executive branch,[6] and political debate more generally.[7]

The formal literature on information acquisition and signaling, at least within political science, is less concerned with the substantive content of expertise and more with the properties that define the general relationship between policies and outcomes. Hence, expertise in these models constitutes the acquisition of information about the mathematical functions that translate policies into outcomes, both of which can assume numerical values. Much of this literature envisions a linear, additive relationship, where all chosen policies yield outcomes along a policy continuum that can be expressed as the sum of the policy and some constant, which typically is interpreted as a stochastic shock.[8] Expertise, according to this formulation, is knowledge of the true value of the stochastic shock. Knowing its value, the expert can assess with certainty how any particular policy translates into an outcome. By knowing her preferences over outcomes, the expert can deduce her most preferred policy as well as the relative utility she would derive from any other policy. To see this, assume that an expert has an ideal point of outcome 6 and that the stochastic shock has a value of 5. Under such conditions, the expert should recommend the enactment of policy 1, as $1+5=6$, thus recovering her ideal outcome. This mapping function is an example of "perfect invertibility."

Recently, however, a number of scholars have criticized this specification on the grounds that it too easily converts nonexperts into experts.[9] In these models, expertise amounts to knowledge of a single piece of information: the unit shift that characterizes the translation of all policies into all outcomes. Hence, by learning how any single policy translates into any

3. Crawford and Sobel 1982.
4. Gilligan and Krehbiel 1987, 1990; Krehbiel 1992.
5. Callander 2008; Huber and Shipan 2002.
6. Gailmard and Patty 2012.
7. Austen-Smith 1990.
8. According to the canonical formulation (see Gilligan and Krehbiel 1987), the mapping process from policies to outcomes is given by $x = p + \omega$, where x is the outcome, p is the policy, and ω is a stochastic shock.
9. Callander 2008; Hirsch and Shotts 2008.

single outcome, the nonexpert can appropriate all the information of the expert and thereby assess how every policy translates into every outcome. Observing that policy 2 yields outcome 4 also tells you that policy 3 yields outcome 5, that 4 yields 6, that 5 yields 7, and so on, which is akin to saying that "a patient may acquire complete medical expertise upon hearing a single diagnosis from a doctor."[10] With principals able to appropriate this expertise so easily and use it for their own purposes, it is not clear why any agent would ever pay the costs of its acquisition.[11]

At the other end of the spectrum are noninvertible mapping functions. Suppose p and q are two policies regarding the same one-dimensional issue (e.g., education). In this case, learning how policy p translates into an outcome x does not provide a layperson with *any* insight as to what outcome will be produced by any alternative policy $q \neq p$. This also seems like an unrealistic portrayal of the mapping process in the policy domain. If a layperson is told that spending $1 billion on primary education in Kentucky will lead to average class sizes of 30 students per teacher, he will probably have a good sense of what class size to expect from allocating $1.01 billion to the same purpose.

In between the extremes of perfectly invertible and noninvertible mapping functions are partially invertible functions, which allow a layperson to extract *some* information about the likely outcome of policy $q \neq p$ when told that policy p produces outcome x. Additionally, one would expect that the amount of information that can be extracted should be decreasing as q gets farther away from p, a characteristic known as "proportional invertibility." To see the intuition behind it, consider a simple example. An expert reveals how a change of the minimum wage to $7.25 translates into the national unemployment rate. Knowing this single translation and that the mapping process is proportionally invertible, the layperson can readily assess how a minimum wage of $7.24 or $7.26 might influence the national unemployment rate. Similarly, albeit with less confidence, the layperson can conjecture how a minimum wage of $7.00 or $7.50 is likely to translate into a national unemployment rate. But this single translation yields relatively little insight about the effect of a minimum wage of $15, and nearly none whatsoever about the outcome associated with a minimum wage of $50.

10. Callander 2008.
11. In these models, the first mover can convey his information noisily through partitions, in which case the layperson appropriates the information and shifts policy to her ideal point only in expectation.

In addition to characterizing the acquisition of expertise under conditions of uncertainty, the existing formal literature provides an account for the stakes involved in any policy issue. By stakes, we mean the extent to which minor changes in policy translate, in expectation, into relatively major changes in outcome.[12] In expectation, the magnitude of expected differences in outcomes increases in direct proportion to the size of the differences in their associated policies and the slope of the mapping function. At one extreme, when the slope is zero, players can expect all policies to deliver exactly the same outcome. But as the slope assumes larger and larger values, players can expect the outcomes associated with different policies to diverge more and more. Indeed, as the slope shifts ever steeper, the smallest policy alterations can induce massive changes in outcomes.

These three qualities—partial invertibility, proportional invertibility, and policy stakes—figure prominently in our own theory of congressional-presidential relations. But before offering a more explicit definition of each, we must make one important adjustment to all the formal theories on information acquisition in public policy making.

ONE POLICY, MULTIPLE OUTCOMES

Though it explores different kinds of mathematical functions that chart the mapping of policies into outcomes, the political economy literature on information acquisition exclusively posits one policy as generating one outcome. In reality, policies generate heterogeneous outcomes. Policies routinely yield outcomes for a particular district or state that look quite different from the outcome for the nation as a whole. For instance, some policies generate substantial effects at the local or state level, but have a more limited impact on national outcomes. Changes in trade regulations for frozen concentrated orange juice, for instance, may yield dramatic results for citrus growers in Florida, but are unlikely to have major consequences for the national economy. Likewise, federal grants and aid for disaster relief may materially improve lives in specific communities without having much of an impact on the country as a whole. Conversely, other policies may have substantial effects on the national level but a more minor effect on particular states or districts. Enacting sanctions against a foreign state, for instance, may have major consequences for the country's standing in the international system, but is unlikely to have any significant

---

12. We do not invoke the more colloquial understanding of stakes as the extent to which any particular policy "matters" to a person, collective, or institution.

implications at the state or district level. Thus, when we think about how policies manifestly change the world, we should allow for the possibility that a single policy can affect a particular state or district in ways that look quite different for the nation as a whole.[13]

Just as a single policy might produce at least two different types of policy outcomes, one national and the other local, so might these outcomes differ in significance for members of Congress and presidents. Precisely because they serve the nation as a whole, presidents view national outcomes as paramount.[14] For as Woodrow Wilson wrote in the 1908 Blumenthal Lectures that he delivered at Columbia University, the president "is the only national voice in affairs . . . He is the representative of no constituency, but of the whole people."

Members of Congress, meanwhile, are an altogether different beast. As David Lewis and Terry Moe point out, "As national leaders with a broad, heterogeneous constituency, Presidents think in grander terms than members of Congress," who themselves tend to evaluate policy "on the special (often local) interests that can bring them security and popularity in office."[15] In *Federalist* No. 10, Madison wrote that the Constitution designs the nation's institutions to maintain a proper balance between local and national interests. Should congressional representatives have constituencies that are too large, he said, legislators will be insufficiently

13. This distinction between national and local outcomes roughly equates to the distinction commonly made between public goods and pork barrel spending, about which a great deal has been written (for recent papers, see Battaglini and Coate 2008; Volden and Wiseman 2007). This latter literature, however, is engaged in a conceptually different enterprise than our own. Whereas these other scholars investigate the conditions under which legislators devote fewer or greater revenues, raised either through taxes or debt accumulation, on what might be called local and national projects, they do not explicitly consider the influence of informational asymmetries between political actors on the ultimate distribution of these revenues. We, by contrast, are primarily interested in the propensity of legislators to support a proposer's policy (in our case, the president's) given different clear informational asymmetries and different assessments of the relative importance of these outcomes.

14. Presidents, of course, do value some local outcomes more than others. For reasons having to do with the winner-take-all design of the Electoral College, for instance, presidents assign greater importance to outcomes in swing states than in safe states. Similarly, as party leader, presidents tend to direct more federal benefits to the states and districts represented by copartisans in Congress (Berry et al. 2010). For the most part, however, presidents show disproportionate interest in certain districts and states because they want to remain in office and exercise control over their party, factors that are central to their ability to advance a policy agenda that, from their perspective, best serves the country. Parochial considerations do not grip the president's attention nearly as much as they do members of Congress. Rather, in the White House, concerns about national outcomes predominate.

15. Lewis and Moe 2010, 370–371.

familiar with how congressional policy affects their constituents. On the other hand, if constituencies are too small, representatives will be "unduly attached" to local interests and "too little fit to comprehend and pursue grand and national objects." Madison endorsed the federal system as a way to ensure that members of Congress place at least some weight on both the national and local consequences of policy, while explicitly acknowledging the concern regular elections and small constituency sizes could encourage members to privilege local interests over national concerns. When assessing the merits of a particular policy, members of Congress can be expected to evaluate its consequences both for the country as a whole and for their local constituents, whereas presidents focus intently on national considerations.

These features of bargaining between the president and Congress lead us to our model. In two substantive ways, this model breaks from the most recent theoretical work on information acquisition and signaling. First, it allows for the possibility that a single policy can generate two outcomes— one of which concerns national affairs, the other local. Second, it allows politicians to assign varying levels of importance to these outcomes. By accounting for these important features of our politics, we can simultaneously assess the effects of policy uncertainty, policy stakes, and the relative salience of national outcomes on the president's success when bargaining with Congress. In so doing, we find that as Congress assigns increased significance to national vis-à-vis local outcomes, presidential bargaining success increases.[16]

2.2 *The Model*

We now are in a position to explicate our model of interbranch negotiations, which we will refer to as the Policy Priority Model. After introducing the elements of the game, we explore two aspects of the model. First, we show that an equilibrium exists wherein the President acquires expertise on national outcomes and makes a policy proposal, and the Legislator acquires expertise on local outcomes and enacts a policy. While alternative equilibria exist for differing values of the parameters, this particular equilibrium most directly reflects the relative advantage that the President has in learning national outcomes and that the Legislator has in learning local

---

16. In addition, and as we discuss in greater detail later, our model does not include "signals," as they are thought of in the preceding literature.

outcomes. Subsequently, we derive the comparative statics of presidential success for each of the parameters of the model. In the equilibrium we have outlined, we find that the President has more success when the Legislator places greater value on national outcomes. This comparative static holds regardless of the ideological preferences of the President and the Legislator, and therefore breaks from many previous models that have relied on preference convergence as the mechanism through which presidential influence typically increases. Our model shows that preference convergence will indeed improve the President's success, but it also demonstrates that the President can improve his position even in its absence.

SETUP

We now identify the four main components of our theory: the players, the strategies available to each player, the utility functions of each player, and the function that maps policies onto outcomes. Additionally, we outline the order of play, the solution concept, and other assumptions of the model necessary to generate predictions.

Players. We are interested in the strategic interactions between the president and Congress. The game, therefore, consists of two players—a president and a representative member of Congress. Hence, $I = \{P, L\}$, where P identifies the President, and L identifies the Legislator with whom he will be negotiating. (For future reference, Table 2.1 provides a legend for all notation in the model).

Strategies. In the game, the President and Legislator interact with one another to select a policy on a bounded interval, $p \in [0,1]$. This policy exists on a one-dimensional line, which can be thought of as denoting liberalism and conservatism (with values on the left indicating a liberal policy and values on the right indicating a conservative policy) or monetary commitments (with larger values indicating more expensive policies).

Each policy p results in both a national political outcome $x_1 \in [0, \mu_1]$ and a local political outcome $x_2 \in [0, \mu_2]$. Like the policy itself, each of these outcomes exists on one-dimensional lines. The mapping function from policy to national political outcome is ψ_1, such that $\psi_1(p) = x_1$. Likewise, the mapping function from policy to local political outcome is ψ_2, such that $\psi_2(p) = x_2$. Thus, each policy p produces a pair of relevant outcomes (x_1, x_2) for the players in the game. Both the President and Legislator have preferences over each of these outcomes, but, as we will see later, their

Table 2.1. NOTATION

Notation	Parameter Description
Players, Indexed by i	
P	President
L	Legislator
Outcomes, Indexed by j	
1	National
2	Local
Actions	
S_i	Strategy of player i
A_j	Player has acquired expertise on outcome j
B	Player has acquired expertise on both national and local outcomes
$\varnothing$	Player has not acquired any expertise
$p^i \in [0, 1]$	Policy proposed/enacted by player i
Parameters	
U_i	Utility of player i
x_j	Outcome j of policy
ψ_j	Mapping function from policy to outcome j
$x_j^i \in [0, \mu_j]$	Ideal outcome j for player i
$c_j^i \geq 0$	Cost for player i to acquire expertise on outcome j
$\lambda \geq 0$	The weight placed on national outcomes (relative to local outcomes)
$\mu_j > 0$	Slope of mapping function from policy to outcome j
$z_j \sim U[-k_j, k_j]$	Stochastic shock to policy on outcome j

utility need not weigh the two outcomes equally. The President's most preferred outcome (that is, his ideal point) is denoted (x_1^P, x_2^P), and the Legislator's most preferred outcome is denoted (x_1^L, x_2^L). To simplify notation, the Legislator's most preferred outcome is normalized to $(0, 0)$. Consequently, (x_1^P, x_2^P) can be thought of as the Euclidean distance between the President's and the Legislator's most preferred outcomes.

Each player may pay a cost $c_1 \geq 0$ to acquire expertise about what national outcome any policy p will produce and a cost $c_2 \geq 0$ to acquire expertise about what local outcome any policy p will produce. To allow for the possibility that the President and Legislator may pay different costs to acquire expertise, we denote c_1^P and c_2^P as the costs the President must pay, and c_1^L and c_2^L as the costs the Legislator must pay.

Table 2.2 presents the order of the game, which begins with the President deciding whether to acquire expertise on how policies translate into

Table 2.2. ORDER OF THE GAME

Stage 1.	The President decides whether to acquire expertise on how policies translate into national and/or local outcomes.
Stage 2.	The President proposes a policy p^P.
Stage 3.	The Legislator decides whether to acquire expertise on how policies translate into national and/or local outcomes.
Stage 4.	The Legislator enacts a policy p^L.
Stage 5.	The enacted policy p^L yields an outcome (x_1, x_2), and payoffs are realized.

national and/or local outcomes. The President may choose to acquire expertise on one, both, or neither mapping function. In a slight abuse of notation, $S_P = \{A_1, A_2, B, \varnothing\}$, where A_1 indicates the President has acquired expertise on how policies translate into national outcomes, A_2 indicates the President has acquired expertise on how policies translate into local outcomes, B indicates the President has acquired expertise on how policies translate into both national and local outcomes, and $\varnothing$ indicates the President has not acquired any expertise. After choosing whether or not to acquire expertise, the President then proposes a policy $p^P \in \left[0, \psi^{-1}\left(x_j^P\right)\right]$ that is in the policy space bounded by the Legislator's and the President's ideal outcomes.[17] In total, the President's strategy set is characterized as: $S_P = \{A_1, A_2, B, \varnothing\} \times \left\{ p^P \in \left[0, \psi^{-1}\left(x_j^P\right)\right]\right\}$.

The Legislator observes the President's actions (whether the President acquired expertise, and the President's proposal p^P). She then chooses whether to invest in acquiring expertise on how policies map onto local and/or national outcomes. Subsequently, she enacts a new policy anywhere on the bounded interval, $p^L \in [0,1]$. Thus, the Legislator's available actions are: $\{A_1, A_2, B, \varnothing\} \times \{p^L \in [0, 1]\}$. Because the game is sequential, the strategy set for the Legislator is a mapping function from each action of the President to a set of actions of the Legislator; formally, $S_L = f: \{A_1, A_2, B, \varnothing\} \times \left\{ p^P \in \left[0, \psi^{-1}\left(x_j^P\right)\right]\right\} \to \{A_1, A_2, B, \varnothing\} \times \{p^L \in [0, 1]\}$. The enacted policy p^L yields national and local outcomes (x_1, x_2), and payoffs are realized.

17. We will have more to say about the implications of this restriction later in this chapter. For now, suffice it to say that this restriction rules out the possibility of strategic proposal making by the President.

Player Utilities. Both the President and Legislator are interested in attaining the political outcomes that most closely approximate their ideological preferences. Thus, their utility crucially depends on the distance between a political outcome and their specified ideal point. The President, we postulate, cares only about the national political outcome.[18] Hence, as the gap between the President's preferred national outcome and the actual national outcome increases, the President's utility decreases, which is captured mathematically by the quadrative loss function, $-\left(x_1^P - x_1\right)^2$. Because the President's utility is unaffected by the distance between his preferred local outcome and the actual local outcome, the only other relevant portions of the President's utility function are the costs he may have paid to acquire expertise on how policies translate into outcomes. The President's utility, then, is given by: $U_P = -\left(x_1^P - x_1\right)^2 - \mathbb{I}\{S_P = A_1 \cup B\} * c_1^P - \mathbb{I}\{S_P = A_2 \cup B\} * c_2^P$, where $\mathbb{I}\{S_P = A_1 \cup B\}$ is an indicator for whether the President acquired expertise on national outcomes and $\mathbb{I}\{S_P = A_2 \cup B\}$ is an indicator for whether the President acquired expertise on local outcomes. Note that while the President's utility is unaffected by the location of policy along the local outcome dimension, nothing in the model precludes him from investing in the acquisition of expertise about the mapping of both national and local outcomes. For this reason, two cost expressions rather than just one appear in the President's utility function.

While we restrict the President to care exclusively about national outcomes, we allow for the Legislator to care about both national and local outcomes. The Legislator's utility is defined over the distance between policy outcomes and her ideal points along both dimensions—that is, her utility decreases when either $\left(x_1^L - x_1\right)^2$ or $\left(x_2^L - x_2\right)^2$ increases. The Legislator, however, may not value both outcomes equally. Indeed, such an assumption seems unlikely. We therefore introduce a parameter $\lambda \geq 0$ to scale the relative significance of national vis-à-vis local outcomes. For $\lambda > 1$, more weight is placed on the national outcome than on the local outcome. Conversely, for $\lambda < 1$, more weight is placed on the local outcome than on the national outcome. And for $\lambda = 1$, the two outcomes matter equally to the Legislator's utility. Like the President, the other portions of the Legislator's utility function reflect the costs that may have been paid to

---

18. As we will discuss at greater length, this assumption that the President cares only about national outcomes, and not at all about local outcomes, can be relaxed in a number of ways without affecting the key comparative statics.

acquire expertise. The Legislator's utility is given by $U_L = -\lambda\left(x_1^L - x_1\right)^2 - \left(x_2^L - x_2\right)^2 - \mathbb{I}\{S_L = A_1 \cup B\} * c_1^L - \mathbb{I}\{S_L = A_2 \cup B\} * c_2^L$, where the first two terms identify the relative losses (weighted by $\lambda \geq 0$) associated with policy outcomes that diverge from the Legislator's national and local ideal points, and the latter two terms identify the costs that may have been paid to acquire expertise about either or both of the two mapping functions.

Mapping Functions. Players can only choose policies, but their utilities are defined over outcomes. Before we can derive their optimal strategies, therefore, we first need to characterize how policies translate into outcomes. Depending on the behaviors of the President and Legislator, policy p^L produces outcome j as follows:

$$\psi_j(p^L) = \begin{cases} \mu_j p^L & \text{if } L \text{ is an expert on } j, \text{ regardless of} \\ & \text{whether } P \text{ is an expert;} \\ \mu_j p^L + z_j & \text{if neither } L \text{ nor } P \text{ is an expert on } j; \\ \mu_j p^L + (p^P - p^L)z_j & \text{if } L \text{ is not an expert on } j \text{ but } P \text{ is.} \end{cases}$$

The mappings of policies onto outcomes, you will notice, vary across different subgames, depending upon the acquisition of expertise and the willingness of a lay Legislator to accept the policy proposal of an expert President. In each case, $\mu_j > 0$ is common knowledge and represents the sensitivity of outcome x_j to policy p, whereby larger values indicate greater sensitivity; or, in the language previously used, larger values indicate higher stakes.[19] Last, z_j is a stochastic shock, which characterizes the uncertainty of the policy-making environment (more on this later). Players have common knowledge that z_j is a random variable, distributed uniformly with support $[-k_j, k_j]$.[20] The multiplicative combination of $(p^P - p^L)$ and z_j generates the effect of proportional invertibility discussed earlier,

19. In future work, we might consider a model wherein $\mu_1 > 0$ and $\mu_2 < 0$, which would make gains in national outcomes unavoidably entail losses in local outcomes. Such might be the case, for instance, when thinking about trade policy, wherein lower tariffs benefit the general country but hurt communities that employ the affected domestic industries. When incorporating this possibility into a model that also allows for the President to assign some positive weight on local outcomes, a possibility that we will discuss later, our core comparative statics regarding the effect of λ on Θ would require two limiting assumptions rather than just one. In addition to the President assigning greater weight to national outcomes than the Legislator, changes in λ would have to increase at a faster rate for the President than for the Legislator.

20. We assume a uniform distribution for mere mathematical simplicity. There is no reason to believe that the key comparative statics will change under alternative distributional assumptions.

for as a lay Legislator's enacted policy deviates farther from an expert President's policy proposal, the uncertainty cost (which both the President and Legislator will incur) associated with the variance of z_j increases.

In three cases, different mapping functions characterize how policy p produces outcome j. In the first, the Legislator becomes an expert on outcome j, in which case she pays no uncertainty cost and the mapping function reduces to $\psi_j(p^L) = \mu_j p^L$. This captures the intuition that by acquiring expertise the Legislator knows exactly what outcome a policy will produce, and therefore does not care whether the President's proposal is based on expert information or not, for it tells her nothing that she does not already know.[21]

If neither the Legislator nor the President acquires expertise, then the mapping becomes $\psi_j(p^L) = \mu_j p^L + z_j$. This captures the notion that a lay Legislator does not place any stock in the proposal made by a lay President, and as a result, partial and proportional invertibility of the mapping function is lost, and all policies carry an uncertainty cost equal to the full value of the variance of z_j.

If the Legislator remains a layperson but the President acquires expertise on j, then the mapping function becomes $\psi_j(p^L) = \mu_j p^L + (p^P - p^L)z_j$. By introducing $(p^P - p^L)$, the mapping function becomes partially and proportionally invertible. As $(p^P - p^L)$ increases, the Legislator's enacted policy deviates farther and farther from the President's proposal; consequently, z_j is being multiplied by a larger number, yielding an increasing uncertainty cost. Because $(p^P - p^L) < 1$, however, this cost can never exceed the uncertainty cost that the Legislator pays when both players lack expertise. Hence, when the Legislator is able to guard against some policy uncertainty, she is always better off.

In two of the three scenarios, the Legislator—and, by extension, the President—can avoid paying any uncertainty cost. The first occurs universally in scenario one. As long as the Legislator acquires expertise about the mapping of policy into a particular outcome, she will not face any uncertainty cost along that respective dimension. Even if she does not acquire expertise, the Legislator can nonetheless avoid paying any uncertainty cost by enacting an expert President's proposal exactly; in which case $(p^P - p^L) = 0$, the second half of the term drops out, and the mapping

21. To keep things simple, we have assumed that an expert knows exactly how each policy translates into an outcome. Of course, one could relax this assumption and allow an expert to confront some uncertainty in the policy-making environment—in which case, the mapping function would also include a lower bound on z_j.

function again reduces to $\psi_j(p^L) = \mu_j p^L$, just as in the case where the Legislator acquires expertise on outcome j. Note, however, that she does not necessarily acquire her most preferred policy outcome. The President's proposal, after all, may well generate an outcome that deviates substantially from the Legislator's ideal outcome. It is for this reason that the lay Legislator's calculus about how to respond to an expert President's proposal reflects the standard uncertainty-bias trade-offs in games of noncooperation.

Thus far, we have considered the uncertainty cost structures of a single mapping function. However, central to our theory is the recognition that a policy can generate multiple outcomes, each of which has its own independent mapping function. When we evaluate the uncertainty costs associated with two independent mapping functions, things really get interesting. For instance, if a Legislator acquires expertise about only the local mapping function, she still faces a potential uncertainty cost associated with the national mapping function. Provided that the President has acquired expertise about the national mapping function and proposed a suitably moderate policy, the Legislator can avoid this uncertainty cost by simply enacting a policy that exactly equals the President's proposal. In doing so, she may well be enacting a policy that she knows will generate a local outcome that is less preferred. To the extent that she deviates from the President, she will have to pay an uncertainty cost on the national mapping even as she pays none at all on the local one. Hence, just as the Legislator faces an uncertainty-bias trade-off within each mapping function, so too does she face one across the mapping functions.

Why should the mappings of policies into outcomes vary according to the expertise of the President and Legislator? The intuition here is simple enough. When either the Legislator is herself an expert or she enacts policy that perfectly represents the views of an expert President, she can be expected to write policy that is sufficiently clear and precise so that only a single outcome will be realized. In this scenario, those charged with interpreting and implementing the policy (bureaucrats, interest groups, and judges, none of whom are represented in the model) have no discretion of their own; and, by assumption, they will not substitute their own policy preferences for that of their expert political superior. On the other hand, when a lay Legislator tries her hand at writing policy, she unavoidably introduces ambiguities and imprecisions that permit a variety of interpretations and, by extension, a variety of plausible outcomes.

Note that in this model, acquiring expertise on outcome j does not reveal the true value of z_j to player i (as it does, for instance, in Gilligan and Krehbiel's work).[22] Rather, by acquiring expertise the Legislator inoculates herself against the effect of z_j. In this sense, the acquisition of expertise constitutes the purchase of insurance against uncertainty, rather than the translation of uncertainty into certainty. Hence, z_j itself should be thought of as a lottery that reflects the variety of possible outcomes that a policy written by a lay politician can support. Players, under this formulation, do not update their beliefs about z_j. Rather, by becoming an expert, players no longer play the lottery when selecting a policy.

By analogy, consider what it means to gain expertise about tomorrow's weather. In Gilligan and Krehbiel's formulation, expertise amounts to knowing whether or not it will rain tomorrow. In ours, by contrast, expertise involves the acquisition of an umbrella, and a perfect umbrella at that, such that the expert is completely unaffected by whether or not it rains. The model, thus postulated, draws on economic models of insurance markets wherein purchasers trade off bias (in the form of insurance premiums) against uncertainty (in the form of assumed risk). Here, the Legislator must weigh the costs of enacting a policy that may not reflect her preferences against the uncertainty associated with shifting policy away from an informed President's proposal.[23]

Solution Concept. Because this is a game of complete information, the equilibrium solution concept is Subgame Perfect Equilibrium.

EQUILIBRIUM ANALYSIS

Depending on the values assumed by the parameters x_j^P, μ_j, k_j, c_j^i, this game supports multiple equilibria. What distinguishes these equilibria, in the main, is the identity of the players who acquire expertise about the

---

22. To preserve proportional invertibility, we do not use Gilligan and Krehbiel's characterization of the mapping of policies into outcomes. Other proposed mapping functions, meanwhile, themselves have features that are subject to criticism—such as non-monotonicity and what Callander refers to as "two-point invertibility." In addition to dodging these particular criticisms, our mapping function offers the benefit of being relatively simple and straightforward—properties that are especially appreciated given the added complexities of mapping one policy into not one but two outcomes. Still, future work may want to explore the possibility of characterizing mapping functions as independent Brownian motions (as in Callander 2008), which also are proportionally invertible.

23. Obviously, this allusion only goes so far, as our model does not identify anyone or anything that can be thought of as an insurance provider.

two mapping functions. Our primary interest, however, lies in identifying the conditions under which presidents enjoy greater or lesser policy success, not in discerning when they or their congressional counterparts invest in the acquisition of information. With this goal in mind, we focus on an equilibrium wherein the President invests only in national expertise (and therefore has no knowledge about local outcomes) and proposes the policy that produces his preferred national outcome, and then the Legislator invests only in local expertise (and hence has only imperfect knowledge of national outcomes) and enacts a new policy.

Theorem I. For sufficiently large c_1^L and sufficiently small c_2^L and c_1^P, an equilibrium exists wherein the President acquires expertise on only national outcomes and proposes a policy that produces either his ideal national outcome or, under select circumstances, the Legislator's. The Legislator then acquires expertise on only local outcomes and enacts a policy that either is closer to her ideal point (in the case when the President proposes the policy that produces his ideal point) or that perfectly matches the President's proposal (in the case when the President proposes the policy that produces the Legislator's ideal point).
Proof. See Appendix A.

In order for this equilibrium to hold, two conditions must be met. First, given that the President has learned how policies translate into national outcomes and made a policy proposal to the Legislator, the Legislator must prefer over all other available options to learn how policies translate into local outcomes, to forsake the opportunity to learn how policies translate into national outcomes, and then to enact a new policy. This condition is satisfied when the cost of acquiring expertise about national outcomes, c_1^L, is sufficiently large and the cost of acquiring expertise about local outcomes, c_2^L, is sufficiently small. Second, knowing what the Legislator will do in response to each of the President's strategic options, the President must prefer over all his other options to learn how policies translate into national outcomes (but not local outcomes) and to make a new policy proposal. This will be true when the cost to the President of acquiring expertise on national outcomes, c_1^P, is sufficiently small.

This equilibrium, you will notice, supports two sets of actions by the President and Legislator. In the first, the President proposes exactly his ideal point, $p^P = \psi^{-1}\left(x_1^P\right)$, which the Legislator then amends to some value $p^L < p^P$. Consider, though, the case where p^L generates the outcome $x_1^L = 0$. In this instance, the Legislator amends the President's proposal to such a degree that the outcome, in expectation, generates her own ideal point. Given that this is her optimal strategy, the President would be better off just setting policy exactly at her ideal point and thereby eliminating the uncertainty cost of having a layperson set policy. As a result, there exists a basic threshold at which the President shifts from proposing his ideal point to proposing the legislator's ideal point.[24] When concessions occur, therefore, they amount to capitulation. This fact derives directly from our characterization of the mapping function. Because of proportional invertibility, the willingness of a lay Legislator to shift policy closer to her ideal point depends on the policy proposed by an expert President. Hence, just because the President expects a Legislator to enact a policy that is less than his proposal (thereby incurring an uncertainty cost for both parties) does not mean that the President will simply want to propose that policy himself. For doing so would allow the Legislator, in turn, to shift policy even farther away from his preferred outcome. Hence, it is only when the Legislator would enact a policy sufficiently close to her ideal point that the uncertainty costs incurred by the President outweigh the utility loss associated with just giving the Legislator her ideal point that the President concedes.

Other equilibria, to be sure, can be derived from the model. For the most part, such equilibria rely on parameter values that seem implausible—for instance, that the Legislator's costs of acquiring local expertise are greater than those of acquiring national expertise, and further that the cost to the Legislator of acquiring national expertise is lower than the cost to the President of doing so. In the equilibrium identified in Theorem 1, however, we need only believe that it is quite costly for Legislators to acquire national expertise, relatively cheap for Legislators to acquire local expertise, and relatively cheap for presidents to acquire national expertise.[25] Moving forward, therefore, this equilibrium guides our analysis.

---

24. The exact cut point is given by the inequality $(x_1^P)^2 \geq \left(x_1^P - \mu_1 \left(\frac{\lambda z p^P}{\lambda(\mu_1^2 + z) + \mu_2^2} \right) \right) - \left(p^P \left(\frac{\lambda z p^P}{\lambda(\mu_1^2 + z) + \mu_2^2} \right) \right) z \right)^2$. When this inequality holds, the President prefers to propose the policy that produces his ideal outcome. If this does not hold, then the President prefers to propose the policy that generates the Legislator's ideal outcome.

25. An alternative justification for this equilibrium is the Legislator is incapable of acquiring the level of expertise about national outcomes that a President can acquire. One could capture this in the model by simplifying the Legislator's strategy set to only include the option of acquiring local expertise, and the President's to only including the option of acquiring national expertise.

SINCERE VERSUS STRATEGIC PROPOSAL MAKING

As specified, the Policy Priority Model requires the President to only introduce policies in the interior space between his and the Legislator's ideal point. As a result, the President regularly proposes the policy that produces his ideal national outcome. If we allow the President to propose any policy $p^P \in [0, 1]$, and if we further allow the Legislator to update on any proposal, strategic proposal-making can optimally occur. To see this, notice that the President can anticipate the amount by which the Legislator will amend his proposal. This amount, after all, makes the Legislator indifferent between the relative policy losses to be had (which are weakly decreasing in the policy reduction toward her ideal point) and the uncertainty costs associated with deviating from an expert President's proposal (which are strictly increasing in the same policy shift). The President, therefore, has clear incentives to increase his proposal by exactly this amount, so that the Legislator will subsequently amend it back to his ideal point.[26] Moreover, because of the proportional invertibility of the mapping function, the President will rightly anticipate that the Legislator will not amend this more extreme proposal by an even larger amount. For even though the Legislator knows that the President is asking for more than he really wants whenever he proposes $p^P > \dfrac{x_1^P}{\mu_1}$, she cannot respond in kind without incurring an even larger uncertainty cost. In this sense, the Legislator knows that she is being gamed, but she cannot do anything about it.

By allowing the President to submit any proposal along the entire policy continuum, the equilibrium identified in Theorem 1 and its associated comparative statics do not entirely unravel. If the Legislator simply commits up front to ignoring any proposal that is greater than the President's ideal point, and that therefore reflects not just any expertise acquired but also his effort to negate the Legislator's subsequent ability to amend this proposal, then our equilibrium is no longer subgame perfect, but it is Nash, which is sufficient to support our core predictions regarding λ. Moreover, we can recover subgame perfection in this equilibrium by introducing to the players' respective utility functions costs associated with verifiably extreme proposal making, a move that is broadly

26. Note that this outcome yields an uncertainty cost that both players must pay. Both players, therefore, would be better off if an expert President proposed his ideal point, which the Legislator enacted into law. Because the Legislator cannot commit to this action a priori, however, this Pareto improving outcome is not supported in equilibrium.

consistent with the formal literature on "blame-game vetoes,"[27] and scholars' widespread recognition of the importance of position-taking more generally.[28]

COMPARATIVE STATICS

Although it is useful to sort through the strategic considerations that inform the President's proposal making and the Legislator's lawmaking, our primary interest resides in the comparative statics that relate to presidential success. In our model, presidential success is characterized as the distance between the President's ideal policy $\left(p^P = \dfrac{x_1^P}{\mu_1} \right)$ and the Legislator's enacted policy (p^L). We denote this distance $\Theta^* = \dfrac{x_1^P}{\mu_1} - p^L$. In this section, we derive the comparative statics of presidential success. We relate changes in Θ^* to changes in the stakes of policymaking nationally and locally (μ_1 and μ_2, respectively), the ideological distance between the Legislator and President (x_1^P), the uncertainty of the policymaking process (k_1), and, most importantly, the relative importance of national considerations to the Legislator (λ).

Both x_1^P and μ_1 are fixed parameters. However, p^L is chosen endogenously by the Legislator. In equilibrium, the Legislator will choose a policy that maximizes her expected utility. Given that the President has invested in expertise on national outcomes and proposed a policy that produces his ideal national outcome,[29] and that the Legislator has invested in expertise on local outcomes and enacted a policy, p^L, the Legislator's expected utility is given by:

$$EU_L = \lambda \left[-(\mu_1 p^L)^2 - (p^P - p^L)^2 \left(\frac{k^2}{3} \right) \right] - (\mu_2 p^L)^2 - c_2^L.$$

The first order condition yields:

$$\frac{\partial EU_L}{\partial p^L} = -2\lambda \mu_1^2 p^L + \frac{2}{3} k_1^2 (p^P - p^L) - 2\mu_2 p^L = 0$$

$$\Rightarrow p^L \left(-2\lambda \mu_1^2 - \frac{2}{3} k_1^2 \lambda - 2\mu_2^2 \right) = -\frac{2}{3} k_1^2 \lambda p^P$$

27. Groseclose and McCarty 2000.
28. Mayhew 1974.
29. See Appendix A for a discussion of results when the President does not propose his ideal point.

$$\Rightarrow (p^L)^* = \frac{\frac{1}{3}k_1^2 \lambda p^P}{\lambda \mu_1^2 + \frac{1}{3}k_1^2 \lambda + \mu_2^2} = \frac{\frac{1}{3}k_1^2 \lambda \frac{x_1^P}{\mu_1}}{\lambda \mu_1^2 + \frac{1}{3}k_1^2 \lambda + \mu_2^2}.$$

Plugging $(p^L)^*$ into Θ^*, we find that:

$$\Theta^* = \frac{x_1^P}{\mu_1} - \frac{\frac{1}{3}k_1^2 \lambda \frac{x_1^P}{\mu_1}}{\lambda \mu_1^2 + \frac{1}{3}k_1^2 \lambda + \mu_2^2}$$

$$= \frac{(3\mu_1^2 + 3\mu_2^2)x_1^P}{\mu_1(3\lambda \mu_1^2 + \lambda k_1^2 + 3\mu_2^2)}.$$

Presidential success, then, can be expressed in terms of five parameters: μ_1, μ_2, x_1^P, k_1, and λ. To determine the effect of each of these factors, we take the partial derivative of Θ^* with respect to each.

Theorem 2. The following five comparative statics hold on presidential proposal influence (Θ^*) whenever the President proposes the policy that produces his ideal outcome:

$$\frac{\partial \Theta^*}{\partial \mu_1} \leq 0 \text{ iff } k_1^2 \leq \frac{3\lambda^2 \mu_1^4 + 6\lambda \mu_1^2 \mu_2^2 + 3\mu_2^4}{\lambda^2 \mu_1^2 - \lambda \mu_2^2}.$$

$$\frac{\partial \Theta^*}{\partial \mu_2} \geq 0 \ \forall \mu_2.$$

$$\frac{\partial \Theta^*}{\partial x_1^P} \geq 0 \ \forall x_1^P.$$

$$\frac{\partial \Theta^*}{\partial k_1} \leq 0 \ \forall k_1.$$

$$\frac{\partial \Theta^*}{\partial \lambda} \leq 0 \ \forall \lambda.$$

Proof. See Appendix A.

The degree to which changes in policy affect changes in national outcomes (μ_1) has a contingent effect on presidential influence. Provided that the uncertainty cost is sufficiently small, presidential success increases as changes in policy lead to greater changes in national outcomes. When the cost of uncertainty becomes sufficiently large, however, presidential success decreases as the national stakes of policy change increase.

The other comparative statics yield clearer predictions. Presidential success will decline as the local stakes of a policy (μ_2) increase. Hence, we should expect the President to fare worse in those interbranch negotiations in which minor changes in policy induce relatively large changes in local outcomes. Presidential success also increases as the President's ideal national outcome (x_1^P) converges to the Legislator's.

Of particular interest are the effects of the final two parameters: (1) the uncertainty of national outcomes (k_1), and (2) the weight the Legislator places on national outcomes relative to local outcomes (λ). As uncertainty about national outcomes increases, so too does the President's proposal influence. Similarly, presidential success increases as the Legislator attaches greater importance to national outcomes relative to local outcomes. Both of these comparative statics hold for all values of (k_1) and (λ), respectively. This should come as no surprise. In this equilibrium, the President has expertise about national outcomes while the Legislator does not. Thus, any factor that amplifies the Legislator's uncertainty costs will yield an outcome that more closely approximates the President's preferences.

The left panel of Figure 2.1 displays the comparative statics of k_1 on Θ^*. Fixing μ_1 at 2, μ_2 at 1, x_1^P at 1, and λ at 2, we allow k_1 to vary. We find that for $k_1 = 0$, Θ^* is approximately 0.3. Moreover, Θ^* is strictly decreasing in k_1—that is, presidents always enjoy greater success as the bounds of uncertainty regarding the national outcome increase.

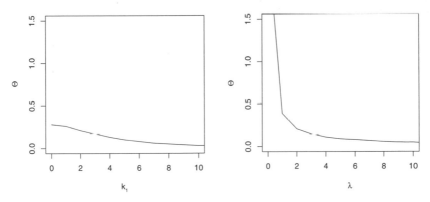

Figure 2.1. COMPARATIVE STATICS OF PRESIDENTIAL BARGAINING SUCCESS.

The left figure shows the comparative statics of k_1, and the right figure shows the comparative statics of λ.

In the right panel of Figure 2.1 we keep μ_1, μ_2, and x_1^P at their previous levels, fix k_1 at 2, and allow λ to vary. Here we find that when $\lambda=0$, Θ^* is 2.5. Again, Θ^* is strictly decreasing in λ. We also find that λ has a substantively larger effect on Θ^* than does k_1, particularly for small values of λ (that is, when Congress goes from placing almost no weight on national outcomes to evenly balancing national and local outcomes). So it would seem that the propensity of members of Congress to vote with the president should be more sensitive to marginal changes in the relative importance they assign to national outcomes than to marginal changes in uncertainty regarding national outcomes of policy.[30]

A PRESIDENT WHO CARES ABOUT NATIONAL AND LOCAL OUTCOMES

It is possible to recover the key comparative static with respect to λ in a model that relaxes the strong assumption that local outcomes do not figure at all in the President's utility. Consider, for instance, a model in which both the President and Legislator each have their own λ parameter: λ_P and λ_L, respectively. In this case, the President's utility function would become $U_P = -\lambda_P\left(x_1^P - x_1\right)^2 - \left(x_2^P - x_2\right)^2 - \mathbb{I}\left\{S_P = A_1 \cup B\right\}*c_1^P - \mathbb{I}\left\{S_P = A_2 \cup B\right\}*c_2^P$, and the Legislator's utility function would become $U_L = -\lambda_L\left(x_1^L - x_1\right)^2 - \left(x_2^L - x_2\right)^2 - \mathbb{I}\left\{S_L = A_1 \cup B\right\}*c_1^L - \mathbb{I}\left\{S_L = A_2 \cup B\right\}*c_2^L$. In this setup, the core comparative statics persist as long as presidents care more about national outcomes than do legislators—that is, $\lambda_P > \lambda_L$.

To see the intuition behind this claim, imagine a world that begins in a time of moderately low levels of λ for both the President and the Legislator—that is, national outcomes are not particularly salient to either group. Then some exogenous event occurs that increases both λ_P and λ_L. The increases to these two parameters may or may not be equal. In this new state of the world, national outcomes are much more relevant to both groups, but the President's concern for national outcomes relative to local outcomes (i.e., λ_P) remains higher than the Legislator's concern (λ_L). Thus, in all states of the world, $\lambda_P > \lambda_L$. In most empirical applications, this assumption is benign.

There is good reason to suspect that, at all times, the President is judged primarily on (and hence cares primarily about) his achievements at the national level. Local events may occasionally figure into his thinking, but

---

30. The same substantive findings hold for alternative parameter values of μ_1, μ_2, and x_1^P.

in the main presidents concern themselves primarily with the national implications of policy. Meanwhile, legislators feel pressure to appeal to the relatively more parochial interests of their constituent base. Therefore, when comparing a President and a Legislator, it seems natural to assume that, at all times, the President places relatively more weight on national outcomes than does the Legislator. If one grants this simple premise, along with the additional assumption that exogenous factors that increase the salience of national outcomes for one political actor also increase the salience of national outcomes for the other actor, then all of our key comparative statics carry through.

COMPARATIVE STATISTICS: OTHER EQUILIBRIA

For different parameter values, alternative equilibria are sustainable. For instance, for sufficiently high c_1^L and c_2^L and sufficiently low c_1^P and c_2^P, an equilibrium exists wherein the President acquires expertise on both national and local outcomes and proposes a policy, and the Legislator acquires no expertise and enacts a policy. In general, all of the main comparative statics hold from the equilibrium specified in Theorem 1.[31] In particular, increasing the uncertainty regarding national outcomes (k_1) or the weight the Legislator places on national outcomes (λ) will still increase presidential success (Θ^*). More generally, these comparative statics hold in any equilibrium in which the President holds an informational advantage regarding national outcomes of policy.

Our core predictions change, however, when the President holds no such informational advantage—that is, when the Legislator acquires expertise on both national and local outcomes, which will occur in equilibrium for sufficiently low levels of c_1^L and c_2^L.[32] In this equilibrium, the President does not acquire any expertise and proposes the policy that corresponds to his ideal national outcome, and the Legislator acquires expertise on both national and local outcomes and enacts the policy that produces her ideal outcome. Because the Legislator always enacts her ideal policy in this equilibrium, the comparative statics identified in Theorem 2 no longer hold.[33] Of particular significance, we find that k_1 and λ have null compara-

31. The one exception concerns the comparative statics on the uncertainty regarding local outcomes (k_2). Whereas before increases in k_2 had a null effect on Θ^*, now they increase presidential success.
32. For a full derivation of the conditions necessary to sustain this equilibrium, see Appendix A, Theorem 3.
33. For a full derivation of the comparative statics of this equilibrium, see Appendix A, Theorem 4.

tive statics on Θ^*. Even in this equilibrium, though, note that the comparative statics do not reverse signs. Thus, for all equilibria in the model, it remains true that increasing k_1 or λ will never impede presidential success. Rather, such increases will only help or have no effect on the President.[34] Indeed, the only parameters that continue to have an effect on Θ^* are x_1^P and μ_1. In this equilibrium, presidential success decreases as x_1^P increases, and increases as μ_1 increases.

Though these alternative equilibria are worth documenting, they have little to say about the contemporary state of American politics. Each of these alternative equilibria, after all, rely on empirically implausible parameter values. For example, the equilibria in which the President holds no informational advantage require that the Legislator be able to acquire national expertise at an extraordinarily low cost. Moving forward, therefore, we restrict our attention to equilibria where the President does hold an informational advantage regarding the national outcomes of policies.

2.3 *Nontechnical Summary*

The Policy Priority Model investigates the bargains that are struck between the president and a representative member of Congress. Ex ante, neither of these players is assumed to agree with the other. Indeed, the whole point of this exercise in theory building is to identify features of politics that bear upon the president's ability to advance his agenda in the face of pre-existing policy disagreement.

In the model, the negotiation process begins with the president making a proposal and ends with Congress enacting a policy. The president's proposal need not be a formal legislative proposal that Congress amends or votes down. In some instances, these proposals are formally made, such as in the budgetary process where the president's annual budget proposal necessarily precedes the final appropriations allocated by Congress. But presidents can also make proposals through informal means, such as in a speech or press release. Even in legislative processes, presidents have ample ways of seeing that their policy initiatives receive a hearing in Congress.

---

34. Null results also arise in models that allow the President to make proposals in the entire policy space, and thereby support strategic proposal making. The null results in these models arise in a subgame perfect equilibrium that we do not analyze.

Our theory begins by recognizing a basic fact of constitutional design: presidents represent the entire country, whereas legislators serve individual districts or states. As a consequence, disputes between presidents and legislators reflect not only disagreements about the optimal policy for either the country as a whole or for some jurisdiction within it, but also disagreements about how to prioritize between these two constituencies. Presidents, it seems fair to assume, care primarily about the nation's welfare. Legislators, by contrast, are regularly torn between what is good for the country and what is good for their district or state—and the two, it bears emphasizing, are not necessarily of a part. Policies that improve the country do not always improve a chosen district or state. Indeed, it is easy to think of policies that may be good for the country (such as free trade) but hurt localities within it; or conversely, policies that benefit a local constituency (such as a public works project) but that hardly affect the nation as a whole. Consequently, if we want to understand the propensity of a legislator to support a president, we must ascertain not only what each politician wants for the nation and locality, but also how each politician priorities between them. Legislative support for the president, as such, hinges as much on what a legislator thinks about policy for a given constituency as on how the legislator thinks about the importance of different constituencies.

To capture these intuitions, the model assumes that policies generate two outcomes: one national, another local. The two politicians, however, disagree about the political relevance of these outcomes. Whereas the president cares about national policy outcomes, the legislator cares about both, albeit not equally. Indeed, the core prediction of the model is that legislators who assign greater importance to national outcomes (and in so doing, appear more "presidential" in their outlook) exhibit higher levels of policy support for the president, all else equal.

In our model, politicians care about policy outcomes, but not policies per se. Hence, we have little to say about negotiations over purely symbolic policy disputes. We recognize, however, that the correspondence between policies (which are the subject of choice) and real-world outcomes (which define players' utility) is uncertain; and, moreover, that learning about the relationship between the two is costly. Hence, the model explicitly accounts for the variable costs of acquiring expertise about the translations of policies into either local or national outcomes. While allowing for these costs to vary in magnitude, nothing about our model prohibits either the president or legislator from acquiring expertise about either the local or national outcomes of a policy. Still, because presidents care only about national outcomes, we might expect them to become experts on the national implications of policy (and not pay the costs of becoming experts on the local implications). And because they care about both national and local outcomes, legislators are more likely than presidents are to acquire expertise on the local implications of policy (though they may prefer to become experts on both the national and local implications).

Having characterized the key players, their utilities, and the order of play, we can identify the optimal policies that a president will propose and the final policies that a legislator will enact. It turns out that some key parameters of the model—parameters, it bears noting, that capture important elements of wartime politics—do not necessarily improve the president's chances of enacting more preferable policies. Under plausible scenarios, the stakes of public policy making can either enhance or diminish presidential success. Hence, just because minor deviations in policy can generate relatively larger changes in outcomes during war than peace does not necessarily play to the president's advantage. Though our model, in the main, confirms previous theoretical work showing that presidents fare better as their preferences converge with those of members of Congress, it also introduces an important wrinkle. When the president's ideal point passes a crucial threshold—one wherein the political uncertainty outweighs the losses in utility associated with policy shifts—the president stops proposing the policy that produces his ideal outcome and instead capitulates to Congress.

The effects of marginal changes in other parameters are more easily interpreted. Like previous theoretical work on interbranch negotiations, we also find that increases in uncertainty about how policies translate into national outcomes improve the president's utility. Most importantly, our model highlights a new parameter that yields clear and crisp predictions about presidential success. We show that presidents are better able to achieve their most preferred outcomes when legislators assign relatively greater importance to national vis-à-vis local outcomes. When they stand by the parochial interests of their constituents, legislators can be expected to vote against the president. But to the extent that they put the interests of the country before the interests of their constituents, legislators can be expected to look favorably on the president's policies. This happens because legislators are relatively uncertain about national outcomes of policies, and the cost associated with this uncertainty increases the more that their policy efforts diverge from an expert president's proposal.

Hence, even when preferences and uncertainty are held constant, policy outcomes better reflect the president's preferences when legislators assign greater importance to national outcomes.

It is worth reiterating the crucial role of expertise in the model. Scholars have written at some length about presidents and their subordinates' superior knowledge about public policy generally, and the national implications of policy in particular.[35] According to Sean Gailmard and John Patty, information serves as the "lifeblood of executive branch action"; and as a result, presidents have access to "information to which Congress and outside observers are not privy."[36]

Precisely because presidents are experts on the national implications of a given policy, they hold an informational advantage over legislators when dealing with national outcomes. When the country enters into a period of war, legislators become more concerned with these national implications. Recognizing that the president knows more about national outcomes, they then defer more to presidential proposals than they would in times of peace, because the uncertainty cost of deviating from the president's proposal is magnified. Thus, even if the president and Congress *disagree* ideologically about the ideal national outcome, legislators will still defer more to the president in war than in peace in order to avoid paying an increased uncertainty cost. In this sense, the president's relative expertise in the national outcomes of policies guarantees congressional deference when the importance of national outcomes increases (as occurs during war).

One could posit a technically simpler model that does not rely upon expertise but instead on ideal point convergence in order to generate its core prediction. Imagine, then, a model that assumes exactly the same form as our own, except that there is no uncertainty about the mapping of policies into either national or local outcomes. In this alternative model, increasing the salience of national outcomes will lead to heightened presidential success, but only if the president and legislator have more ideological comity regarding national outcomes than they do regarding local outcomes; but if the president and legislator disagree more about national outcomes than they do about local ones, then increases in the salience of national outcomes necessarily lead to policy enactments that make the president worse off. By focusing on expertise, our model altogether avoids these entanglements, generating clean predictions that do not rely

35. See, for example, Canes-Wrone et al. 2008; Schlesinger 1973, 2004.
36. Gailmard and Patty 2012, 8, 9.

upon strong (and perhaps unwarranted) assumptions about ideological convergence.

With the Policy Priority Model, we have a basis for believing that wars might augment presidential success. When the nation transitions from peace to war, legislators can be expected to assign greater value to the national implications of policies, and relatively less to the local implications of policies. During war, therefore, both the president and Congress fixate on the national outcomes of policies, which encourages legislators to more closely abide the expertise that presidents retain over how policies map into national outcomes. As a result, and as we discuss at greater length in the next chapter, presidential proposals can be expected to receive a more favorable hearing in war than they do in peace.

2.4 *Conclusion*

The Policy Priority Model captures essential elements of interbranch negotiations. It provides an explicit accounting for how policies translate into outcomes, while also allowing for the possibility that a single policy will generate multiple outcomes of variable importance to presidents and legislators. Moreover, the model recognizes the costs associated with acquiring expertise in how policies translate into outcomes. Unlike previous work on information acquisition, our model explicitly recognizes important differences between the evaluative criteria of legislators and presidents.

The Policy Priority Model cannot be said to favor the president. If anything, it overstates the extent to which Congress influences policy outcomes. None of the collective action problems or transaction costs that routinely undermine legislative initiatives are present. The multiple veto points, complex committee structures, and bicameral nature of Congress that do so much to define the legislative process are utterly ignored. The president, meanwhile, is stripped of his ability to either veto legislation or to forsake the legislative process altogether and strike out on his own. Indeed, in this model the president's only opportunity to affect legislative outcomes comes through his ability to propose policies.

Further, in the model, the utility of legislators in no way reflects a need to support the president simply because he is the commander in chief (a claim often made in the empirical literature on the presidential use of force). Bargaining, in this sense, occurs strictly over policy outcomes, and in no way recognizes the unique obligations that presidents have over certain policy domains.

The predictions that this model generates, therefore, arguably over-state congressional influence, just as they understate presidential influence. For our purposes, though, this fact is largely irrelevant. Our primary goal is not to develop a model that appropriately captures the balance of power across the two branches of government. Nor, empirically, are we interested in evaluating whether it is the president or Congress who exerts the most influence over policy outcomes. Rather, we want to investigate whether policy outcomes more closely approximate the president's preferences—regardless of whether presidential influence, in the main, is large or small—during periods of war than they do during periods of peace. So long as those elements of politics that our model ignores do not correlate with the incidence of war—and for the most part, they should not—we sit on fertile theoretical ground.

The Policy Priority Model supports an eclectic array of predictions that align with previously established empirical regularities on interbranch negotiations. It suggests, for instance, that presidents should experience greater success on policies that centrally concern the nation's welfare, and less success on policies that invoke stronger regional considerations. For this reason, we should expect presidents to fare better on foreign policies—noted primarily for their national outcomes—and worse on domestic policies. Though for decades the so-called two-presidencies thesis attracted a fair measure of controversy,[37] recent research that accounts for the deep endogeneity issues associated with presidential position-taking shows that presidents do in fact fare better on foreign policy than on domestic.[38] Also consistent with our model, members of Congress are more supportive of the president's policy agenda on the subset of foreign policy issues with a distinctly national focus (such as security) than those issues (such as foreign aid and trade) with stronger regional implications.[39]

Suppose, further, that the national media and presidents themselves tend to focus their attention on those policies that, by reference to some fixed criteria, evoke stronger national concerns. If true, then we should expect presidents to experience greater congressional deference on these subsets of policies, a finding that is consistent with a large literature indicating that presidents improve their bargaining leverage by "going public."[40]

37. Compare, for example, the original Wildavsky 1966 and the follow-up Oldfield and Wildavsky 1989.

38. Canes-Wrone et al. 2008.

39. Milner and Tingley 2010, 2011.

40. Canes-Wrone 2006; Kernell 2007; Rudalevige 2002.

Table 2.3. KEY TAKEAWAY POINTS OF THE POLICY PRIORITY MODEL

1.	The model shows conditions under which presidents will increase their success with Congress even in the absence of preference convergence.
2.	Presidential influence increases as members of Congress assign greater importance to national outcomes and less to local outcomes.
3.	By increasing the salience of national outcomes, wars have the potential to increase presidential influence.

By a similar logic, those members of Congress who assign relatively greater importance to national outcomes, all else equal, can be expected to vote in ways that better reflect the president's policy preferences. True to form, a number of scholars have found that party leaders, committee leaders, and members of Congress who plan to run for the presidency tend to vote more consistently with the president than do rank-and-file members of Congress.[41]

In this book, however, we are less interested in exploring all of the various predictions of the Policy Priority Model, and more in using the model to illuminate facets of the particular relationship between war and presidential power. In this regard, three other contributions of the Policy Priority Model stand out as particularly important, and these contributions are summarized in Table 2.3. First, the model shows conditions under which presidents will increase their success with Congress even in the absence of preference convergence—or more specifically, the convergence of players' ideal points. Support for the president derives not from changes in what outcomes a legislator would like to see realized, but instead how she prioritizes these outcomes—a fact that establishes the basis for the second contribution of the Policy Priority Model: the comparative statics on λ identify conditions under which policy will more closely reflect the president's preferences. When members of Congress assign greater importance to national outcomes, and relatively less to local outcomes, presidents can expect to enjoy greater success. Third, and finally, the parameter λ provides a way for thinking about the relationship between war and presidential success. If wars augment the salience of national outcomes, they can be expected to bolster the president's influence.[42] In the next chapter, we provide some basis for believing that they do.

41. Bond and Fleisher 1990; Edwards 1989; Grofman et al. 2002; Jessee and Malhotra 2010.

42. Naturally, we do not rule out the possibility that crises other than wars may have a similar effect on λ. In subsequent chapters we explore some plausible candidates. We do so, however, as merely a supplement to the core empirical analyses that focus on the relationships between war and presidential success in Congress.

CHAPTER 3

The Model's Predictions about Modern U.S. Wars

Though it does not expressly parameterize war, the Policy Priority Model nonetheless offers a way of thinking about the variable willingness of members of Congress to support the president during war and peace. In particular, the model suggests that the relative importance of national policy outcomes (as characterized by the parameter λ) has important implications for presidential success in Congress. To the extent that wars induce positive changes in λ, we should expect them to yield legislative bodies that are more sympathetic to the president's policy agenda. To investigate whether recent wars undertaken by the United States actually have had this effect, we now incorporate many of the historical details about the domestic politics of war that made barely an appearance in the previous chapter.

To make headway, though, we first must answer a basic question: What do we mean by *war?* In the first section of this chapter, we outline a definition of war that focuses squarely on the most significant military operations the United States has undertaken since World War II. Should we fail to find evidence to support our model's predictions in these large ventures, the model is unlikely to have much to say about the extent to which more limited military operations reshape relationships between the president and Congress.

We recognize that all major wars are not identical. The Pearl Harbor attacks on December 7, 1941 propelled the nation into war against the Axis powers, which set into motion an unprecedented unification of the country's resources to its defense, with combat troops dispatched to all corners of the globe. Other wars, such as the Persian Gulf War, posed little or no imminent threat to national security, had fairly narrow and well-defined missions, and did not mobilize the country's economic engines to substantially increase production. Fortunately, the Policy Priority Model suggests a way of evaluating the relative impacts of different wars on presidential success. Because the key parameter of the model is treated continuously, we can distinguish between those wars that in-duce smaller or greater changes in the relative importance of national outcomes. Consequently, we have a theory that does not merely postu-late that presidential success should increase during times of war but provides a foundation for thinking through the heterogeneous impacts of different wars.

Observed differences across wars therefore, provide further opportuni-ties to test our theory and isolate the effects of war on presidential policy influence. To wit, the second section of this chapter describes what the key parameter of the model might look like in the real world. We define more precisely what we mean by the nationalization of policy priorities and what evidence might signify its advancement or decline. Having laid out these criteria, we sort through the specific military ventures that meet our definition of war. We then specify our exact predictions about which wars will induce the largest increases in presidential success, and which wars will contribute more modestly to presidential influence.

We recognize that our explanation for why wars increase presidential success has its competitors. Mechanisms that have little to do with the nationalization of politics (such as the costs of war, public opinion, and the state of the economy) may be responsible for congressional accom-modation to the president during war. Indeed, within our own theory we can find competing explanations that center on the relative uncertainty of policy making during periods of war and peace. In the last section of this chapter, therefore, we briefly outline these alternative explanations and then suggest some critical tests that will allow us to distinguish them from ours.

3.1 *Defining War*

When are we at war? Or, more to the point, when are we not?[1] In the mod-ern era, hundreds of thousands of troops are stationed around the globe. In some regions, such as the demilitarized zone separating North and South Korea, multiple battalions of troops have stood poised for battle for over a half-century. A Cold War loomed for nearly as long, during which time the world's two superpowers came to the very brink of nuclear war at least once. Since World War II, the United States has launched hundreds of small and midsize deployments to every continent in the world, with

---

1. For an extended discussion of these questions, see Dudziak 2012.

Beirut, Grenada, El Salvador, Haiti, Bosnia, Kosovo, and Libya representing some of the more recent targets of military action. The U.S. military regularly works in concert with the United Nations patrolling, and in some cases exercising force in, regions of the world that are wracked by ethnic violence and political instability. Given its hegemonic status, the United States constantly monitors emergent threats to the nation's economic and political interests from anywhere around the globe. And if those were not enough, modern presidents have waged "wars" against terrorism, drugs, poverty, piracy, cancer, and polio.

Should we construct a definition of war that encompasses all of these preparations and actions, then we will never recognize the incidence of peace. For the purposes at hand, this effectively rules out the possibility of examining the impact of war on congressional voting behavior, at least in the modern era. Thus, for purely practical reasons we take a much more restrictive view of war. Following a host of other scholars,[2] we distinguish from all other "wars" World War II, the Korean War, the Vietnam War, the Gulf War, and the wars in Afghanistan and Iraq that followed the attacks on September 11, 2001. By any metric, these constitute the most significant military actions taken by the United States in the modern era. These five wars further distinguish themselves from other international showdowns—most obviously the Cuban Missile Crisis—when two states appeared on the verge of battle, but either no or only infrequent fighting actually occurred, as well as those purely symbolic "wars" that were waged not against armies but security threats, social ailments, and bodily diseases.

Having selected our wars, we now need to determine when they began and when they ended. This also turns out to be less than straightforward. By the time the United States entered World War II, European nations had been fighting for the better part of two years. During this time, both with and without Congress's formal consent, Roosevelt had directed a steady stream of material support to England. The beginnings of other wars are also difficult to pinpoint. The United States began sending military "advisers" to Indochina as early as 1950; by the early 1960s, the U.S. military capacity in the region had steadily expanded. And after 9/11, the better part of three weeks passed before the president initiated action to retaliate against the Taliban regime in Afghanistan.

2. See, for example, Clark 2006, and Epstein et al. 2005.

Identifying when wars end can be just as problematic. Long after fighting came to a halt in Europe in 1945, U.S. troops remained stationed on the continent, as the United States grappled with how to handle the emergent new world order. And as of this writing, the military campaigns in Iraq have all but ceased, while those in Afghanistan are rapidly declining.

Recognizing these complexities is one thing. Becoming incapacitated by them is quite another. In the interest of moving us along, then, the following criteria inform our selection of starting and ending points for war. War begins when actual fighting that involves U.S. troops either commences (in the case of World War II, Korea, the Persian Gulf, and the post-9/11 era) or rapidly escalates (in the case of Vietnam). For our purposes, therefore, World War II does not begin until after Pearl Harbor, when the United States formally entered the war. The post-9/11 era does not begin until October 7, 2001, when Congress authorized the use of force and U.S. troops entered Afghanistan. The Vietnam War does not formally begin until the spring of 1965, with the commencement of Operation Rolling Thunder, the first major military venture after the Gulf of Tonkin. War ends when a formal peace treaty is signed, regardless of whether U.S. troops remain stationed in the region or intermittent fighting continues. With these rules, the following dates delineate the beginnings and ends of each of our wars: World War II, December 7, 1941, to August 14, 1945; Korea, June 27, 1950, to July 27, 1953; Vietnam, February 7, 1965, to January 27, 1973; Persian Gulf, January 16, 1991, to April 11, 1991; and Afghanistan beginning October 7, 2001.[3]

This definition of war supposes that the nation is either at war or is not. Thus, we do not distinguish those periods in which the nation's military resources are directed to a single war effort—as was the case, for instance, in the Persian Gulf War—from other periods in which the nation is involved in multiple wars simultaneously. On March 20, 2003, with a war already being waged against Taliban insurgents in Afghanistan, President George W. Bush took the nation to war against Iraq. Our definition, however, does not permit distinctions between periods, for the war in Afghanistan remained ongoing while the United States prosecuted another war in Iraq. Just as we do not distinguish between the Pacific and European fronts of American involvement in World War II, we also do not distinguish between the periods

3. With one exception, these dates replicate those in Epstein et al. 2005. Although they identify a period of peace that preceded the Iraq war in 2003, we treat the entire period after the outbreak of war in Afghanistan as an uninterrupted war.

when the United States was involved militarily only in Afghanistan from when troops also descended on Iraq. Therefore, we will henceforth refer to the period after military operations commenced in Afghanistan in 2001 as the "post-9/11 wars."

Admittedly, our definition of war has its limitations. Most obviously, it does not distinguish mobilization and demobilization efforts, the varying levels of our military engagements, or the changing size and immediacy of foreign threats. We can and will compare the effects of different wars on different congresses. For the most part, however, changes in the size or scope of a given war lie beyond the scope of the analysis that follows. Of equal concern, our definition does not distinguish between different peacetime periods. Though the nation watched Europe erupt in flames in 1939, stood on the brink of nuclear war in 1962, heralded the demise of the Soviet Union in 1989, and then sporadically intervened into the post–Cold War regional crises of the latter 1990s, all of these periods are defined as peaceful, and nothing in our definition permits comparisons between them.

Our definition of war also has advantages. First, it zeroes in on those military actions that have the best chance of reconstituting the domestic polity. If legislative behavior is insensitive to U.S. involvement in these wars, it seems unlikely that members of Congress are affected by participation in smaller military campaigns. Second, the definition eschews the extraordinary measurement difficulties of systematically accounting for the smaller deployments and diplomatic standoffs that populate so much of the modern era. Whereas our chosen wars reveal a natural breakpoint in the historical data, a more encompassing definition would require an even more arbitrary and elusive dividing line between periods of war and peace. Third, to the extent that it allots all kinds of military actions and threats to periods of "peace," our definition constitutes something of a hard test for the proposition that members of Congress adopt a more deferential posture vis-à-vis the president during war. Operationally, what we are calling peace may, in fact, not be peaceful at all. If so, then the evidence reported in subsequent chapters most likely understates the true impact of war on congressional voting behavior. And fourth, our definition bears more than a passing resemblance to those employed by previous scholars, and hence provides some basis for comparison.

3.2 *Which Equilibrium Are We Playing?*

Depending on the parameter values assumed by x_j^i, μ_j, λ, and c_j^i in the Policy Priority Model, different behaviors and outcomes will emerge in equilibrium (see Chapter 2). For the most part, these equilibria produce substantively similar comparative statics. In particular, any equilibrium in which the president has an informational advantage regarding the national outcomes of policies produces the key comparative static that, as the legislator places more weight on national outcomes (i.e., as λ increases), the president experiences greater success (i.e., Θ^* decreases). This result holds regardless of the other player's decisions about whether to acquire expertise on local outcomes.

It is important to recognize, however, a basic fact about the empirical exercise we are about to embark on. When conducting comparative statics on λ, we are exploring the effect of marginal changes in the relative importance of national outcomes on presidential success, contingent upon the president retaining informational advantages about these national outcomes. If λ becomes sufficiently high, however, we may actually jump from one equilibrium to another.[4] By assigning a sufficiently large value to national outcomes, members of Congress will prefer to pay the cost of acquiring national expertise over the uncertainty of relying on the president. Moreover, in this new equilibrium, our main comparative static does not hold. When the Legislator becomes informed about national outcomes, the President himself will not pay the cost of acquiring expertise only to be ignored by the Legislator. As a consequence, the President's leverage disappears, and increasing the salience of national outcomes may or may not help the President in his negotiations, which explains the weak inequalities in Theorem 2.

For understanding contemporary politics in the United States, we argue, the relevant equilibrium is one in which the President *does* have an informational advantage regarding national outcomes. We base our argument on two observations. First, for the President to lose his informational advantage in equilibrium, it must be the case that the Legislator need pay a very low cost to acquire expertise on national outcomes (c_1^L). But if expertise costs are functions of institutional structure—and they assuredly are—then we can infer something about which equilibrium we are playing

---

4. The precise threshold is a complex—and largely unintuitive—function of five parameters.

by observing the material world we inhabit. It seems uncontroversial that at present the administrative state is expressly designed to facilitate the transmission of information about national issues to presidents, and that to the extent the administrative state responds to congressional concerns, it is by addressing their more parochial interests. To be sure, members of Congress can extract information about the relationship between policies and national outcomes. The point here is simply that Congress lacks the deep infrastructure to support such inquiries. By contrast, members of Congress have built substantial administrative capacity to facilitate the acquisition of information about the local implications of public policy making, making these inquiries relatively cheap. These basic facts about existing institutions—and the cost structures they imply—suggest that we do in fact inhabit a world defined by the equilibrium identified in Theorem 1 in Chapter 2.

Second, it bears emphasizing that the core predictions of the model hold so long as the Legislator fails to acquire the same *level* of expertise as the President. Strictly speaking, for our equilibrium to hold, the President need only know more about the national mapping than Congress—not that Congress knows nothing at all. Indeed, in the context of the model, the President knowing more than Congress is isomorphic to a model in which the Legislator does not have the option of investing in national expertise. Here again, we take it as incontrovertible that, at least on the national implications of public policy, presidents know more than members of Congress.

3.3 *Measuring the Prioritization of National Outcomes*

All major wars bring the nation's health and security into stark relief. In an effort to stamp out threats to the nation's sovereignty, vital interests, and security, wars affirm citizens' shared status as Americans and underscore their common heritage, values, and shared fates. During war, American flags are raised, anthems are sung, and a sense of solidarity sets in. Major wars rather consistently prompt citizens and politicians to express solidarity with the president, eschew partisan labels, and reaffirm their allegiance to the nation.[5]

---

5. See Brody 1991 and Mueller 1973 for a more extended discussion of the "rally-'round-the-flag" phenomenon.

Beyond merely symbolic calls for national unity, wars also emphasize the need for members of Congress to prioritize national political outcomes over policy outcomes that favor their local constituencies. As the historian James Sparrow notes, "no moral equivalent could lay claim to national obligation more effectively than war."[6] During major wars, members shift their attention away from policy outcomes that benefit local citrus farmers or textile manufacturers, and instead place greater weight on how policy outcomes affect the nation as a whole. Debates about education, housing, labor–management relations, and the like lose their local color and become wrapped in larger conversations about the nation's ability to meet a perceived foreign threat and compete internationally.

The Policy Priority Model trains our attention on this last dimension of the domestic politics of war. The model predicts that a representative legislator will support policies that more closely approximate the president's preferences when she attaches greater importance to the national implications of public policy making. Within the model, the parameter λ represents the relative importance of national and local policy outcomes. But, of course, we do not observe the values of λ directly.[7] To ascertain

6. Sparrow 2011, 26.
7. Undaunted, some political scientists have tried to isolate the effect of constituency characteristics on members' voting behavior. Indeed, a modest but resilient literature in American politics explores the relationship between district-level and state-level characteristics on members' voting behavior. Largely descriptive in nature, this empirical literature examines how constituency factors correlate with members' roll call votes. Though weakly informed by theory and unable to draw firm causal inferences, this research nonetheless provides some insights into the strength of the relationships between a variety of demographic measures of local constituencies and observed patterns of voting on Capitol Hill. Building on this literature, we did investigate whether the observed correlations of some constituency characteristics—particularly those that are distinctly local in nature and that, themselves, are unlikely to be affected by the outbreak of war—and members' voting behavior attenuates when the nation enters war. The results, however, did not indicate any clear pattern either across wars, parties, or chambers of Congress. Indeed, when looking at the correlations between characteristics such as percentage of union membership or farmers within a district or state, the results were notably sensitive to model specification, convincing us that this was not an especially profitable avenue of distinguishing among our different wars. Even if we had uncovered reasonably stable and consistent findings, it is not altogether clear what we could have made of them. For starters, finding evidence of a diminished wartime relationship of one local characteristic does not rule out the possibility of the emergence of another. In addition, lacking any clear measure of distinctly national considerations, we could not claim to have demonstrated an increase in λ per se. Finally, because the true relationship between any local or national consideration and members' voting behavior is unobservable, we cannot say that a steeper slope in the estimated relationship during one period or another—which is all that a correlation indicates—says anything about the quality of representation offered by the member to any particular interests, be they local or national.

whether any given war is likely to alter presidential success, we must identify a set of tangible characteristics of wartime politics that correlate with, induce changes in, or serve as proxies for the salience that legislators assign to national policy outcomes.

Changes in a legislator's prioritization of national and local outcomes may either be induced or directly conceived. It is quite possible that citizens come to an independent judgment about the importance of an ongoing war effort, to which members of Congress, ever fearful of the next election, pay continual homage. In this sense, reevaluations of national priorities occur at the behest of a watchful and informed public. Alternatively, members of Congress may come to their own judgments about a war's relevance for policy disputes that pit the welfare of their constituents against the welfare of the nation as a whole. In this sense, members are seen with a great deal more autonomy than standard characterizations of the electoral connection typically allow.[8] Because it does not expressly model a representative voter, the Policy Priority Model provides little insight into which source is more likely. Strictly as a matter of measurement, though, we want to allow for both possibilities.

We therefore look to five types of evidence. The first type consists of public appeals and speeches made by members of Congress. Here, we canvass the rhetoric that members of Congress use to justify their votes, both in the speeches that they make on the floors of Congress and in written remarks they submit for publication in the *Congressional Record*. Where possible, we examined the *Congressional Record* during the weeks immediately before and after the beginning of war. We supplemented this research with two kinds of secondary accounts of the policy debates that occurred during times of peace and war. First, we canvassed biographies of presidents and congressional leaders to assess the ways in which these figures characterized lawmaking as the nation moved into and out of war. Second, we searched the *New York Times* for coverage of congressional activity during the same time periods.

Our primary objective has been to identify the kind of appeals members of Congress make to their congressional colleagues, their constituents, and the president. We are interested in assessing the extent to which members justify their behavior by invoking national concerns as opposed to local interests. Should we find that, during war, members of Congress regularly invoke their districts' interests to explain their positions for or

8. Mayhew 1974.

against policy proposals, the war is unlikely to have been accompanied by sizable increases in λ. On the other hand, if, during some other war, members frequently justify their votes by asking their constituents to put the nation's interests above their parochial concerns, the increase in λ is likely to have been more significant. Where we find similar patterns within a given war across all these sources, we have some confidence in our characterization of the extent to which war altered the weighting that members placed on the national (relative to local) implications of policy.

We remain cognizant of the difficulties of divining motivations from public statements. When issuing public appeals, members of Congress have ample incentive to dissemble. Imperfect as they may be, these public statements at least hint at changes in λ, if only because politicians regularly articulate the reasons why they vote for or against a given policy, and these reasons often signify the relative importance of national and local priorities.

Of course, members of Congress can affirm their commitment to national ends while also professing to stand up for their local constituents. A spirit of self-sacrifice and national pride can coexist with assertions of local prerogatives. As observers, though, we can at least gauge the relative emphases that members place on these two imperatives. Occasionally, members will come right out and openly admit that they are casting votes that, while good for the country, will hurt their constituents, or, alternatively, that they value local concerns more than those of the federal government. More often, members assert a positive case either for uniting in common cause with the rest of the country or for standing by the legitimate interests of their district or state. What members do not say can often reveal as much about their underlying motivations as what they do say. Thus, as much as the content of public statements, we also seek to characterize the tenor of the arguments members deploy in the public sphere.

We further recognize that the ways in which members justify their votes at the commencement of war may be a product of war itself. Members may articulate greater support for the president and emphasize the need for national unity precisely because war has fixated their attention on the national implications of policy. Members' speeches then constitute data about the degree and magnitude of shifts in congressional support for the president, just as other kinds of data do so in the chapters that follow. In using this criterion to evaluate relative changes in λ, we recognize that we run the risk of overdetermining the results of our subsequent empirical tests. However, to the extent that members' public justifications for votes cast in Congress are sincere revelations of the relevant considerations they used when deciding how to vote, this criterion is the most direct way of measuring relative changes in members' emphasis on national concerns.

We also consult contemporary media accounts and the secondary historical literatures on each of these wars. From these sources, we look for descriptions of a wartime domestic polity that fit two broad categories. In the first, politicians and citizens are seen rallying behind a common purpose, affirming their shared interests and common bonds, and reasserting a distinctly national identity. The clarion call of "Country First" is affirmed, again and again. Though policy disagreements may surface, the sources of such disagreements are not regionally specific preferences or priorities. Rather, such disagreements center on how the nation should go about meeting the threat posed by an enemy that intends harm on the entire nation. In the second, by contrast, politicians and citizens do not shy away from asserting their own parochial interests and celebrating the diversity and dissent that defines so much of the nation's history. Though they may not disparage the war effort per se, and certainly not the soldiers who stand on its front lines, citizens and politicians nonetheless routinely raise what they perceive to be legitimate concerns about how policies affect local communities around the nation.

We also assess the state of public opinion during each of these wars under the assumption that the values that members of Congress assign to local and national outcomes either reflect or inform the views and priorities of their constituents. Again relying on accounts found in the *New York Times,* we track two aspects of public opinion during each of our wars. First, we examine observed levels of patriotism. Clearly, patriotism invokes some sentiments, ranging from xenophobia to national pride, that have little to do with our conception of λ. A defining element of patriotism, however, is an abiding belief that the good of the nation trumps the good of the individual. Patriots, as such, willingly sacrifice their private, parochial concerns for the nation's well-being. As Kosterman and Feshbach put it, patriotism reflects the extent to which individuals experience a sense of "attachment to the nation" that reorients their perceived interests and priorities.[9] The prevalence of patriotism in World War II, commentators at the time explained, could be found in citizens who "subordinated or shelved" their "aims and values" in order to meet the threat posed by

9. Kosterman and Feshbach 1989, 271.

the Axis powers.[10] Assessments of patriotism, then, provide some indication of the extent to which these wars increased the salience of national vis-à-vis local policy outcomes. In our survey of the secondary historical literatures on these wars, we look for descriptions of contemporary levels of patriotic sentiment, as expressed in parades, national songs, and other national symbols.

As a second reading of public opinion—and, by implication, of members' voting behavior—we track changes in perceptions of the "most important problem" facing the nation.[11] When a substantial segment of the population identifies national security and foreign affairs as among the country's chief concerns, they are likely to reevaluate the relationships between policies and outcomes. For example, rather than arguing on behalf of education reform on the basis of augmenting the life chances of groups that historically have faced discrimination, citizens may equate education reform with the nation's ability to keep pace with foreign competitors. Similarly, gas prices may have less to do with one's personal finances and more to do with American dependence on foreign oil. Wars that shift the public's attention to foreign affairs, therefore, are likely to increase the importance of distinctly national policy outcomes. To assess these shifts, we examine the changes in the percentage of Gallup Poll respondents who identify war and foreign affairs as the nation's most important problem in polls conducted immediately before and after war begins. Large shifts in the percentage of respondents who identify war as the most important problem suggest that the war has substantially reoriented the public's evaluation of the implications of policy changes.[12] Although these data are not perfect,[13] in contrast with other public opinion data, they are available for almost the entire time period under investigation. Further, these

10. Blumer 1943, 226, 229; Cantril 1951, 1172, 1178; both cited by Leff 1991, 1297.
11. In principle, these data are available back to 1935. Unfortunately, as Smith (1980) discusses, the surveys were conducted irregularly and infrequently before 1946, requiring us to exclude World War II surveys from the analysis.
12. The Policy Agendas Project at the University of Texas has recoded the open-ended responses to the Gallup Poll's question into twenty-three categories, ranging from crime to labor to agriculture to foreign trade. We combine these more specific categorizations into three broad classifications of issues: war (which combines "defense" and "international affairs"), social issues ("civil rights," "health," "labor," "education," "social welfare," and "housing and development"), and economic issues ("macroeconomics"). We investigate patterns of responses while war was occurring, and in the years immediately preceding and after a war. For additional details, see http://www.policyagendas .org. We gratefully acknowledge T. Jens Feeley, Bryan D. Jones, and Heather Larsen for these data.
13. See, for example, Wlezien 2005.

data require us only to assess changes over short periods of time (i.e., the years immediately before, during, and immediately after war), which relaxes the assumptions needed to make comparisons across wars.

Lastly, we look to some of the specific features of war that are likely to induce members of Congress to assign greater importance to national vis-à-vis local outcomes. Specifically, we assess the extent to which wars present imminent security threats. Facing an enemy that has demonstrated its ability to attack stateside and that has expressed patently imperial designs, U.S. citizens and politicians are particularly likely to support those policies that strengthen the country, even when they introduce substantial costs for their own communities and personal livelihoods. Conversely, when confronting a distant and more ethereal threat, U.S. citizens and politicians are less likely to forsake their parochial interests for the good of the nation. So while the presence of an imminent security threat is not, in itself, a direct measure of the nationalization of politics, it is a likely prerequisite for policy priorities to change in ways that lead to increased presidential success.

None of these measures, summarized in Table 3.1, offers an unobstructed view of λ in action during each of our wars. Members' rhetoric is often fickle, insincere, and idiosyncratic. The contemporary views of journalists and subsequent reflections of historians have biases of their own. The expressed views of the public may diverge from those of their elected representatives in Congress. Objective facts about war can be

Table 3.1. PROXIES FOR THE PRIORITIZATION OF NATIONAL OUTCOMES

Criteria	Rationale	How Measured
Congressional affirmations of national interests	Most direct measure of members' increased emphasis on national vis-à-vis local concerns	Public statements by members of Congress at the beginning of war
Congressional expressions of national unity	Affirming/asserting a shared national identity	Contemporary media and secondary historical accounts
Public displays of patriotism	Suggests subversion of parochial interests for the good of the country	Contemporary media and secondary historical accounts
Public attentiveness to war	Indicates how war reorients the public's attention to policy issues	Gallup Poll "Most important problem"
Imminent threat to national security	Security threats amplify national concerns and reduce local ones	Contemporary media and secondary historical accounts; statements by public officials during war

understood in widely different ways. And the quality and availability of data that relate to our five measures varies widely across our wars. Hence, we should not bank on any single measure yielding incorruptible claims about the relative weightings of local and national outcomes that inform members' voting behavior. However, after surveying all of these measures, we should have a reasonable basis on which to assess changes in politicians' criteria for evaluating public policy in war and peace—and hence to generate predictions about the extent to which members' voting behavior during World War II, the Korean War, the Vietnam War, the Persian Gulf War, and the post-9/11 wars conform to presidential preferences.

3.4 *Characterizing the Wars*

We do not purport to offer an exhaustive accounting of these wars. Nor do we intend to uncover anything new about them. Our objective here is far more modest. By canvassing the kind of evidence already discussed— assessments of the type of public speeches made by politicians, reflections by historians, and survey research on patriotism and national priorities— we offer some general characterizations of our wars. Though these assessments may be familiar and, we suspect, uncontroversial, they serve an absolutely vital function. They establish a foundation for predicting the relative impact of different wars on presidential policy success—and hence, for linking the Policy Priority Model to the empirical tests that follow.

WORLD WAR II

World War II ranks highly across all our criteria for assessing the extent to which members placed increased emphasis on national policy outcomes. The war inspired a degree of national pride and patriotism perhaps never before seen in the nation's history; it was waged against an enemy with broad imperial designs, and evoked expressions of solidarity from citizens and members of Congress alike. As Sparrow put it, World War II converted traditions of "regionalism, localism, and religious pluralism" into a "genuine national polity."[14] By all indications, this war established the benchmark against which our other wars are to be compared.

When Japanese planes attacked Pearl Harbor on December 7, 1941, the United States promptly suspended an ongoing debate about the nation's

14. Sparrow 2011, 8.

limited interests in Europe's conflict and launched headlong into war. The *Richmond Times-Dispatch* wrote, "America has been shocked into unity in a single Sunday afternoon. The bombs which came hurtling down yesterday without warning from Japanese warplanes upon our Pacific bases have closed the debate over the country's course."[15] Even staunch isolationists in Congress threw their support behind the president. Doris Kearns Goodwin details that, upon learning of the attacks:

> Senator Arthur Vandenberg of Michigan, who had struggled long and hard against American involvement in the war, phoned the White House to tell the president that "he would support him without reservation." Even Representative Hamilton Fish of New York, one of Roosevelt's severest critics, urged the American people to "present a united front in support of the President." After months of vacillation, confusion, and hesitation, the U.S. was committed at last to a common course of action.[16]

Immediately after the bombing of Pearl Harbor, the federal government declared war on the Axis powers. The president and members of Congress promptly united behind the nation's defense, publicly affirming the dual imperatives of self-sacrifice and the collective good. Representative George Dondero (R-MI) told his colleagues in the House that "there are no political parties in the United States today. The defense of our country and our liberty is at stake."[17] Representative Harry L. Haines (D-PA) was even more explicit about his increased interest in national policy outcomes: "The people I have the honor to represent are aroused and will not disapprove of my stand in thinking of my country first."[18] Or as House minority leader J. W. Martin (R-MA) put it, "There is no politics here. There is only one party when it comes to the integrity and honor of the country."[19]

In his first address to the nation upon the declaration of war, Roosevelt said:

> Together with other free peoples, we are now fighting to maintain our right to live among our world neighbors in freedom and in common decency, without fear of assault . . . Every single man, woman, and child is

15. Editorial, "Japan Strikes and America Answers," *Richmond Times-Dispatch,* December 8, 1941.

16. Goodwin 1995, 295.

17. December 8, 1941. http://www.presidency.ucsb.edu/ws/?pid=16056

18. Speech given on the floor of the House, December 9, 1941, *Congressional Record.*

19. C. P. Trussell, "Congress Decided," *New York Times,* December 8, 1941.

a partner in the most tremendous undertaking of our American history. We must share together the bad news and the good news, the defeats and the victories—the changing fortunes of war.[20]

Seeking to unify the nation behind the war efforts, the president continued: "The lives of our soldiers and sailors—the whole future of this Nation—depend upon the manner in which each and every one of us fulfills his duty to our country."

In the week following the Pearl Harbor attacks, the nation witnessed a presidency in ascendance. Roosevelt declared that he was "the final arbiter in all departments and agencies of the government."[21] Renowned journalist Walter Lippmann likely had this in mind when he published a column in the *Washington Post* on December 9:

> Congress should remove all legislative restrictions which prevent the President as Commander in Chief from employing our armed forces and our munitions whenever he and his advisers find it most advisable to use them. No war of this character can be won if the total power of the Nation is not freely available to those who are responsible for the strategical direction of the war. If they cannot be trusted to use all of our forces wisely, they cannot be trusted to use any of our forces wisely.[22]

Or as the historian James McGregor Burns observed, "As wartime Commander in Chief, Roosevelt could exert power over the American economy and society transcending any he previously wielded, even in the first heady days of the New Deal."[23]

Buttressing the president's exhortations were the grave and imminent security threats facing the nation. With the bombing of Pearl Harbor, the United States appeared more vulnerable to foreign attacks than at any time since the War of 1812. In a single day, the Imperial Japanese Navy managed to sink four U.S. battleships, seriously damage four more, destroy 188 U.S. aircraft, and kill 2,402 servicemen and citizens. The Japanese caught the U.S. government entirely by surprise on its own soil. Like no single event in the nation's history, this attack exposed the nation's vulnerability to foreign aggression, just as it punctured claims for isolationism that had held such sway on Capitol Hill.

---

20. Fireside chat, December 9, 1941, http://www.presidency.ucsb.edu/ws/?pid=16056.
21. Quoted in Burns 1970, 417.
22. "Wake Up, America," *Washington Post,* December 9, 1941.
23. Burns 1970, 417.

The foreign threats did not end with Japan. Germany declared war against the United States before Roosevelt could so much as assess the damage done to his naval fleet. Earlier in the war, Adolf Hitler had regularly professed his intention to build a new German Empire and prophesized that "the year 1941 will bring consummation of the greatest victory in [German] history." If the United States was to survive, it would need to wage a war on two fronts, facing two enemies with demonstrably imperial designs.

To meet these challenges, Roosevelt sought to connect virtually every policy instrument to the war effort. Every policy initiative, foreign and domestic, was part and parcel of the war effort. Thus, the only way to understand the merits of any particular policy initiative was by reference to its contributions to the men and women fighting abroad. As the president put it in the fall of 1942, when defending a budget proposal before Congress: "in a true sense there are no longer non-defense expenditures. I cannot tell what powers may have to be exercised to win this war."[24] In this war, the president argued, partisan and parochial interests had to accede to national exigencies. Under the president's leadership, the national project became the erection and then fortification of an "arsenal of democracy."

Most members of Congress heeded the president and promptly turned their attention to tax hikes, price controls, and wage ceilings. The arguments on behalf of these policy initiatives had little to do with the benefits they would deliver to local constituencies. For most communities, in fact, these policies produced significant hardships. Rather, members of Congress rallied behind these policies because they were seen as integral to the war effort particularly, and the nation's well-being more generally. Of congressional efforts to institute price controls, legal scholar Joseph Aidlin wrote:

> Every economic factor, every instrument of production, every hour worked, every item sold and service rendered, every material used bears directly upon the effectiveness of the prosecution of the war . . . It cannot be questioned that "in the interest of national defense and security and necessary to the effective prosecution of the war" the stabilization of prices, prevention of speculation and of unwarranted and abnormal increases in prices and rents, the elimination and prevention

24. September 7, 1942. The Public Papers and Addresses of Franklin D. Roosevelt, 1942 volume. http://quod.lib.umich.edu/p/ppotpus/4926593.1942.001?rgn=main; view=fulltext.

of profiteering and hoarding, and the other stated objectives of the Emergency Price Control Act are vitally necessary.[25]

By virtually every marker, citizens during World War II were filled with patriotism. As the *New York Times* wrote in summer 1942, "If the measure of a people's patriotism is their demand for flags, then American loyalty has leaped into the heights since Pearl Harbor."[26] The mayor of Chicago urged residents to display American flags,[27] and New York flag manufacturers were "besieged" with requests for more. The depth and longevity of American patriotism were credited with ending labor strikes[28] and compelling judges to reduce the sentences of felons who sold war bonds while in prison.[29] At one stretch, the Secretary of the Treasury's office received nearly 200 submissions daily from patriotic citizens who penned short tunes intended to inspire people to purchase war bonds.[30] According to newspaper headlines, patriotism even swept "over racial lines,"[31] and "through institutions and 'fired' inmates' hearts."[32]

As hagiographies like *The Greatest Generation* and *Saving Private Ryan* extoll, World War II was a time when Americans made difficult sacrifices to aid the nation's war efforts. Indeed, the very meaning of patriotism, and the terms by which public debate proceeded, involved the subversion of parochial interests in the name of collective security and national identity. As Leff wrote:

> The public-spirited wartime community of World War II holds a cherished place. It is nostalgically recalled as *our* "finest hour," when Americans freely sacrificed selfish desires . . . in common purpose. During World War II, Americans glorified in the feeling that they

25. Aidlin 1942, 654.
26. "Demand for Flags Called 'Terrific'; Requests at Retail Stores Here Increase as Patriotic Fervor Gains Momentum," *New York Times,* August 2, 1942.
27. "Mayor Urges Homes, and Businesses, Firms to Display Our Flag," *Chicago Tribune,* December 16, 1941.
28. "War Labor Board Wins in First Case; Appeal to Patriotism Brings A.F.L. Machinists Back to Work in Holland, Mich.," *New York Times,* January 23, 1942; "Buffalo Strikers Heed Patriotism; Vote to Return to Magnesium Plant and Put Wage Issue in Hands of the WLB," *New York Times,* July 19, 1942.
29. "Sold Bonds While in Prison; Patriotism Wins Probation," *Milwaukee Journal,* June 16, 1945.
30. Frances Long, "Patriotism Strikes High Note as 200 Persons Pen War Bond Ditties Daily," *Milwaukee Journal,* November 10, 1943.
31. "Patriotism Sweeps Over Racial Lines; More War Work Demanded," *Pittsburgh Post-Gazette,* September 26, 1942.
32. "War-Born Changes in Prisons Hailed; WPB Reports Patriotism Has Swept Through Institutions and 'Fired' Inmates' Hearts," *New York Times,* November 22, 1943.

were participating in a noble and successful cause by making "sacrifices." In common parlance sacrifice did not require the suffering of terrible loss. It instead comprehended a range of activities—running the gamut from donating waste paper to donating lives—in which narrow, immediate self-interest was subordinated to the needs of the war effort.[33]

This spirit of self-sacrifice and national beneficence, though, would not last forever. When the war finally ended, citizens—and with them, members of Congress—turned their attention to issues at home. Housing shortages plagued residents in cities around the country, labor unions conducted major strikes in the coal, railroad, and automotive industries, and price controls frustrated residents everywhere. As David McCullough noted, "A populace that had been willing to accept shortages and inconveniences, ceilings on wages and inadequate housing since 1941—because there was a 'war on'—seemed desperate to make up for lost time."[34] In March 1946, for instance, the administration proposed an increase in margins for trading in cotton futures. Though members of Congress went along with price controls during the war, they balked when peace returned. The *New York Times* reported that about twenty southern senators from cotton states resisted these efforts, arguing that the measure "would squeeze out small traders and depress the price [of cotton], hurting the small growers."[35] Concerns about local outcomes had returned, in force.

As long as troops were fighting and dying on the battlefield, members of Congress were willing to privilege national policy interests. But once the war had been won, these same members willingly and forcefully reasserted the independent interests of their local constituencies. Somewhat ironically, then, by winning the war the president depleted a key source of his policy influence—namely, the propensity of members of Congress to worry more about the interests of the nation, and less about the parochial concerns of their district or state. Not coincidentally, perhaps, Democrats' failure to deliver outcomes to their constituents cost them control of Congress in the 1946 midterm elections and nearly put the presidency in Republican hands in 1949.

33. Leff 1991, 1296.
34. McCullough 1992, 470.
35. "Group of Southern Senators Urged Anderson to Block Bowlers' Proposal," *New York Times,* March 17, 1946.

KOREA

According to all of our criteria, the Korean War did not alter the terms by which members of Congress evaluated public policy to nearly the degree that World War II had. Though evidence certainly exists of moderate changes in each of our five proxies for the nationalization of policy debates, the nation's utter preoccupation with national priorities in World War II assuredly did not resurface in full form in 1950.

The end of World War II ushered in the Cold War, the decades-long standoff between the world's two superpowers. It would not take long for the simmering conflict between the United States and the Soviet Union to come to a head. In 1945, the Korean peninsula was divided along the 38th Parallel, with U.S. troops occupying the southern region and Soviet troops occupying the north. Three years later, South Korea elected its first president and formally adopted an anti-Communist constitution, and North Korea established a Communist government headed by Kim Il-Sung. Shortly thereafter, both Soviet and U.S. troops withdrew from the territory they had occupied.

The Soviet withdrawal, however, proved to be short lived. On June 25, 1950, North Korean forces invaded South Korea, and U.S. State Department officials declared that the "United States [would] hold Russia responsible for the Communist North Korean war against the independent South Korean Republic that [the United States] and the United Nations brought into being and have supported."[36] Two days later, President Truman announced that U.S. forces would return to Korea to combat Communist aggression. As Truman recalled in his autobiography, "Communism was acting in Korea, just as Hitler, Mussolini and the Japanese had ten, fifteen, and twenty years earlier. I felt certain that if South Korea was allowed to fall, Communist leaders would be emboldened to override nations closer to our own shores."[37]

When launching the Korean War, members of Congress did not stand in the president's way, but they did not go out of their way to support him. Congress did not enact a formal authorization of war, and its domestic agenda, for the most part, appeared unaffected by the war. To see this, consider what members had to say about a tax cut bill that was being debated in the House in the summer of 1950, when the war began. The

36. "Washington Holds Russia to Account," *New York Times,* June 25, 1950.
37. Truman 1956, 2:332–333.

measure called for more than $1 billion in excise tax cuts, which would be offset by a $433 million increase in corporate taxes. Whereas World War II had significantly changed members' perception of the domestic economy, Representative Jacob Javits (R-NY) encouraged his colleagues to proceed with the bill as they would if war had not commenced. "Certainly the commitments we have undertaken so far in respect of Korea and the Far East has necessitated no major reform of the fiscal picture. Hence, I believe we should go right ahead and act on this bill as we would ordinarily in the absence of the Korean situation."[38] Despite the President's opposition, the bill easily passed the House the next day and was taken up by the Senate Finance Committee the following week.[39]

Superficially, the public appeared at least cognizant of the war. According to Gallup Poll data, the public became notably more concerned about foreign policy and national security after the war had commenced. In 1951, nearly 20 percent more respondents identified war as the nation's most important problem than in 1949. Although 20 percent of respondents identified social issues as the country's most important problem in 1950, fewer than five percent did so in 1951.

Though it did fix the public's attention on foreign affairs, the Korean War did not evoke anything like the levels of patriotism witnessed less than a decade before. Sandler writes that "Korea did not unleash great surges of . . . patriotic sentiment in the United States."[40] Though they dutifully registered their support for the president, Americans felt little compunction to set aside their local and more private concerns for the good of the nation. Sandler goes to on explain:

> the war rested . . . easily on the United States, for as in the Second World War the homeland was spared its ravages. Military conscription took her sons, but most of them went to Europe, although more than 30,000 would lose their lives in Korea. But there was no rationing, no censorship, not even a reduction in automobile production. In fact, the war produced an economic boon that more than paid for the increased wartime taxes . . . The vast majority of Americans simply accepted the war, after the initial burst of patriotic fervor in the summer of 1950, as one further consequence of global leadership in the fight against Communist aggression.[41]

38. June 28, 1950, *Congressional Record.*
39. John D. Morris, "House, 375–14, Votes Billion Excise Cut," *New York Times,* June 30, 1950.
40. Sandler 1999, 7.
41. Ibid., 9.

North Korean troops could not be seen lining up on the U.S. borders, and North Korean leaders could not be heard professing their intention to not merely defeat but also conquer the United States. The logic of U.S. intervention, instead, rested on the containment of a rather nebulous Communist threat—a threat that, momentarily at least, resided several thousand miles from home. Hence, whereas most Americans had equated the " 'day of infamy' at Pearl Harbor with an attack on hearth and home," the historian Robert Leckie notes, "during the Korean War, no clerk or waiter would have dared explain away his inability to fill an order by snapping, 'Say, don't you know there's a war going on?' For during Korea much of the American public refused to admit there was a war on."[42]

Not surprisingly, contemporary media accounts revealed a domestic citizenry largely unperturbed by war. In the fall of 1951, the *Los Angeles Times* lamented that the youth have "plenty of patriotism for America but can't get fired up over the war in Korea. They would defend their homeland to the last ditch but can't stretch that same patriotism across an ocean."[43] Just a few days later, the *Baltimore Sun* reported on an Armistice Day event in which a young veteran of the Korean War "sound[ed] a call for the resurrection of the old-fashioned brand of patriotism."[44] Acts of patriotism could be detected. But for the most part, they constituted idle curiosities rather than a deep sense of obligation to national purposes.

In 1952, with his public approval ratings in tatters, Truman declined to run for another term, and Republicans won control of the White House and Congress beneath a pledge to end the war. Yet when they did, in the summer of 1953, there were no victory celebrations or parades as there had been in the summer of 1945.[45] For their part, members of Congress seemed reluctant to celebrate the war's end, and some appeared wary of the terms of the truce. Representative Dewey Short (R-MS) claimed that he "felt we could never have permanent peace with a divided Korea. I hope for the best. I am fearful it is only a temporary thing." Senator Alexander Wiley (R-WI) anticipated that the truce "would not be greeted with the sort of unrestrained joy or optimism which have marked the close of other hostilities," most likely referring to World Wars I and II, but rather "it is

42. Leckie 1996 [1962], 89.
43. Mary Ann Callan, "Forum Reflects Strong Feeling of Patriotism," *Los Angeles Times,* November 8, 1951.
44. "Korea Veteran Asks Return of Old-Fashioned Patriotism," *Baltimore Sun,* November 12, 1951.
45. For one description, see Parmet 1999 [1972], 314–315.

met by an attitude of grim realism that we have only opened a new chapter in a long book—the fight for peace." Prominent Democrats agreed, including Senator and 1952 Vice Presidential Nominee John Sparkman who said the truce "doesn't bring us to the end of our troubles."[46] The end of the war in Korea, while providing a moderate victory for the Eisenhower administration, was not accompanied by a reorientation of the public's—or Congress's—priorities, perhaps because neither had changed appreciably while the war was being waged.

VIETNAM

In the main, the Vietnam War did little more to alter members' evaluations of public policy than did the Korean War. Indeed, across these two wars, evidence of heightened national priorities appears in equally short supply. Neither reveals anything like the transformation of the domestic polity experienced during World War II.

In stark contrast with World War II, the beginning of the Vietnam War did not inspire overt displays of bipartisanship, national pride, or unity. Even before the United States escalated its war effort, members of President Johnson's own party showed signs of dissent on how to proceed in Vietnam. Senators Wayne Morse (D-OR) and Ernest Gruening (D-AK) were "agitating for withdrawal of U.S. forces from the conflict," while "at the other extreme, Senator Thomas J. Dodd, Democrat of Connecticut, is demanding extension of the war to North Vietnam."[47] The *New York Times* reported that while Republicans planned to contest the administration's position on foreign policy in the 1964 elections, "the Democrats . . . have been firing all the big guns—against themselves."[48] Many political elites, including Senator Richard B. Russell (D-GA), suggested that patriotism did not require support for the war, and that one should not "imput[e] or impl[y] a lack of patriotism or courage to those who see their duty in another way and continue to oppose the war in Vietnam."[49]

Nor did Johnson attempt to link the war effort to other items on his policy agenda, as Roosevelt had done so often during World War II. To the contrary, Johnson was warned by Senate Majority Leader Mike Mansfield (D-MA) that continued military involvement in Vietnam threatened his

46. "Armistice Hailed as Victory for U.N.," *New York Times,* July 27, 1953.
47. John D. Morris, "Policy in Vietnam Divides Senators," *New York Times,* March 21, 1964.
48. Max Frankel, "Democrats with Doubts," *New York Times*, March 26, 1964.
49. Tom Wicker, "Senator Russell: 'Win or Get Out,'" *New York Times,* April 20, 1966.

domestic agenda. "In the end," Mansfield wrote, "I fear that this course . . . will play havoc with the domestic program on the administration."[50] Likewise, as VanDeMark writes, Johnson appeared "uneasy and uncertain about [his] larger troop proposal" and therefore "aimed to conceal its dimensions from the bureaucracy, Congress, and public, hoping to limit political pressure for escalation and therefore danger to his domestic agenda."[51]

Not coincidentally, members of Congress did not see cause for proclaiming the overriding importance of national policy outcomes. Quite the contrary: members remained largely preoccupied with the consequences of policy for their local constituencies. At times Johnson appealed to the nation's shared identity and common values, but the appeals usually fell flat. In July 1965, for instance, Johnson said that in this war "our national honor is at stake," but as the *New York Times* reported, "a majority of Congress still sees [U.S.] commitment in the limited and conditional terms set forth by President Kennedy."[52]

This is not to say that the American public was oblivious to the expansion of the war effort in 1965. In 1964, a plurality of respondents (approximately 45 percent) identified social issues as the nation's most important problem. By 1965, however, that figure fell by more than half (to around 18 percent). Meanwhile, the percentage of respondents who identified war as the nation's most important problem increased from 30 percent in 1964 to 50 percent in 1965, a figure that remained remarkably stable for the remainder of the Johnson administration. Indeed, it would not be until 1972 that defense and international affairs receded into the background, and Americans' attention turned to economic issues.

If Korea motivated only lukewarm displays of patriotism, Vietnam yielded none whatsoever. Just a year after the war's outbreak, grumblings about an ill-advised and ill-fated military venture pervaded the press. Before long, protests materialized across the country. In the spring of 1966 the *New York Times* reported that "[President] Johnson, described by aides as deeply troubled by the turmoil and the effect it is having on American opinion, pressed for patience and understanding in both Vietnam and the

50. Letter, March 24, 1965, Johnson Library: White House Central Files, EX ND 19/ CO 312, April 12, http://www.presidency.ucsb.edu/vietnam/showdoc.php?docid=86

51. VanDeMark 1995, 105.

52. E. W. Kenworthy, "Johnson's Policy in Vietnam—Four Positions in Congress," *New York Times*, July 24, 1965.

United States."[53] Crucially, public debates about patriotism did not emphasize the imperatives of subverting private, parochial interests to national
imperatives. Quite the opposite, the war protests of the mid- and late-
1960s suggested that patriotism might best be understood as an expression
of dissent, independence, critical thinking, and the celebration of multicul-
turalism and regional differences.

More than most, veterans noticed the absence of patriotism from public discourse. When covering the American Legion's annual convention in
the summer of 1966, *New York Times* reporter Tom Wicker encountered
World War II veterans who compared their combat experiences with the
current war efforts. The veterans said that the spirit at American Legion
events was more downtrodden than in years past. "The fun really is a little
forced now, the vital spirit on the ebb, the parades less rousing, the great
conclaves rather melancholy, because the world has turned and the great
themes of the Legion—the nation, patriotism, war itself—are not as they
were."[54] Even decades later, the planning and the design of the Vietnam War
memorial in Washington, D.C., was defined by a complete lack of patriotic
sentiment. Bodnar writes, "The final design for the memorial was more of
an expression of grief and sorrow than a celebration of national unity or the
glorious triumph of the nation . . . this design glorified neither the nation nor
the sacrifices of foot soldiers for magnificent national causes."[55]

Amid the difficulties that stemmed from an unpopular war, President
Johnson, like President Truman before him, declined to seek another
term in office. As was the case when Truman's successor brought the Korean War to a close, the end of the Vietnam War was not met with fanfare
or feelings of triumph. If anything, citizens and their elected officials were
merely relieved that the distractions of the distant, poorly executed, costly
war were removed so that they could devote their full attention to the
more immediate concerns of a struggling domestic economy.

PERSIAN GULF

Like the previous two wars, the Persian Gulf War did not substantially
alter members' evaluations of public policy. Displays of patriotism and

53. Max Frankel, "Johnson Appeals for Unity in War," *New York Times*, May 22,
1966.
54. Tom Wicker, "A Melancholy Link to Yesteryear," *New York Times*, August 31,
1966.
55. Bodnar 1992, 4.

national solidarity could be found, but with the war's onset, a vaunted spirit of self-sacrifice did not grip the nation, nor could members of Congress be heard admonishing their constituents to set aside their private, parochial concerns for the good of the nation. Change, such as it was, appeared moderate in magnitude.

On August 2, 1990, Iraqi forces under the leadership of Saddam Hussein invaded their tiny oil-rich neighbor Kuwait. President George H.W. Bush promptly condemned the invasion as "naked aggression" that "will not stand," and the United Nations called for trade and economic sanctions against Iraq. Fearing that Iraq might soon invade Saudi oil fields, President Bush, at the behest of Saudi King Fahd bin Abdul Aziz Al Saud, sent an initial force of 50,000 troops to Saudi Arabia as part of Operation Desert Shield.

The buildup in the Persian Gulf region continued through the fall of 1990, reaching a peak of nearly 550,000 troops. Meanwhile, U.S. attempts at diplomacy faltered. In November, the U.N. Security Council set a January 15, 1991, deadline for Iraq to withdraw its forces from Kuwait, at which time member states would use "all necessary means" to forcefully remove Iraqi troops. On January 12, both chambers of Congress passed the Authorization for Use of Military Force Against Iraq Resolution, which provided President Bush with the authority to commit U.S. troops to war. Of the authorization to the use of force in Iraq, long-time *New York Times* contributor R. W. Apple Jr. wrote, "[Congress] gave Mr. Bush the benefit of the doubt, but they could express no profound national commitment."[56] Nor could much enthusiasm for war be found outside of Congress. In the South, "traditionally a fortress of patriotism . . . support [for the war] often seems to be qualified, hemmed in by doubts and qualms and conditions. It may not be the kind of support likely to see President Bush through a long, difficult war."[57]

Iraq failed to comply with the terms of the U.N. resolution, and thus began an extensive bombing campaign on January 17, which marked the beginning of the Persian Gulf War. Though the president called upon the public to support the war, he did not ask that anyone set aside their local interests in the service of a larger good. Nothing about the war effort itself, at least for members of Congress, elevated the importance of

56. R. W. Apple Jr., "Bush's Limited Victory," *New York Times,* January 13, 1991.
57. B. Drummond Ayres Jr., "Across the South, a Clash of Doubt and Fervor," *New York Times,* January 9, 1991.

national policy outcomes. From the war's outset, the *Washington Post* reported, "The national mood is one of somber disquietude, rather than the righteous indignation that in the past often bound Americans together in martial pique."[58]

Nor, apparently, did the war alter the ways in which members of Congress evaluated the national and local impacts of policy. Amid a deepening economic recession and the prospect of a costly war, members might have been persuaded to raise taxes. Instead, "memories of last year's budget imbroglio appeared too fresh for lawmakers to consider new taxes to pay for the Persian Gulf War."[59] Furthermore, we could not find any other evidence that the Persian Gulf War encouraged members of Congress to attach greater importance to national policy outcomes, as congressional debates continued to center around the same parochial and partisan interests.

The war *did* increase Americans' attention to issues of defense and international affairs. As Mueller reports, "two weeks into the war, 37 percent [of Americans] called it the most important problem facing the country."[60] Throughout the war, citizens freely expressed their abundant patriotism. Yellow ribbons, Whitney Houston's stirring rendition of the national anthem, and Lee Greenwood's new hit "God Bless the USA" defined popular culture in the winter of 1991. However, these displays of patriotism did not require the kind of self-sacrifice and suppression of parochialism that so characterized the domestic polity in World War II. As the *New York Times* reported, these symbols were "ambiguous, flaunted with equal fervor by supporters and opponents of the war. If there is a unifying thread to the country's conflicting sentiments about the war in the gulf, it is a conviction that this generation of soldiers should not be treated as shabbily as were the combatants in Vietnam."[61] Though the conflict may have united Americans' support for the military, it did not reorient Americans' views about how best to evaluate public policy.

Crucially, perhaps, in this war the nation's security did not hang in the balance. The United States itself was not attacked, nor was there any threat of it being so, either then or in the future. While the Iraqi regime

58. Rick Atkinson, "A Defining Moment in History," *Washington Post,* January 15, 1991.

59. David S. Cloud, "Partisanship Likely to Drive Any Debate on New Taxes." *CQ Weekly Online,* January 26, 1991, 239–241.

60. Mueller 1994, 73.

61. Alessandra Stanley, "War's Ribbons Are Yellow With Meaning of Many Hues," *New York Times,* February 3, 1991.

regularly and roundly criticized the United States, its leaders did not express any intention of bringing the fight to American shores. Instead, the overriding justification for the war centered on oil and regional stability—real and legitimate interests, but not the sort that can be expected to wholly displace politicians' concerns for their local constituents.

On February 29, 1991, the Allied forces liberated Kuwait City. Six weeks later, on April 11, Iraq assented to the terms of the U.N. agreement that formally brought the war to a close, less than three months after it had begun. Upon the war's end, the nation's attention quickly turned to a deepening domestic recession.

POST-9/11 WARS

With the terrorist attacks of September 11, 2001, and the subsequent military operations in Afghanistan, the nation reconsidered its policy priorities in ways not seen since World War II. Both spontaneous and planned expressions of patriotism could be found everywhere. Politicians publicly affirmed their commitment to distinctly national ideals, and citizens and soldiers alike worried about the nation's security.

The day after nineteen hijackers seized four American aircraft, crashing two into the twin towers of the World Trade Center in lower Manhattan, Congress reconvened, shaken by the events of the day before. As the *New York Times* reported, "The Congress that reopened today was transformed into a unity government, its bitter divisions erased overnight by the worst act of terrorism on American soil and the widespread sentiment that the nation was at war." Eager to express their solidarity, members of both parties gathered on the steps of Capitol Hill to sing "God Bless America." "Everything has changed," declared Senator Kent Conrad (D-MT), while Senator John Breaux (D-LA) predicted that "the political war will cease."[62] In the wake of the attacks, the nation's attention turned to the president.

On October 7, members of Congress authorized the use of military force in Taliban-controlled Afghanistan, which was suspected of harboring many of the terrorists responsible for the 9/11 attacks. Congress understood that this was a new kind of war, and one that would require swift action and new intelligence. Later in October, Congress passed the USA PATRIOT Act, which authorized an unprecedented expansion of gov-

62. Alison Mitchell and Richard L. Berke, "After the Attacks: The Congress; Differences Are Put Aside as Lawmakers Reconvene," *New York Times,* September 13, 2001.

ernment surveillance into the activities of private citizens. In a very real sense, this was a war that would be waged both abroad and at home.

When voting on domestic policies, members of Congress openly recognized the importance of coming together in common cause. More than once, members admitted voting with the president and against their districts' interests. Consider, for instance, the debate that occurred in the fall of 2001 over whether to grant the president trade-promotion authority. Under this legislation, the president would have the ability to negotiate trade agreements directly with foreign governments, bypassing Senate confirmation. A similar bill had failed several times during the Clinton administration, and it was seen as an important test of President Bush's power just months after the 9/11 attacks. More than thirty House Republicans who previously had voted against the bill now voted to support it, including vulnerable members from districts whose constituents opposed the measure. Representative Cass Ballenger (R-NC), for instance, said that his vote to support the bill "was not the smartest vote [he'd] made in [his] life," but he "felt it was [his] duty to support the president," while Representative Adam Putnam (R-FL) said that choosing between the demands of citrus farmers in his district and the pressure of the president "made [him] want to throw up."[63]

On 9/11, U.S. citizens endured a stateside attack for the first time since World War II. The 9/11 attacks came seemingly out of nowhere and implicated an altogether nebulous enemy, one that resided not only in distant caves and desert encampments but also, potentially, within our midst. On September 30, Attorney General John Ashcroft told reporters: "We believe there are substantial risks of terrorism still in the United States of America. As we as a nation respond to what has happened to us, those risks may in fact go up."[64] Again and again, executive officials emphasized that the key question centered not on whether another attack would occur stateside, but when.

Not surprisingly, in the aftermath of the 9/11 attacks, the public was much more likely to rate national security as the country's "most important problem." Indeed, by 2002 the public prioritized war to an extent not seen since 1972, the final year of the Vietnam War. Though few would have predicted that military involvement in Afghanistan would become

63. Joseph Kahn, "House Supports Trade Authority Sought by Bush," *New York Times,* December 7, 2001.
64. James Dao, "Defense Secretary Warns of Unconventional Attacks," *New York Times,* October 1, 2001.

the longest war in U.S. history, the nation's attention remained fixated upon national security considerations, even as the attacks rattled the foundations of the U.S. economy.

The fall of 2001 saw the most significant upsurge in patriotism and national camaraderie since World War II. Charitable giving skyrocketed in the weeks and months following the 9/11 attacks. Major League Baseball instituted a practice of singing "God Bless America" at every professional game. "Madison Avenue is wrapping itself in red, white and blue in an outpouring of patriotism not seen in mainstream advertising since World War II," reported the *New York Times*.[65] Later that fall, "national pride—from flags flying in between the spiderwebs and scarecrows to patriotic costumes replacing Jack the Ripper—[became] a part of Halloween decor."[66] Even Hollywood, typically a bastion of liberalism, appeared caught up in a fever of patriotism:

> Not since World War II has there been such a patriotic fervor in Hollywood. Flag waving, once scorned by Hollywood executives as behavior befitting the Archie Bunkers of the nation, is now visible everywhere, and scripts that denigrate the government, the Army or the C.I.A. are unlikely to see the light of day.[67]

Americans' patriotic sentiments were more than momentary arousals. By the president's own account, the 9/11 attacks "shocked Americans into a passionate sense of commitment that is both more widespread and less superficial than most recent fevers of patriotism. The new sense of national peril, the erosion of the sense of security the United States has relied on for 200 years, has begotten a new national unity."[68] The 75th annual Macy's Thanksgiving Day Parade was "transformed by patriotic pomp and recast as a raucous affirmation of New York's resilience in the face of tragedy. Lady Liberty replaced Tom Turkey at the front of the procession; the red and white candy canes in Santa's sleigh wore ribbons of red, white and blue; and a waving Mayor Rudolph W. Giuliani drew far more cheers than

65. Stuart Elliott, "Madison Avenue Rides Wave of Patriotic Fervor," *New York Times*, October 8, 2001.

66. Jane Gordon, "Frightening Time for a Frightening Holiday," *New York Times*, October 14, 2001.

67. Bernard Weinraub, "The Moods They Are A'Changing In Films; Terrorism Is Making Government Look Good," *New York Times*, October 10, 2001.

68. R. W. Apple Jr., "Nature of Foe Is Obstacle in Appealing for Sacrifice," *New York Times*, October 15, 2001.

either Barney or the Rugrats."[69] The 2002 Superbowl was a "day of flags and footballs,"[70] and prior to the June Belmont Stakes it was reported that "American patriotism drives even the naming of racehorses."[71]

The 9/11 attacks and the war in Afghanistan that followed galvanized the nation. The United States confronted a new enemy that threatened its way of life, and whose leaders espoused a commitment to no less than "the extinction of America."[72] The actual material threat that the likes of Al Qaeda posed to America remained a matter of some dispute. In the minds of most politicians and Americans, however, it was a threat that radically shifted their priorities from local to national policy outcomes, for at least as long as the bulk of the fighting was in Afghanistan; and even during the early stages of another war in Iraq that would begin roughly eighteen months later.

3.5 *Key Expectations*

All our wars stand some chance of augmenting the president's influence over public policy, but as we attempt to make clear in this chapter, some of these wars should increase presidential influence more than others. The Policy Priority Model sets forth a framework for thinking about the conditions under which war increases the president's influence over lawmaking. To the extent these conditions vary, so should the president's bargaining position with Congress.

Reflected in a variety of dimensions, which are summarized in Table 3.2, World War II and the post-9/11 wars fixated politicians' attention on the national implications of public policy, often to the exclusion of more localized considerations. In so doing, these wars should have provided the presidents then in office with substantial increases in congressional support. In contrast, we expect that Korea, Vietnam, and the Persian Gulf wars had more limited effects on presidential influence. None of these wars presented an immediate security threat to U.S. citizens. Though Korea and Vietnam were accompanied by large numbers of casualties, they did

69. Andrew Jacobs and Shaila K. Dewan, "A Parade Steeped in Pageantry, With a Core of Patriotism," *New York Times,* November 23, 2001.

70. Richard Sandomir, "Sports Media; A Day of Flags and Footballs," *New York Times,* February 4, 2002.

71. Jim Squires, "Trying to Win the Triple Crown—and Our Hearts," *New York Times,* June 6, 2002.

72. Mullah Mohammed Omar, November 15, 2001, interview with the British Broadcasting Corporation, http://news.bbc.co.uk./2/hi/south-asia/1657368.shtm.

Table 3.2. WAR AND THE PRIORITIZATION OF NATIONAL OUTCOMES

War	Public Statements	National Unity	Patriotism	Most Important Problem	Imminent Threat	Summary
World War II	High	High	High	(not available)	High	HIGH
Korea	Low	Low	Moderate	Moderate	Low	MODERATE
Vietnam	Low	Low	Low	Moderate	Moderate	MODERATE
Persian Gulf	Moderate	Moderate	High	Moderate	Low	MODERATE
Post-9/11 wars	High	High	High	High	High	HIGH

Note: Entries reflect the relative levels of each of the five criteria we use to evaluate the extent to which war increased the emphasis of members of Congress on national policy outcomes relative to local outcomes.

not nationalize policy outcomes in ways similar to World War II and the post-9/11 wars. Though the beginnings of the Korean and Persian Gulf wars, in particular, received widespread popular support, they did not evoke deep and persistent feelings of patriotism and self-sacrifice.

As we turn to empirical testing, we expect to find large and more consistent evidence of heightened presidential influence in World War II and the post-9/11 wars, and more limited evidence in the Korean, Vietnam, and Persian Gulf wars.

3.6 *Competing Explanations*

Ours, of course, need not be the only explanation in town. Indeed, previous scholarship has identified other features of war that might correlate with presidential success. As it turns out, though, the predictions generated from our model stand in contrast to those that emerge from using these other factors. None of these alternative explanations provides a basis for expecting World War II and Afghanistan to yield comparatively larger increases in presidential success than other major wars. Having performed our empirical tests, therefore, we will have some basis upon which to evaluate these competing explanations, and to determine whether our own theory passes muster.

ATHEORETICAL CLAIMS

Virtually all of the existing competing explanations lack theoretical grounding. Rather then derive predictions from a well-specified model, these explanations gesture toward factors that, for reasons that are typically ill-specified, may augment the president's ability to advance his policy agenda during times of war. That they lack theoretical grounding , though, does not mean that these explanations are in any sense wrong. As best we can, then, we need to account for them and identify the ways in which their predictions differ from our own.

The first and perhaps simplest competing explanation focuses on the costs, whether real or perceived, of voting against a wartime president. By this account, members of Congress may experience some sense of obligation to support the president whenever a substantial number of troops stands in harm's way. Such a sense may derive from objective concerns about electoral retribution if, for instance, citizens are prone to punishing elected officials who stand in the way of a wartime president. Alternatively, members of Congress may simply have an abiding sense of duty to vote with a wartime president that has nothing to do with the independent views of their constituents. Either way, this explanation suggests that all major wars ought to trigger heightened congressional support for the president—and to do so by roughly equal magnitudes.

Other explanations more naturally generate predictions about the heterogeneous effects of war. Consider, for instance, the relative human toll of war. John Mueller, and many others since, argued that public support for war specifically, and the president by extension, wanes as casualties mount.[73] To the extent that members' voting records reflect public sentiment, Congress may be willing to grant more deference to wartime presidents when casualties are low.[74] If so, we should observe the highest levels of congressional accommodation to the president during the Persian Gulf War, during which the fewest number of war-related deaths occurred (382 deaths), and Congress should have been most hostile to the president's proposals during World War II, in which over 400,000 American military personnel perished. Moreover, as all wars proceed and death tolls mount, congressional accommodation to the president should wane.

Alternatively, Congress may support the president to a greater degree when war mobilization efforts are high. By this account, each member's propensity to stand with the commander in chief is contingent upon the sheer size of the war effort he is charged with coordinating. There are, of course, a variety of ways in which one might characterize a war's "size." It should come as no surprise that these measures correlate highly with one another. As gauged by the percentage of the U.S. population that served in the military during each of the conflicts, the World War II congresses should be the most accommodating, while the Persian Gulf and post-9/11 congresses should be the least so. Characterized instead by the financial costs of war, as measured by inflation-adjusted dollars, World War II stands head and shoulders above the rest, followed by the Vietnam War, and then the Korean, Persian Gulf, and post-9/11 wars trailing far behind. Measured as the percentage of the nation's gross domestic product (GDP) in the wars' peak years, war costs for World War II comprised 35.8 percent of the GDP, the Korean and Vietnam Wars comprised 4.2 percent and 2.3 percent, respectively, and the Persian Gulf and post-9/11 wars both constituted less than one percent of the nation's GDP during the war's peak year.

73. Mueller 1973.
74. For our purposes we focus exclusively on war-related deaths.

We still have not exhausted the possible alternative explanations to our theory. Wartime increases in presidential success may hinge upon the existence of a healthy proportion of copartisans filling House and Senate seats. By this account, the stimulating effects of war on presidential power are confined to those members of Congress who are already predisposed to support the president, and hence the wars that he wages. Should this be true, then presidents who led the nation through World War II, Korea, and Vietnam should have enjoyed marginally greater increases in success in Congress than those who held office during the Persian Gulf and post-9/11 wars.

Finally, congressional support for the president may be predicated upon the existence of broad public support for the president. There are at least two ways in which this might work. First, the outbreak of war may boost public support for the president and, by extension, his legislative agenda; perennially attuned to their constituents' opinions, members of Congress assume a more sympathetic posture to the president. By this account, wars do in fact augment presidential influence, but their proximate effect is on public opinion. Alternatively, wars may simply activate new, or perhaps augment existing, costs associated with voting against a popular president. Whereas members of Congress may feel reasonably free to vote against a popular president during times of peace, they may be reticent to do so as long as he is coordinating a major military campaign abroad. In this sense, it is the interaction between war and preexisting public support for the president that enhances the prospects of Congress enacting the president's policy agenda. Though one can readily conceive of different conceptual models that relate war, public opinion, and presidential influence, the point prediction is reasonably clear: wars ought to have the greatest effect on presidential power when they are accompanied by large increases in public support for the president. Using this criterion, the post-9/11 wars would have constituted the largest boon to presidential success in Congress, while World War II and the Persian Gulf War would have provided significant but smaller increases in public support. Presidential success during the Korean and Vietnam wars, however, would have increased only modestly.

Table 3.3 summarizes the data that led to these competing predictions about the effects of war on presidential success in Congress. Again, we lack a well-specified theory about why presidential success in Congress should depend on any of these factors. As such, we do not want to put them on equal footing with our own predictions. Still, it will be of some

Table 3.3. COMPETING EXPLANATIONS FOR PRESIDENTIAL SUCCESS DURING WAR

War	Financial Costs		War Deaths[c]	% Citizens Participating in War	Proportion of President's Party in Congress	Presidential Approval[d]
	Total expenses[a] (billions)	% of GDP[b]				
World War II	4,100	35.8	405,399	11.3	0.6	13
Korea	341	4.2	36,574	3.5	0.6	9
Vietnam	738	2.3	58,209	4.6	0.7	4
Persian Gulf	102	0.3	382	0.9	0.4	18
Post-9/11 wars	297	0.7	5,105	0.3	0.5	38

[a] In 2010 inflation-adjusted dollars. *Source:* Stephen Daggett, 2010, "Cost of Major U.S. Wars," Congressional Research Service, Document RS22926, http://www.fas.org/sgp/crs/natsec/RS22926.pdf.

[b] Entries reflect war costs as a percentage of the gross domestic product (GDP) during the peak year of the war. *Source:* Stephen Daggett, 2010, "Cost of Major U.S. Wars," Congressional Research Service, Document RS22926, http://www.fas.org/sgp/crs/natsec/RS22926.pdf.

[c] *Source:* Anne Leland and Mari-Jana Oboroceanu, 2010, "American War and Military Operations Casualties: Lists and Statistics," Congressional Research Service, Document RL32492, http://www.fas.org/sgp/crs/natsec/RL32492.pdf.

[d] Entries represent the increase in presidential approval at the beginning of war, as measured by the change in the percentage of Gallup poll respondents who approve of the job the president is doing between the most recent poll conducted before war and the first poll conducted at the war's beginning. Larger entries indicate a larger spike in presidential approval that coincided with the beginning of war. *Source:* Roper Center, http://webapps.ropercenter.uconn.edu/CFIDE/roper/presidential/webroot/presidential_rating.cfm.

concern if we uncover evidence that corresponds more closely to one of the rank orderings of war in Table 3.3 rather than those generated from the Policy Priority Model.

A THEORETICAL CLAIM

Let us not forget one last competing explanation. Unlike the others, this one *is* grounded in theory. In fact, it comes from the Policy Priority Model itself.

The model, you will recall, predicts that a representative legislator will exhibit greater support for the president when the uncertainty of the national mapping process increases. War may have just this effect. Indeed, by expanding the range of possible outcomes associated with any particular policy, wars necessarily increase uncertainty. During a fight against the Nazis, communists, foreign aggressors, or terrorists, policy changes can have effects that are not imaginable during times of peace. When the United States enters a war, the nation's sovereignty and the security of its citizens suddenly hinges, at least in part, on the domestic and foreign policy initiatives undertaken by the federal government; and when the United States is exiting that war, such outcomes are removed from political debate, thereby simplifying the task for all politicians of assessing the national implications of policy change.

When comparing our various wars, it is not at all clear that predictions on the basis of uncertainty look especially different from predictions on the basis of the nationalization of politics. Though assuredly for different reasons, World War II and the post-9/11 wars both induced large changes in both of the model's parameters, while the remaining wars induced more modest changes. Hence, unlike all the atheoretical explanations we have entertained, the mechanisms drawn from our own model yield observationally equivalent predictions about the relative magnitude of effects of our different wars on presidential influence.

When distinguishing across policy spheres, however, it may be possible to distinguish these two mechanisms. On foreign policy matters, the onset of war induces substantial changes in uncertainty, but only modest changes in the relative salience of national outcomes. Precisely because the nation is at war, after all, the range of possible outcomes of foreign policies expands, suggesting an increase in policy uncertainty. But precisely because foreign policy already has a strong national component, the onset of war is unlikely to substantially change the salience of national versus local outcomes. In this sense, a substantive reading of the nationalization of politics provides strong reasons to believe that the president's foreign policy initiatives will enjoy a greater measure of support within Congress than his domestic policy goals, but *not* that wars will increase the marginal probabilities that Congress will enact his foreign policy agenda.

On domestic policy matters, by contrast, the predictions of the two model parameters look quite different. Here, the onset of war has a relatively modest effect on uncertainty, but potentially a large effect on the evaluative criteria that members of Congress rely on when casting their votes. When the nation goes to war, the range of possible outcomes of domestic policies may not change much at all. As we have seen, however, the terms by which members of Congress consider these policies may shift quite substantially.

Clearly, no single comparison of domestic and foreign policies during periods of war and peace will prove dispositive. But if the preponderance of evidence suggests that congressional accommodation to wartime presidents is either most pronounced in domestic policy initiatives, or that it carries over to both policy domains, then marginal changes in the salience of national outcomes ought to be a relevant theoretical mechanism at work. On the other hand, should this accommodation be restricted to foreign policy, we may want to shift our bets over to uncertainty being the relevant mechanism at work.[75]

CRITICAL TESTS

In Table 3.4, we identify how predictions that relate to the nationalization of politics, our preferred explanation, compare with other plausible claims. When considering atheoretical counterarguments, we focus on the evidence of congressional accommodation to the president across wars. For every counterargument, there is at least one war where their predictions differ from our own. The relevant critical test between our two theoretically informed arguments concerns the wartime changes in congressional support for the president across different policy domains. In hopes of further clarifying what it is about war that induces at least some members of Congress to support the president when otherwise they would oppose him, we will regularly refer back to these competing predictions in the empirical studies that follow.

75. These two mechanisms, of course, are not mutually exclusive. Should we observe accommodation in both domestic and foreign policy, we certainly cannot rule out the possibility that both are contributing to the president's wartime successes within the legislative arena.

Table 3.4. CRITICAL TESTS

Explanation	Empirical Distinction from Our Core Argument
Total war expenses	Predicts large increases in presidential success during the Vietnam War; does not predict large increases in presidential success during the post-9/11 wars
War costs as % of GDP	Does not predict large increases in presidential success during the post-9/11 wars
War deaths	Predicts large increases in presidential success during the Korean and Vietnam wars; does not predict large increases in presidential success during the post-9/11 wars
Mobilization	Predicts possible increases in presidential success during the Korean and Vietnam wars; does not predict large increases in presidential success during the post-9/11 wars
Presidential party in Congress	Predicts largest increases in presidential success during the Vietnam War; does not predict large increase in presidential success during the post-9/11 wars
Increase in presidential approval	Predicts largest increases in presidential success during the Persian Gulf War
Uncertainty	Predicts large increases in presidential success in foreign policy; uncertain impact on presidential success in domestic policy

3.7 *A Closing Note on Theory Testing*

Before we turn to data, let us be clear about exactly what we will be testing. Strictly speaking, in one equilibrium where the legislator acquires expertise about the local mapping and the president acquires expertise about the national mapping, the Policy Priority Model predicts that increases in the nationalization of politics generate policies that more closely approximate the president's preferences. In another equilibrium wherein the president acquires expertise about both mapping functions, the same comparative statics hold. In a third equilibrium, however, the model predicts that changes in the nationalization of politcs will not have any bearing on a legislator's propensity to vote in ways that reflect the president's policy preferences. When the legislator acquires expertise about both mapping functions and the president acquires expertise in neither, the comparative statics on the nationalization of politcs are null. For reasons outlined above, therefore, we offer as our first maintained hypothesis that we inhabit a world wherein presidents have expertise about the mappings of policies into national outcomes.

Note further that the Policy Priority Model, strictly speaking, is silent about the influence of war. Whether as a conditioning state or a parameter within the players' utility functions, war does not appear in the model. Rather, we quite deliberately constructed a very general model of inter-branch politics. Because this is a book about the wartime president, how-ever, we must find way to link our general model to the incidence of war. As a second maintained hypothesis, therefore, we stipulate that wars increase the salience of national outcomes and decrease the importance of local ones, albeit to varying degrees. To be sure, other events (such as smaller military ventures, attacks on U.S. citizens abroad, or economic recessions) may have similar effects. In this sense, our theoretical model could be applied to a wide range of phenomena. Our interest in the model, however, is instrumental rather than intrinsic. So while we entertain the possibility that other events can change politicians' assessments of the relative importance of national and local outcomes—and in subsequent chapters we show evidence that at least one, the 1957 launching of the Soviet satellite *Sputnik,* did—our primary intention is to use the model to illuminate what it is about war that encourages at least some members of Congress to stand behind their president.

It is the combination of our theory and maintained hypotheses that allows us to generate predictions about the relevance of war for public policy making—and predictions, it is worth recalling, that differ from those made by other plausible claims about wartime lawmaking. Because war is not expressly parameterized in the model, there is no way around this fact. Hence, all the empirical analyses that follow constitute tests of three simultaneous propositions: (1) members of Congress are more likely to vote with the president when they assign relatively greater importance to national vis-à-vis local outcomes of public policy making; (2) major wars induce such changes, albeit to different degrees; and (3) during our period of study, presidents have greater expertise about the mapping of policies into national outcomes.

Imagine that in the real world of politics members of Congress are no more accommodating to the president during war than they are during peace. What, exactly, does this tell us? Three possibilities present them-selves, each of which are observationally equivalent with the others. First, the theory might be correct, but one of our arguments about which equilib-rium characterizes domestic politics in the twentieth century is misguided, or the effect of war on members' assessments of the relative importance of national and local outcomes is wrong. In this case, we will have said something potentially important about interbranch negotiations, but one (or both) of our maintained hypotheses is wrong. Second, presidents and

Congress may acquire expertise in exactly the ways we postulate, and wars may influence the evaluative criteria that members employ in exactly the way we postulate, but our theoretical characterization of these criteria is flawed. In this case, we will have identified a potentially interesting curiosity about war, but we cannot claim to have established its relevance to presidential success. Third, neither the theory nor the maintained hypotheses might be correct. Unavoidably, then, the precise meaning of a possible null finding remains deeply ambiguous.

Empirical findings that support the predictions laid in Table 3.4 are more easily interpreted. For presidential success to increase in war, both our theory and our maintained hypotheses must be true. Therefore, evidence that is consistent with our core predictions must corroborate both. To be sure, there may be other theories or other maintained hypotheses that also support the patterns in the data we see. And, moving forward, scholars would do well to develop such theories and maintain hypotheses, and to offer critical tests that permit distinctions among them. This would be the work of a discipline, not a single study. For our own study, it is important merely that we retain a measure of clarity about the stakes involved in all the empirical tests that await.

PART III

Empirical
Investigations

CHAPTER 4

Spending in War and in Peace

Congress's two most important responsibilities are writing the nation's laws and passing its budgets. Of late, the two responsibilities have melded into one. During the modern era, members have taken to embedding a wide range of policy initiatives into appropriations, which enjoy the advantage of coming before Congress every single year. Policy and budget debates, therefore, are often interchangeable, making annual appropriations a vitally important arena for presidents to pursue their policy initiatives.

In addition to being substantively important, budgets constitute an ideal venue in which to test the main proposition that members of Congress more closely accommodate presidential preferences in war than in peace, and that they do so because of presidential expertise. In its structure, the Policy Priority Model represents something of a distillation of the appropriations process. Since the enactment of the Budget and Accounting Act of 1921, the president has been responsible for composing a complete budget proposal, which is submitted to Congress in February of each year, and which initiates the actual authorization and appropriations process.[1] Producing the president's budget is no trivial undertaking. In multiple volumes and thousands of pages, the president's budget identifies funding levels not just for individual agencies, but also for individual projects and employees within those agencies. The president then supplements specific requests with extensive policy and legislative recommendations, detailed economic forecasts, and exhaustive accounts on the performance and finances of federal agencies and programs. When they ultimately get around to crafting a final budget, members of Congress rely upon the president's budget more than any other document for information about operations within the federal government—another fact that resonates well with the Policy Priority Model.[2]

---

1. For a useful discussion of early efforts to build a budgetary clearance apparatus, see Neustadt 1954.
2. Schick 2000, 90, 189–193.

Substantial efforts are made to ensure that the president's budget reflects his policy priorities. Rather than submit requests directly to Congress, agencies seeking federal funding must submit detailed reports to the Office of Management and Budget (OMB). Working at the behest of the president, the OMB then clears each of these reports to ensure that they reflect the chief executive's policy priorities.[3] When they reveal discrepancies, officials at the OMB either return the reports to the agencies for subsequent amendment or simply edit the documents themselves. The end product, then, is a proposed budget that closely adheres to the president's policy agenda.

Appropriations present a reasonably clear opportunity to assess Congress's variable willingness during war and peace to support the president— and to do so without introducing the substantial identification issues endemic to previous research on war and presidential power. First, and perhaps foremost, budgets allay the deep endogeneity issues associated with presidential position taking. Presidents may act strategically when they issue their budget proposals, and later in this chapter, we will explicitly account for this possibility. Notice, though, that presidents must issue a budget every single year, and that Congress must subsequently enact a final set of appropriations. Unlike the traditional legislative process, the appropriations process does not permit presidents to remain silent on particularly controversial bills or members of Congress to refuse to cast judgment on presidential proposals.[4] Every year, presidents must propose a budget, members of Congress must dispose of it, and we, as observers, have a basis upon which to gauge the difference.

This leads to a second advantage of using budgets to assess presidential influence in war and peace. In the legislative process, bills regularly undergo substantial amendments, with final enactments yielding hazy and diluted renderings of original proposals. This makes it difficult to measure the difference between what the president wanted on a particular legislative initiative and what (if anything) he got.[5] But with budgets we avoid

---

3. A small number of agencies do not submit budgets directly or only to the OMB. Examples include the U.S. Sentencing Commission and the International Trade Commission (Lewis 2004).

4. Though Congress can delay formal approval of the budget (and frequently has done so), it ultimately has always passed an annual budget, even if late.

5. And if it is difficult to measure the difference between what the president wanted on a particular legislative initiative and what (if anything) he got, comparing these differences across policy domains is impossible. We are left with a rather impoverished basis upon which to gauge presidential success in war and peace. At best, we can try to infer the president's core policy preferences from vague public pronouncements, set some arbi-

these entanglements because the president must take a public position on the amount of money to be allocated to an executive agency and members of Congress must decide how much to actually award. The difference between these quantities thus constitutes a clear and continuous measure of presidential success, which can be readily compared across policy domains. The more that members of Congress wish to accommodate the president's proposal, the smaller the observed differences between proposed and actual appropriations. Should members decide to give the president exactly what he wants, these differences will vanish altogether.

For our purposes, the central question focuses first on whether these differences systematically vary in times of war and peace, and second on whether the patterns across wars and policy domains comport with our theoretical expectations laid out in Chapter 3. In the main, we find support for our key predictions. On average, final appropriations more closely reflect presidential proposals during times of war than during times of peace. Among our wars, the largest effects appear in World War II and the post-9/11 wars, where we find sizable effects in both foreign and domestic policy. What is more, the estimates do not appear to be an artifact of any particular characterization of the differences between proposed and final appropriations, of strategic proposal making, or of any single model specification.

4.1 *Data*

In the empirical analyses that follow, the unit of observation is a particular agency and/or program budget in a particular year. The data set spans seventy-four years, covering 1933 to 2006 inclusive. Over this time period, we track budgetary proposals and allotments for the same seventy-seven agencies that Roderick Kiewiet and Mathew McCubbins analyzed in their seminal work on delegation.[6]

As can be seen in Table 4.1, the agencies and programs in our data set address a wide range of policy areas. Twenty of them focus on defense policy, while the remaining fifty-seven cover a variety of foreign and domestic policies. Hence, for example, the list includes funds to cover all aspects of military construction as well as the Office of Education, which,

---

trary threshold for presidential success, assume that the thresholds we set across bills are constant, and then denote each enactment as a presidential win or loss.

6. Kiewiet and McCubbins 1991. To extend the data set back to 1933, we also include a handful of the predecessors to agencies in the Kiewiet and McCubbins data set. None of the key findings presented here depend upon their inclusion.

Table 4.1. AGENCIES AND PROGRAMS INCLUDED IN THE BUDGETARY DATA SET

Program/Agency	Years of Existence	Program/Agency	Years of Existence
Food and Drug Administration	1933–2006	HUD Housing Programs	2004–2006
Weather Bureau	1933–1966	Rural Waste Water and Disposal Grants	1968–1995
Geological Survey	1933–2006	Small Business Administration Business Loan and Investment Fund	1971–1989
Census Bureau	1933–2006	Consumer Product Safety Commission	1975–2006[a]
Federal Bureau of Investigation	**1937–2006**	Occupational Safety and Health Administration	1974–2006[a]
Immigration and Naturalization Service	1933–2006[a]	Commodity Futures Trading Administration	1977–1991
Federal Prison System/Bureau of Prisons	1933–1942[a]	Environmental Protection Agency	1975–2006
Federal Prison System/Bureau of Prisons	1943–2006	Drug Enforcement Administration	1975–2006
Customs Service/Bureau of Customs	1933–2006	National Highway Traffic Safety Administration	1972–2006
Bureau of the Public Debt	1933–1945[a]	National Science Administration/National Science Foundation	1954–2006
Bureau of the Public Debt	1946–2006	Department of Justice/Legal Activities and General Administration	1933–1985
Secret Service	1933–2006	Department of Justice/Legal Activities	1986–2006
Bureau of Internal Revenue/Internal Revenue Service	1933–2006	General Services Administration	1948–1985
Patent Office	1933–1998	General Services Administration	1986–1995[c]
Coast and Geodetic Survey	1933–1966	General Services Administration	1996–2006
National Bureau of Standards	1933–1973	Civil Aeronautics Authority/Civil Aeronautics Board/Federal Aviation Administration	1940–2006
Bureau of Narcotics	1933–1969	Federal (Power) Energy. Regulatory Commission	1933–1985
Bureau of the Mint	1933–1992	Federal (Power) Energy. Regulatory Commission	1986–2006[a]
Bureau of Labor Statistics	1933–1991	Interstate Commerce Commission	1933–1996
Labor Standards/Employment Standards	1935–1968[a]	Nuclear Regulatory Commission	1977–2006

Agency	Dates	Agency	Dates
Extension Service	1933–2006	Federal Communications Commission	1936–1985
Farmers Home Administration	1949–1967	Federal Communications Commission	1986–2006[a]
Soil Conservation Service	1937–1995	Federal Trade Commission	1933–2006
Forest Service	1933–2006	Securities and Exchange Commission	1936–2006
Bureau of Reclamation/Reclamation Service	1933–1994	**Coast Guard**	**1933–2006**
General Land Office/Bureau of Land Management	1933–2006	Federal Maritime Commission	1964–1985
National Park Service	1933–2006	Federal Maritime Commission	1986–2006[a]
Bureau of Indian Affairs	1933–2006	**War Department**	**1933–1948**
Fish and Wildlife Service	1942–2006	**Navy Department/Naval Establishment**	**1933–1948**
Bureau of Mines	1933–1996	**Military Establishment**	**1937–1948**
Bonneville Power Administration	1939–1975	**DOD Independent Agencies**	**1949–1959**
Office of Education/Department of Education	1933–2006	**DOD Office of the Secretary of Defense**	**1949–1959**
National Oceanic and Atmospheric Administration	1972–2006	**DOD Department of the Army**	**1949–1959**
Vocational Rehabilitation	1933–1968	**DOD Department of the Navy**	**1949–1959**
National Aeronautics and Space Administration	1961–2006	**DOD Department of the Air Force**	**1949–1959**
Corps of Engineers	**1933–2006**	**Military Assistance**	**1955–2006**
Military Construction	**1960–2006**	**Defense Procurement**	**1961–2006**
Economic Development Administration	1967–2006	**Defense (Military) Personnel**	**1961–2006**
Rural Electrification Administration	1938–1994	**Defense Operations and Maintenance**	**1961–2006**
Atomic Energy Commission	1949–1975	**Defense Research and Development**	**1961–2006**
Public Health Service	1933–1969	**Administration of Foreign Affairs**	**1958–2006**
HUD Commission Planning and Development/ Community Planning and Development	1973–2006	International Organizations and Conferences	1958–2006
HUD Housing Programs	1977–1999	**International Commissions**	**1958–2006**
HUD Housing Programs	1998–2006[b]		

Note: Bold type indicates a defense agency (as opposed to a nondefense agency). Programs and agencies tracked from 1933–2006.
[a]Salaries and expenses only.
[b]Housing for special populations only.
[c]Consumer Information Center allocation only.

as the predecessor to the Department of Education, oversaw all aspects of the federal government's involvement in education policy.

The agencies also vary greatly in size, as measured both by the number of personnel working within them and the size of their annual budgets. Some of these agencies are quite large, such as the Food and Drug Administration, the Federal Bureau of Investigation, and the Bureau of Indian Affairs. Others are relatively small, such as the Federal Power Commission and the Federal Trade Commission. Some agencies, such as the Food and Drug Administration (FDA), the Occupational Safety and Health Administration (OSHA), and the National Aeronautics and Space Administration (NASA), are well known. Others, such as the Rural Waste, Water, and Disposal Grants, are more obscure.

Table 4.1 also shows the years for which budgetary data are available for each agency or program. In total, we have 3,201 observational units, which is significantly less than the possible number of cases supported by this data set (77 agencies times 74 years, yielding 5,698 observations). In a few rare instances data on the president's budgetary request for a particular agency in a particular year are simply not available. More commonly, though, an agency does not exist in a given year, either because the date precedes its establishment or because the date appears after the agency's merger with another agency, internal division, or outright termination. We also recognize that in the first year of a president's first term, the official budget proposal comes from the previous president. We therefore drop these observations, limiting the sample to the last three years of a president's first term, and all four years of the president's second term.

For each agency-by-year observation, we identify the president's budget proposal and the actual appropriations allotted to that agency (standardized to 1983 dollars). For the years 1948 to 1985, we use data collected by Rod Kiewiet and Mathew McCubbins. Brandice Canes-Wrone furnished data from 1986 to 2001.[7] For the years 1933 to 1947 and 2002 to 2006, we collected data from the *Congressional Record*. For each fiscal year, the Senate document entitled "Appropriations, Budget Estimates, Etc" lists the president's proposal (referred to as the budget estimate) and the amount appropriated, broken down by agency and/or program. In some cases, data on the full appropriations to an agency are not provided. In these cases, accordingly, we use the salaries and expenses allotted for the agency (as noted in Table 4.1). Additionally, a handful of agencies

7. We cross-checked all these data, which Senate documents showed to be accurate.

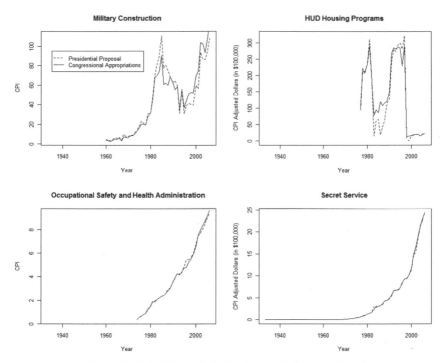

Figure 4.1. TIME SERIES DATA: PRESIDENTIAL BUDGET REQUESTS AND CONGRESSIONAL
APPROPRIATIONS FOR FOUR AGENCIES.

Presidential requests are shown by the dashed lines, and congressional appropriations are shown by the solid lines. The dollar amounts are standardized to 1983 figures. Consumer Price Index (CPI) presented in adjusted 1983 dollars (in $100,000).

have changed names over time (such as the General Land Office, which became the Bureau of Land Management in 1948). In these cases, we treat the agencies as a continuously operating unit.[8] Only when an agency splits, merges, or dies does it fall out of our data set.

Figure 4.1 tracks the allocation of real dollars requested by the president and appropriated by Congress for four elements of our data set: military construction, Department of Housing and Urban Development (HUD) programs, OSHA, and the Secret Service. Because different elements are observed for different time periods, the data set is unbalanced. But as long as the presence or absence of agencies is uncorrelated with war, we need not worry about the selection process that generated our sample.

8. Estimating models that treat such agencies as different does not change any of the substantive results.

Inspecting the data, we see that the president generally requests more money (as shown by the dashed line) than Congress allocates (as shown by the solid line) in any given year. And in some instances, such as military construction in the 1980s, congressional appropriations substantially trailed presidential requests. There are exceptions to this pattern, however. For instance, Congress regularly appropriated more money for HUD housing programs than the president requested.

Just as the differences between presidential proposals and actual appropriations vary within agencies and programs, so too do they vary across agencies and programs. Viewed in terms of either absolute or proportional differences, presidential proposals in military construction and HUD housing programs diverge more from actual appropriations than do those for OSHA or the Secret Service. For reasons that will be explained below, all our estimates about the impact of war on presidential success come from changes within, rather than across, agencies and programs.

When considering all the observations in our data set, the president requests on average $4,382,662 per agency each year, while Congress allocates $4,368,323, an overall difference of $14,339. When looking at the absolute value of the differences between presidential requests and congressional appropriations for each agency and year, we find substantial variation. Though the median difference is just $1,924, the mean is $202,000, and the standard deviation is roughly $1 million. Though these differences represent absolute values, in the vast majority of cases Congress appropriates less than the president requests. Forty-eight out of seventy-seven agencies received less money from Congress per year than the president requested. Likewise, Congress granted fewer real dollars per agency than requested by the president in fifty-five out of seventy-four years. (Note that the fact that adjustments to the president's budget proposals consistently run in one direction is itself broadly consistent with the Policy Priority Model.)

As Table 4.2 shows, budgets routinely increase during war. On average, presidential budgetary requests increase by $3.3 million per agency-year during war, and likewise Congress's approved budget increases by $3.5 million. Note further that in times of war Congress allocates slightly more money per agency-year than the president requests (by $19,691); during times of peace, Congress allocates less per agency-year than the president requests (by $26,629). The same trends hold when these data are disaggregated into defense agencies and nondefense agencies. Presidential budgetary estimates increase, on average, from $1.4 to $1.7 million during war

Table 4.2. DESCRIPTIVE STATISTICS

	Wartime	Peacetime	Difference
Presidential proposals			
Total	$20,011,888	$16,721,495	$3,290,393
Defense agencies	18,307,561	15,367,199	2,940,362
Nondefense agencies	1,704,327	1,354,296	350,031
Congressional appropriations			
Total	19,986,823	16,510,322	3,476,501
Defense agencies	18,240,558	15,130,993	3,109,565
Nondefense agencies	1,746,265	1,379,329	366,936
Difference between proposals and appropriations			
Total	25,065	211,174	−186,108
Defense agencies	67,002	236,206	−169,203
Nondefense agencies	−41,937	−25,032	−16,905

Note: Values denote the average real dollars (scaled to 1983) per agency per year for each of the categories.

for nondefense agencies, and from $15.4 to $18.3 million for defense agencies. Likewise, congressional appropriations increase from $1.4 to $1.7 million for nondefense agencies, and from $15.1 to $18.2 million for defense agencies. These figures indicate that presidents receive an additional $16,905 more than they requested during war years for nondefense agencies, and that the gap between a president's request and Congress's appropriations decreases by just under $170,000 for defense agencies. Further disaggregating the data by agency, we find that fifty-two out of seventy-six agencies have higher presidential proposals during war, fifty-three out of seventy-six agencies have higher congressional appropriations, and the gap between these two values (proposals and appropriations) is smaller during war in forty-two out of seventy-six agencies.

4.2 *Primary Analyses*

In this section, we outline our empirical strategies for testing our primary, theoretically informed predictions. We then present our main results, which broadly conform to expectations.

EMPIRICAL STRATEGY

Dependent Variable. Our dependent variable characterizes discrepancies between proposed and final appropriations for different agencies in different years. The distribution of these differences, it turns out, reveals substantial skewness. In our main models, therefore, we take the natural logarithm of these differences. Though we explore a wide variety of specifications, our preferred version of the dependent variable is the natural log of the absolute value of the difference between proposed and final appropriations for each agency in each year—that is, $\ln(|Prop_{it} - Approp_{it}| + 1)$.[9] Larger values of this variable indicate greater discrepancy between what the president requested and what Congress ultimately granted, and smaller values indicate less discrepancy.[10] When interpreting the effects of any particular covariate, positive values indicate an expansion of the difference between proposed and final appropriations, while negative values indicate a contraction.

War. Periods of war are identified by the criteria laid out in Chapter 3. To be identified as a war year, the nation must have been at war when appropriations were proposed. Hence, 1941 is not coded as a war year, because the United States did not enter World War II until after the Pearl Harbor attacks of December 7. Meanwhile, 1991 is coded as a war year, as Bush issued his proposal while the Gulf War remained ongoing, even though Congress set final appropriations after that war had ended.[11]

High and Moderate Nationalization Wars. To further distinguish different types of wars, we separate our five wars into two categories: those in which national priorities were high, and those in which national priorities were modest. Following from Table 3.2, World War II and the post-9/11 wars constitute high nationalization wars, while Korea, Vietnam, and the Gulf War constitute moderate nationalization wars. Under this rubric, peace years constitute periods of low nationalization.

Control Variables. Obviously, the likelihood that Congress accommodates the president's requests depends on a great deal more than the condition of peace or war. Most importantly, perhaps, it depends on just how much

---

9. We also will discuss other plausible characterizations of the dependent variable.

10. This characterization comports with other spatial models of the budgetary process, including Canes-Wrone 2006, Ferejohn and Krehbiel 1987, and Kiewiet and McCubbins 1988. In each of these models, the president is assumed to have an ideal appropriation amount for a given unit at a given time period, and the utility he derives from actual appropriations decreases in their distance from his ideal point.

11. The variable *War* identifies the following calendar years: 1942–45, 1951–53, 1965–73, 1991, and 2002–2006 (when our panel ends). None of our findings change significantly when the Persian Gulf War is excluded from the analysis.

money the president requests. At the margin, we expect that Congress will look more favorably on smaller requests than larger ones. We therefore control for the logged value of the president's proposal for each agency in each year.

Congress's response to the president surely also depends on the level of political support that he enjoys within its chambers. Presidents who confront congresses with large numbers of ideological or partisan supporters are likely to secure appropriations that more closely approximate their requests than presidents who face off against congresses dominated by the opposition party. Following Kiewiet and McCubbins, we therefore control for the percentage of House seats held by the president's party in each year.[12]

We further account for the state of the economy. In particular, we include three economic indicators: the average unemployment rate during the year when appropriations are proposed and set, the national growth rate since the previous year, and the total budget deficit from the previous year. We do not have strong expectations about how each of these variables will relate to the outcome of interest. It seems plausible that the president's ability to convince Congress to meet his budgetary requests will depend on the perceived severity of unemployment problems and the levels of available revenues.

Finally, in all our statistical models we include fixed effects, that account for all observable and unobservable time-invariant characteristics of individual agencies and presidents. Identification in the model, therefore, comes from changes in appropriations within agencies and within presidential administrations. Such changes, of course, could arise from changes in presidential proposals, final appropriations, or some combination of the two. Hence, if Congress always delivers the president a fixed percentage of his request for a particular agency, then this agency will not contribute to the estimated effect of war (or any other time-varying

---

12. Kiewiet and McCubbins 1985. Partisanship, of course, plays no role in the Policy Priority Model. We also have estimated models that control for the distance between the president's and the median House member's NOMINATE score, which characterizes the degree of preference convergence across the branches of government, which itself *is* implicated by the theory. Though these models furnish comparable results, for two reasons we are reluctant to rely on them. First, DW-NOMINATE scores are partly a cause and partly a consequence of the very phenomenon we seek to explain—legislative support for the president's positions (Clinton 2007). Second, presidential DW-NOMINATE scores are highly unreliable because of the small and nonrandom sample of bills on which presidents take positions (Treier 2010).

covariate of interest). If Congress delivers a fixed percentage of presidential requests for all agencies, then the effect of war (and all other time-varying covariates) will not be identified.

Statistical Models and Key Predictions. In concert with our characterizations of major modern wars, the Policy Priority Model makes two key predictions. First, wartime budgets generally will more closely approximate presidential preferences than will peacetime budgets. We refer to this as Hypothesis 1. Second, the budgets during World War II and the war in Afghanistan will more closely approximate presidential preferences than those in the Korean, Vietnam, and Gulf wars (see Chapter 3). We refer to this as Hypothesis 2. To test these hypotheses, we employ two statistical models, which we estimate via least squares. The first model takes the following general form:

(4.1) $\quad y_{it} = \beta_0 + \beta_1 War_t + \beta_2 Prop_{it} + \beta_3 CongSupp_t + ECO_{t,t-1}\Psi + D_i + P_t + \varepsilon_{it},$

where y_{it} characterizes the discrepancy between the president's proposed budget (*Prop*) and Congress's final appropriations (*Approp*) for agency i in calendar year t (or fiscal year $t+1$),[13] *War* identifies whether appropriations were proposed during times of war, *CongSupp* identifies the level of partisan support for the president in Congress, *ECO* is a vector of covariates that characterize the state of the economy, D_i is a vector of agency-specific fixed effects, P_t is a vector of president-specific fixed effects, and β_0 and ε_{it} are constant and error terms, respectively. To account for any serial correlation, and to recover standard errors that are robust to arbitrary forms of heteroskedasticity, we cluster the standard errors on agencies.[14] The second model is nearly identical to the first, but distinguishes between high and moderate nationalization wars:

(4.2) $\quad y_{it} = \beta_0 + \beta_1 HighNatWar_t + \beta_2 ModNatWar_t + \beta_3 Prop_{it}$
$\qquad\qquad + \beta_4 CongSupp_t + ECO_{t,t-1}\Psi + D_i + P_t + \varepsilon_{it}.$

---

13. In the first year of a president's first term, the official budget proposal comes from the previous president. We therefore drop these observations, limiting the sample to the last three years of a president's first term, and all four years of the president's second term.

14. For a longer discussion of the merits of clustering, see Petersen 2009 and Wooldridge 2006. We recognize that within any given year, presidential proposals for different agencies may not be independent of one another. Facing budgetary constraints, presidents may trade increased spending proposals for one agency for decreased spending on another. When clustering the standard errors on fiscal year rather than agency, the standard errors increase very slightly. The main results we report, however, carry through entirely.

Table 4.3. KEY PREDICTIONS

Hypothesis 1	Appropriations more closely match presidential requests during war than during peace.
Statistical model 4.1	$\beta_1 < 0$
Statistical model 4.2	$\beta_1 < 0$
Hypothesis 2	Appropriations more closely match presidential requests among those wars where the nationalization of politics is relatively high than those where it is relatively moderate.
Statistical model 4.2	$\beta_2 < \beta_1$

The first model allows us to test Hypothesis 1: wartime budgets will more closely approximate presidential preferences than will peacetime budgets. Specifically, in Model 4.1, Hypothesis 1 predicts that $\beta_1 < 0$. Meanwhile, the second model allows us to test both Hypothesis 1 and Hypothesis 2. Specifically, in Model 4.2, Hypothesis 1 predicts that $\beta_1 < 0$, and Hypothesis 2 predicts that $\beta_2 < \beta_1$. These key predictions are summarized in Table 4.3.

TESTING HYPOTHESIS 1: COMPARING WAR AND PEACE

Column 1 of Table 4.4 presents our preferred estimate of the impact of war on Congress's willingness to abide the president's budgetary requests. The effect, as expected, is negative, substantively large, and statistically significant. During periods of war, differences between proposed and final appropriations attenuate substantially. Taking the inverse log of the point estimate, this translates into a roughly 26 percent decrease in the average discrepancy between proposed and final appropriations for our sample of agencies during the period under investigation.

The other variables in the model also behave as expected. Presidents who confront congresses with a larger number of House copartisans enjoy higher levels of budgetary success than do presidents who must work with a larger number of partisan opponents—an effect that is substantively large and statistically significant. Congress demonstrates greater accommodation to the president's proposed budget when national growth rates are large, and less accommodation when available revenues (as measured by budget deficits) are relatively scarce.[15] Consistent with expansionary fiscal policy during periods of unemployment, presidents also experience more accommodation from Congress when unemployment rates are

---

15. The first two estimates are both statistically significant, and the latter estimate just misses standard thresholds for statistical significance ($p = .147$).

Table 4.4. COMPARING WAR AND PEACE

	Logged Differences	Accounting for Asymmetries
All Wars	−0.300 (0.129)**	−0.495 (0.199)**
House Seat Share	−2.190 (0.744)***	−3.300 (1.074)***
ln(Unemployment)	−0.360 (0.135)***	−0.615 (0.189)***
Real Deficit	0.090 (0.057)	0.305 (0.134)**
Real GDP Growth	−2.341 (1.028)**	−3.000 (1.450)**
ln(Proposal)	1.055 (0.105)***	0.982 (0.150)***
(Intercept)	0.761 (1.538)**	−5.414 (2.472)**
N	3201	3201
R^2	0.74	0.32
MSE	2.11	3.84

Note: Entries are linear regression coefficients with standard errors shown in parentheses. In column 1, the dependent variable is $\ln(|Prop_{it} - Approp_{it}| + 1)$. In column 2, the dependent variable is $\ln(|Prop_{it} - Approp_{it}| + 1)$ if $Prop_{it} > Approp_{it}$, and zero otherwise. Though not reported, all models include president and agency/program fixed effects.
*** indicates $p < .01$; ** indicates $p < .05$; * indicates $p < .10$, two-tailed tests.

high.[16] We also find that Congress appropriates monies that more closely approximate smaller budgetary requests than larger ones—another effect that is substantively large and highly statistically significant. Finally, the agency and presidential fixed effects, which are not reported to conserve space, are both jointly significant.

The second column of Table 4.4 considers a characterization of the dependent variable that distinguishes instances when Congress appropriates larger amounts than the president requests from instances when Congress appropriates smaller amounts. The logic for doing so is straightforward enough. When Congress refuses to appropriate the full amount of money requested for a specific agency, it clearly constrains the agency's ability to either perform at a level of activity that the president would like or to pursue specific policy functions that constitute presidential priorities. But given the president's ability to influence, ex post, how monies are spent— whether by discouraging bureaucrats from vigorously enforcing their mandate, reprogramming or transferring funds from one account to another, or simply impounding funds, as was done for much of the period under investigation—Congress may have a difficult time inducing agencies to either more vigorously pursue their mandate or to administer a larger number of policy activities. Congressional influence, under this account, constitutes

16. The effects of these economic variables are also observed when they are either represented individually or as subsets within the models.

a greater influence as a constraint than as a stimulant to executive activity. Congress can readily impede executive functioning, but it has a much more difficult time either galvanizing existing executive functions or jumpstarting altogether new ones. To account for this asymmetry, we generate a dependent variable that continuously measures final appropriations that are lower than the president's proposal but treats appropriations that exceed proposals as equivalent to ones that exactly meet them—that is, $|Prop_{it} - Approp_{it}| = \ln(|Prop_{it} - Approp_{it}| + 1)$ if $Prop_{it} > Approp_{it}$, and zero otherwise. The results, presented in column 2, compare well with those observed in our preferred specification. Once again, we find a negative, substantively meaningful, and statistically significant relationship between war and the observed discrepancy between proposed and final appropriations.

ROBUSTNESS CHECKS

As empirical findings go, those presented in Table 4.4 are remarkably robust. We have estimated a wide variety of models that use alternative versions of the dependent variable, include alternative sets of control variables, and consider periods of the time series when budget proposals may better reflect presidential preferences. In the vast majority of instances, our core findings hold.

Alternative Characterizations of the Dependent Variable. Though they are not reported, we have estimated still more models that employ a variety of other characterizations of the dependent variable. For instance, we have estimated models that consider the logged absolute value of the difference between proposed and final appropriations as a percentage of the president's proposal for each agency in each year—that is, $ln(|Prop_{it} - Approp_{it}|/Prop_{it} + 1)$. Once again, we find that final appropriations more closely approximate presidential proposals during war than during peace.

With respect to war, nothing especially important rides on the decision to take the logarithmic transformations of the dependent variable. We reran the models with the dependent variable as the raw differences between proposed and final appropriations in columns 1 and 2—that is, as $|Prop_{it} - Approp_{it}|$, and as $(|Prop_{it} - Approp_{it}|)$ if $Prop_{it} > Approp_{it}$, and zero otherwise. Once again, we recover comparable estimates for our main covariate of interest, war. In all three cases, the point estimates for war are negative; in two of the three cases, they are statistically significant. In the one case where the estimated effect of war is insignificant—that is, in the version that accounts for asymmetric effects of overappropriations and underappropriations—the recovered p value is .18. But because the estimates associated with other regressors in this model, notably House partisan support and deficits, attenuate substantially, and in some cases actually switch signs, we have less confidence in the face validity of these specific results.

We also have examined the dependent variable as the proportion of the president's proposal that is enacted into law—that is, $Approp_{it}/Prop_{it}$. In an effort to address the possibility of asymmetric effects associated with underappropriations and overappropriations, we also have set an upper limit on this proportion at 1, such that $y_{it} = Approp_{it}/Prop_{it}$ if $Approp_{it}/Prop_{it} < 1$, and $y_{it} = 1$ otherwise. And finally, we also have used a measure developed by Brandice Canes-Wrone in her study of the impact of public appeals on Congress's willingness to abide the president's budgetary proposals.[17] Canes-Wrone estimates the absolute value of the difference in annual percentage changes in presidential proposals and annual percentage changes in final appropriations—that is, $|([Prop_{it} - Prop_{it-1}]/Prop_{it-1}) - ([Approp_{it} - Approp_{it-1}]/Approp_{it-1})|$. Every one of these alternative specifications furnished comparable results.

Model Specification. Just as the main results associated with war are robust to a variety of different characterizations of the dependent variable, so too do they hold across a host of alternative model specifications. We have estimated models that exclude the president's proposal from the regressors, include the raw value of the president's proposal, include subsets of the economic variables, account for the partisan composition of the Senate as well as (or in lieu of) the House, exclude the substantial number of president and agency-specific fixed effects, and include controls for periods of unified and divided government, election years, each agency's budget authority from the previous year, the president's public approval ratings, and the president's year and term in office. In nearly every instance, the main results hold.[18] Again and again, the models support the

---

17. Canes-Wrone 2006.
18. The general results do appear to be sensitive to the inclusion of a control variable for unemployment. When this variable is excluded from models that span the entire time series, the estimated effect of war approaches zero. This finding, however, appears to be an artifact of the historically high unemployment rates during Roosevelt's first two terms in office. When dropping unemployment from the model but limiting the sample to the post–World War II era, the estimated effect of war remains negative and statistically significant, as it also does when unemployment is included for this shorter time series.

contention that presidents enjoy higher levels of budgetary success during periods of war than during peace.

We also recognize the possibility that presidential proposals and Congress's final appropriations are themselves functions of the public's demand for government activism. Indeed, the public's appetite for government spending may frame interbranch disagreements about budgetary priorities. If this appetite itself varies during times of war and peace—as it surely does—then the evidence presented thus far may overstate the independent influence of war on the president's budgetary success. To investigate this possibility, we estimated models that included a control for "public mood," as developed by James Stimson.[19] None of the results change. Indeed, the effect of war and every other covariate remains virtually identical, while the mood measure itself registers a null effect.[20] The relevance of war in budgetary politics does not appear to conflate with public attitudes toward spending, at least as captured by this measure.

Accounting for Changes in Budgetary Clearance. As Richard Neustadt documented in his classic article on budgetary clearance, the president did not immediately assume full control over the proposal-making process the moment that Congress granted it to him in 1921.[21] Rather, the construction of budgetary clearance procedures constituted a work in progress, with the most significant strides being made in 1939 when the Bureau of the Budget was officially recognized as an agent of the president with new, comprehensive oversight powers, and 1947 when James Webb, Truman's new Director of the Budget, overhauled and strengthened the budgetary review process. In principle, budgetary proposals made before 1945, and especially before 1938, may only weakly represent the president's policy views. If so, changes in observed levels of congressional accommodation to presidential proposals during this period may say very little about presidential success.

19. Stimson 1999. Aggregating citizens' responses to a wide array of survey items, Stimson tracks annual changes in the public's demand for government services. The measure is available only back to 1952. When looking at the restricted period between 1952 and 2006, we again find that Congress enacts budgets that more closely resemble presidential proposals during war than during peace.

20. The mood measure does correlate positively with aggregate spending. It is not surprising, then, that mood does correlate with the version of the dependent variable that merely distinguishes cases where Congress appropriates less than the president's request. Even here, the effect of war remains negative and significant.

21. Neustadt 1954.

To account for this possibility, we reestimated our main models for the post-1938 and post-1946 periods. The recovered estimates associated with war are indistinguishable from those presented in Table 4.4. Whereas the coefficient for war for the entire time series is −0.30 with a standard error of 0.13, the coefficient and standard error for the post-1938 period are −0.28 and 0.13, respectively; and for the post-1946 period, they are −0.34 and 0.13, respectively.

TESTING HYPOTHESIS 2: COMPARING TYPES OF WARS

The estimated results for Equation 4.1 provide strong support for Hypothesis 1: presidents enjoy greater budgetary success in times of war than they do in times of peace. We now turn our attention to the second empirical implication generated in Chapters 2 and 3: presidents enjoy greater budgetary success in those wars wherein the country places greater weight on national outcomes than they do in wars wherein the country places relatively less weight on national outcomes. To test Hypothesis 2, we reestimate Equation 4.1 with an added interaction term to distinguish the effects of the two types of wars. The results are presented in Table 4.5.

Columns 1 and 2 of Table 4.5 replicate the models estimated in Table 4.4, except this time we disaggregate World War II and the post-9/11 wars

Table 4.5. COMPARING TYPES OF WAR

	Logged Differences	Accounting for Asymmetries
Moderate Nat'l Wars	−0.263 (0.129)**	−0.421 (0.200)**
High Nat'l Wars	−0.854 (0.332)*	−1.600 (0.551)**
House Seat Share	−2.179 (0.744)***	−3.277 (1.075)***
ln(Unemployment)	−0.608 (0.191)***	−1.119 (0.306)***
Real Deficit	0.107 (0.056)*	0.338 (0.135)**
Real GDP Growth	−2.275 (1.036)**	−2.868 (1.476)*
ln(Proposal)	1.051 (0.105)***	0.974 (0.150)***
(Intercept)	−2.496 (1.575)	−4.512 (2.482)*
Prob $\beta_2 = \beta_1$	.07	.03
N	3,201	3,201
R^2	0.74	0.31
MSE	2.12	3.84

Note: Entries are linear regression coefficients with standard errors shown in parentheses. In column 1, the dependent variable is $\ln(|Prop_{it} - Approp_{it}| + 1)$. In column 2, the dependent variable is $\ln(|Prop_{it} - Approp_{it}| + 1)$ if $Prop_{it} > Approp_{it}$, and zero otherwise. Though not reported, all models include president and agency/program fixed effects.
*** indicates $p < .01$; ** indicates $p < .05$; * indicates $p < .10$, two-tailed tests.

from the Vietnam, Korean, and Persian Gulf wars. So doing, we find that the main effects of both *High λ Wars* and *Moderate λ Wars* are negative and statistically significantly different from zero for both characterizations of the dependent variable. Consistent with Hypothesis 2, we also find that these two estimated effects are significantly different from one another. Indeed, the estimated effects for *High λ Wars* are roughly 3 to 4 times larger in magnitude than those for *Moderate λ Wars*, suggesting that at least with regards to budgetary politics, the differences observed across wars can be just as significant as those observed between periods of war and peace. The coefficients on each of the control variables, meanwhile, are consistent with the results of Table 4.4.

WAR-SPECIFIC ESTIMATES

To further flesh out our findings, Table 4.6 replicates our main model but disaggregates war into all its constituent elements: World War II, Korea, Vietnam, Persian Gulf, and the post-9/11 wars. The results, for the most part, conform to the basic patterns in Tables 4.4 and 4.5. In the first column of Table 4.6, the point estimates from World War II and the post 9/11 wars are roughly three times as large as the other wars. Though the differences

Table 4.6. VARIATION ACROSS WARS

	Logged Differences	Accounting for Asymmetries
World War II	−0.831 (0.354)**	−1.381 (0.583)**
Post-9/11 Wars	−1.334 (0.518)**	−4.202 (1.018)***
Korean War	−0.189 (0.199)	−0.015 (0.260)
Vietnam War	−0.354 (0.189)*	−0.401 (0.239)*
Gulf War	−0.122 (0.262)	−1.069 (0.674)
House Seat Share	−2.182 (0.769)***	−3.550 (1.109)***
ln(Unemployment)	−0.599 (0.199)***	−0.995 (0.318)***
Real Deficit	0.105 (0.056)*	0.336 (0.135)**
Real GDP Growth	−2.331 (1.094)**	−3.562 (1.581)**
ln(Proposal)	1.050 (0.106)***	0.970 (0.151)***
(Intercept)	−2.488 (1.579)	−4.482 (2.488)**
N	3,201	3,201
R^2	0.74	0.31
MSE	2.11	3.84

Note: Entries are linear regression coefficients with standard errors shown in parentheses. In column 1, the dependent variable is $\ln(|Prop_{it} - Approp_{it}| + 1)$. In column 2, the dependent variable is $\ln(|Prop_{it} - Approp_{it}| + 1)$ if $Prop_{it} > Approp_{it}$, and zero otherwise. Though not reported, all models include president and agency/program fixed effects.
*** indicates $p < .01$; ** indicates $p < .05$; * indicates $p < .10$, two-tailed tests.

are not statistically significant, the estimated effect for World War II is slightly smaller than the one for the post-9/11 wars. The evidence of war's influence on the president's budgetary success is not confined to these two wars. The point estimates for the Korean, Vietnam, and Persian Gulf wars are all negative. Of these wars, only in the case of Vietnam is the effect statistically significant, but then only marginally so.

Once again, the recovered estimates, both of war generally and of each separate war, are generally consistent across each of our characterizations of the dependent variable. Moving forward, we focus on our preferred specification, $\ln(|Prop_{it} - Approp_{it}| + 1)$, which is found in the first columns of Tables 4.4, 4.5, and 4.6.

INTRAWAR VARIATION

We also have estimated a variety of models designed to account for changes in Congress's propensity to support the president over the course of a war. Given the short duration of rally effects, for instance, one might expect that Congress's propensity to stand behind the president would be short lived, and, moreover, that once the costs of war (both financial and human) materialize, members of Congress would become emboldened to vote against the president. If true, then evidence of heightened presidential influence should be confined to the first year or two of an ongoing military venture.

We do not find any support for such a supposition. Indeed, to the extent that we find any evidence of a temporal effect, it suggests that appropriations more closely approximate presidential proposals later in a war rather than earlier. For example, when estimating the same model as shown in column 1 of Table 4.4 but adding a simple counter for the number of years that had passed since the onset of war, we observe a negative effect that just misses standard thresholds of statistical significance ($p = .106$). Other models that include indicator variables for each year of a war or that isolate only the first year of a war generate comparable effects. In no instance do we find any evidence that congressional accommodation is confined to the early stages of a war.

These findings are not mere curiosities. Indeed, they speak directly to the concern that war might just proxy for increased public support for the president (see Chapter 3). As a historical matter, the president's approval ratings spike during the early periods of each of these wars. Thus, that evidence of congressional accommodation to the president is not confined to these early periods weighs in favor of our preferred explanation about the nationalization of politics.[22]

4.3 *Strategic Proposal Making*

The most nettlesome problem associated with this kind of analysis is the possibility—indeed, the probability—that presidential proposals do not represent the president's actual preferences about how federal monies are allocated. Presidents do not lock themselves in a hermetically sealed room, safely removed from politics' mephitis, while crafting their proposals. To the contrary, presidents are acutely aware of their political surroundings. When contemplating how much to ask for any individual agency, presidents and their advisers maintain a steady gaze on how the larger polity will receive their requests. Just as a seasoned negotiator will open any negotiation with a low-ball offer, presidents, in anticipation of Congress's next move, may request higher (or lower) levels of appropriations in an attempt to ultimately secure their ideal outcomes.

A GENERAL STATEMENT OF THE PROBLEM

The Policy Priority Model, as currently specified, does not support the issuance of strategic appeals (see Chapter 2). Rather, the model predicts that when presidents make a proposal they will either propose their ideal policy; or they will entirely capitulate and propose congress's. However, we should not presume that the Policy Priority Model constitutes the underlying data-generating process for budgetary politics. As a general matter, presidents have incentives to ask for more money than they truly believe is optimal when they anticipate that Congress will not fulfill their budgetary requests. Consequently, an empirical model that attempts to estimate the gap between the presidents' ideal budget allocations and Congress's final appropriations needs to account for the possibility that presidents' budgetary proposals do not necessarily equal their ideal budgets.

That presidential proposals may not constitute an exact rendering of the president's sincere policy preferences does not mean that our recovered

---

22. We also have estimated models that simply control for the president's public approval ratings. Though such data are only available for a subset of our time series, their inclusion does not bear substantively upon the recovered estimates of war, providing still further support for our argument about the relevant quality of wars that induce heightened presidential success in Congress.

estimates are necessarily biased. If, for instance, presidents consistently request a fixed portion more (or less) than they would like, all of the estimates from Tables 4.4 and 4.5 appropriately interpret the impact of war on presidents' ability to secure appropriations that reflect their sincere (though unobserved) preferences. Indeed, there is good reason to expect that presidents behave exactly this way. Rather than stating their sincere preferences up front, presidents present their budget proposals as an initial volley, fully expecting Congress to adjust spending to a more middling position.[23] As long as the same strategic considerations inform presidential decisions about budget proposals during conditions of peace and war, our existing least squares regressions constitute a perfectly defensible estimation strategy.

If the strategies of writing peacetime and wartime proposals systematically differ from one another, however, are our claims about the impact of war on the president's budgetary success unavoidably misguided? The answer depends upon how these strategies are adapted to war's onset. The most likely scenario suggests that we have underestimated the impact of war. Consider the following: if presidents anticipate that Congress will be more obliging in war than in peace, wartime presidents may recommend deeper cuts into those administrative agencies that they oppose and higher increases for those agencies they support. If so, then observed differences between wartime proposals and final appropriations may be no smaller than, and perhaps may even exceed, the observed differences between peacetime proposals and final appropriations. Note, however, that Congress has not assumed an equally critical stance in war as in peace. Rather, presidents anticipate the reception they are likely to receive in both conditions and adjust accordingly. Consequently, any comparison of the differences between proposals and final budgets in war and peace that fails to account for this strategic behavior—including our own—will understate the extent to which wars fortify the president's influence in budgetary politics.

What, then, would have to be true in order for our estimates of the impact of war on the president's budgetary success to be upwardly biased? Imagine the following: when presidents go to war, their primary concern lies with maintaining a fragile base of domestic support; given the extraordinary stakes involved in war, presidents avoid taking controversial actions or positions at home. If true, wartime presidents may be espe-

---

23. Schick 2007, 92–95.

cially inclined to advance policies that already enjoy widespread support at home, and to proactively diffuse any potential disputes that might distract from their war effort. Members of Congress may then enact a final budget that more closely resembles the president's proposal. They do so, however, not out of concern for the war per se, but rather because wartime presidents go out of their way to placate their opponents, the net result of which is a substantially less controversial presidential budget proposal.

On its face, it seems highly unlikely that presidents assume a meek and appeasing posture at home while brandishing the sword abroad. Indeed, the first chapter's brief survey of wartime actions paints an altogether different picture—one of presidents boldly and unapologetically seizing power at home, insisting again and again that one domestic reform after another is needed to ensure military victory. In an abundance of caution, though, we shall not dismiss the faint possibility that presidents, at least when it comes to budgets, temporarily scale back their ambitions at home while troops are fighting and dying on the battlefield.

WHO ACCOMMODATES WHOM?

That final appropriations more closely approximate presidential proposals could be evidence of one of three scenarios: (1) during war, members of Congress go out of their way to accommodate presidential preferences; (2) during war, presidents go out of their way to accommodate congressional preferences; or (3), during war, both members of Congress and presidents go out of their way to accommodate each other's preferences. To argue that presidential influence increases during war, we are laying our bets on the first scenario. Unfortunately, all three scenarios produce observationally equivalent predictions with respect to our key finding.

By investigating trends in presidential proposals during war and peace, we can make some headway in distinguishing among these possibilities. If during war, for instance, we find that presidents scale back their proposals, particularly those involving domestic agencies and programs, then confidence in our preferred interpretation necessarily erodes. On the other hand, if presidential proposals remain constant during war, then it is hard to tell a plausible story in which our results derive from heightened presidential accommodation of Congress during periods of war. If presidential proposals increase during war, then the recovered estimates may actually understate the extent to which wars augment presidential influence over budgetary outcomes.

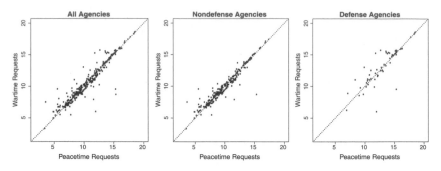

Figure 4.2. PRESIDENTIAL BUDGET REQUESTS DURING WAR AND PEACE.
Limiting the analyses to the six presidents (Roosevelt, Truman, Eisenhower, Johnson, Nixon, and George H. W. Bush) who submitted budget requests during times of both peace and war, we calculated the average agency budget requests for each president during peacetime and wartime. The x-axes in the plots represent presidents' average peacetime requests, and the y-axes represent presidents' average wartime requests. Amounts shown are the logged values of the budget requests in 1983 dollars. Points located above the 45-degree line indicate that a president requested more agency funds during wartime than during peace; points below the line indicate that he requested less.

Take a look at Figure 4.2, which plots the average peacetime and wartime proposals for each agency within those presidential administrations for which both conditions are observed. The y-axis denotes wartime values, and the x-axis denotes peacetime values. By construction, observations from those presidents who served only in times of peace or war (including Eisenhower, Kennedy, Ford, Carter, Reagan, and Clinton) are excluded from the analysis, as they do not contribute to our estimates of the impact of war. If presidents recommend the same proposal amounts, on average, during times of war and peace, then the observations should cluster around the 45-degree line. If they request less during war than during peace, they will appear below the 45-degree line. If they request more, they will appear above it.

As is plain, most observations for all proposals (left panel), as well as the subset of defense (right panel) and nondefense (middle panel) proposals, are clustered right around the 45-degree line. Those that stray almost always do so above the 45-degree line. In Table 4.2 we already saw that average peacetime requests were roughly 30 percent smaller than those during wartime. When limiting the analysis to the subset of presidents who held office during periods of both war and peace, as we do in Figure 4.2, the effects are even greater. For these presidents, wartime proposals were more than twice as large as peacetime proposals overall. Nondefense-related proposals roughly doubled and defense proposals tripled when moving from periods of war to peace.[24] Systematically, these presidents asked for higher appropriations during war than during peace.

When estimating regressions that posit presidential proposals as a function of war along with agency and president fixed effects, the recovered effect of war is positive and statistically significant. During war, presidents request, on average, 60 percent more for defense-oriented programs and agencies, and 19 percent more for domestic programs and agencies than they do during peace. But after accounting for some basic controls, the difference between peacetime and wartime proposals disappears. When adding to these models our full bevy of political and economic controls, the estimated effect of war hovers around zero and does not approach statistical significance.

It seems clear, then, that presidents do not scale back their wartime budgetary requests. Presidents may even increase them. This fact bodes well for our preferred interpretation. For in conjunction with the findings from Table 4.4, this fact suggests that Congress appropriates amounts that better reflect presidential proposals during war than during peace, even though presidential requests, depending on how they are characterized, either remain the same or increase. These results look a lot like what we would expect from heightened congressional accommodation to the president.

ESTIMATES FROM INSTRUMENTAL VARIABLES MODELS

Instead of directly gauging the extent of strategic proposal making on the basis of trends in actual peacetime and wartime proposals, in principle it is possible to account for such unobserved behavior within our main statistical models. In practice, though, it is nearly impossible. Indeed, to make inroads on the problem of strategic proposal making (which, increasingly, appears to be less and less of a problem) in this way, we would need to identify factors that encourage a president to request higher spending on some agencies and lower spending on others during periods of war and peace for reasons that have nothing to do with his expectations on how these requests will be received.

We have taken a stab at the problem, but in interpreting the findings caution is clearly warranted. Given the observed trends in peacetime and

---

24. Average overall requests during peace were $1,994,758 versus $5,094,777 during war. For defense programs and agencies, average requests increase by $8,167,029 when moving from peace to war, whereas nondefense requests increase by $636,188.

wartime proposal making, we doubt that the estimates presented thus far are an artifact of strategic proposal making; for reasons that will become clear, we remain equally skeptical that the particular modeling strategies we discuss below correct for the (unlikely) sources of bias therein. Still, we recognize that scholars who analyze budgetary politics regularly employ these techniques. Some may take comfort in the fact that the estimates from instrumental variables models look broadly consistent with those from the reduced form equations.

Our primary task is to isolate the variation in presidential proposals that has nothing to do with presidents' expectations of subsequent congressional behavior. To do this, we need to identify and then make the case for some plausible instruments. Following Kiewiet and McCubbins, we use as our instruments a collection of variables that identify how long a president has held office when a proposal is issued.[25] To wit, we estimate the following system of equations:

(4.3) $$Prop_{it} = \beta_0 + \beta_1 War_t + \beta_2 CongSupp_t + \beta_3 T_t + ECO_{t,t-1}\Psi_1 \\ + T_t + Yr_t + D_i + P_t + \varepsilon_{1it}$$

(4.4) $$y_{it} = \beta_4 + \beta_5 War_t + \beta_6 \widehat{Prop}_{it} + \beta_7 CongSupp_t + ECO_{t,t-1}\Psi_2 \\ + D_i + P_t + \varepsilon_{2it}$$

where each of the characters and subscripts remain as they were defined in Model 4.1. Notice that in the first equation, we estimate presidential proposals for agency i in year t as a function of all the same covariates used to predict the difference between proposed and final appropriations. The key difference, and what allows us to identify this system of equations, is the addition of T_t and Yr_t, which specify first-term presidents and the year of each term during which proposals are made and budgets set.[26] As before, ε_{1it} and ε_{2it} are error terms, and standard errors are clustered by agency.

For this system of equations to generate unbiased estimates of β_6, the impact of war on the president's budgetary success, T_t and Yr_t must satisfy two requirements. First, they must be correlated with the size of the president's budget, which they are. Each of our instruments generates estimates that are substantively large and statistically significant, both individually and jointly. First-term presidents request smaller budgets than do second-term (and in the case of Roosevelt, third and fourth term) presidents. And

---

25. Kiewiet and McCubbins 1991.
26. Comparable results are recovered when using only T_t or Yr_t as instruments.

over the course of a single presidential term, presidents request larger and larger budgets.

The second requirement is that T_t and Yr_t influence y_{it} only through $Prop_{it}$, and hence both are uncorrelated with ε_{2it}. Ultimately, the case for T_t and Yr_t meeting what is called the "exclusion restriction" for instrumental variables must be based on theory. It is worth recognizing, then, that presidents are more apt to recommend cuts in agencies and programs when they first assume office. Presidents do so, after all, because a greater portion of these programs and agencies employ people not of their choosing who pursue mandates not of their making. Irrespective of their expectations about how Congress will receive their proposals, presidents should propose systematically lower proposals in the first year of their first term in office. As Allen Schick observes, "presidents tend to take their boldest budget steps early in their term."[27] Over time, presidents have ample opportunities to reorganize and staff their bureaucracy to their liking. Having done so, presidents can be expected to request more spending. Moreover, and this is crucial, they do so regardless of their expectations about whether Congress will actually comply, something that we do not observe. Technically, as long as $Prop_{it}$ operates independently of ε_{it} through T_t and Yr_t it satisfies the exclusion restriction.[28]

In Table 4.7, we report the main estimates from equations 4.3 (in column 1) and 4.4 (in column 4). The results for the first stage of the equation are encouraging. Individually, our instruments are highly significant; and jointly, they generate an F-statistic that exceeds conventional instrumenting norms. Moreover, the pattern of results broadly conforms to our rationale for employing these particular instruments.

The point estimates on all of the control variables appear remarkably similar to those from Models 4.1 and 4.2. Though the standard error on

27. Schick 2007, 109.

28. Of course, this is not the only rationale one could offer for the relevance of year-of-term effects in budgetary politics. If, for instance, presidents have greater incentive to pander to public opinion in election years, as some have argued (Canes-Wrone et al. 2001), and if in pandering presidents propose budgets to which members of Congress more closely adhere, then the argument for T_t and Yr_t satisfying the exclusion restriction is patently violated. Two facts temper this concern. First, we do not find any evidence in our models of heightened presidential success in presidential election years. Second, it bears remembering that presidents and members of Congress serve altogether different constituencies. Hence, even if they both have incentives to pander, and even if this pandering amounts to more than just across-the-board spending increases, it is not at all clear that presidents and members of Congress will converge on a preferred set of budgetary priorities.

Table 4.7. STRATEGIC PROPOSALS

	Second-Stage Results			First-Stage Results		
	Model 1	Model 2	Model 3	Model 1	Model 2	Model 3
All Wars	−0.302 (0.130)**			−0.102 (0.065)		
Moderate Nat'l Wars		−0.269 (0.131)**			−0.095 (0.066)	
High Nat'l Wars		−0784** (0.309)			−0.177 (0.129)	
World War II			−0.807 (0.314)**			−0.139 (0.168)
Post-9/11 wars			−1.231 (0.500)**			0.266 (0.177)
Korean War			−0.101 (0.221)			0.036 (0.126)
Vietnam War			−0.346 (0.188)*			−0.170 (0.085)**
Gulf War			−0.141 (0.262)			−0.037 (0.148)
House Seat Share	−1.702 (1.016)*	−1.846 (1.006)*	−1.866 (1.047)*	−1.175 (0.431)***	−1.213 (0.438)***	−1.332 (0.449)***
ln(Unemployment)	−0.323 (0.134)**	−0.551 (0.174)***	−0.093 (0.031)***	−0.209 (0.059)***	−0.242 (0.088)***	−0.221 (0.091)**
Real Deficit	0.097 (0.057)*	0.109 (0.057)*	−0.088 (0.055)	0.076 (0.022)***	0.078 (0.023)***	0.072 (0.023)***
Real GDP Growth	−2.622 (1.015)***	−2.477 (1.022)**	−3.192 (1.038)***	0.894 (0.476)*	0.912 (0.477)*	0.787 (0.497)
ln(Proposal)	1.276 (0.224)***	1.203 (0.219)***	0.998 (0.287)***			
Year 1				−0.271 (0.057)***	−0.262 (0.060)***	−0.246 (0.062)***
Year 2				−0.109 (0.047)**	−0.101 (0.049)**	−0.091 (0.050)*
Year 3				−0.059 (0.043)	−0.056 (0.043)	−0.059 (0.043)
First Term				−0.524 (0.048)***	−0.518 (0.050)***	−0.499 (0.052)***
(Intercept)	−6.209 (3.437)*	−4.789 (3.357)	−2.413 (4.378)	14.708 (0.219)***	14.772 (0.254)***	14.787 (0.255)***
N	3,201	3,201	3,201	3,201	3,201	3,201
R^2	0.74	0.74	0.74	0.93	0.93	0.93
MSE	2.12	2.11	2.11	0.86	0.86	0.86

Note: Entries are linear regression coefficients with standard errors shown in parentheses. Columns 1–3 report the results of the second stage of the Two-Stage Least Squares model, while columns 4–6 report the results of the first stage of the model. The dependent variable is $\ln(|Prop_{it} - Approp_{it}| + 1)$. Columns 1 and 4 pool across wars. Columns 2 and 5 consider the impact of wars with low nationalized politics and the incremental effect of wars with high nationalized politics. Columns 3 and 6 consider the impact of each war individually. Though not reported, all models include fixed president and agency/program effects. T_t and Yr_t serve as instruments. The F-statistic for T_t and Yr_t is 23, which satisfies the requirement for strong instruments.
*** indicates $p < .01$; ** indicates $p < .05$; * indicates $p < .10$, two-tailed tests.

baseline requests increases substantially (which is to be expected), its associated point estimate remains highly statistically significant. Most importantly, the estimated effect of war remains large, negative, and statistically significant. Columns 2 and 5 confirm similar findings as those found in column 1 of Table 4.5, and the results of columns 3 and 6 align closely with the results in column 1 of Table 4.6. This again highlights the finding that the effect of war appears especially pronounced in World War II and the post 9/11 wars.

Strictly speaking, instrumental variables recover only the local average treatment effect of war, not the overall average effect. By leveraging exogenous variation in presidential proposals that tangentially relates to presidential preferences, as we do in Table 4.7, we may not be recovering a quantity of interest. Though it is possible to tell a story that links year- and term-fixed effects to presidential preferences—indeed, that is exactly what we have tried to do in this section—our chosen instruments are not themselves direct measures of presidential preferences. It is possible, then, that estimates based on them—consistent and unbiased, though they may be— simply do not speak to Congress's propensity to accommodate genuine presidential preferences during periods of war and peace.

Unfortunately, given our basic research strategy, it is difficult to conceive of an alternative instrument that directly accounts for exogenous variation in presidential preferences. Any observable measure of presidential preferences unavoidably reflects both the president's sincere preferences *and* his expectations about future congressional behavior. To see this, consider the use of identifiers for each president as an instrument. To be sure, different presidents harbor systematically different preferences over budgetary outlays. Moreover, this particular instrument appropriately skirts the impossible challenge of measuring presidents' sincere preferences directly. Instead, it merely recognizes that these preferences vary across presidential administrations. To argue that this instrument satisfies the exclusion restriction, however, one must be convinced that all the variation in congressional accommodation to presidential proposals comes from differences in proposals that are observed across presidents and across periods of peace and war. If there are idiosyncratic features of congressional-presidential relations for which the regression does not account—and there surely are—then the exclusion restriction is violated, and we cannot claim to have corrected for any persistent estimation bias.

Instruments that exploit differences in presidents' preferences present still more problems. Whereas before we examined variation within presidential administrations, now we must leverage variation across administrations, which should further erode our confidence in the recovered estimates. Unfortunately, there is no way around this. Lacking a direct measure of presidential preferences that varies within presidential administrations, we have no choice but to substitute the president fixed effects in the main equation for either the equivalent or some other measure that is subsumed by these fixed effects (such as the party identification of the president) in the first stage.

For what it is worth, we have estimated models that substitute president fixed effects as instruments rather than controls in the main regression of interest. In so doing, we again find that congressional appropriations better reflect presidential proposals during war than during peace. Given the rather extraordinary assumptions that these regressions require, we are not inclined to put much stock in them. Still, when evaluated within the larger context of findings from a diverse assortment of statistical models, these estimates may allow us to infer that strategic proposal making, if not ephemeral, is not the only reason why congressional appropriations converge on presidential proposals during times of war.

4.4 *Distinguishing between Two Theoretically Informed Causal Mechanisms*

By estimating separate models for defense and nondefense programs and agencies, we have an opportunity to intuit the key mechanism at work here. If the nationalization of politics, as signified by λ, constitutes the primary reason for heightened congressional accommodation to the president during war, then we should observe effects that are at least as large in nondefense related programs and agencies as in defense ones. On the other hand, if heightened uncertainty, as signified by the parameter z_j, is the determining factor, then the effects should be concentrated in defense programs and agencies.[29]

In Table 4.8, we distinguish budgets for defense and nondefense agencies. In both instances, the effect of war is negative and substantial. More

29. Note that expectations about differences in the impact of war on presidential success within different policy domains are analytically separate from expectations about differences in overall presidential success across policy domains. For a related analysis of the latter issue, see Canes-Wrone et al. 2006, who find that appropriations in foreign policy more closely approximate presidential preferences than do appropriations on domestic policy. For papers that examine the variable levels of presidential success within foreign policy, see Milner and Tingley 2010, 2011.

Table 4.8. DEFENSE VERSUS NONDEFENSE SPENDING

	OLS		2SLS	
	Defense Agencies	Non-Defense Agencies	Defense Agencies	Non-Defense Agencies
War	−0.325 (0.207)	−0.308 (0.154)**	−0.272 (0.254)	−0.306 (0.156)*
House Seat Share	−4.245 (1.638)**	−1.823 (0.822)**	−4.878 (1.714)***	−0.993 (1.61)
ln(Unemployment)	−0.173 (0.233)	−0.385 (0.151)***	−0.866 (0.812)	−0.346 (0.149)**
Real Deficit	0.081 (0.067)	0.093 (0.072)	0.086 (0.072)	0.106 (0.073)
Real GDP Growth	−6.378 (4.952)	−1.772 (0.968)**	−5.395 (5.131)	−2.220 (0.935)***
ln(Proposal)	1.136 (0.147)***	1.065 (0.121)***	0.274 (0.974)	1.418 (0.233)***
(Intercept)	−4.312 (2.771)	−3.251 (1.784)**	13.316 (19.710)	−8.491 (3.645)**
N	614	2,587	614	2,587
R^2	0.77	0.71	0.74	0.71
MSE	1.97	2.15	2.20	2.17

Note: Results for ordinary least squares (OLS) and two-stage least squares (2SLS) regressions reported. Entries are linear regression coefficients with standard errors shown in parentheses. The dependent variable is $\ln(|Prop_{it} - Approp_{it}| + 1)$. Though not reported, all models include fixed president and agency/program effects. *** indicates $p < .01$; ** indicates $p < .05$; * indicates $p < .10$, two-tailed tests.

to the point, wars have comparable effects on Congress's willingness to abide presidential proposals for defense and domestic agencies alike. Indeed, the point estimates associated with war are identical: −0.33 in defense policy (Model 1A) and −0.31 in nondefense policy (Model 1B). Given the differences in sample sizes, the standard errors are quite a bit smaller in the latter case than in the former; hence, the estimate for nondefense policy is significant, while that for defense policy is not. Models 2A and 2B replicate the instrumental variable techniques employed in Table 4.7 for defense and nondefense agencies, respectively. Though the effects of war are negative for both subsets of observations, they are statistically significant in only those models that concern nondefense programs and agencies.

Across these models, most of the other covariates perform similarly in both defense and nondefense policy. Higher partisan support augurs well for presidential proposals, no matter the agency type, as do smaller proposals themselves and heightened economic growth. Unemployment rates bear only on Congress's deliberations over domestic agency proposals. And this should not surprise, for when unemployment rates are high, Congress has cause to accommodate presidential requests over domestic agencies that might dampen the negative effects of joblessness, but little reason to privilege presidential requests over foreign and defense agencies that address the problem only through their own hiring practices.

Collectively, these findings lend credence to Aaron Wildavsky's observation that during war the agencies responsible for foreign and domestic policy alike make much of the security implications of their activities. Throughout the appropriations process, Wildavsky observes, "the temptation to say that almost anything one can think of has implications for national defense is overwhelming and few agencies have been able to resist it."[30] The findings presented in Table 4.8 suggest that when wars confer national defense priorities upon domestic policy agencies, members of Congress take heed.

4.5 *A Comment on Endogenous War Making*

When estimating models of war making, scholars routinely worry about the plausibly endogenous relationship between domestic politics and international relations, and with some justification. Decisions about war may well reflect, rather than cause, domestic support for the president. Indeed, we ourselves have written at some length about how the timing and frequency of military deployments is conditioned by the level of partisan support for the president within Congress.[31] In principle, then, expectations about y_{it} may themselves be a function of our key explanatory variables in equations 4.1 and 4.3.

Before this concern burrows too deeply into our psyche, it is worth recognizing a few points about this particular project. First, the previous research that emphasized an endogenous relationship between war making and congressional support included within its definition of war the hundreds of small-scale military deployments undertaken by presidents during the modern era. By setting a much higher threshold for what constitutes war, we significantly increase the salience of foreign considerations. Whereas political developments at home might influence presidential decisions about smaller-scale deployments, they are less likely to do so in massive military campaigns. Is it really plausible to argue that Bush waged war in Afghanistan because he expected Congress to look kindly on his domestic policy agenda rather than because he sought to avenge the 9/11 attacks? Indeed, the one case where the onset of war and the fate of the president's policy agenda probably were linked—that is, Vietnam, which is discussed at length in Chapter 7—suggests that the president escalated a military venture not

30. Wildavsky 1984, 122.
31. Howell and Pevehouse 2007.

to leverage expected congressional support for new policy initiatives, but to ward off opposition to his past domestic achievements.

Second, for this particular source of endogeneity to generate biased estimates of the effects of war, it must be the case that our measure of war and the error term in equation 4.1 are correlated. Note, though, that we already have controlled for precisely the kinds of domestic sources of support for the president to which the larger literature on war making calls our attention—in particular, the state of the economy and the partisan composition of Congress. Of course, it is always possible that there remain unobserved (and perhaps unobservable) variables that correlate with both the incidence of war and the differences between proposed and final budgets. Given this possibility, we may only know the true effect of war on budgetary success when the great institutional review board in the sky approves a randomized field trial for massive military campaigns. In the meantime, the findings in this chapter come about as close as we are likely to get to the truth.

Finally, it is worth identifying the scope conditions of this particular problem. We recognize that lots of decisions about how our wars were waged may well have origins within Congress generally, and within concerns about the fate of domestic policy achievements more specifically. Presidents, for instance, may have refused to escalate certain campaigns until after Congress had passed key domestic policy initiatives. But again, recall an important aspect of our definition: wars are either ongoing or absent, and nothing is done to differentiate how precisely they are being waged over time. Concerns about endogeneity only concern the president's decision to begin and end these particular wars. These specific decisions for these specific wars, we suggest, have a great deal more to do with events abroad than political developments at home. To the extent that domestic politics are in play, our statistical model does a reasonable job of accounting for them.

4.6 *Conclusion*

When analyzing federal budgets, we find considerable evidence in support of the Policy Priority Model. Congressional appropriations more closely adhere to the president's preferences during war than during peace. Moreover, those wars that had the largest impact on members' prioritization of national outcomes yielded the biggest effects on presidential success. During World War II and the post-9/11 wars, congressional budgets more closely approximated presidential preferences than during the Korean, Vietnam, or Persian Gulf wars.

These results appear remarkably robust. We find consistent effects in: (1) models that include a wide assortment of control variables, most importantly agency and presidential fixed effects, (2) models that characterize the difference between presidential proposals and final appropriations in different ways, (3) models that explicitly account for the possibility of strategic proposals, and (4) models that distinguish between defense and nondefense policies. The conclusion that wars generally, and World War II and the post 9/11 wars in particular, augment presidential success does not hinge upon any single set of estimates.

For a variety of reasons, the analyses in this chapter constitute a hard test for the proposition that wars augment presidential success in Congress. For starters, we are examining a domain over which presidents exert relatively little influence. Perhaps more than any other policy-making venue, members of Congress wield extraordinary authority over the appropriations process. Additionally, none of the analyses in this chapter account for supplemental appropriations, which increasingly are used to fund the ground-level operations of war. Rather, we focus exclusively on regular appropriations that are made to agencies that can be observed in times of war and peace.[32] Nor do the models presented in this chapter discriminate among different programs or initiatives conducted by administrative agencies. If one thinks that interbranch bargaining over appropriations concerns not only the amount of money allotted to different agencies but also how these monies are actually spent, then our empirical tests would appear as rather blunt instruments for assessing presidential influence in war and peace. Finally, the challenges of managing a wartime economy may simply negate opportunities for presidential influence. Wars stimulate government spending like nothing else does.[33] Given the sheer magnitude of wartime

32. In addition to funding policies that are more closely tied to the war effort itself, supplemental appropriations also present a host of statistical modeling issues. Whereas the president must submit a formal budget proposal every year, and Congress, in turn, must enact a final set of appropriations, supplemental appropriations are by definition entirely voluntary. So being, their inclusion introduces all of the selection biases endemic to the traditional legislative process. Moreover, because presidents do not submit a formal proposal for supplemental appropriations, there is no obvious way to include them in the models presented herein. Admittedly, supplemental appropriations may substitute for some elements of the general budget. It is not at all clear that their exclusion from the analysis biases our results in favor of our predictions. Rather, for reasons already recognized in the text, by excluding supplemental appropriations from the tests, we most likely have reduced the chances of observing wartime budgets that more closely approximate presidential proposals.

33. As Steven Bank, Kirk Stark, and Joseph Thorndike recognize, "There is simply no other government activity that requires as much revenue as fighting a war" (2008, xiv).

budgets, presidents may have an especially difficult time overseeing their allocation. Indeed, one of the possible consequences of heightened wartime spending is that federal funds are distributed in ways that do a poorer job of reflecting presidents', or any other political actors', policy objectives.

It is of some consequence that the appropriations process yields such consistent evidence of heightened presidential success during war. Appropriations, however, are not the only venue in which to evaluate the central claims of the Policy Priority Model. The most obvious alternative is roll call votes, to which we turn in the next chapter.

The United States spent no less than $4 trillion (in 2009 real dollars) fighting World War II. In just its first eight years, the war in Afghanistan drained $1 trillion from the federal government's coffers. The intervening wars in the latter half of the twentieth century also came with substantial price tags: $320 billion for the Korean War, $686 billion for Vietnam, and $96 billion for the Gulf War (Schick 2007; Staudt 2011, Table 1.1, 13). The total costs of war may be higher still, especially when one accounts for the retraining and health care costs for veterans, the aid needed to rebuild conquered nations after a war terminates, funds given to business contractors, interest on the debt, and numerous other macroeconomic costs. When accounting for these expenditures, Stiglitz and Bilmes (2008) put the combined short-term and long-term costs of the war in Afghanistan at more than $7 trillion.

CHAPTER 5

Voting in War and in Peace

Having scrutinized the appropriations process, we now turn to members' votes on legislation. In this chapter, we employ a variety of statistical techniques to compare legislators' voting records over time. We then assess the extent to which members compile voting records during wartime that better reflect the president's preferences than those observed in peacetime.

In particular, we compare members' voting records on the universe of roll call votes undertaken as the nation transitioned into and out of war. To be sure, this approach comes at a cost—namely, an inability to explicitly model the president. But by considering all roll call votes, rather than the subset on which the president takes a clear position, we can readily assess whether members compile voting records that better correspond to the president's ideological orientation when the nation enters war, and less well when it exits war. Moreover, this approach avoids the deep measurement and selection problems endemic to research that infers presidential positions from policy pronouncements—which are often vague, and always strategic—and then compares final policy outcomes with the president's desired outcome.

A basic intuition structures the analyses in this chapter: if a conservative president takes the nation to war, particularly one that increases the salience of national outcomes, we ought to observe a shift in members' voting records to the ideological right. When this war ends, we then should witness a shift to the ideological left. When a liberal resides within the White House, members of Congress should shift in exactly the opposite direction as the nation enters and exits such wars.[1]

---

1. Note that this supposes that the president's preferences are external to the pivotal actors in Congress, who, depending on the model, include the median member of the chamber, the median member of the majority party, and the veto override pivot. Of the wartime presidents we investigate—Roosevelt, Truman, Eisenhower, Johnson, Nixon, G. H. W. Bush, and G. W. Bush—this assumption seems justified, with the possible exception of Eisenhower. We discuss his case in more detail later.

In the main, the evidence we present in this chapter corroborates such expectations. The outbreak of the 2001 war in Afghanistan, for which we have the most reliable estimates of legislative behavior during peace and war, coincided with a major shift to the ideological right in members' voting behavior. Moreover, these shifts do not appear to be an artifact of changes in the agenda, party control, the electoral calendar, rising conservatism across all levels of government, other factors that preceded the terrorist attacks on 9/11 and precipitated the war, or our choice of identification strategies. We also find similar effects when limiting the sample of votes to purely domestic legislation or bills that were the most visible or highly contested.

Examining prior wars, we find that the U.S. entry into World War II coincided with a significant shift to the ideological left; the end of the war, however, evoked a significant shift to the ideological right, away from the orientation of the president then in office. We find limited evidence that the beginning of the Korean War induced Congress to vote in ways that better reflected the ideological leanings of President Truman, and the end of the war coincided with a significant shift away from President Eisenhower. We find no consistent evidence that the beginnings of the wars in Vietnam and the Persian Gulf induced members to vote in ways that better reflected the preferences of the presidents then in office; the end of the Vietnam War yielded a Congress less inclined to reflect the ideological orientation of its president. Finally, we find no consistent evidence of movement away from President George H. W. Bush upon the end of the Persian Gulf War.

5.1 *Data and Methods*

Commensurate with the expectations described in Chapter 3, this chapter compares congressional voting behavior in times of war and peace. The best source of data about legislator voting behavior is the roll call record, which indicates whether members of Congress supported or opposed each of the hundreds of items on which Congress voted. Unsurprisingly, these data reveal, among other things, that Democratic members tend to vote with Democrats, and Republicans vote with Republicans; and across parties, significant differences in voting patterns are observed. During their long careers in the Senate, we know that Senators Jesse Helms (R-NC) and Ted Kennedy (D-MA) were ideologically quite different, and that Kennedy and George McGovern (D-SD) were more similar. By analyzing these roll call data in a systematic way, we can recover estimates of roll call records that quantify the ideological differences between legislators and describe the distribution of preferences within a chamber.

Scholars have devised a variety of techniques for recovering estimates of legislator ideologies using roll call data.[2] The most widely used methods are DW-NOMINATE and its Bayesian analogue.[3] Both methods produce similar estimates of legislative voting behavior. For reasons that we explain below, we use the Bayesian approach, which Joshua Clinton, Simon Jackman, and Doug Rivers introduced to political science. The intuition behind these statistical procedures is that members who vote together often are more ideologically similar than members who usually vote differently. On a given roll call vote j, legislators have a choice between supporting the bill and opposing the bill, in which case the status quo is the reversion point. The proposal's ideological location is given by ζ_j and the status quo location is given by ψ_j, which are located in the policy space $\mathbb{R}_d$, where d denotes the relevant dimension of the policy space. Legislators have utilities over the status quo and the proposal, and choose the option that provides them with the greater utility. In other words, legislators will choose the option that most closely approximates their preferences.

As is standard in political science and economic models of choice, the Clinton-Jackman-Rivers scores assume that legislators have quadratic utility functions with normally distributed errors. More formally, the utility for legislator i from the proposal j is given by $U_i(\zeta_j) = -|x_i - \zeta_j|^2 + \eta_{ij}$, and the utility from the status quo is given by $U_i(\psi_j) = -|x_i - \psi_j|^2 + v_{ij}$, where $x_i \in \mathbb{R}_d$ represents the ideal point of legislator i. Legislators are assumed to vote for the proposal ($y_{ij} = 1$) if $U_i(\zeta_j) > U_i(\psi_j)$, and to support the status quo ($y_{ij} = 0$) otherwise. Finally, we assume that the errors η_{ij} and v_{ij}, or the stochastic components of legislator utility have a joint normal distribution such that $E(\eta_{ij}) = E(v_{ij})$ and $\text{var}(\eta_{ij} - v_{ij}) = \sigma^2$, and these errors are assumed to be independent across both legislators and roll calls.

The roll call data are composed of n legislators voting on m roll call items, where each legislator i must choose between a "yea" position and a "nay" position on roll call j, as described previously. This specification results in a probit model, $P(y_{ij} = 1) = \Phi(\beta_j x_i - \alpha_j)$, where $\Phi(\bullet)$ is the standard

---

2. All congressional roll call data for this project were obtained from Keith Poole's Web site at http://voteview.com.

3. For descriptions and applications of these techniques, see Poole and Rosenthal 1997, and Clinton et al. 2004, respectively.

normal cumulative density function, β_j is an item discrimination parameter that indicates how well roll call j distinguishes liberals and conservatives, α_j is the item difficulty parameter that describes the position of a legislator who is indifferent in voting yea or nay on roll call j, and x_i corresponds to legislator i's ideal point. The item discrimination parameter captures the notion that some roll call votes are more informative about legislator preferences than others. For instance, roll call votes that are closely contested provide more information about who is liberal and who is conservative than roll call votes that succeed (or fail) by overwhelming margins. Consequently, the former vote is "weighted" more heavily in the calculation of member ideal points. The item difficulty parameter characterizes the ideological location of the legislator who is indifferent between supporting or opposing the proposal in question, where more extreme (either large positive or large negative) parameter estimates indicate a more ideologically extreme proposal.

As mentioned previously, member ideal points are recovered through Bayesian estimation, which provides a coherent framework for characterizing uncertainty in parameter estimates. The Markov chain Monte Carlo (MCMC) algorithm begins at an arbitrary starting point and alternates among simulating the ideal points, bill parameters, and legislator utilities. The joint density of model parameters α_j, β_j, and x_i is estimated from the data. By iterating this process many times once the Markov chain has "converged," or reached a steady state, we can characterize the full posterior distribution of the model parameters. For instance, repeated sampling from the posterior distribution of a legislator's estimated ideal point provides many possible estimates of the legislator's ideology, and the density of this sample of posterior estimates characterizes the distribution of the estimate of the legislator's ideal point. Based on the variance of these posterior distributions, which characterizes the uncertainty associated with the estimates, we can then make probability statements about the likelihood that, for instance, Ted Kennedy was a more liberal senator than George McGovern.

EMPIRICAL STRATEGY

When the nation enters and exits war, do members of Congress shift their voting behavior with respect to the ideological direction of the president? To answer this question, ideally we would like to observe identical members of Congress voting on identical bills immediately before and immediately after the outbreak of war, when other potential confounders might be constant. In such a setting, vote switching could plausibly be attributed to the influence of war. Unfortunately, such data do not exist. After a rather exhaustive search of the roll call record during the days and weeks straddling the onset and termination of our wars, we could not find a single instance of Congress voting on the exact same bill during periods of both war and peace.

Lacking a natural experiment, we turn to the next best option. Rather than selecting a handful of ideal comparisons, we split the universe of roll calls based on the presence or absence of war. Whenever possible, we restrict the sample to a single congress and thereby control for the many contextual factors that have been the subject of previous scholarship on congressional voting behavior. By analyzing the universe of congressional roll calls within these time frames rather than the subset of bills on which presidents have taken public positions, we substantially reduce the selection biases that plague previous research on war and congressional voting behavior.

Our empirical analyses are conducted at both the chamber and individual levels. If a particular war induces members of Congress to vote in ways that better reflect the ideological leanings of the president, we expect to observe aggregate shifts in member ideal points. Thus, we employ a series of one-tailed t-tests to assess whether the chamber mean is statistically significantly different during war than during peace. We likewise use one-tailed Wilcoxon signed rank tests to determine whether the median ideal point of the chamber is significantly different during war than during peace. Second, for each war we identify the number of individual members who accumulate voting records that are statistically significantly different during war compared with during peace. Using these figures, we calculate the probability that the number of statistically significant shifts in the hypothesized direction could have been observed by chance. Small values of these probabilities suggest that the outbreak of war led members to vote in ways that were more consistent with the ideological leanings of the president.

Although we expect to find evidence of an overall war effect on member voting behavior in Congress, we also expect the magnitude of these effects to vary across wars (as we argued in Chapter 3 and empirically demonstrated in Chapter 4). In particular, we expect to find that some wars yielded Congresses that were considerably more inclined to reflect the ideological orientation of the president then in office, but other wars had more modest effects on the extent to which members of Congress

Table 5.1. EXPECTED SHIFTS IN ROLL CALL VOTING BEHAVIOR

War	President's Ideological Orientation	Expected Direction of Shift	Expected Magnitude of Shift
World War II			
Beginning	Liberal (−)	Liberal (−)	Large
End	Liberal (−)	Conservative (+)	Large
Korea			
Beginning	Liberal (−)	Liberal (−)	Modest
End	Conservative (+)	Liberal (−)	Modest
Vietnam			
Beginning	Liberal (−)	Liberal (−)	Modest
End	Conservative (+)	Liberal (−)	Modest
Persian Gulf			
Beginning	Conservative (+)	Conservative (+)	Modest
End	Conservative (+)	Liberal (−)	Modest
Post-9/11 Wars			
Beginning	Conservative (+)	Conservative (+)	Large

shift their voting behavior in the ideological direction of the president. Table 5.1 summarizes our expectations for the findings we report in this chapter.

INTERTEMPORAL COMPARISONS OF ROLL CALL VOTING RECORDS

Our chosen approach faces two key challenges. First, it rules out the possibility of explicitly modeling the president. Because we examine all roll calls cast in a Congress, rather than the subset upon which the president took a clear position, we cannot identify where, exactly, the president resides along an ideological continuum. By analyzing multiple wars conducted by presidents with very different ideological orientations, we can identify whether members of Congress shift in the general direction of the president then in office. But because the president takes relatively few positions on roll call items over the course of any particular Congress, and because interpretations of these thin voting records confront deep selection endogeneity issues, we cannot precisely measure each member's relative proximity to the president during war and peace.[4] Second, we cannot compare peace and wartime ideal points that have been estimated independently. Indeed, it is well documented that ideal points estimated with

4. For an extended discussion of this problem and a proposed solution, see Treier 2010.

different sets of data cannot be directly compared because the latent scales may have shifted or stretched.[5]

Though the first challenge lacks a clear remedy, the second challenge can at least be mitigated. To meaningfully compare estimates from separate samples of roll call votes, scholars typically recommend the use of "bridge" observations,[6] which serve as fixed reference points against which ideal point estimates can be compared. Using this bridging approach, previous scholars have compared preference estimates between presidents, Senators and Supreme Court Justices, bureaucrats and members of Congress, and state legislators and members of Congress.[7]

Our chosen empirical strategy does not require us to compare different actors across different settings, but rather the same actors across different time periods—transitioning either from peace to war, or from war to peace. Because we do not need to make comparisons across both time and institutions, we simply assume a fixed scale across the prewar and postwar time periods, and that two actors' positions remain constant across both periods. The Clinton et al. (2004) approach to ideal point estimation described previously requires only two restrictions to identify the model. By holding constant the ideal points of two actors and assuming a fixed scale across both time periods, therefore, we facilitate intertemporal comparisons of member ideal points.

The trick, then, is to identify bridge actors whose willingness to support different bills is plausibly unaffected by war. Though we explore a variety of options, we place the greatest confidence on those estimates that use interest groups to link peacetime and wartime congressional voting records. During war, interest groups are less likely than any other political actor to assume different positions on pending bills. Moreover, as Keith Poole

5. For instance, an extremely liberal member of Congress may have an ideal point estimate of −1 during one Congress and −1.5 in another. It is possible either that the scale of all members of Congress shifted in the negative direction, or that it expanded such that the variance of scores in the latter Congress is larger than in the former (Bafumi et al. 2005; Clinton et al. 2004; Jackman 2001; Martin and Quinn 2002).

6. See Bailey 2007, and Bailey and Chang 2001. Scholars have recommended other approaches, which are less suited to our own purposes. Martin and Quinn (2002), for instance, allow estimates to trend smoothly through time, but their growth models are assumed rather than estimated, rendering this technique inappropriate for the task at hand. Clinton et al. (2004) analyze the 107th Senate to determine whether Senator James Jeffords voted differently after his defection from the Republican Party. They do so, however, by comparing differences in Jeffords's ideological rank, which is not a quantity of interest in the present study.

7. Some notable studies employing these techniques include Bailey and Chang 2001, Clinton and Lewis 2008, and Shor et al. 2010.

demonstrated in an analysis of interest group positions on congressional roll call votes, interest groups' ideological orientations are generally consistent and stable over time.[8]

Following Poole, Rosenthal, and Treier,[9] we rely upon the American Conservative Union (ACU) and Americans for Democratic Action (ADA) as our bridges. The use of these interest groups offers several practical benefits. First, both groups take a fairly large number of positions (generally, forty to fifty) per chamber during each Congress, which enables us to estimate their ideal points precisely. Second, whereas some organizations such as the American Civil Liberties Union and the National Rifle Association are concerned primarily with roll calls that address a specific issue domain, the ACU and the ADA take positions that span a wide range of issues. Because we assume unidimensionality, it is important that a fuller complement of issues define the continuum over which legislator estimates are compared, such that any shifts between the prewar and postwar estimates can be meaningfully described as "liberal" or "conservative."

Of course, there are potential downsides to assuming that any actor's preferences remain constant over time. For several reasons, however, the assumption appears justified in this instance. First, we track the positions of interest groups and legislators within short periods of time, never more than two years. Second, the ACU and the ADA are the nation's oldest existing conservative and liberal interest groups, which suggests some degree of ideological consistency that may not exist among organizations with shorter histories. Third, though interest groups may be strategic in their selection of roll calls,[10] the recovered estimates should be consistent as long as the interest groups take ideologically consistent positions on the key votes that they select during peace and war.[11]

---

8. Poole 1981.

9. Poole and Rosenthal 1997; Trier 2010.

10. Fowler 1982; Snyder 1992.

11. To test this assumption more directly, we estimated a heteroskedastic item-response model (see Lauderdale 2010) using the entire set of roll call votes and interest group positions in the 107th Congress. This procedure recovers legislator-specific estimates of σ^2, where larger values indicate that the legislator's position on any given roll call vote is predicted less well by their ideal point estimate along the primary dimension. The mean values of σ^2 for the 107th House and Senate are 1.08 (standard deviation = 0.37) and 1.04 (standard deviation = 0.24), respectively. The ADA and ACU have estimates of σ^2 that are smaller than these figures in both the House (ADA = 1.01, ACU = 1.01) and Senate (ADA = 1.01, ACU = 1.02), providing support for our assumption that interest groups take relatively consistent ideological positions over the course of a single Congress.

To see how our bridging technique works in practice, consider the analysis of the 107th Congress. First, we split the set of roll calls for the 107th Congress at the date on which the war in Afghanistan began (October 7, 2001). We then construct separate matrices for the prewar and postwar roll calls in both the House and Senate in which the rows correspond to legislators and the two interest groups.[12] Column entries indicate whether the legislator or interest group supported or opposed each bill. By estimating the above statistical model in an unidentified state, we generate member ideal points for the roll call votes that occurred before October 7, 2001. The data are postprocessed to constrain the ideal point estimates to have mean zero and unit variance, where negative ideal points identify more liberal members and positive ideal points identify more conservative members.[13] After recovering the prewar estimates, we estimate the postwar ideal points for all members of Congress while constraining the estimates of the ACU and ADA to equal their prewar estimates. We then compare the prewar and postwar estimates at both the individual and chamber levels.

A HARD TEST OF PRESIDENTIAL SUCCESS IN CONGRESS

Given our empirical approach, it would not be surprising to find null effects. By virtually all accounts, congressional voting behavior is remarkably stable over time. As Keith Poole remarks, "based upon the roll call voting record, once elected to Congress, members adopt an ideological position and maintain that position throughout their careers—once a liberal or moderate or conservative, always a liberal or moderate or conservative."[14] To substantiate such claims, Poole and Rosenthal analyzed roll call voting behavior of all House and Senate members who served more than one term in the 1st through 96th congresses. So doing, they found that members' voting records are highly correlated over time.[15] Upon observing remarkable patterns of consistency in roll call voting behavior among legislators who served in post–Civil War congresses, Poole and Rosenthal later concluded: "Whatever forces are working to produce spatial stability have been operating on both chambers with equal intensity. Contemporary

---

12. Members who served for short intervals of a given Congress were dropped from the analysis.
13. We fit a one-dimensional item-response model, running 300,000 iterations after discarding the first 50,000, and thinning by 500.
14. Poole 2007, 435.
15. Poole and Rosenthal 1997.

members of Congress do not adapt their positions during their careers but simply enter and maintain a fixed position until they die, retire, or are defeated in their ideological boots."[16]

Scholars also have shown that a variety of contemporaneous shocks do not affect the stability of members' voting behavior. Herbert Asher and Herbert Weisberg analyzed House votes from 1949 to 1972 and argued that any changes in voting behavior were "evolutionary" rather than immediate and dramatic.[17] Upon examining votes in four policy areas—national debt, foreign aid, school construction, and civil rights—they concluded that "the forces of continuity predominate in congressional voting" to such a degree that "stability" was the "central characteristic of legislative decision making."[18]

For the most part, the available evidence supports the claim that members cling to their ideologies for the entirety of their careers. Though abstention rates may increase, retiring legislators exhibit no less stability than their colleagues who seek reelection.[19] Legislators who serve in multiple offices compile similar voting records across all of them, even when they serve different constituencies.[20] Though redistricting can alter the composition of House members' constituencies, it does not appear to affect their voting behavior.[21]

The principal exception concerns members who switch parties and who, scholars have shown, subsequently change their voting behavior.[22] In addition, Jeffrey Jenkins found that members of the Confederate House who had previously served in the U.S. House exhibited little ideological stability, even in the face of federal invasion of their districts.[23] Jenkins attributes these findings to the lack of a stable party system in the Confederacy,

16. Poole and Rosenthal 2007, 97.
17. Asher and Weisberg 1978, 423.
18. See also Carmines and Stimson 1989.
19. Herrick et al. 1994; Lott 1987, 1990; Lott and Bronars 1993; Poole and Romer 1993; Poole and Rosenthal 1997; Vanbeek 1991. Rothenberg and Sanders (2000) provide evidence that House members *do* exhibit significant changes in roll call behavior upon their decision to retire or after their defeat in a primary. Carson et al. (2004), however, argue that the Rothenberg and Sanders analysis suffers from omitted variable bias, and they present evidence from a better-specified version of the model that is consistent with prior research.
20. Grofman et al. 1995; Hibbing 1986; Poole and Romer 1993; Poole and Rosenthal 1997.
21. Poole 2007; Poole and Romer 1993.
22. McCarty et al. 2001; Nokken 2000; Nokken and Poole 2004.
23. Jenkins 2000.

suggesting that Poole's contention that members "die in their ideological boots" is contingent upon the existence of stable parties.

The lesson from these studies is clear: comparisons of individual members over short periods of time—and especially those that focus on trends within a single congressional term among members who did not switch parties—can be expected to reveal overwhelming stability in individual voting behavior; moreover, no external event, very much including war, is likely to dislodge members from their chosen ideological footings. Accordingly, the empirical tests that follow constitute a stringent test of the proposition that members' voting behavior is different during war than during peace.

5.2 *Post-9/11 Wars and the 107th Congress*

Consistent with expectations, members of the Congress voted in ways that better reflected President George W. Bush's preference upon the commencement of the war in Afghanistan in October 2001. In Figure 5.1 we plot the densities of members' estimated peacetime and wartime ideal points in the 107th Congress. The dashed lines indicate the peacetime scores, and the solid lines indicate the wartime scores. Scores are arbitrarily scaled from −2 to 2, where larger values indicate more conservative voting behavior. Both distributions are bimodal, with Democrats populating the left portion of the distribution, and Republicans the right. In both the House (left panel) and Senate (right panel), we see marked shifts to the right. In the House, the movement appears to be concentrated among Republicans, while in the Senate both parties shift rightward. The unconstrained mean and median shifts in the House were +0.54 and +1.28 respectively; in the Senate, they were +1.21 and +1.26.[24]

The Policy Priority Model supports predictions about when a representative member of Congress will support a generic president during a generic war. Because it does not characterize Congress as a collective decision-making body, it has less to say about the distributional effects of war across

24. Additional summary statistics for all of the analyses can be found in Appendix C. However, readers should not compare the cell entries across rows because the magnitudes of the mean and median shifts cannot be meaningfully compared across chambers or congresses. In addition, the number of members exhibiting significant movement cannot be compared across chambers or congresses because the number of roll call votes with which estimates were calculated vary widely. Ideal points are estimated much more precisely when there are large numbers of roll call votes, and thus there are likely to be many more significant shifts when both the prewar and postwar ideal points are estimated with high degrees of precision.

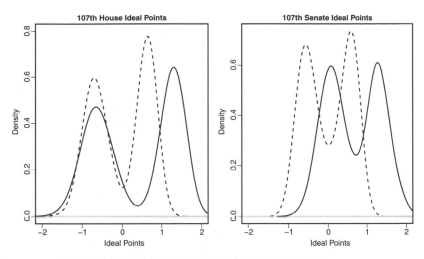

Figure 5.1. AGGREGATE SHIFTS IN VOTING BEHAVIOR IN THE 107TH CONGRESS.

The dashed lines reflect the distributions of ideal points estimated using roll call votes cast before the war in Afghanistan began on October 7, 2001. The solid lines reflect the distributions of ideal point estimates using roll call votes cast after the war began. The American Conservative Union (ACU) and the Americans for Democratic Action (ADA) are the bridge actors used to link the two time periods. Positive ideal points indicate more conservative voting behavior, and negative ideal points reflect more liberal voting behavior.

different members of Congress.[25] In the real world, though, it is perfectly reasonable to expect that war has heterogeneous effects on members' inclinations to support the president. In Figure 5.2, therefore, we again plot the prewar and postwar scores for every member of the 107th House and Senate. This time, however, individual scores before the outbreak of war are aligned on the x-axis, and wartime scores appear on the y-axis. If a member's voting behavior did not change at all, then she will locate right on the 45-degree line. Scores above the 45-degree line indicate movement in the conservative direction, and scores below the 45-degree line reveal movement in the liberal direction. Observations whose peacetime and wartime scores are significantly different from one another at $p < .001$ are solid, and the rest are shaded.

Plainly, the vast majority of members in both chambers appear above the line. Indeed, all 95 members of the Senate and 323 of the 362 members of the House who reveal statistically significantly different prewar and postwar

25. According to the model, the marginal effect of λ is decreasing in x_p, suggesting that wars have a bigger impact on members of Congress who align, ex ante, more closely with the president. We do not know whether this effect carries over to a richer model with more than one legislator.

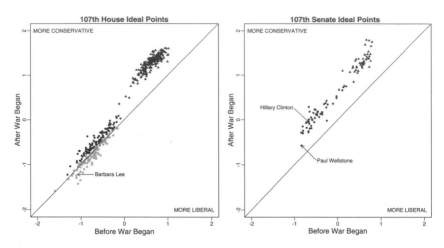

Figure 5.2. INDIVIDUAL SHIFTS IN VOTING BEHAVIOR IN THE 107TH CONGRESS.

The x-axes represent member ideal points based on roll call votes cast before the beginning of the war in Afghanistan on October 7, 2001, and the y-axes represent ideal points
estimated using roll calls cast after the beginning of the war. Members whose points fall
along the 45-degree line demonstrate perfectly consistent ideological voting patterns in
the prewar and postwar periods. Republican members are represented by triangles and
Democratic members by circles. Members whose prewar and postwar ideal points are
statistically significant at $p < .001$ are shown in bold.

scores document movement in the conservative direction. As points of
reference, therefore, we have identified a handful of individual members.
Compare, for instance, the locations of two Senate Democrats: Hillary
Clinton and Paul Wellstone. The latter, clearly, is located to the left of the
former, indicating a significantly more liberal voting record. Importantly,
though, Wellstone is much closer to the 45-degree line than is Clinton, suggesting the outbreak of war had less influence on his voting behavior.

These Senators' public comments about the war are consistent with
the observed differences in their voting records. The day after the 9/11
attacks, Clinton declared her intention to:

> stand united behind our President as he and his advisers plan the nec-
> essary actions to demonstrate America's resolve and commitment . . .
> I have expressed my strong support for the President, not only as the
> Senator from New York but as someone who for 8 years had some sense
> of the burdens and responsibilities that fall on the shoulders of the hu-
> man being we make our President.[26]

26. *Congressional Record* 2001, S9288.

At the time, nothing similar could be heard from Wellstone. One year later, in spite of the prevailing political winds that led to a historic level of midterm success for Bush and the Republicans, Wellstone was one of only four Democratic Senators seeking reelection to oppose the authorization for the use of force in Iraq.[27] Wellstone insisted, "Right now, despite a desire to support our president, I believe many Americans still have profound questions about the wisdom of relying too heavily on a pre-emptive, go-it-alone military approach."[28] Problematic as Bush's wars were, Wellstone further argued, they provided little justification for rethinking the merits of a broader class of policy initiatives.

FOREIGN AND DOMESTIC POLICY

In addition to pooling all roll call votes into pretreatment and posttreatment conditions, we also distinguish subsets of votes in different policy domains. In particular, we examine changes in voting behavior in domestic and foreign policy. Substantively interesting in its own right, the distinction also helps elucidate what it is about war that alters congressional voting behavior. If heightened uncertainty about the mapping of policies onto outcomes is the relevant mechanism, then observed changes in the members' voting record should appear especially acute in foreign policy. But if changes in the assessments of national outcomes are the key, then wartime effects should be more pronounced in domestic policy.

To classify roll call votes as either domestic or foreign policy, we used an automated text classification algorithm.[29] Domestic issues were defined narrowly, consisting of roll call votes that occurred on issues not related to national security or defense, foreign policy, or any sovereign state; bills that did contain such references were classified as foreign policy votes. We then estimated separate peacetime and wartime ideal points for each

27. In contrast, most other Democrats appeared to fear opposing the president's security agenda. House minority leader Richard Gephardt (D-MO) attributed the historic midterm Republican gains to the public support for the president in the aftermath of the 9/11 terrorist attacks: "You've got a president at 65 percent approval," he said. "I think part of that comes from 9/11. The whole country's rightful reaction to the horrible attack on our country, that whole cluster of issues are still out there." Adam Nagourney, "With Big Election Gains, G.O.P. Takes Control of Domestic Agenda," *New York Times,* November 6, 2002.

28. *Congressional Record* 2002, 19025.

29. As a check on the automated procedure, we also coded the bills for the 107th Senate by hand. The coding procedures agree on over 88 percent of the bill classifications. Moreover, to the extent there was disagreement, this was principally related to whether a bill should be coded as "domestic" or "procedural," or "foreign" or "procedural."

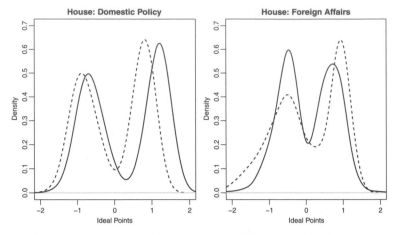

Figure 5.3.   SHIFTS IN CONGRESSIONAL VOTING BEHAVIOR ACROSS POLICY DOMAINS.

Plots show the distribution of ideal points in the 107th House before and after the beginning of the war in Afghanistan, using the American Conservative Union (ACU) and the
Americans for Democratic Action (ADA) to link the two time periods. Dashed lines
reflect the distribution of ideal points before the war in Afghanistan began, and the solid
lines reflect the distribution of ideal points after the war began. Across both domestic
and foreign policy domains, there is evidence of shift in members' voting behavior in the
conservative direction that coincides with the beginning of war.

member of Congress in each policy domain, restricting bridge observations to the subset of key votes within each domain.

Results for the 107th House are presented in Figure 5.3.[30] In domestic
policy (left panel), we again find widespread evidence of rising conservatism. Indeed, when looking at this subset of bills, the effects appear even
more pronounced and far-reaching than in the entire sample, when a shift
appeared among Republican members of Congress. In foreign policy, however, the observed changes are not nearly so clear. Though the variance of
the distribution shrinks somewhat upon the outset of war, Democrats vote
somewhat more conservatively, while Republicans vote somewhat more
liberally. The median members show hardly any movement at all.

These results support our contention that it is changes in the salience of
national outcomes, rather than changes in uncertainty, that constitute the
key mechanism by which wars induce shifts in members' voting behaviors.
It is possible that our assumptions about the stability of our bridge actors

30. Results are substantively similar for the 107th Senate within domestic policy. Because only a handful of foreign policy roll call votes were held in the Senate (eighty-three,
only nineteen of which took place before the war), we cannot reliably compare changes in
Senate voting behaviors across policy domains.

may not hold within some policy domains. If, for instance, the ADA and ACU became more conservative in foreign policy after the outbreak of war, but held steadfast to their prewar positions on domestic policy, then the observed differences across policy domains may be an artifact of our modeling strategy. But seeing such strong evidence of a wartime shift in domestic policy, we have further reason to conclude that changes in the ways in which members evaluate public policy outcomes represent the salient feature of wartime congressional support for the president.

ROBUSTNESS CHECKS

For all sorts of reasons, the 107th Congress provides a nearly ideal venue in which to examine the impact of war on members' voting behavior. For starters, the impetus for war was plausibly exogenous. In addition, lacking both impending threat of war (as characterized the beginning of World War II) or the steady buildup of troops (as in Vietnam), the dividing line between peace and war in 2001 is quite clear. Furthermore, because the war began almost midway through the congressional term, large numbers of roll call votes are available for us to generate precise estimates of members' peacetime and wartime ideal points. And because all the votes come within a single Congress, we hold constant most (though not all) intra-institutional influences on voting.

Of course, by relying on observational data, we unavoidably confront important challenges to causal inference. As we will describe, however, the findings are remarkably robust. For instance, they do not appear to be an artifact of our choice of bridge actors, changes in the agenda, sample of roll call votes analyzed, other factors that preceded the 9/11 terrorist attacks, uniformly rising levels of conservatism across all levels of government, or natural differences observed over the course of a congressional calendar. Additional figures and methodological details can be found in Appendix D.

Estimation Procedure. Supplementing our first estimation procedure, we employed a second approach to recover peacetime and wartime estimates of members' ideal points. Rather than estimating separate prewar and postwar member ideal points, we constructed a single matrix per chamber in which each legislator appears in two rows: one that reflects their roll call votes before the war began, and one that indicates their roll call votes after the war had begun. Because they link members' prewar and postwar voting records, each of the interest groups appear on just one row.[31] The

31. This is the general approach used in Bailey 2007 and Shor et al. 2010.

results of this procedure are substantively identical to those reported in the previous section.

Selection of Interest Group Bridges. Though the magnitude of the shifts identified are sizable, they are not driven by the choice of bridge actors. We have outlined several reasons underlying our choice of the ACU and ADA, but it is possible that the conservative shifts we observe are due to peculiarities in the ways in which the interest groups selected their key votes. To test whether our results are a function of interest group movement, we replicated the analysis but substituted the American Federation of Labor and Congress of Industrial Organizations (AFL-CIO) for the ADA. We again found that members of Congress had more conservative wartime voting records.

We also have estimated models that rely on more than two bridge actors. In addition to the ACU and ADA, we used the AFL-CIO, the League of Conservation Voters (LCV), the National Right to Life Council (NRLC), the American Civil Liberties Union (ACLU), the National Farmers Union (NFU), and the Public Interest Research Group (PIRG), all of which report key votes during the entire 107th Congress.[32] Upon estimating House ideal points in this way, we again find evidence of a shift in members' voting records in the conservative direction, though the magnitude of the shift attenuates somewhat. In the Senate, the results look nearly identical to the estimates that rely exclusively on the ACU and ADA.[33] For reasons we lay out in Appendix D, we are reluctant to use a larger collection of interest group bridges as a general estimation strategy. The results from the 107th Congress, however, at least suggest that our primary findings do not depend on the specific number or composition of interest group bridges.

We also examined whether our results are a function of the kinds of bills on which the interest groups rated legislators. We reestimated prewar and postwar ideal points for members of Congress using only the votes which either or both the ADA and ACU identified as a key vote. Even with these small subsamples of votes, we observe sizable shifts in the conservative direction.

---

32. The number of roll calls on which these groups took positions varied widely: ACU (fifty), ADA (forty), AFL-CIO (twenty-one), LCV (twenty-two), NRLC (ten), ACLU (fifteen), NFU (fifteen), and PIRG (twenty-eight).

33. Because the NRLC and NFU did not take any roll call positions in the 107th Senate, we exclude them from the estimation procedure. The number of positions for the remaining groups is as follows: ACU (forty-four), ADA (thirty-eight roll calls), AFL-CIO (twenty-nine) LCV (twenty-four), ACLU (five), and PIRG (twenty-eight).

Changes in the Agenda. Our ideal point estimates, we recognize, may confound systematic shifts in the congressional agenda. This possibility takes two general forms. First, the onset of war may have coincided with wholesale changes in the kinds of issues considered by members of Congress. This is of some concern, as the ideological shifts in the conservative direction may simply denote equivalent agenda changes in the opposite direction. The second concern is that our estimates do in fact capture some differences in member voting behavior before and after the war began, but that the war opened up an entirely new dimension of ideological conflict that is not captured by the main liberal-conservative dimension. If true, then our recovered estimates may not reflect substantively meaningful changes in legislative behavior. To address these dual concerns, we conducted two sets of supplementary analyses.

The first check accounts for a historical fact about the 107th Congress. On May 24, 2001, Senator James Jeffords defected from the Republican Party and thereby handed control of the chamber to the Democrats, and the change in leadership may have shifted the agenda to the ideological left. Should this be true, the changes that we observe may conflate the commencement of war with the shift in partisan control that occurred much earlier in the year. We therefore replicated the original analysis with the full set of wartime data, but we limited the peacetime roll call votes to the period after Jeffords switched his party affiliation. Our substantive findings remained unchanged.

As a second check, we examined the distribution of roll call vote cutpoints in the 107th Congress. The cutpoints are calculated using the item parameters that are generated simultaneously with legislator ideal points. If the findings we observe are due to changes in the agenda, then we should observe shifts in the distribution of cutpoints to the ideological left upon war's beginning. Instead, we find that the distribution of cutpoints shifted to the ideological right.[34] As a consequence, to the extent that our results reflect changes in the agenda, they understate the true extent to which members shifted to the ideological right at the onset of war.

More substantively, we also investigated the contents of bills voted on in the 107th Congress.[35] In so doing, we found little evidence that the presence of war induced significant changes in the kinds of issues taken up by

34. See Figure A.D5.
35. These data were collected by David W. Rohde and are available at https://www.msu.edu/~pipc/pipcdata.htm.

Congress. To be sure, the wartime Congress considered more items related to national defense, foreign policy, and government operations and justice. However, these increases came largely at the expense of roll call votes that dealt with appropriations. Every other area of domestic policy was virtually unaffected by the presence of war.[36]

Finally, war could spawn a whole new set of issues that is orthogonal to the main liberal-conservative dimension that usually characterizes so much of congressional voting behavior. We examined this possibility by estimating legislator ideal points in both one and two dimensions. During the prewar period, a single dimension correctly predicts over 91 percent of the votes in both the House and the Senate, and a second dimension correctly classifies another 1 percent. The same patterns hold true for the wartime period. Compared with a single dimension, a second dimension correctly classifies 1 percent more of the House roll call votes, and 1.78 percent more of the Senate roll call votes. These results further allay concerns that the shifts in roll call patterns that we have observed are due to the presence of an additional agenda that is orthogonal to the main dimension along which we characterize legislative voting behavior.

Subsets of Roll Call Votes. Though we do not find evidence that war induced members to vote differently on foreign affairs issues relative to domestic items, the observed findings could be driven by changes in the way members voted on purely symbolic items, while compiling more consistent voting records on substantive and/or significant issues. To explore this possibility, we reestimated member ideal points using interest groups to bridge the prewar and postwar periods, and we distinguished substantive and significant votes in two ways. First, we considered the subsets of bills that received coverage in the *New York Times* and/or the *Wall Street Journal*. Second, we restricted the sample to include only "strategically significant" bills by using a measure of closeness that accounts for different passage thresholds.[37]

Focusing our attention on these significant and substantive bills—those votes that received the most public attention and for which legislators had the most at stake—largely confirmed our main findings. Indeed, three out of the four analyses yielded evidence of large wartime shifts in voting behavior in the conservative direction. This result suggests that while mem-

36. See Table A.D1.
37. More specifically, we included bills with competitiveness ratings of 0.90 and above. These data come from Krehbiel and Woon 2005.

bers of Congress granted solid support for the president on matters related to the conduct of military activities in Afghanistan, the support extended well beyond the realm of purely symbolic gestures of national unity.

Defining the Beginning of War. We define the beginning of war as the date coinciding with major troop deployments, not the underlying events that precipitated the deployments. Hence, we select October 7, 2001, as the beginning of the war in Afghanistan. We recognize, however, that changes in members' voting behavior may not have coincided perfectly with the outbreak of war. Perhaps members lurched to the right in the immediate aftermath of the 9/11 terrorist attacks. Alternatively, members' shift to the ideological right may have occurred later in the war. And finally, and perhaps most importantly, we must examine whether factors having nothing to do with the war precipitated the observed shifts.

To explore these possibilities, we reestimate member ideal points using arbitrary dates during 2001 to distinguish "control" and "treatment" conditions—specifically, the first and fifteenth of every month between May and November 2001. We then calculate the magnitude of the observed shifts for each set of estimates in the House and Senate. In the House, we find that the magnitudes of the shifts steadily increase as we use cutpoints later in the year; in the Senate, the largest "treatment effect" is observed using October 1 as the arbitrary cutpoint, which then begins to attenuate for the remainder of October and November. Although these data do not allow us to discern whether different members moved just once though at different times, or whether members moved together but repeatedly during this time period, they do support two conclusions. First, factors unrelated to the war are probably not responsible for the observed shifts in voting behavior. Second, members continued to tack to the ideological right in the weeks and months that followed the 9/11 attacks.

Rising Conservatism and War. Perhaps the shifts observed after the outbreak of the war in Afghanistan had less to do with the president per se and more to do with a rising conservatism evoked by war.[38] To investigate this possibility, we examine changes in voting behavior in the California legislature during the same time period.[39] Using the same estimate technique

38. We will be able to speak to this issue more fully by examining previous wars undertaken by Democratic presidents.
39. The California legislature has the advantage of furnishing a large number of roll call votes in the 2001–02 session, high-profile liberal and conservative interests groups

already described, we find that, rather than observing a shift in the conservative direction upon the outbreak of war, members of the California assembly compiled strikingly more *liberal* voting records.[40] Whatever these findings signify, they certainly weigh against the notion that the Afghanistan war evoked a uniform and widespread conservative reaction that had little to do with the president.

Congressional Voting Behavior and the Electoral Calendar. It is entirely possible that the shifts we observe have little to do with the outbreak of war and instead reflect typical changes in the voting patterns of members of Congress over the course of a congressional term. To investigate this possibility, we generate and compare ideal points for the first and second sessions of three congresses during which no major military actions occurred: the 95th (Carter, 1977–78), 99th (Reagan, 1987–88), and 103rd (Clinton, 1993–94).

Examining each of these three congresses, we find little systematic evidence of changing patterns in voting behavior over the course of a single congress. To the extent that aggregate changes are observed, the movement occurs in the direction opposite the ideological position of the president—a finding that may reflect member posturing in anticipation of midterm losses. Were this pattern to hold for the 107th Congress, members would have more liberal voting records after the war began, and all the evidence suggests that the opposite occurred.

CORRELATES OF INDIVIDUAL DIFFERENCES
IN VOTING BEHAVIOR

Though the Policy Priority Model focuses on the negotiations between a single president and a single representative legislator, we do not rule out the possibility that wars have a different impact on different members of Congress. The data themselves underscore this point. The variance of the wartime estimated ideal points is actually larger than the peacetime ones, particularly among Democrats, suggesting that members of the 107th Congress were not merely lining up behind the president the moment that

---

(the California League of Conservative Voters and Chamber of Commerce, respectively), and a Democratic governor (Gray Davis) then under its watch.

40. These shifts occurred at the same time that every single congressional representative from California who showed significantly different voting patterns during this period (both Senators and thirty-seven of fifty-one members of the House, Republicans and Democrats alike) shifted in the conservative direction after the war began.

the United States launched the Afghanistan war. Moreover, as Figure 5.2 makes clear, the size of the shifts in members' estimated ideal points varies markedly both across chambers of Congress and across parties.

In this section, we explore some plausible predictors of the magnitude of the shifts observed during war and peace, as depicted in Figure 5.2. The findings in this section offer more than a palliative to the generally curious. They provide a face-validity test for our overall modeling strategy. To the extent that the correlates of vote shifts conform to our intuitions about the subject, we can proceed with still greater confidence that we are recovering something of value. Moreover, the estimates from these regressions will provide a basis for new bridging strategies to be employed in other wars.

We begin by investigating the relationship between the differences in members' peace and wartime scores and President Bush's 2000 vote share in their political jurisdictions. So as not to impose any functional form assumptions on the relationship between Bush's prior vote share and the estimated shifts in members' voting behavior, we estimate generalized additive models that are fit using cubic smoothing splines. In particular, we estimate the following model: $y_i = \alpha + \sum g_i(X_i) + \epsilon_i$, where α is a constant term, ϵ is an error term, and X_i identifies Bush's vote share in jurisdiction i. The model recovers estimates of $g_i(X_{i,j})$ for every value of $X_{i,j}$. Figure 5.4 displays the shapes of the fitted functions. The x-axis is the share of the vote Bush received in states or districts. The mean of the estimates for $g_i(X_i)$ is set to zero, so the y-axis indicates how much movement a member with a given vote share exhibited compared with the average shift. Where the fitted lines slope upward, members of Congress exhibited greater movement than average as their constituents supported Bush at higher levels. A downward-sloping line indicates that members were less inclined to vote with the president as Bush's vote share increased. The dotted lines represent the 95 percent confidence intervals, and the hash marks along the x-axis indicate observations.

Among Democrats in both chambers, the relationship between votes for Bush and changes in member voting records is both positively sloped and monotonic, suggesting that Democrats from districts and states that supported Bush by larger margins were more responsive to the outbreak of war, whereas Democrats who represented constituents who supported Bush by lower margins held more closely to their prewar ideologies. The plots for House Republicans show that, for the most part, the relationship is negatively sloped in those portions of the distribution where the

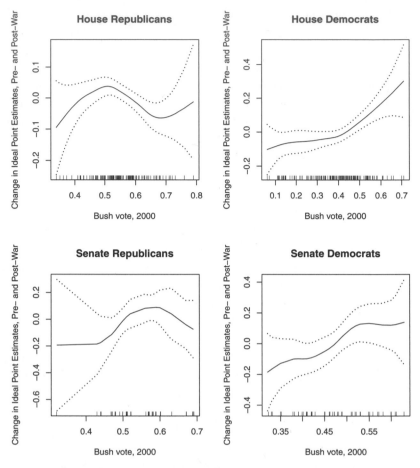

Figure 5.4. PRESIDENTIAL VOTE SHARE AND CHANGES IN MEMBER VOTING BEHAVIOR IN THE 107TH CONGRESS.

Bivariate generalized additive models estimated. The x-axes represent the Republican share of the two-party presidential vote in the 2000 election, and the y-axes reflect changes in ideal point estimates before and after the beginning of the war in Afghanistan, where larger positive numbers suggest larger shifts in the conservative direction. The dotted lines represent the 95 percent confidence intervals around the estimate, and the tick marks along the x-axes indicate observations.

observations are most concentrated. The correlation between presidential vote share and changes in voting behavior are more ambiguous among Senate Republicans, however.

Similar relationships for Democrats are observed in a multivariate context. We estimate a set of linear regressions that posit change in members' ideal points (y_i) as a function of members' distance from the chamber median and its quadratic, their seniority, a linear expression of Bush's prior vote share, and indicators for whether members were veterans of the U.S. military, served on a committee primarily concerned with foreign policy or national security, were a party leader, or represent constituents in New York or Pennsylvania (the sites of the 9/11 attacks). In addition, to account for the extent to which electoral pressures might differ between members of the House and Senate, we include an indicator in the Senate regressions for whether the Senator is up for reelection in the subsequent election cycle (2002).[41]

The results are displayed in Table 5.2. We observe a statistically significant, positive effect associated with Bush's prior vote share for Democrats in both the House and Senate, and point estimates that approach zero for Republicans in both chambers. In addition, we find that liberal House Democrats exhibited smaller ideological shifts than moderate House Democrats, while conservative House Republicans and moderate Senate Democrats exhibited greater movement in the conservative direction. House Democrats from New York and Pennsylvania, sites of the 9/11 attacks, also exhibited greater movement in the conservative direction. We also find a significant and positive effect for Republican Party leaders in the Senate, and while we observe a negative and significant effect among House Democrats who were veterans of military service, the opposite relationship holds for Senate Democrats.

We find little evidence of any other systematic relationships between member characteristics and changes in voting patterns. Length of service does not appear to have any relationship with the difference between a member's prewar and postwar voting record, though the coefficient estimate is negatively signed in three of the four regressions. Likewise, membership on a committee that is responsible for foreign policy or national security legislation is not significantly related to changes in legislative behavior that correspond with the presence of war. In the Senate, members of both parties who faced reelection in 2002 demonstrated smaller shifts in voting behavior, yet these estimates were not significantly different from zero. We also are reluctant to make much of this result given that these

---

41. The model takes the form $y_i = \alpha + X\beta + \varepsilon_i$, where X is a matrix of the covariates we have discussed and β is a vector of parameter estimates for the relationship between each covariate and change in ideal point estimates. Other plausible covariates, such as public approval of the president, are not available at the district or state level for all observations during the time period under investigation.

Table 5.2. REGRESSION RESULTS

Independent Variables	House Democrats	House Republicans	Senate Democrats	Senate Republicans
Bush vote, 2000	0.03 (0.01)**	0.01 (0.01)	0.15 (0.05)***	−0.00 (0.07)
Distance from median	−0.64 (0.17)***	0.58 (0.12)***	0.79 (0.30)**	−0.06 (0.50)
Distance from median (squared)	0.20 (0.06)**	−0.67 (0.10)***	−0.32 (0.16)**	0.05 (0.30)
Time in office (decades)	−0.03 (0.02)	−0.02 (0.01)	−0.04 (0.03)	0.01 (0.04)
Veteran	−0.08 (0.04)**	−0.03 (0.02)	0.19 (0.06)***	0.09 (0.10)
Committee[a]	0.03 (0.03)	0.02 (0.02)	0.03 (0.06)	−0.04 (0.09)
Party leader[b]	0.12 (0.12)	−0.05 (0.06)	0.02 (0.13)	0.41 (0.15)***
Site of attack[c]	0.10 (0.04)**	−0.04 (0.03)	0.08 (0.16)	−0.23 (0.21)
Reelection[d]			−0.19** (0.07)	−0.13 (0.09)
(Intercept)	0.41 (0.16)***	0.92 (0.07)***	−0.05 (0.33)	1.39 (0.33)***
N	210	216	50	49
Adjusted-R^2	0.14	0.32	0.31	0.08
MSE	0.20	0.13	0.19	0.25

Note: Entries are linear regression coefficients with standard errors shown in parentheses. The dependent variable is the change in member ideal point estimates once the war in Afghanistan began on October 7, 2001, where larger values indicate larger shifts in member voting behavior.
*** $p<.01$; ** $p<.05$; * $p<.10$, two-tailed tests.
[a]In the House, these committees include the Committees on Armed Services, Foreign Affairs, Homeland Security, Intelligence, and Veterans' Affairs. In the Senate, they include Armed Services, Foreign Relations, Intelligence, and Veterans' Affairs.
[b]We define party leaders as the House speaker and majority and minority leaders and whips, and the Senate majority and minority leaders and whips.
[c]Indicates whether the legislator represents constituents living in New York or Pennsylvania.
[d]Indicates whether the Senate seat is up for reelection in 2002.

Senators' voting behavior during this term may also reflect additional strategic factors that are motivated by electoral concerns.

Because war disproportionately affects communities with a large military presence, we also estimate the above models with several different covariates that are related to the military interests in members' districts or states. We find no relationship between changes in member voting behavior and the percentage of the population that then served in the military or was a veteran of military service. Finally, we find no evidence that members from safe seats exhibited larger or smaller shifts in voting behavior than members who won more narrow election victories in their most recent election.

5.3 Earlier Wars

We now investigate whether earlier wars furnish additional evidence in support of our expectations about congressional voting behavior during wartime. Figures 5.5 and 5.6 display our aggregate findings across all of the wars we examine. Figure 5.5 shows the extent to which congressional voting records shift in the ideological direction of the president in office at the war's beginning, and Figure 5.6 does the same for congressional voting behavior at the end of war. The x-axis represents the magnitude of the shift in voting records and is scaled such that larger positive values indicate larger movements in the direction of the president, while negative values indicate movement away from the president's ideological orientation. The large solid dots represent the average effect of each war in each chamber, which are obtained by aggregating the shifts in member voting behavior across every method we used to identify changes between peacetime and wartime. The horizontal bars indicate the 95 percent confidence intervals. The dashed vertical line is zero, which indicates that war did not produce an observable impact on member voting behavior. Because we cannot measure the magnitude of member shifts across wars, our main interests are in observing whether the estimated effects are consistent across both chambers within a given war, and that the confidence intervals do not include zero.

For each of the major modern wars that preceded the Afghanistan war, we confront new identification problems. To analyze the Vietnam and Persian Gulf wars, we must pool observations across congresses so that we have a sufficient number of roll call votes on both sides of the transitions between peace and war. The beginning of the Vietnam War, moreover, is contested, and the end is conflated with Watergate. For these reasons alone, the results that follow are more provisional than those recovered from the Afghanistan war.

The biggest challenges, though, concern our use of bridge observations. Interest groups did not identify "key votes" for the congresses that served during World War II and the Korean War.[42] Due to its short duration

---

42. Though the ADA began issuing congressional ratings in 1947, the ACU did not do so until 1971. A conservative interest group, Americans for Constitutional Action, preceded the ACU, but it did not begin to issue ratings until 1959.

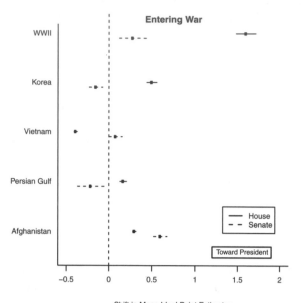

Figure 5.5. AVERAGE EFFECTS OF WAR INITIATIONS ON CONGRESSIONAL VOTING BEHAVIOR.

The points represent the mean shifts in chamber ideal point estimates, which are obtained by aggregating the results from the analyses using interest group and member bridges. The horizontal lines are the 95 percent confidence intervals of the estimated shifts. The vertical dashed line represents no shift in member voting behavior. If the outbreaks of wars induce members of Congress to vote in ways that better reflect the preferences of the president, we expect to find large positive shifts (that is, shifts toward the president's position) in voting behavior. The average effects for World War II and the Korean and Persian Gulf wars are calculated using member bridges only; the effects for the Vietnam and Afghanistan wars are aggregated from the analyses that use members and interest groups to facilitate intertemporal comparisons of voting behavior.

(January 16–April 11, 1991), the Persian Gulf War does not contain an adequate number of interest group roll call positions taken during the war. In place of interest groups, we apply criteria described in Appendix B to identify individual members of Congress whose voting records are least likely to have been affected by the onset of war, and who therefore serve as plausible bridge observations for World War II, the Korean War, and the Persian Gulf War.

WORLD WAR II

Apart from the bridging issues we have discussed, our analysis of World War II has a number of commendable properties. First, the war itself—or

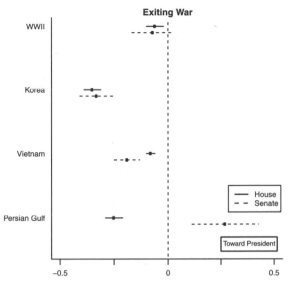

Figure 5.6. AVERAGE EFFECTS OF WAR TERMINATIONS ON CONGRESSIONAL VOTING BEHAVIOR.
The points represent the mean shifts in chamber ideal point estimates, which are obtained by aggregating the results from the analyses using interest group and member bridges. The horizontal lines are the 95 percent confidence intervals of the estimated shifts. The vertical dashed line represents no shift in member voting behavior. If the terminations of wars induce members of Congress to vote in ways that less reflect the preferences of the president, we expect to find large negative shifts (that is, shifts away from the president's position) in voting behavior. The average effects for World War II and the Korean and Persian Gulf wars are calculated using member bridges only; the effects for the Vietnam War are aggregated from the analyses that use members and interest groups to facilitate intertemporal comparisons of voting behavior.

more exactly, the U.S. entry into the war—has reasonably clear beginning and end points. Because Congress did not anticipate the Pearl Harbor attacks, the war's beginning also is likely to be exogenous to the congressional agenda. Because Democratic presidents held office at the war's beginning and end, we have an important basis of comparison to the Afghanistan war, when a Republican president held office.

World War II should have had a substantial impact on congressional voting. More exactly, we expect that members of the 77th Congress voted more liberally once the United States declared war against the Axis Powers, and that members of the 79th Congress voted more conservatively after the Japanese surrender in August 1945. We find support for both expectations. All three analyses support the claim that both the 77th House and Senate voted more liberally after the United States entered World War II. The results using subsets of domestic and foreign policy legislation are a bit weaker: we find consistent evidence that members of the House voted more liberally upon the beginning of war, but the results for the Senate are less robust. We are somewhat hesitant to stake much on the results of the bill subsets, however, because each chamber cast on the order of one-fifth as many roll call votes as in the 107th Congress, and limiting the analyses to domestic and foreign policy items substantially shrinks the pool of bills with which we can assess changes in voting patterns. Nevertheless, the evidence supports our prediction that the outbreak of World War II yielded a Congress that voted in ways that better resembled the ideological preferences of President Roosevelt.

Because the military conflict in Afghanistan is ongoing, at least as of this writing, our analysis focuses exclusively on voting behavior at the war's outset. For all our other wars, however, we can examine changes in members' voting behavior as the nation transitions from war to peace. Note that in World War II, Truman rather than Roosevelt presided over the end of the war. The change in leadership, however, did not disrupt the basic patterns in the data. Consistent with our predictions, members were *more* likely to support Truman as long as the war was ongoing. We find that the end of World War II yielded a Congress less willing to vote in ways that reflected the preferences of President Truman.[43] Each of the analyses that use all roll call votes shows shifts in the conservative direction on the conclusion of World War II, though the findings for the Senate fall just short of statistical significance at conventional levels. In addition, all the analyses of domestic policy legislation show significant shifts in the conservative direction, though our findings for foreign policy issues are a bit more tentative.

KOREA

Once again, we rely on members of Congress as our bridges for the Korean War. As with World War II, different presidents presided over the beginning (Truman) and end (Eisenhower) of the Korean War, though in this case the presidents were members of different parties. If the Korean War

---

43. We include only those roll call votes cast during Truman's presidency.

induced members to vote in ways that better reflected the president's ideology, we should see members of the 81st Congress moving in a liberal direction (toward Truman) at the war's onset, just as do members of 83rd Congress (opposite Eisenhower) upon the war's end. For reasons already discussed, however, we do not expect that the Korean War altered the relationship between Congress and the president in as significant ways as World War II and the Afghanistan war.

Our findings are largely consistent with expectations. Though the results show that the onset of the Korean War induced a liberal response from members of the House, neither set of Senate results reveals comparable changes. Indeed, members of the Senate appear to have voted in a *more conservative* manner upon the war's commencement. We find similar inconsistencies when examining the subsets of domestic and foreign policy legislation.

Our results suggest that members of Congress were less likely to vote in ways that reflected Eisenhower's preferences once he fulfilled his campaign promise to bring the Korean War to a close. Upon war's end, members of the 83rd House and Senate moved in the liberal direction—away from the president's ideological orientation. Such results also appear when examining purely domestic bills.

In tandem, signs of heightened presidential success appear rather limited during the Korean War. We find mixed evidence of congressional accommodation to President Truman upon the beginning of the war, while members of Congress were less likely to vote in ways that reflected President Eisenhower's ideology upon the end of the war. Eisenhower also is somewhat of an unusual case compared with the other presidents we examine in this chapter, as he is the one president perhaps best characterized as an ideological moderate. Thus, the conservative shifts we observe at war's end may indicate that Congress took genuinely moderate positions on most issues, and, in fact, are not an indication of wholesale rejection of the president's policy positions. Once we admit this possibility, we are left with meager evidence that the Korean War dramatically expanded the president's influence over congressional voting behavior.

VIETNAM

Unlike World War II and the Korean War, interest group positions are available for us to compare voting behavior before and after the Vietnam

War.[44] The Vietnam War, nonetheless, presents several unique challenges of its own. First, unlike the other wars we examine, the gradual escalation of U.S. involvement makes it difficult to identify a clear start date. Following the lead of other scholars, we mark February 7, 1965, as the beginning of the Vietnam War, which corresponds with the execution of Operation Flaming Dart, the first large-scale military initiative after the Gulf of Tonkin Resolution. We fully recognize, though, that one could readily make a case for other transition dates. Second, the war both begins and ends quite early in new congressional sessions. Consequently, we lack sufficient numbers of peacetime and wartime roll calls to compare members' voting records within a single Congress. We address this problem by combining the second session of the 88th Congress (1964) and the first session of the 89th (1965), and the second session of the 92nd Congress (1972) and the first session of the 93rd (1973). We further limit the analyses of these pooled samples to those members who served in both congresses. Unfortunately, by selecting observations across congresses, these comparisons less effectively control for the intra-institutional factors that previous scholars have identified as important predictors of members' voting behavior.

We do not anticipate that the Vietnam War augmented presidential influence in Congress to a significant degree, and the data broadly comport with our expectations. We find no evidence that the beginning of the Vietnam War yielded a Congress more willing to vote in ways that reflected the president's ideological orientation. In the House, we find consistent and robust evidence that members voted more *conservatively* upon the beginning of the war, when a liberal president held office; voting behavior in the Senate, meanwhile, is not statistically different between the two time periods. This pattern of findings reappears when examining subsets of domestic and foreign policy legislation.[45]

We do find that with the Vietnam War's termination, the voting records of members of Congress shifted in the liberal direction—that is, away

44. However, because the ACU did not issue congressional ratings until 1971, we use positions taken by Americans for Constitutional Action (ACA) for the 88th and 89th Congresses. The ACA is a reasonable substitute because it was founded in the mid-1950s as the conservative analog to the ADA, and it also takes a large number of issue positions on a wide range of bills. Scaling a number of interest groups based on their congressional ratings issued from 1969 to 1978, Poole (1981) also shows that the ACA and the ACU were virtually identical ideologically.

45. These findings are broadly consistent with those in Stimson (1999), which show that liberalism within Congress peaked in the early to mid-1960s.

from the ideological orientation of the president then in office. In the analyses that include all roll call votes cast in 1972 and 1973, members of Congress compiled significantly more liberal voting records upon the end of the war. Because the end of the war coincided with President Nixon's deepening political troubles due to the Watergate scandal, however, the observed differences may also reflect members' efforts to distance themselves from an unpopular president.

Taken together, the patterns we observe for congressional voting behavior before, during, and after the Vietnam War are consistent with our expectations. The evidence we have assembled here weighs against the proposition that President Johnson received increased support from Congress once the war began. And, although President Nixon likely enjoyed greater support during the war than after its conclusion, personal scandal rather than armistice may be responsible for the observed changes in voting behavior.

PERSIAN GULF WAR

The Persian Gulf War presents many of the same challenges as the Vietnam War. The war began immediately after a new Congress (the 102nd) was seated, so we lack sufficient prewar roll call votes to examine changes in voting behavior within a single Congress. We therefore cull votes across the last year of the 101st Congress (1990) and the first year of the 102nd Congress (1991), and we restrict the analysis to members who served in both Congresses. In addition, the war's short duration prevents us from using interest group positions to anchor our comparisons. Thus, our analyses rely exclusively upon member bridges, identified through the criteria described earlier.

In the main, we find little systematic evidence that the Persian Gulf War induced members of Congress to vote in ways that better reflected the preferences of President George H. W. Bush. Upon the beginning of war, our results for the House *do* suggest the presence of a war effect, but we find exactly the opposite relationship in the Senate. These results also hold for our analysis of bills that concerned purely domestic policy items. Upon the end of the Persian Gulf War, we see that both patterns are reversed. Members of The House shifted in the liberal direction, away from the position of the president, while members of the Senate compiled more conservative voting records. These results show that the war may have increased presidential support in the House, but that support did not extend into the Senate.

On the whole, these results suggest that the Persian Gulf War induced either modest or no changes in members' voting behavior. Whatever evidence of a wartime effect may exist, however, it pales in comparison to what we observe for World War II and the post-9/11 wars.

5.4 *World War I and the Relevance of Stateside Attacks*

Whether analyzing budgets (as we do in the previous chapter) or actual roll call votes (as we do in this chapter), the most consistent evidence of congressional accommodation to the president appears in World War II and the Afghanistan war. These also happen to be the two modern wars in which the United States suffered a stateside attack. The presence of imminent security threats—very much including those that successfully reach the nation's shores—can be expected to increase the salience of national considerations, and thereby augment the chances that the president's agenda will receive a favorable hearing in Congress. A stateside attack, however, does not constitute a precondition for the emergence of the kinds of politics that favor the president. In this sense, World War I provides a useful point of comparison. Like World War II, World War I unleashed many of the same forces that nationalize politics—a carefully orchestrated propaganda campaign, widespread calls for self-sacrifice, a spike in patriotic sentiment, and the like. But unlike World War II, the enemy never struck within the nation's borders.

From its beginnings in 1914, the Great War stood at the center of American political debate. Woodrow Wilson, honoring the Monroe Doctrine, initially committed to a policy of neutrality. The president, however, quickly drew fire from critics on both sides of the war issue. Those on the Left argued that Wilson had not taken advantage of the opportunity to negotiate a peace settlement between the Allied and the Central Powers. His secretary of state, William Jennings Bryan, resigned in protest in 1915 over what he saw as Wilson's unwillingness to profess his sympathies with the Allies. On the Right, however, Theodore Roosevelt complained that Wilson had not gone far enough to prepare the United States for war, or to protect and defend northwest Europe against unjust German attacks.[46] The American people initially appeared unwilling to support a U.S. entry into the war, and in 1916 Wilson was reelected on the slogan "he kept us out of war."

46. Kennedy 2001; Roosevelt 1915.

In the months after his reelection, however, Wilson would find it increasingly difficult to sustain a policy of isolationism. Following the sinking of the *Lusitania* in 1915, American ships continued to come under attack from German U-boats. With the revelation in March 1917 that the Germans had sought to form an alliance with Mexico against the United States, the Wilson administration had little choice but to enter the Great War. On April 2, 1917, Wilson sought a congressional declaration of war, calling upon nothing less than the "the organization and mobilization of all the material resources of the country" in order to "make the world safe for democracy."[47] The president solicited dramatic increases in military personnel, universal conscription, and massive tax increases. In so doing, the president awakened the national consciousness.

Given that World War I preceded the period of modern polling, we cannot provide as thorough an accounting of the proxies for the nationalization of politics that appear in Chapter 3. All signs, though, point to a dramatic increase. World War I, after all, reveals many of the same features of World War II, which is our standard-bearer for heightened national considerations. As Corwin tells us, World War I is best understood as a "prologue and rehearsal" to World War II.[48] "World War II is World War I writ large; and F.D.R.'s conduct of it is Mr. Wilson's conduct of World War I writ large."[49] Or as Clinton Rossiter observed, in World War II, "the mould of 1917–18 was rarely broken; the grooves were simply cut a little deeper."[50]

Partly through government cultivation, and partly through the spontaneous actions of citizens and civic organizations, expressions of patriotism, affirmations of national solidarity, and a unifying spirit of self-sacrifice swept the land. During World War I, Uncle Sam made his debut on military recruitment posters. The federal government urged Americans to support their country by purchasing Liberty Bonds and War Savings Stamps, knitting socks for soldiers, consuming grains other than wheat, launching careers in nursing, and planting "victory gardens." The Committee on Public Information, organized to disseminate propaganda and rally support for the war, played a key role in mobilizing public support as it "closely monitored purity of thought and opinion, defined patriotism in narrow, bombastic terms, utilized all instruments of communication, made all public gathering

47. Woodrow Wilson, "Speech before Congress," April 2, 1917.
48. Corwin 1957, 237.
49. Corwin 1956, 777.
50. Rossiter 2005 [1948], 265.

places sites of indoctrination, and defined all dissent as treason."[51] Most every aspect of private life—from what one cooked in the kitchen to what one said among friends—was linked to the war effort. As such, citizens worried a great deal more about the fate of the nation and less about the welfare of their own households and communities. This clearly was a war that supported the preconditions for enhanced presidential success in Congress.

Because the president did not submit budget requests prior to the Budget and Accounting Act of 1921, we cannot extend the analyses in Chapter 4 to World War I. Using the basic bridging strategies employed for World War II, the Korean War, and the Persian Gulf War, however, we can investigate whether members of Congress voted in ways that better reflected President Wilson's preferences upon the beginning of war, and less well upon the end of the war. Because World War I began (April 6, 1917) and ended (June 28, 1919) early enough in new congressional terms, we lack sufficient numbers of peacetime and wartime roll calls. Thus, to assess changes in voting behavior upon the beginning of war, we analyze the voting behavior of members who served in both the 64th and 65th Congresses, and we evaluate behavior upon the end of war using members who served in both the 65th and 66th Congresses. In the absence of interest group positions, we again use members of congress as our bridges.

Upon the beginning of the war, both sets of bridging criteria indicate that Senators shifted to the left of the ideological spectrum. The estimated mean shifts are −0.15 for Republicans and −0.55 for Democrats, both of which are statistically significant. In the House, where only one bridging strategy was possible, the observed shifts are not statistically different from zero. Comparable findings appear at the end of the war. Both estimates for the Senate show significant movement in the conservative direction—that is, away from the preferences of President Wilson. In the House, meanwhile, the estimated effects are indistinguishable from zero.

Of course, all the usual caveats still apply. These estimates rely upon members of Congress as bridges rather than interest groups. Moreover, these estimates pool observations across congresses rather than tracking changes in members' voting records within a single Congress. As a consequence, we have less confidence in the findings for World War I than we do for those in the Afghanistan war. Still, the movements we observe in the Senate are broadly consistent with our theoretical expectations, and they provide at least suggestive evidence that a stateside attack does not consti-

---

51. Gary 1999, 19–20.

tute a prerequisite for engendering the kinds of wartime politics that, we posit, are responsible for increased levels of congressional accommodation to the president.

5.5 *War and Other Crises*

We recognize that major wars may constitute elements of a larger class of phenomena that induce systematic changes in congressional support for the president. Indeed, it remains unclear whether the findings we observe above are products of the peculiarities of war, or whether crisis events more generally affect the extent to which members of Congress compile roll call voting records that are more consistent with the president's preferences. To investigate this, we look at instances of other types of events (foreign crises, smaller military deployments, and presidential scandals) that might encourage members of Congress to vote in ways that better reflect the ideological leanings of the president.

We used two main criteria to select these crisis events. First, to ensure that there are sufficient numbers of roll call votes with which to characterize legislator voting behavior before and during a crisis event, the event should have occurred roughly midway through a congressional session. Second, we restrict our attention to crises that occurred since 1971 so that the ACU and ADA can be used as bridge actors. These criteria rule out the inclusion of events such as the assassination attempt on President Reagan, which occurred just weeks after his inauguration; news of the Iran-Contra affair, which broke at the end of the 99th Congress; and the 2008 financial crisis, which occurred at the end of the 110th Congress and whose beginning date is ambiguous.

Using these rules, we selected the Iran hostage crisis, which began on November 4, 1979, during the 96th Congress; the commitment of troops to Lebanon beginning August 24, 1982, during the 97th Congress; U.S. participation in the United Nations peacekeeping mission in Bosnia, beginning December 20, 1995, during the 104th Congress; and the revelation of President Clinton's affair with Monica Lewinsky, which occurred on January 17, 1998 and clouded Clinton's presidency for the remainder of the 105th Congress. All of these events permit comparisons within single congresses using interest groups as bridges.

If crises involving foreign affairs and military commitments to small-scale operations increase the weight that legislators assign to national policy outcomes, we should see evidence of shifts in the liberal direction in

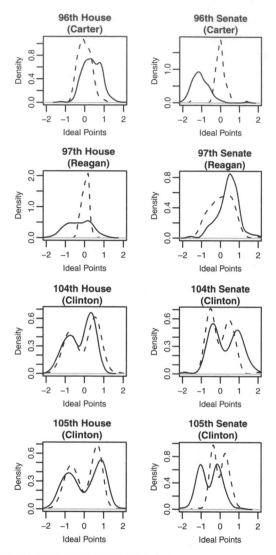

Figure 5.7. SHIFTS IN CONGRESSIONAL VOTING BEHAVIOR DURING OTHER CRISIS EVENTS.

Each row of plots depicts shifts in congressional voting behavior that correspond with four other "crisis events": the Iran hostage crisis (began November 4, 1979, during the 96th Congress), the commitment of U.S. troops to Lebanon (began August 24, 1982, during the 97th Congress), the deployment of U.S. troops to assist with peacekeeping operations in Bosnia (began December 20, 1995, during the 104th Congress), and the revelation of President Clinton's affair with Monica Lewinsky (news of the scandal broke on January 17, 1998, during the 105th Congress). Dashed lines reflect the distribution of ideal points for roll call votes before the beginning of the crisis events, and the solid lines reflect the distribution of ideal points for votes cast after those dates. The American Conservative Union (ACU) and the Americans for Democratic Action (ADA) were used to link the time periods.

the 96th and 104th Congress, and in the conservative direction during the 97th Congress. Presidential scandals, on the other hand, may persuade legislators to focus more intensely on their local concerns, perhaps in an attempt to distance themselves from the president and demonstrate their ability to serve district needs in spite of the president's distractions. Thus, if presidential scandals weaken presidential influence in Congress, we should observe shifts in the conservative direction in the 105th Congress.

Using the same estimation procedure used to identify patterns of roll call behavior during conditions of war and peace, we find little systematic evidence (shown in Figure 5.7) of congressional accommodation to the president. In none of these cases are consistent effects observed across the House and Senate. Indeed, in every case that movement is detected toward the president's ideological orientation in one chamber, movement away from the president is detected in the other. Although these particular examples clearly do not exhaust the possibilities of crises (military or otherwise) that implicate the president, the collective evidence presented here suggests that U.S. involvement in large wars has the potential to alter patterns of congressional voting in ways that these smaller affairs do not.

5.6 *Conclusion*

Within the context of our theory and maintained hypothesis, this chapter examines the extent to which wars induce changes in congressional voting behavior. Analyzing every major war in which the United States has participated since World War I, we find that frequently the beginning of war yields a Congress more inclined to vote in ways that reflect the ideological orientation of the president then in office. Upon the end of war, however, the voting records of members of Congress take a turn in the opposite direction. This evidence is consistent with our general claim that wars increase presidential success in Congress.

This chapter also provides broad support for our more specific predictions, outlined in Chapter 3, that some wars increase presidential success more than others. At the outset of World Wars I and II and the Afghanistan War, members of Congress began to vote in ways that better reflected the ideological orientations of the presidents then in office. But evidence for the beginnings of the Korean, Vietnam, and Persian Gulf wars is more mixed. Members of Congress did not line up behind the president in consistent ways. With the termination of every war we analyzed, members of Congress shifted away from presidents—suggesting that whatever "honours and emoluments" wars had to offer the president (to borrow from Madison), they were promptly withdrawn when these wars ended. Still further, the evidence for the shifts away from presidents is more robust the greater the wartime boon to presidential power. The key feature of war implicated by the Policy Priority Model—the nationalization of policy outcomes—does well in explaining why some modern wars induced changes favorable to the president, but others reconstituted the relationships between presidents and members of Congress in less consistent, and certainly less obvious, ways.

In several important respects, this chapter complements the budgetary findings. It provides a more explicit test for the extent to which wars have a heterogenous effect on voting behavior in Congress. The approach used here also allows us to address the behavior of Congress more generally, extending well beyond the realm of appropriating presidential budget requests. And finally, these findings avoid the deep endogeneity issues associated with presidential position taking, which plague previous quantitative explorations of the impact of war on congressional voting behavior.

By design, the analyses in this chapter have limitations of their own. Most obviously, they do not permit explicit evaluations of the president's location during war and peace. Hence, although we can assess whether members adjust their voting behavior in ways that broadly comport with the president's ideology, we cannot measure the precise distances between members' ideal points and the president's. Similarly, not all of our estimates are equally reliable. We place the greatest confidence in those based on interest group bridges within a single Congress, and less weight on those that pool votes across congresses or rely on members of Congress to serve as bridges.

Despite these limitations, our chosen methodological approach makes some headway on a problem of more general interest to scholars of political institutions: how do major events, including war, alter the separation of powers between Congress and the president? We employ a technique that uses interest groups to facilitate intertemporal comparisons in congressional voting behavior. Other research could make use of this approach to examine, for instance, the effect of changes in the economy on congressional voting behavior, or whether bureaucrats or judges adjust their behavior when a new president occupies the White House.

The findings we offer represent something of a challenge to the literature that focuses exclusively on member characteristics, constituencies, and the intra-institutional organization of Congress as predictors of member vote choices—and that, holding these quantities fixed, emphasizes the ideological stability of members' voting patterns. In particular, we find that war has the capacity to alter—sometimes in a dramatic fashion—the voting records of members of Congress. Members of Congress may indeed "die in their ideological boots," but over the course of these members' careers, wars can profoundly recast their relationships with presidents.

CHAPTER 6

Case Studies I: Illustrations

The previous two chapters presented a variety of estimates of the variable repercussions of war on congressional voting behavior. The findings speak broadly to war's general effects on domestic and foreign policy, differences between the transitions from war to peace and from peace to war, and the heterogeneous impacts of different modern wars on presidential influence. For the most part, however, those chapters ignored the particular elements of public policy—the very subjects of political debate.

So rather than continue to quantify the landscape of peacetime and wartime policy making, we now examine individual cases of actual lawmaking. Those that appear in this chapter—Wilson's domestic policy achievements in World War I, Roosevelt's effort to quash anti-labor legislation at the outbreak of war as well as his extraordinary influence over domestic policy during the war's course, and Bush's efforts to reform border security and, by implication, immigration policy—match up quite nicely with the primary arguments and evidence presented in earlier chapters. In the main, these studies bear witness to the various ways in which wars can alter the terms of political debate, highlighting national priorities while tempering local ones. In doing so, these cases illustrate the effect that wars can have on presidential influence.

Not all of our cases merely confirm what has already been argued and established. In particular, cases in the next chapter—the federal government's sudden entry into education policy in 1957, Johnson's efforts to protect elements of his Great Society during the early stages of the Vietnam War, and Bush's failed attempt to reform Social Security in 2005—in one way or another challenge the purest distillations of our arguments and evidence. In various ways, these studies identify important limitations of our claims, and still others introduce altogether new political dynamics to congressional-presidential bargaining during peace and war.

We do not pretend that these cases constitute a representative sample of domestic policy disputes during war and peace. They do not. Rather, we selected these cases for the light they could shed on our main theoretical assertions and empirical findings. Most of these studies allow us to witness the Policy Priority Model in action, played out in real time with real politicians. Some of these studies also shed light on elements of the domestic politics of war about which the Policy Priority Model says very little. Happily, all the studies recover some of the political drama, personalities, and strategizing that are lost in the regression coefficients and density plots that constitute the core offerings of earlier chapters.

6.1 *The First Total War*

The spectacle and experience of war reshaped citizen Woodrow Wilson's thinking about the appropriate division of powers between Congress and the presidency. When President Woodrow Wilson later waged one of his own, not only was his thinking about a more expansive wartime president affirmed, but so was that of members of Congress.

WILSON'S CONVERSION

Woodrow Wilson is among the very few presidents to have written rather extensively on the proper forms of executive, legislative, and judicial powers before taking office. In his first major publication, *Congressional Government,* Wilson heralded Congress's supremacy—albeit a Congress remade in the image of Britain's parliament. As he put it, "Our constitution . . . practically sets [Congress] to rule the affairs of the nation as supreme overlord."[1] For Wilson, executive (and by implication presidential) independence merely frustrated Congress's practical capacity to address contemporary challenges, and of "making [Congress's] authority complete and convenient."[2] To guard against such eventualities, Wilson enlisted extraconstitutional institutions, in particular strong parties. The discipline imposed by such parties, Wilson thought, would temper executive independence and allow Congress to dispose of the "ever widening duties and responsibilities" appropriately laid before it as the federal government's first among unequal branches of government.

Later in life, though, Wilson would repudiate such claims, and the advent of war was the primary reason for him doing so. Watching the Spanish-American War convinced Wilson of the importance of the president

1. Wilson 1901 [1884], 312.
2. Ibid., 314.

assuming a primary role in both the foreign and domestic governance of the nation. War, Wilson noted in the preface to a revised version of *Congressional Government* published in 1901, established both the practical need and principled justification for "the greatly increased power and opportunity for constructive statesmanship given the President."[3] The president alone, in Wilson's judgment, could provide the necessary unity and voice that the nation required during war. When a nation was at war, Wilson now insisted, "its Executive must of necessity be its guide: must utter every initial judgment, take every first step of action, supply the information upon which it is to act, suggest and in large measure control its conduct."[4]

The exigencies of war, Wilson recognized, ushered in a presidency with far-reaching influence over both the foreign and domestic affairs of the country. The president's wartime leadership, Wilson concluded:

> will have a far reaching effect on our whole method of government. It may give the heads of the executive departments a new influence upon the action of Congress. It may bring about, as a consequence, an integration which will substitute statesmanship for government by mass meeting. It may put this whole volume hopelessly out of date.[5]

In this extraordinary admission, Wilson counseled his reader to set aside *Congressional Government* when the nation stood at war, for this book, which established Wilson's academic reputation, provided few insights into the workings of a wartime government.

Not surprisingly, Wilson gave the presidency pride of place in his subsequent masterpiece *Constitutional Government*. As the only elected individual representing a truly national electorate, as the leader of his party, as the only individual with the gravitas needed to allay the concerns of foreign states, and as the administrator of executive powers that are at once personal and absolutely essential to all matters of governance, the president was uniquely equipped to lead the nation and to assemble in common purpose the various institutions of government that the Founders worked so hard to separate. For Wilson, the president alone could provide the vision that the country needed in order to meet the challenges of its day—a rapidly expanding industrial force, the assimilation of millions of new European immigrants, and, soon enough, the advent of total war. Hence, notes Sidney

3. Ibid., xi.
4. Ibid., xi–xii.
5. Ibid., xii–xiii.

Pearson in his introduction to *Constitutional Government*, "Presidential leadership occupied the most exalted position in Wilson's hierarchy of political virtues."[6]

In *Constitutional Government*, as in *Congressional Government*, arguments about one branch's primacy are embedded in a more general critique of the Constitution. And in this regard, Wilson's view stood largely at odds with the most important wartime president of the previous century, Abraham Lincoln. For Lincoln, wars strained the constitutional order, beckoning presidents to act in ways that are best thought of as extraconstitutional. When taking such actions, Lincoln insisted, presidents owed Congress and the citizenry something of an apologia. Having temporarily abandoned the Constitution in service of the nation's and perhaps the Constitution's survival, presidents must submit themselves to the judgment of their peers, who have every right to renounce their actions and perhaps throw them from office. For Wilson, by contrast, wars (and other urgencies that warranted a government response) demanded revisions to the constitutional order itself. Wilson did not agonize about the relaxation of the constitutional limits of presidential power during war. For Wilson, these limits, and the Constitution more generally, must be understood within the historical context within which presidents ruled. Representing the entire citizenry, presidents must reinterpret, and thereby remake, the Constitution to serve a larger public good. Lincoln viewed the Civil War as something of an interruption to the everyday business of a president who must protect the office as the office was intended to be. Wilson, throughout his presidency, aligned himself with, in the words of his fellow Progressive Henry Jones Ford, "the work of the people, breaking through the constitutional form."[7]

In Wilson's political science, a system of governance based on mechanistic checks and balances and a fixed conception of constitutional strictures was unsustainable. The world would not wait on political institutions working against one another or a constitution written by men long since dead. Rather than adhere to outdated constitutional notions, Wilson insisted, government must adapt to its surroundings and reconstitute itself and its relation to the citizenry according to the dictates of material wants and needs.

> Government is not a machine, but a living thing. It falls, not under the theory of the universe, but under the theory of organic life. It is accountable

6. Wilson 2002 [1908], xlvi.
7. Ford 1898, 292–93.

to Darwin, not Newton. It is modified by its environment, necessitated by its tasks, shaped by its functions by the sheer pressure of life.[8]

And should it fail in this regard, Wilson thought, the government would suffer the fate of the ammonites, trilobites, and famed mastodon.[9] To survive, the federal government, with the president at its helm, must remake itself "from age to age by changes of life and circumstance and corresponding alterations of opinions."[10] The presidency must be whatever the people and the times require of it.

Of course, evolution and teleology are not synonymous. The executive's ascendance in the hierarchy of government, though eminently justified, is not guaranteed. To correct both the Founders' and his own past errors, Wilson recognized, presidential foresight and initiative would be crucial. Having rejected a static and highly constrained view of the presidency in favor of a "machinery of constant adaptation," Wilson the scholar encouraged presidents to view their office as "anything [they have] the sagacity and force to make it."[11] Soon enough, Wilson the president would heed his own counsel.

FROM THINKING ABOUT WAR TO WAGING IT

By unleashing the technologies that produced human carnage the likes of which the world had never seen, the Great War of 1914 would forever change the way nations went to war. For all parties involved, success on the battlefront depended on the massive production of ammunition, guns, and armor. As such, domestic industries had to be redirected and in some cases remade to this end. For President Wilson to make a difference on the war's western front, which lay some 3,000 miles from Washington, D.C., he would need to first secure control over events and activities at home.

The origins of the U.S. involvement in World War I are well known.[12] On January 31, 1917, Germany announced its policy, which would take effect the next day, of sinking without warning or provocation all merchant ships bound for France or England. The Kaiser hoped that the unrestricted deployment of its U-boats would starve the English population before the United States could gather the men and material needed

8. Wilson 2002 [1908], 56.
9. For more on Wilson's general views of presidential power, see Tulis 1988, and Zentner 1994.
10. Wilson 2002 [1908], 22.
11. Ibid., 8.
12. Classic accounts include May 1959; Millis 1935; Smith 1965.

to turn the war in the Allies' favor. The gambit was not foolhardy. Two and a half years into the war, English food stocks were rapidly dwindling, and isolationist currents continued to run strong in the United States. In the previous presidential election, Wilson had vowed to keep the United States out of Europe's war. Moreover, before it could adequately respond to Germany, the United States would have to amass stockpiles of weapons on a timetable that just decades prior would have been unfathomable.

Propitiously, at least from Germany's standpoint, Wilson did not immediately declare war. In fact, Wilson twice went before Congress to reaffirm his commitment to peace and neutrality. But with rising losses of merchant vessels and, crucially, the concurrent outbreak of revolution in Russia and the interception of a German telegram urging Mexico to wage war against the United States, Wilson finally steeled himself for combat. On April 2, 1917, he went before Congress requesting a declaration of war. The president recognized that success demanded "the organization and mobilization of all the material resources of the country."[13] The nation's entire industrial strength must be harnessed in pursuit of a single objective: the rapid and copious supply of arms needed to defeat the Central Powers of Germany and Austria-Hungary. While calling for changes to the tax code, the imposition of new loyalty measures, the appropriation of funds for the fastest arms buildup the nation had ever seen, and conscription, Wilson emphasized the newfound powers that war appropriately delivered to the executive branch. Deference is warranted, Wilson insisted, to "the branch of the Government upon which the responsibility of conducting the war and safeguarding the nation will most directly fall."[14]

In an effort to rally support for the war and expand the president's influence over the domestic polity, Wilson's administration issued public appeals that expressly subsumed local interests to national imperatives. Quite suddenly, even the most private of activities were linked to national interests. Propaganda posters beckoned women to plant "war gardens" in their backyards, to can food in their kitchens, to conserve bread in their dining rooms, and to knit socks in their living rooms. In the name of saving civilization no less, citizens were asked to purchase "liberty bonds," to contribute to chocolate funds, and to donate books to their libraries. Patriotism required frugality, temperance, and financial savings. Where one worked, how one spent money, with whom one spoke and about what

13. Leonard 1918, 36.
14. Ibid., 38.

were all linked to the overriding importance of winning a foreign war run by the nation's commander in chief.

Throughout the eighteen-month involvement of the United States in World War I, Wilson maintained unprecedented control over the domestic economy.[15] An extraordinary number of congressional statutes vested in the president newfound control over economic and social affairs at home for the duration of the emergency. To manage these affairs, the president created a panoply of war agencies. The War Industries Board, headed by the enigmatic Bernard Baruch, worked with numerous industries to ensure the continual production of munitions, food stock, and machinery that were deemed essential for the war effort. The National War Labor Board oversaw labor–management relations in just about every aspect of the domestic economy. A host of other agencies—the Fuel Administration, the Railroad Administration, the Food Administration—maintained strict oversight over wages, prices, production levels, allowable profits, product standardization, and much, much more within specific industries. For example, throughout the U.S. involvement in the war, the Fuel and Food Administrations wielded:

> the power to regulate by license the importation, manufacture, storage, mining, or distribution of necessaries; the power to purchase, store, and sell certain foods; the power to take over factories, packing houses, pipe lines, mines, or other plants, and operate the same; the power to fix a minimum price of wheat; the power to limit, regulate, or prohibit the use of food materials in the productions of alcoholic beverages; the power to fix the price of coal and coke and to regulate the production, sale, and distribution thereof.[16]

None of these activities—taken by the president and his subordinates, and sanctioned by Congress—would have been tolerated by the courts or citizenry absent the U.S. entry into war.

Moreover, the regulatory activities of these agencies appropriately fulfilled Wilson's conception of a wartime presidency. During the war, Wilson deliberately forsook some of the naked power grabs he associated with Lincoln's prosecution of the Civil War, preferring instead to enlist the voluntary cooperation of Congress and the people. Nevertheless, once Wilson committed the nation to war, he saw it as his war to prosecute and

15. For a longer treatment of this subject, see Kennedy 2004, 93–143.
16. Corwin 1947, 81–82.

his war to win. Whether by dint of persuasion or command, in Wilson's mind the domestic polity was meant to bend to his will as long as troops fought and died on the nation's behalf.

Consider, for example, Wilson's exhortation to the American Federation of Labor in November 1917, wherein the president asked attendees to temporarily abandon strikes as a method of advancing their material self-interests. Though he insisted that he would not quash the rights of labor with the heavy hand of government during the war, and that he would demand as much of management as he did of labor, the president laid plain his expectation that the war mobilization would not be interrupted. What superficially appeared as a conciliatory speech ended with the following zinger:

> I have to come away [from Washington] and talk to men who are up against the real thing and say to them, "I am with you if you are with me." And the only test of being with me is not to think of me personally at all, but merely to think of me as the expression for the time being of the power and dignity and hope of the United States.[17]

I am willing to honor your interests, Wilson told them, so long as those interests conform to my own. For as long as the war continued, the president and the president alone would embody nothing less than the "power and dignity and hope of the United States." Is it any wonder that Wilson's administrative stewards demanded a level of loyalty to the president that would threaten the very foundations of democratic governance?[18]

If, according to Wilson's constitutionalism, executive power justifiably expands during war, it is less clear whether such power must contract in peace. True, virtually all of Wilson's wartime agencies were disbanded shortly after Germany's surrender in the late fall of 1918. Wilson did not argue that the most draconian regulations set during war should persist in peace. Still, the impact of Wilson's wartime policies and administrative agencies proved lasting. Efforts to raise money through bonds and

---

17. Leonard 1918, 76.

18. As numerous other scholars have documented, suppressions of civil liberties—through the control of the mail, the arrest and detention of individuals suspected of supporting insurrection, the propagandizing of the Committee on Public Information, the establishment of an extralegal network (the American Protective League) to support federal agents in their efforts to identify and prosecute individuals who represented a threat to the nation's internal security, and the vigilantism such policies and agencies encouraged—represent some of the most troubling dimensions of Wilson's wartime presidency. See, for example, Kennedy 2004, 45–92; Stone 2004, 135–234.

an income tax, notes the historian David Kennedy, "occasioned a fiscal revolution in the United States."[19] The principle of progressive taxation, whereby revenues were collected on the basis of individuals' and corporations' ability to pay, became a central component of the political landscape. Whereas before the war the government had collected most of its revenues through excise and customs taxes, after the war it primarily relied upon taxing incomes, profits, and estates. It is difficult to see how any of this could have happened absent the war. Again, David Kennedy notes, "Without the crisis and the huge financial demands it put upon the government, that shift in incidence and the accepted legitimacy of such a degree of progression in the tax system might have come about much more slowly."[20]

More generally, these agencies established a precedent for an altogether new partnership between government and business—a central tenet of the Progressive Movement in which Wilson was cast as a protagonist. Under Wilson's leadership through World War I, the government told businesses what they could produce, by what standards, and at what price. The government waged routine propaganda campaigns to root out disloyalty, discourage gross consumption of certain food products, and encourage the purchase of government bonds at low interest rates.[21]

In World War I, the dependence of U.S. troops abroad on the continued production of munitions on domestic assembly lines established the principled basis for the expansion of presidential power at home. The administrative agencies born of this dependence established a template for another president who, just 20 years later, would confront familiar foes bent on taking savagery to altogether new heights. As Corwin would write at the height of World War II, Wilson's presidency established "precedents for presidential dictatorship in time of war or of grave international crisis—a condition of affairs that is likely to remain a factor of our daily lives for many years to come."[22]

19. Kennedy 2004, 112.
20. Ibid., 112.
21. Reflecting on the Great War just a decade after armistice, Mark Sullivan bemoaned the war's lasting influence on the level of government intervention into what had previously been genuinely private spheres of life. "Every business man was shorn of dominion over his factory or store, every housewife surrendered control of her table, every farmer was forbidden to sell his wheat except at the price the government fixed. Our institutions, the railroads, the telephones and telegraphs, the coal mines, were taken under government control. The probation of individual liberty in the interest of the state could hardly be more complete" (1933, 5:489).
22. Corwin 1956, 783.

LESSONS

In World War I, we see a vast illustration of the capacity of war to reach deeply into the domestic polity and to alter the very terms by which politicians understand and evaluate policy alternatives. While total war wreaked havoc on the European continent for several years, Wilson insisted that those struggles were not of the United States's making and not in the immediate interest of the United States to resolve. But the moment he switched positions, he committed fully to the war effort. He did not merely call upon the valor and sacrifice of the soldiers who would be sent into battle. He spoke to labor and management, to housewives and gardeners, to farmers and businessmen, insisting that their labors were now endowed with new meaning and national import. Success on the battlefield, he argued, hinged upon the productive capacities of assembly-line workers, the willingness of housewives to turn to their gardens rather than to grocery stores for produce, and the curtailment of criticism in the media.

By successfully linking domestic activities to national concerns about sovereignty and security, Wilson established the groundwork for some rather extraordinary domestic policy achievements. He introduced widespread changes to the federal government tax code. He wholly remade the administrative state. He reorganized and restructured vast segments of American industry. Absent the war and the changes to the domestic polity that it brought, it is difficult to even conceive of these policy changes.

In broad outline, then, World War I confirms the central argument of this book. In war, concerns about the local implications of policies abate, while concerns about national implications intensify. Hence, through war the president found the means by which to strengthen his bargaining authority with Congress.

6.2 *Pearl Harbor and National Labor Policy*

At the end of 1941, President Franklin D. Roosevelt's labor agenda was up against the ropes. After two terms of advancing the rights of labor, the president now confronted a Congress intent on restricting the incidence of strikes. Hoping to ward off a substantial policy setback, the president lent his support to a compromise industrial relations bill. On December 3, 1941, however, the House defeated this moderate labor bill; in its place, the lower chamber substituted a much more aggressive anti-strike bill, which enjoyed broad support among Republicans and southern Democrats, and the Senate was expected to quickly follow suit. But when the Japanese air force struck Pearl Harbor on December 7, the momentum behind these bills quickly dissipated, just as the president recovered his own influence over domestic policy. Roosevelt immediately called for an emergency National Labor Management Conference to discuss nonlegislative means to resolve the problem of strikes in the defense sector. He created the National War Labor Board (NWLB), which retained unprecedented power to intervene in labor disputes that could potentially undermine the war effort. He then blocked pending anti-strike legislation and fortified his domestic political coalition. Without the advent of war, scholars generally recognize that none of this would have been possible.[23]

AN EMERGENT LABOR PROBLEM

Late in Roosevelt's second term of office, strikes had begun to pose a significant political dilemma for the president. On the one hand, labor unrest threatened Roosevelt's efforts to mobilize the nation's economy in support of the ongoing war in Europe. Following the German occupation of Paris, Roosevelt pushed for legislation to expand the size of the U.S. navy and to increase the supply of aircraft and destroyers to Britain.[24] To meet these goals, the speed and volume of industrial production would have to increase dramatically. Labor unions, however, stood in the way. Sensing the opportunity to extract greater concessions from management, unions threatened to strike, a possibility that significantly complicated the president's ability to pursue his broader defense goals.[25] But still, the president opposed the enactment of new restrictions on the rights of labor that were gaining traction among a conservative coalition of legislators.[26] The president worried that anti-strike legislation would only increase the incidence of strikes and weaken domestic production. Moreover, for both political and policy reasons, the president opposed the repeal of his New Deal labor reforms. In the lead-up to the 1942 midterm elections, the president had no interest in alienating the core of his political base, yet he remained committed to his New Deal legislative achievements. Roosevelt therefore faced a delicate balancing act. He needed to reduce the frequency of labor

23. For debates about the centrality of World War II in the construction of federal labor policy, see Sparrow 1996; Workman 2000, 2002.

24. For a longer discussion of these efforts, see Morison 2002.

25. Brinkley 1995; Workman 2000.

26. For a comprehensive analysis of the anti-labor coalition formed between Republicans and southern Democrats, see Katznelson et al. 1993.

strikes that threatened to disrupt the domestic economy and rouse political support for anti-strike legislation. At the same time, he needed to curry the ongoing support of labor.

Throughout 1940 and 1941, Roosevelt attempted to deal with the labor issue through nonlegislative means. In May 1940, he established the National Defense Advisory Committee (NDAC), appointing Sidney Hillman as the head of its Labor Division. Hillman had played a prominent role in the founding of the Congress of Industrial Organizations (CIO) and had run the Amalgamated Clothing Workers of America. Not coincidentally, he also was an ardent supporter of Roosevelt.[27] Hillman's Labor Division initially demonstrated some success at resolving labor disputes, but its efforts were plagued throughout 1940 by divisions within the CIO. John L. Lewis, the leader of the United Mine Workers (UMW), and Phillip Murray, the head of the CIO, both openly criticized Hillman and his Labor Division. Lewis, in particular, attempted to drive a wedge between labor and the president. When he failed to do so in December 1940, Lewis gave up the presidency of the CIO, but continued to attack Hillman as a lackey of the administration.

In late 1940, Hillman's health waned, and with it his ability to control the strike problem. By February 1941, monthly strikes had more than doubled, walkouts were on the rise, and more than 100,000 defense workers had walked off the job. Additionally, in just the previous month the number of man-days of idleness rose from 625,000 to 1,000,000.[28] Sensing NDAC's incapacity, conservative legislators began to attack the unions, introducing a number of legislative actions in the House and Senate. Supporters of the administration were able to block these bills by tying them up in committee, but political pressure for action mounted. The National Association of Manufacturers (NAM) with the support of anti-labor legislators, publicly called for stricter anti-strike legislation, including the repeal of the Wagner Act.[29] As strikes proliferated, so did the sense of national crisis. To head off unfavorable legislative action, Roosevelt launched new initiatives expressly designed to reduce strikes in the defense sector.

In early 1941, Roosevelt issued an executive order creating the National Defense Mediation Board (NDMB). The NDMB quickly racked up a

27. Fraser 1991; Josephson 1952.
28. "President Opposes New Strike Curbs," *New York Times,* April 2, 1941, 1.
29. See, for example, NAM statements recorded in Henry N. Doriss, "Congress Attitude on Strikes Cools," *New York Times,* April 2, 1941, 16; "President Opposes New Strike Curbs," *New York Times,* April 2, 1941, 1.

series of successes. Less than two weeks after the NDMB's creation, its chairman announced the resolution of one of the longest and most visible defense sector strikes between the Allis-Chalmers Manufacturing Company and the United Automobile Workers (UAW), and the CIO. After a seventy-five-day strike, NDMB mediators managed to negotiate an agreement in just over two days.[30] At the same time, the NDMB actively helped settle two other major defense industry strikes involving more than 500,000 men. Shortly thereafter, the Ford Motor Company's shutdown, which affected more than 100,000 workers, ended with Henry Ford acquiescing to virtually all UAW demands.[31]

In the aftermath of the NDMB's early successes, legislators' expressed vitriol against the strikes began to cool. In more than three days of mid-April hearings, senior government officials testified before the House Military Affairs Committee about the effectiveness of the NDMB. They cited the success of the NDMB in ending major strikes and preventing new walkouts. Labor Secretary Perkins also argued that she anticipated the termination of existing stoppages. Accordingly, she announced that the administration would not call for any changes to existing labor laws.[32]

To be sure, some anti-labor legislators continued to press their case for anti-strike legislation. Senator Greg Ball (R-MN) and Representative Carl Vinson (D-GA) both introduced bills that would institute a mandatory thirty-day "cooling off period" before a strike and give statutory authority to the NDMB. But after the Vinson bill passed the House Naval Affairs Committee, Secretary of War Henry Stimson sent a letter to the Senate Labor Committee declaring his opposition to the legislation as long as "other methods of preventing interruption prove effective."[33] By late April, the NDMB had succeeded in ending virtually all the major defense strikes, and the public outcry for action died down considerably. For the time being, members of the House and Senate shifted their priorities to other matters.[34]

30. W. H. Lawrence, "Agreement to Long Allis Strike Won by Mediators," *New York Times,* April 7, 1941, 1.

31. Louis Starks, "Hope of Ford Peace Told by Mediators," *New York Times,* April 6, 1941, 37; Louis Starks, "Ford Agents Meet Murray on Strike," *New York Times,* April 9, 1941, 1.

32. Doriss, "Congress Attitude."

33. "Stimson Opposes Anti-Strike Bill," *New York Times,* April 21, 1941, 3.

34. For a comprehensive account of NDMB's successes during this period, see Workman 2000, 247–249.

LABOR STRIFE AT THE PRECIPICE OF WAR

The NDMB enjoyed unimpeded success throughout the summer of 1941. Even the small number of ardent Communists in the CIO began to express solidarity with the government after the German invasion of the Soviet Union on June 22, 1941.[35] By July, virtually all unionists and labor leaders accepted the necessity of cooperating with the NDMB in support of the war effort.

By late fall, however, the fragile labor–management peace began to fracture. Union leaders demanded "closed" or "union" shops in which employment was contingent upon active union membership. Labor leaders insisted that closed shops merely constituted an issue of fairness: they prevented free-riding on union activities who bore the brunt of political and economic opposition. By forcing at least some workers to join unions against their will, however, closed shops raised altogether new issues of fairness, which broad segments of the American public rejected.[36] Empowering labor unions in their fight for recognition from management was one thing. Putting the political interests of unions above the free and independent choices of workers, though, was quite another.

The confrontation over closed shops came to a head in November 1941 when John L. Lewis demanded the extension of the UMW closed shop contract to all the "captive mines" that were owned by major steel companies. Although the captive mines constituted an integral component of the nation's steel production capacities, members of the NDMB worried about the precedent that would be created by granting closed shop rules on such a high-profile case. Instead, the NDMB offered Lewis a maintenance-of-membership plan, under which employees were required to join the union but only had to pay dues so long as union leaders succeeded in negotiating contracts with management. Viewing the captive mines dispute as an opportunity to press for union security throughout the entire steel sector, Lewis balked.[37] Despite three personal appeals by the president, Lewis continued to press the issue and eventually called for walkouts.[38]

Following two strikes in the steel mines, on November 3, 1941, the NDMB ruled against Lewis and the UMW. Several days later, Roosevelt

35. Lichtenstein 1977.
36. "The President Speaks Out," *New York Times,* November 15, 1941, 16.
37. Lichtenstein 1977, 220–21. For a more complete discussion of Lewis' motives and strategy, see Dubofsky and van Tine 1977.
38. See, for example, Roosevelt's "Letter to John L. Lewis on the Captive Coal Mines Strike," on October 26, 1941, http://www.presidency.ucsb.edu/ws/?pid=16028.

backed the board's decision, claiming, "I tell you frankly that the government of the United States will not offer, nor will Congress pass legislation ordering a so-called closed shop."[39] On this policy dispute, the public clearly stood behind their president. In a Gallup poll from the first week of November, 60 percent of respondents opposed the coal walkout, and only 8 percent lent their support. Meanwhile, no less than 70 percent of respondents expressed an unfavorable opinion of John Lewis.[40]

Even in the face of such popular dissension, the UMW was not forced to relinquish its prior claims. Quite the contrary: its financial reserves, its critical role in the CIO, and the sheer size of its membership rolls all made the UMW one of the most powerful unions in the country. When the NDMB rejected Lewis's demands, therefore, it provoked the withdrawal of all CIO representatives from the NDMB, which threatened the board's ability to settle disputes and prevent strikes. Additionally, the decision prompted Lewis to call for another walkout in the coal mines. Faced with large-scale closures and a fight with the entire CIO, Roosevelt backed down. Rather than seize control over the mines, the president created a special arbitration board that was nearly guaranteed to grant the UMW the closed shop in the captive mines. Though Lewis ended the strike on November 22, the president's actions destroyed the credibility of the NDMB as an effective institution. As the *New York Times* editorialized on November 25, "it has been demonstrated that if a labor union leader does not like the board's decision the Administration will get him another board."[41]

Faced with both the refusal of the CIO to return to the NDMB and the public outrage over the closed shop issue, Congress reentered the fray. At the time, two major legislative proposals were circulating in Congress. The first was the Vinson bill, which had passed the House Naval Affairs Committee earlier in the year and provided for a mandatory thirty-day cooling off period before defense strikes. Representative Howard Smith (D-VA) introduced the second, more draconian proposal. Smith's plan would ban mass picketing, maintain open shop rules where they existed, protect workers against violence, and permit defense strikes only with the

39. As quoted in Bernstein 1969, 763–764.

40. George Gallup, "60% Are Opposed to Coal Walkout," *New York Times,* November 20, 1941, 33. For a longer discussion of public opinion on New Deal labor policy, see Schickler 2009.

41. Editorial. *New York Times,* November 30, 1941.

support of a majority of a plant's employees.[42] Neither of these proposals, however, satisfied Roosevelt, who resisted any efforts to restrict his ability to oversee labor–management relations. The president therefore met with leaders of the Labor Committee to draft a compromise bill that would provide for a sixty-day cooling off period, mediation, and the explicit authority for the president to seize plants whenever he deemed necessary.[43]

In late November 1941, Congress appeared poised to enact the Labor Committee bill favored by Roosevelt. According to Majority Leader John McCormack (D-MA), the Democratic "party was unified and had the votes to pass the Labor Committee bill."[44] But last-minute lobbying efforts by John Lewis and the CIO backfired badly. Quite suddenly, public opinion (and with it congressional sentiment) turned drastically against labor, scuttling the coalition behind the Labor Committee bill. In its place, the House, on December 3, 1941, overwhelmingly passed the harsher Smith Act along with two additional amendments: one that forbade the importation of pickets into a strike zone and another that banned from union rolls "any officials or organizers who had committed a crime of moral turpitude or who are members of the Communist party or a Nazi bund."[45]

When asked what had changed the situation so quickly, Representative Robert Ramspeck (D-GA) pinned the blame squarely on the unions. Ramspeck, who had introduced the administration's bill in the Labor Committee, pointed to "John L. Lewis. He is responsible, because of his arrogance."[46] Though some union members recognized the failure of their lobbying campaign, they could not reverse course. After the House passed the revised Smith bill, the Senate was expected to follow suit and pass equivalent legislation. Although several senior labor policy advisers recommended that he assemble a national conference on labor–management relations, Roosevelt rejected the idea on the grounds that the chasm between labor and management had grown too great.[47] On December 6, 1941, the president's labor policy lay in ruins.

42. Frederick R. Barkeley, "Labor Situation Holds up House," *New York Times,* November 17, 1941, 10.

43. Ibid.

44. "House Strike Bill Expected to Pass." *New York Times,* November 30, 1941, 53.

45. Henry N. Dorriss, "A Sweeping Bill," *New York Times,* December 4, 1941, 1.

46. Ibid.

47. William H. Davis, Sidney Hillman, and Labor Secretary Frances Perkins all encouraged the president to pursue a conference before Pearl Harbor; nevertheless, Roosevelt

PEARL HARBOR AND THE REASSERTION
OF PRESIDENTIAL CONTROL

Pearl Harbor reinvigorated the president's ability to shape labor policy. Within days, John L. Lewis and virtually every other important labor leader pledged that they would not strike for the duration of the war.[48] With the onset of war, neither the AFL nor the CIO wanted to appear in opposition to the federal government and especially not the commander in chief.[49] Sensing opportunity, on December 10, Roosevelt called for the very conference he had repudiated just weeks earlier. Gathering senior labor and industry spokesmen, the president announced his intention to develop a framework for creating a replacement to the NDMB, which would be charged with overseeing labor–management disputes during the war.

In many ways, however, securing the support of labor was the least of Roosevelt's problems. Indeed, it is not at all clear that the outbreak of war was even needed to garner labor's cooperation. The passage of the Smith Act in the House had already convinced the CIO to reconsider its aggressive posture vis-à-vis the president. At the time, it was business and industry leaders who were least disposed to working with the administration. Anticipating the enactment of favorable legislation, groups like the National Association of Manufacturers preferred to let the process play out on Capitol Hill. Even in the days after the attacks on Pearl Harbor, pro-business leaders continued to publicly promote anti-strike legislation.[50]

Undeterred, the president continued to press his case. When announcing the conference, Roosevelt confidently stated that "it is not expected that there will be any hesitation on the part of either labor or industry."[51] The president also moved quickly to block Senate action on the Smith Act. He

---

cited the willingness of Phillip Murray of the CIO to back John H. Lewis, making negotiations between business and labor impossible (Workman 2000, 250).

48. For a discussion of the effect of the war on labor leaders, see Lichtenstein 1977, 221. For an example of changes in labor leaders' rhetoric and demands, compare Philip Murray's comments in W.H. Lawrence, "War Spurs Bill to Curb Strikes," *New York Times,* December 7, 1941, 30, to his statement in W.H. Lawrence, "President Moves for Labor Peace," *New York Times,* December 11, 1941, 34.

49. Workman 2000, 251.

50. Lawrence, "President Moves for Labor Peace." New York Times, December 11, 1941, 34; Even after the attack on Pearl Harbor, the NAM released a statement arguing that "the President's labor-industry conference would delay a real solution of the labor problem by legislation."

51. As quoted in Workman 2000, 251.

focused his initial appeals on Elbert Thomas (D-UT), the Senate Education and Labor Committee chairman who had previously promised a vote on pending anti-strike bills within the week. The administration encouraged Thomas to delay hearings and votes on the Smith bill until after the conference. On December 11, Thomas relented, stating, "I can't imagine anyone interfering with the President's scheme."[52] Thomas further agreed to delay hearings on the Smith bill until the conclusion of the conference.

The conference convened on December 17. The agenda, set by the president, solicited participants' endorsement of three broad principles: (1) the ban of strikes or lockouts in defense industries during the war, (2) greater speed in arms production with extended operating hours for all factories, and (3) the establishment of a governmental arbitration board that would settle all labor–management disputes.[53] Both sides agreed in principle to the no-strike and no-lockout provisions as well as the creation of a newly empowered arbitration board. Deliberations, however, quickly stalled over the closed shop issue. Industry leaders hoped to delegate the issue to Congress, which had already demonstrated a propensity to reduce the rights of labor. Labor leaders, by contrast, rightly feared that Congress would ban the closed shop altogether. When talks deadlocked over the issue, Roosevelt declared the conference over. He then issued a public statement noting his acceptance of the conferees' recommendation to create a dispute arbitration board and the conferees' pledge to refrain from strikes and lockouts for the duration of the war.[54]

In early January, Roosevelt created the National War Labor Board (NWLB) by executive order. Although the NWLB retained the basic tripartite structure of the NDMB, its formal powers exceeded those of the NDMB. Whereas the NDMB formally relied on voluntary mediation efforts, the NWLB could mandate binding arbitration. Critically, the NWLB also retained jurisdiction over the union security issue.[55] Although several conservative senators wanted to move forward with legislation, Senator Thomas used his powers as Education and Labor Committee chairman to block the Smith anti-strike bill and other pending legislation. The committee never held a vote on the Smith bill. In fact, at no point during the war

52. Lawrence, "President Moves for Labor Peace." See also Bernstein 1969, 773–75.
53. Ibid.
54. "Official Text of President's Plea for Management Labor Accord," *New York Times,* December 18, 1941, 14.
55. For detailed accounts of the powers and responsibilities of the NWLB, see Livernash 1961 and Seidman 1953.

did the committee even hold hearings on the bill or on the issue of labor strikes.[56] While tempering the demands of labor, the president simultaneously quashed, once and for all, congressional efforts to enact strict antistrike legislation.

Although Roosevelt appeared on the brink of legislative defeat in early December 1941, the attack on Pearl Harbor provided him with an opportunity to reassert his primacy over labor policy. He unilaterally created the NWLB, blocked Senate consideration that just weeks earlier seemed a lock on passage, and strengthened his domestic political coalition, all in the name of national defense. The fallout of these actions, moreover, would be felt for years to come. Almost all labor historians agree that Roosevelt's policy stance significantly enhanced his control over labor–management relations throughout the war. Moreover, these historians concede that the creation of the NWLB and the failure of Congress to enact restrictive legislation established the foundations for union expansion well after the war ended.

LESSONS

The labor–management episode reveals three related themes that are central to this book. First, and most obviously, the outbreak of war significantly enhanced the president's bargaining leverage in ongoing legislative deliberations. Relegated to the peripheries of congressional debates over the Smith bill on December 3, 1941, the president was thrust back into the center on December 7. With the outbreak of war, members of Congress did not want to appear out of step with the president's policy agenda. In part, this was because members feared publicly opposing a president whose job approval ratings had just surged. More to the point, members did not want to do anything that might complicate the president's efforts to meet the security threat that had finally reached the nation's shores.

This leads to the second point: the president's private information about the nature of the foreign threat and the policies that were required to meet it enhanced his ability to advance his policy agenda. The president could credibly claim to possess a better understanding of the wartime implications of labor–management policy. This superior knowledge of how policy would map into outcomes during a period of war persuaded

56. "Senate Block Insists on Strike Ban Law," *New York Times,* December 24, 1941; "Fate of the Smith Bill," *New York Times,* March 3, 1942, 22; "Strikes Nil, No Law Needed Now, War Production Chiefs Testify," *New York Times,* March 19, 1942, 18.

at least some key members of Congress to switch positions and lend the president their support.

Third, and finally, the president's wartime success came not through the enactment of new legislation that select members of Congress had previously foiled, but instead through the derailment of legislative provisions that the president himself opposed. When we think about the impact of war on presidential power, we must recognize not only the propensity of members of Congress to promptly consider and vote in favor of presidential initiatives but also their decision to delay or vote against bills that the president opposes. In this instance, Congress got out of the business of labor–management relations altogether, abandoning a bill that seemed destined to pass just days earlier and permitting the president to forge onward by exercising his own unilateral powers.

6.3 *Roosevelt and All the Resplendence of a Wartime Presidency*

Roosevelt's wartime achievements did not end with the NWLB. Over the course of the war, Roosevelt exerted extraordinary influence over the domestic polity—so much so, in fact, that opponents of the president complained of the emergence of a dictatorship within their midst. The charge could not be dismissed as mere hyperbole. As Clinton Rossiter wrote in 1948, "Future historians will record that in the course of the second World War the Presidency of the United States became the most powerful and distinguished constitutional office the world has ever known."[57]

Assuming the presidency in the depths of economic depression and leaving it at the height of a war that would claim the lives of nearly 70 million people, Franklin Roosevelt did not offer a grand view of the office that he would do so much to transform. During his time in office, the president preferred to act, challenge the adjoining branches of government to counter, adjust when necessary, and then act again. In so doing, Roosevelt managed to profoundly alter the executive branch, plunging headlong into policy domains that had never before been the province of government action, displacing pleas for limited government by classical liberals with a solemn commitment to ensure the welfare of average citizens, and, some argue, ushering in the modern era of the American presidency. It is difficult to

---

57. Rossiter 2005 [1948], 266.

conceive of Roosevelt accomplishing nearly so much without the great crises that stood as bookends to his presidency.

Abroad, the killing of soldiers and the destruction of territory that had characterized the world's first modern war was being taken to altogether new heights in its second. Six times as many Americans fought overseas in World War II as had in World War I, and nearly four times as many American soldiers died. At home, Wilson's forays into the domestic economy had established the precedent for Roosevelt's reconstitution of the relationship between the state and private industry. In his war mobilization effort, Roosevelt picked up where Wilson left off, coaxing and (when necessary) ordering American industry to produce at levels that few—including the Axis powers of Europe and Asia—thought possible.

ACTION, ACTION, ACTION

Throughout World War II, the president independently seized, Congress conferred,[58] and the courts willingly approved[59] a wide range of emergency powers to do such things as set prices and wages; regulate labor–management relations; require workers in "non-deferrable" employment to be transferred into either the armed forces or jobs deemed essential to the war effort; impose martial law on an entire state (Hawaii); force new workers into unions in any place of employment already covered by a union contract; requisition private property; mandate the length of a work week; demand under threat of criminal punishment that specific businesses meet orders placed by the government; suspend or amend regulations governing radio communications; ration food, tires, gasoline, and other scarce commodities; oversee the quality and quantity of goods produced by different industries; and, where necessary, assume primary control over the production of plants deemed central to the war effort. During Roosevelt's wartime presidency, the line between public and private spheres of life did not merely blur. It vanished.[60]

Roosevelt launched a massive public relations campaign designed to rally public support for the war. By support, the administration meant a great deal more than a willingness to affirm the president's decision to wage war

58. Particularly important legislative delegations of power to the president during World War II include the Price Control Act of 1942 and the War Labor Disputes Act of 1943. For an accounting of prior legislation, much of which was enacted either during World War I or the Great Depression, see Koenig 1944, 67–96.

59. See, for example, *Yakus v. United States,* 321 U.S. 414 (1944).

60. For detailed treatment of Roosevelt's actions at home during World War II, see Goodwin 1995; Harris et al. 1984; Kennedy 2001; Polenberg 1972; Vatter 1985.

abroad. Once again, all things parochial were castigated while all things national were exalted. Citizens were meant to deny their private interests in the service of a larger public good, to suppress their individual desires, habits, and routines for the sake of the war effort. In a very real sense, the war was being waged at home just as much as it was on the battlefronts in Europe, Africa, and the Pacific. Both through the deliberate design of the federal government and the independent sentiment of the larger public, a genuine sense of war-mindedness took hold—one that enlisted every citizen in an epic struggle against fascism, and one that posited the U.S. soldier as the benchmark for measuring sacrifice. Citizens were asked to "think of themselves as personally connected to the battlefront and to imagine the repercussions of their every action for the combat soldier."[61] Hence, as one wartime propaganda poster intoned, housewives must "buy wisely, cook carefully, store carefully, and use leftovers" because "where our men are fighting, our food is fighting." With a ghoulish image of the Third Reich in the background and a brawny arm wielding a wrench in the foreground, another poster implores, "Stop the monster that stops at nothing. PRODUCE to the limit! This is your war!"

Like Wilson, Roosevelt relied upon a small army of wartime administrative agencies to realize his policy agenda at home. Some, such as the War Production Board, were expressly modeled after World War I administrative agencies, in this case the War Industries Board. Others, such as the Office of Emergency Management, were created via some blend of congressional and presidential actions during the lead-up to the U.S. entry into the war. But most—including the Office of Price Administration, the National War Labor Board, the National Housing Agency, the Board of Economic Warfare, the War Manpower Commission, the Office of Defense Transportation, the Office of Economic Stabilization (which subsequently became the Office of War Mobilization), and the Office of Censorship, to name but a few—came into being after Pearl Harbor. Most of these agencies, moreover, were born not from congressional statutes but from executive orders and other unilateral directives that enabled the wartime president to extend the reach of the federal government into just about every facet of American life.

Important elements of the domestic war mobilization effort were run through the military itself. Military purchasing bureaus issued hundreds of billions of dollars worth of contracts for all kinds of supplies, from raw

61. Sparrow 2011, 12.

steel and aluminum to aircraft and tanks. Consequently, they left a deep and lasting impression upon the nation's industrial machinery, both in the kinds of products rolling down assembly lines and in the fortunes of specific corporations. The sheer size of these military orders had an immediate impact on the living standards of average civilians. "By one estimate," notes David Kennedy, "fulfilling all the army and navy orders would cut civilian consumption to 60 percent of its level in 1932, the darkest year of the Depression."[62]

Still, overall government war spending had a fantastically positive effect on the consumption patterns of average citizens. During the war, Kennedy continues:

> most Americans never had it so good. They started half a million new businesses. They went to movies and restaurants with unhabitual frequency. They bought books, recordings, cosmetics, pharmaceuticals, jewelry, and liquor in record volumes. Racing fans wagered two and a half times more on the horses in 1944 than they had in 1940.[63]

Government spending during World War II, some economic historians argue,[64] ultimately amounted to a far greater stimulus to the domestic economy than the relatively fledgling, piecemeal efforts of the New Deal. Rather than the military sector displacing the civilian sector during World War II, both abounded in tandem.

As had World War I, World War II unleashed a flurry of presidential orders that curbed First Amendment protections of speech and assembly. The Office of Censorship, established under an executive order issued less than two weeks after the bombing of Pearl Harbor, monitored communications with foreign states. The same office also established codes of conduct for domestic newspapers and radio outlets. The Office of War Information assumed the responsibilities of World War I's Committee on Public Information, that of publicizing and propagandizing the war at home.[65]

Other presidential orders reshaped relationships between different ethnic groups and their government. Most famously, Roosevelt in the months after Pearl Harbor approved orders to intern Japanese Americans living on the West Coast—a decision that probably represents the greatest stain on his presidency. Under the auspices of the War Relocation Authority,

62. Kennedy 2001, 627–628.
63. Ibid., 646.
64. See, for example, Bernstein 1987; Stein 1984; Vatter 1985; Vernon 1994.
65. See Stone 2004, 235–307.

the Roosevelt administration forcibly detained and relocated over 100,000 Japanese descendants, resident aliens and citizens alike.[66] The vast majority of these individuals spent years in war relocation camps in western and mountain states. The military exclusion order that justified their relocation remained in place for almost the entire duration of the war. When they were finally released, each internee was given $25 and a train ticket to their former hometown.

Though Japanese Americans absorbed hard blows during World War II, other racial and ethnic groups, in particular African Americans, witnessed slight advancements. Under pressure from the National Association for the Advancement of Colored People (NAACP) and the Urban League, which repeatedly threatened to march on Washington, D.C., Roosevelt issued a series of directives that addressed concerns about racial discrimination in the military. Under executive order 8802, a newly established Fair Employment Practices Committee (FEPC) retained modest powers to investigate and, where appropriate, remediate employment discrimination in the defense industries.[67] As originally constituted, the agency had modest resources to investigate discrimination claims, operated without clear standards of discrimination, and lacked direct enforcement powers. Under continued pressure from civil rights groups, however, Roosevelt issued subsequent orders that increased the number of FEPC committee members and salaries, required that all government contracts (not just defense contracts) include nondiscrimination clauses, and made the agency directly beholden to the president.

Though substantively austere, Roosevelt's actions symbolically were spectacular. Most immediately, they demonstrated the gains to be had from organized political protest. Roosevelt's executive orders galvanized the civil rights movement, sparking massive growth in the NAACP's membership and the establishment of the Committee of Racial Equality. Over the longer term, Roosevelt's orders established important precedent for the federal government's recommitment to addressing the plight of African Americans, which paved the way for the desegregation of the military and, more distantly, the 1964 and 1965 Civil Rights Acts.

Whether in the service of or to the detriment of civil liberties and rights, Roosevelt's wartime record was very much the equal of Wilson. Each of

66. For a comprehensive treatment of this subject, see Robinson 2001.
67. For more specifics on Roosevelt's wartime actions on civil rights, see Morgan 1970 and Nathan 1969.

these presidents used his war not merely as a pretext for either advancing or derogating civil rights and civil liberties; rather, the exigencies of war served as their primary justification. Concerns about the loyalties of Japanese Americans and imminent stateside attacks by their native country served as the first—and only—rationale for rounding up and imprisoning tens of thousands of residents who had done nothing at all against either the U.S. government or its peoples. Rising demand for African American labor in both domestic industries and the military provided the impetus for A. Phillip Randolph's Urban League to threaten a march on Washington if certain demands were not met. Roosevelt ultimately met these demands not because of an abiding commitment to civil rights but because he feared the distraction of domestic protests during the war. The story of civil rights in the United States during the 1940s cannot be told without accounting for war.

WARTIME POWERS CLAIMED

How do the extraordinary actions taken during World War II—economic and social—speak to the longstanding relationship between war and presidential power? Or more narrowly, how do they figure into Roosevelt's thinking on the matter? Unlike Lincoln and Wilson, Roosevelt left us with no full confessional or treatise on the linkages between war and presidential power. However, in Roosevelt's day-to-day negotiations with Congress, we find numerous appeals to war—to the material challenges it posed and to the unique powers it supposedly confered upon presidents. Though his worldview was less well formulated than Wilson's, Roosevelt nonetheless supported the notion that foreign wars established a principled basis for presidential activism and concurrent judicial and congressional deference.

The political fallout of the Emergency Price Control Act provides a case in point. Enacted in early 1942, the Price Control Act created the Office of Price Administration (OPA), which was charged with setting prices and rents that it considered "generally fair and equitable" for the duration of World War II. Businesses that sold commodities in excess of the prices set by the OPA could be prosecuted in criminal court or sued in civil court. A special tribunal called the Emergency Court of Appeals was granted exclusive jurisdiction to hear challenges to OPA rulings.

Roosevelt supported legislative efforts to eliminate profiteering, hoarding, inflation, and other disruptive market conditions. But in the president's mind, the Price Control Act retained the seeds of its undoing. By allowing the OPA to set prices for only a portion of domestic commodities, the act kept the OPA from adequately controlling any prices. From the president's vantage point, a price control regime that exempted such important food items as butter, cheese, and other dairy products, as the Price Control Act did, was doomed to failure.

On September 7, 1942, Roosevelt spelled out his objections and gave Congress three weeks to repeal all the act's offending provisions limiting the president's ability to establish price ceilings on farm products.[68] "If Congress should fail to act, and act adequately," Roosevelt warned, "I shall accept the responsibility and I will act." With that, Roosevelt stipulated his intention to disregard a statute he had signed into law earlier that year, which he now had the constitutional responsibility to faithfully execute.

Not surprisingly, the president's power grab raised alarm bells among members of Congress, even among copartisans. Senator Prentice Brown (D-MI), while endorsing the president's policy objective, demurred on his intended legislative method: "I think the President has ample authority to control wages, but I am doubtful about the extent of his authority to set aside a provision of an act of Congress."[69] Another traditional Senate ally, George Norris (I-NE), expressed the hope that the president "would not make a mistake like that—it would raise hell in Congress, and it would give those who have been crying "dictatorship" all of these years another chance to renew their attacks."[70] Senator Pat McCarran (D-NV) openly worried about the consequences of Roosevelt's threats on the Congress's perceived autonomy: "If the president can set aside or freeze the action of Congress, then the legislative branch of our democracy is on the way out. If he can set aside laws the Congress passes, then there is no need for Congress."[71]

Such arguments, however, held little sway with the president, for whom the exigencies of war established a clear and principled basis for usurping congressional powers. After offering vague references to the Constitution and unspecified statutes, the president in his speech insisted that he retained the power "to take measures necessary to avert a disaster which would interfere with the winning of the war." It mattered little that this "disaster" was purely domestic in nature; the front lines of the war extended

68. The full text of this speech, which is quoted rather extensively below, is available in *Congressional Record—House,* 1942, 1052–1055.
69. Ben Gilbert, "Wage, Price Sacrifices Life Ahead, Says Roosevelt," *Washington Post,* September 6 1942, 6.
70. "Norris Condemns Price-Decree Talk; Action by President to Override Act Would Anger Congress, Says Nebraskan," *New York Times,* September 7, 1942, 8.
71. Ibid.

to the home front. "The prevention of a spiraling domestic economy is a vital part of the winning of the war itself." As part of winning the war, the president insisted, he retained the ultimate "responsibility to the people of this country to see to it that the war effort is no longer imperiled by threat of economic chaos." With this declaration, Roosevelt shattered all distinctions between a president's well-regarded authority to reroute troops from one battlefield to another and his more tenuous claims over the domestic economy. In war, Roosevelt insisted, these powers are one and the same, falling with equal ease under the president's authority as commander in chief.

The dictates of modern warfare, wherein success on the battlefront depended as much on the production of food stocks and machinery as on the valor of men, delivered a booster shot to the commander in chief clause.[72] As the president explained:

> This total war, with our fighting fronts all over the world, makes the use of Executive power far more essential than in any previous war. . . . We are fighting a war of survival. Nothing can yield to the over-all necessity of winning this war, and the winning of the war will be imperiled by a runaway domestic economy.

Managing the war effort now meant managing the home front. Distinctions between military and social or economic policy were a thing of the past.[73] Being crucial elements of the war effort itself, daily tasks at home suddenly fell squarely within the purview of presidential control.

---

72. In his survey of events leading up to the U.S. entry into World War II, Louis Koenig elaborated on this argument. Penned at the height of the war, his observations are worth quoting at length: "Success in the construction of an efficient military machine requires an ambitious organization of the home front. The machine is an omnivorous consumer of economic materials. With these it must constantly be fed. The feedings must be prompt and in ample measure. It is essential, then, that the President, if he is to meet his responsibilities as Commander in Chief, have at his service the power to arrange the economy according to a plan by which it will satisfy military needs. Without that power, his military authority would be weakened by a serious lack of control over the sources of supply" (Koenig 1944, 67).

73. Or as Roosevelt noted in his second wartime fireside chat, just after submitting to Congress a draft of what would become the Price Control Act, the current war offered "one front and one battle where everyone in the United States—every man, woman and child—is in action . . . That front is right here at home, in our daily tasks." Radio address by FDR, April 28, 1942. Or as Senator La Follette put it, "the role of Congress in time of war is a difficult one. Sweeping powers must of necessity be concentrated in the hands of the Commander in Chief so that he may direct with dispatch and decision the striking power of the nation. In total war the home front is an integral part of the fighting front." See Robert M. La Follette Jr., "A Senator Looks at Congress," *Atlantic Monthly,* 172, no. 1, July 1943, 92.

Presidential powers over the domestic economy secured in war must necessarily lapse in peace. As Roosevelt attempted to make clear, the authority he claimed to annul objectionable domestic legislation applied only for the duration of war. In no way did he intend to establish precedent for future peacetime presidents to annul provisions of laws with which they disagreed and thereby make a mockery of the constitution's "take care" clause. "I will use my powers with the full sense of responsibility to the Constitution and to my country," Roosevelt insisted. "I shall not hesitate to use every power vested in me to accomplish the defeat of our enemies in any part of the world where our own safety demands such defeat . . . [But] when the war is won, the powers under which I act will automatically revert to the people of the United States—to whom those powers belong." Roosevelt never explained why such powers should revert to the people, who never exercised them in the first place,[74] but no matter, for his point is clear. The president sought to assuage concerns of an emerging dictatorship, insisting that with the war's cessation, powers of nullification would no long reside within the president's grasp. Presidential power must expand in war, but so too must it contract in peace.

We cannot know whether Roosevelt would have followed through on his threat to unilaterally annul the objectionable provisions of the Price Control Act. Within a month, Congress delegated the needed authority for the president, with Executive Order 9250, to suspend the restrictions on farm price ceilings. That he would claim the authority at all is evidence enough of the president's expansive views of his war powers. As Senator Jacob Javits, a great proponent of the 1973 War Powers Resolution, would later write, "Roosevelt's assertion could be easily read as a call for a new set of power relationships that would bypass Congress altogether and establish a government based on the connection between President and people. We would, under such terms, live in an elective monarchy."[75] Neither as cautious as Lincoln nor as thoughtful as Wilson, Roosevelt emphatically asserted powers during war that would have made Madison shudder.

LESSONS

At every turn, World War II reshaped the terms by which citizens and politicians evaluated the merits of policy. As in World War I, national

74. The notion that presidential power derives from the people, however, has deep roots in Progressive thinking. As Henry Jones Ford puts it, the president is "the elect of the people, the organ of the will of the nation" (1898, 214).

75. Javits 1973, 231–232.

policy considerations displaced local ones, with virtually every domain of public and private life becoming tied to the massive war effort. And as the Policy Priority Model predicts, this shift played to the president's benefit. Though he certainly suffered his share of defeats, and though not all policies perfectly reflected his preferences, Roosevelt managed to exercise a measure of influence in war that had eluded him in peace. This newfound influence even extended into domains of public policy that previously had been understood as exclusively domestic in nature.

6.4 *The Immigration Provisions of the USA PATRIOT Act*

The 9/11 attacks left the nation, public and government reeling. The stock markets shut down, rumors churned about additional terrorist attacks, and every commercial aircraft stood grounded. Makeshift memorials popped up on city streets and flag sales skyrocketed as the country mourned its dead.

Action clearly was needed, and fast. So just forty-five days after the terrorist attacks, Congress enacted the Uniting and Strengthening America by Providing Appropriate Tools Required to Intercept and Obstruct Terrorism Act of 2001 (the USA PATRIOT Act, more commonly known as the Patriot Act), the single most important antiterrorism bill in decades. The act substantially strengthened the federal government's intelligence-gathering activities, surveillance procedures, and controls over money laundering. The act went farther still: a variety of its provisions simultaneously centralized power within the executive branch and advanced key components of President George W. Bush's domestic policy agenda—immigration policy and border security—in ways that extended well beyond terrorism prevention. By so doing, this landmark legislation has constituted yet another example of Congress yielding to a president when concerns shifted decidedly from the local to the national.[76]

BACKGROUND

Long before Bush assumed office in 2001, scholars and politicians recognized the need for new antiterrorism initiatives. The most recent legislation on counterterrorism—the Antiterrorism and Effective Death Penalty Act

---

76. David Mayhew (2005) identifies the USA PATRIOT Act as one of the fifteen most significant pieces of legislation passed in the 107th congressional session.

of 1996 and the Defense against Weapons of Mass Destruction Act of 1996—had increased funding for law enforcement targeting terrorism, increased penalties for terrorist crimes, and streamlined deportation of immigrant criminals. The remainder of America's antiterrorism legislation had been enacted during the Cold War era—the Foreign Intelligence Surveillance Act of 1978 (FISA), the Electronic Communications Privacy Act of 1986 (ECPA), the Money Laundering Control Act of 1986, and the Immigration and Nationality Act of 1952 (INA), among others. According to many, these laws did not amount to an effective response to evolving terrorist threats. In the late 1990s, noted one report, multiple blue-ribbon commissions highlighted the federal government's lack of preparedness for a possible terrorist attack. Attempts were made to improve antiterrorism policy, but, "largely due to civil liberties concerns, [Congress] did not pass legislation to correct the problems that would ultimately be addressed in the USA Patriot Act."[77]

Bush, meanwhile, retained a longstanding interest in large-scale immigration reform. This interest had less to do with terrorism deterrence, and more to do with the economic implications of illegal immigration. Among many proposed reforms, the president emphasized a need for increased border security, the establishment of a temporary worker program, an increase in Immigration and Naturalization Service (INS) funding, and aggressive deterrence programs such as Operation Hold the Line.[78] Consistent with these objectives, Bush proposed an additional $500 million to fund new personnel in the INS and the splitting of the INS into two agencies, allowing one to focus exclusively on border enforcement.

Despite his longstanding interest in immigration reform, Bush made little headway on the issue during the early months of his presidency. The high point of his efforts came on September 5, when he met with President Vicente Fox of Mexico and discussed possible solutions to the problem of illegal border crossings. At the time, though, no substantial reform efforts had made their way onto Congress's legislative agenda.

---

77. Ibid., 437.

78. The goal of Operation Hold the Line was "to prevent illegal immigration through deterrence. This called for more fencing, border patrol agents, technology, lighting and surveillance equipment to be implemented in four phases." See Andrew Becker, "Mexico: Crimes at the Border. Immigration Timeline," http://www.pbs.org/frontlineworld/stories/mexico704/history/timeline.html.

SEPTEMBER 11, 2001

Among the many effects on the domestic political arena, the 9/11 attacks provided an unique opening for both antiterrorism and immigration reform. By most accounts, these attacks "breathed new life into the proposals Congress had previously considered by turning abstract flaws in terrorism preparedness into stinging indictments of how the system was broken."[79] The civil liberties concerns, while still present for some, no longer stood in the way of new legislation, and members of Congress wholly embraced the need for decisive action.[80]

Consequently, the Patriot Act moved quickly through Congress. James Sensenbrenner (R-WI) introduced the bill on the House floor on October 23, 2001, and the president signed it into law a mere three days later. With the accelerated timetable, the bill bypassed both the committee process and floor debate. The bill received near unanimous support in both chambers, passing 357–66 in the House, and 98–1 in the Senate.[81] The obstacles that had previously held up antiterrorism reform had vanished, as the country focused its attention on the prerequisites of national security. Indeed, where the legislative branch had previously stood in the way of antiterrorism policy reform, the events of 9/11 led "Congress to act as a rubber stamp,"[82] approving nearly every request made by the Bush administration.

The Patriot Act addressed the concerns raised by the blue-ribbon commissions, revising and extending existing statutes governing computer fraud, foreign intelligence gathering, wiretapping, criminal procedure, and immigration. Many reforms that had previously been blocked for their civil liberties infringements became prominent features of the act. Title II drastically expanded the scope and availability of wiretapping and surveillance orders, removed many of the requirements about who could be targeted for surveillance, and diminished the warrant requirements associated with terrorism investigations. Title III sought to reduce the flow of laundered money to terrorist organizations by tightening record-keeping requirements for financial institutions and authorizing seizure of terrorist

79. McCarthy 2002, 437.
80. As quoted in Kranich 2009.
81. HR 3162: Uniting and Strengthening America by Providing Appropriate Tools Required to Intercept and Obstruct Terrorism (USA PATRIOT ACT) Act of 2001, 107th Congress, 2001–2002, http://www.govtrack.us/congress/bills/107/hr3162.
82. McCarthy 2002, 439.

assets.[83] Title VIII increased the criminal penalties for terrorism and redefined terrorism in considerably broader terms. Title IX streamlined communication between the Federal Bureau of Investigation (FBI) and the INS regarding foreign intelligence information, and centralized the process through the Director of Central Intelligence (DCI).

The terrorist attacks also opened the door for significant immigration reform. Title IV, in particular, addressed border security and immigration reform. Much of its content had clear connections to antiterrorism policy. For instance, one of the troubling revelations of the 9/11 attacks was that "hijackers had entered the United States on legal visas," which "showed a need for terrorist-related immigration reforms."[84] In response, Subtitle B, section 414 imposed a more rigorous screening process for obtaining visas and ensuring their integrity and validity. Additionally, and pursuant to the president's direction, section 411 retroactively amended the Immigration and Naturalization Act to prevent aliens who were part of any foreign organization or group that endorsed terrorist activity from entering the United States. Correspondingly, the definition of "terrorist activity" now incorporated the assistance of terrorist objectives by third parties.[85]

Consistent with the president's wishes, the act also reformed immigration policy to prevent illegal entry into the United States. The most notable of these reforms appeared in Subtitle A, which increased security along the nation's northern border. Section 401 authorized the attorney general "to waive any cap on personnel assigned to the Immigration and Naturalization Service on the Northern border." Section 402 authorized appropriations to "(1) triple the number of Border Patrol, Customs Service, and INS personnel (and support facilities) at points of entry and along the Northern border; and (2) INS and Customs for related border monitoring technology and equipment." The latter part of this section allotted an additional $50 million each to the INS and the U.S. Customs Service. Section 403 amended the INA "to require the Attorney General and the FBI to provide the Department of State and INS with access to specified criminal history extracts." Section 404 "eliminate[d] certain INS overtime restrictions."[86] These provisions sought to protect the country

83. Ted Bridis and David Rogers, "Agency Proposes Much Broader Antiterror Laws," *Wall Street Journal,* September 20, 2001, A3.
84. McCarthy 2002, 438.
85. See USA PATRIOT Act, http://www.govtrack.us/congress/bills/107/hr3162.
86. Ibid.

against potential terrorist threats, and by most accounts, they succeeded; by tightening border security, the country was better prepared to prevent terrorist attacks from individuals in the United States illegally or through use of fraudulent documents.

But the Bush administration had larger goals in mind. The primary immigration provisions of the Patriot Act included increased numbers of border troops and increased funding to border security more generally. Nothing in the Patriot Act required that the additional troops or funds be tied to antiterrorism efforts. Indeed, reports confirmed that "the Justice Department has used many of these antiterrorism powers to pursue defendants for crimes unrelated to terrorism, including drug violations, credit card fraud, and bank theft."[87] By increasing the number of INS agents and reducing the restrictions on deployment protocols along the northern border with Canada, sections 401 and 404 provided the raw manpower to install programs very similar to Operation Hold the Line, which Bush had long desired but had not been able to implement. By allocating essentially uncapped levels of funding to the INS for border control, the Patriot Act and subsequent legislation also increased border security funding from nearly $5 billion in 2001 to over $10 billion in 2007—making good on another of the president's campaign pledges.[88]

The Patriot Act also centralized power within the executive branch. By increasing INS funding and autonomy, the act ensured that future immigration policy would come from this agency rather than legislative initiative. Additionally, the attorney general gained considerable influence over not only antiterrorism policy but also immigration policy more generally. By giving the attorney general "unfettered discretion to determine who is a terrorist,"[89] the act vested extraordinary new powers over the detainment and detention of illegal immigrants, broadly construed.

LESSONS

By all accounts, the Patriot Act would not exist had the 9/11 terrorist attacks not occurred. It would be a mistake, however, to understand the act strictly in terms of 9/11. Congress did not draft this act anew in forty-five days. Rather, Congress, under the president's direction, stitched together provisions that had been circulating for years but had failed to find their

87. Kranich 2009.
88. U.S. Immigration Support, "Immigration Reform," n.d., http://www.usimmigrationsupport.org/immigration-reform.html.
89. McCarthy 2002, 449.

way into law. Substantively, these provisions concerned more than just antiterrorism policy; indeed, a nontrivial portion of them extended to immigration policy more generally.

For the act's critics, these facts constitute key points of evidence. As Michael McCarthy notes, detractors of the Patriot Act regularly point out that "many of the new powers granted in the Act extend beyond terrorism per se" and "that many provisions were drawn from other legislation proposed before September 11." As he puts it, "the government took advantage of a national crisis to abrogate powers long desired, but politically unacceptable in peacetime."[90] Similarly, in a committee hearing convened to discuss related matters on September 24, 2001, Representative Bob Barr (R-GA) stated that law enforcement urged swift passage as a means of "taking advantage of what is obviously an emergency situation to obtain authorities that it has been unable to obtain previously."[91]

We have nothing to say about whether the Patriot Act is good policy, as nothing about our theory or statistical evidence speaks to the quality of legislation enacted during peace or war. For good or ill, though, the act clearly reveals how a president can leverage security concerns to expand his power and advance his policy agenda. There are, of course, limits to this expansion. The act excluded important elements of Bush's immigration agenda, particularly the temporary worker program. And when Bush attempted in 2007 to build upon his earlier immigration achievements and create such a program, members of Congress sharply objected. For at least the short term, however, the 9/11 attacks constituted a clear boon to presidential power. In this instance, the relevant counterfactual was not a law that did not reflect the president's wishes; rather, it was no law at all.

6.5 *Final Remarks*

In these four cases, we see different elements of the Policy Priority Model at play. In two world wars, presidents wrested control from Congress and shaped policy in ways that better suited their interests. At Roosevelt's behest, Congress backed off a widely popular labor policy at the moment the nation plunged into war. In the aftermath of the 9/11 attacks, Bush

90. Ibid., 450–451.
91. Legislative Proposals Designed to Combat Terrorism: Hearing before the House Committee on the Judiciary, 107th Congress (September 24, 2001), 2001 WL 1143717, *Congressional Record.*

managed not only to alter the content of immigration policy but also to strengthen his control over its implementation.

For the most part, these cases comport with our main theoretical arguments and statistical findings. National security concerns find their way into a diverse assortment of domestic policy debates. Political actors do not merely debate the merits of policy, but the very terms by which policies are meant to be evaluated. Presidents and members of Congress expressly worry about the local and national implications of policy initiatives—and when national concerns prevail, so do presidents.

Of course, the nationalization of politics does not constitute the only source of these presidents' wartime policy achievements. In various ways, factors entirely outside of the Policy Priority Model—the personalities and policy agendas of the presidents in office, members' concerns about the electoral costs of challenging the president, specific facts about the military campaigns then under way—played their parts in these unfolding dramas. The Policy Priority Model certainly does not identify the exclusive reason for presidents' intermittent wartime success. But as the cases in this chapter make clear, the model does identify a crucially important one. Indeed, absent the extraordinary changes in the criteria by which legislators evaluated domestic policy, it is difficult to conceive of Wilson, Roosevelt, or Bush accomplishing as much as they did.

CHAPTER 7

Case Studies II: Challenges

Not every theoretical insight finds purchase in the real world. Nor does every data point lie directly on the regression line. In this chapter, therefore, we present examples of cases that do not fit quite so cleanly into our theory. We see presidents failing in war and succeeding in peace, and in at least one instance, the Policy Priority Model has almost nothing to say about such discordant events. So whereas the case studies in the previous chapter confirmed our primary argument and evidence, the case studies in this chapter, in one way or another, challenge them.

7.1 *The Federal Government Enters the Public Education Business*

At the end of World War II, the federal government resided at the periphery of education policy, which remained decidedly a state and local concern. Almost all federal education funds supported the construction, operation, and maintenance of school buildings for the children of federal employees who typically worked on military bases. The federal government did support several larger programs that provided assistance to veterans for higher education, most notably the Serviceman's Readjustment Act, commonly known as the G.I. Bill of Rights. At the time, though, the federal government did not support any significant programs for elementary or secondary education.[1]

Facing classroom shortages and inadequate local funding in the late 1940s, members of Congress began to push for greater federal involvement. During a 1948 floor debate on a House bill that would augment federal aid to education, Senator Lister Hill (D-AL) complained:

---

1. For a more detailed enumeration of the federal programs affecting education at the state and local levels of government, see Charles A. Quattlebaum, *Federal Educational Activities and Educational Issues before Congress,* House Document 423, 82nd Congress, 2nd Session, 1952.

Mr. President, bills similar to this one have been before the Senate for many years. . . . Year after year, the committee has held hearings. Year after year, the committee has spent weeks considering the bill, attempting to reconcile differences, attempting to wipe out inequities, attempting to bring forth the best possible bill to provide Federal aid, with the primary responsibility for education still continuing in the States.[2]

That particular bill died early in the legislation process, as would many successors. Indeed, ten years hence Senator Hill reiterated the same theme as he introduced his own federal aid legislation.[3] For a decade, federal education bills came before the House and Senate, and for a decade, every one of them failed. By intermittently linking federal involvement in education to predominant concerns about religion, communism, and segregation, opponents managed to keep the federal government out of public education.[4]

In 1958, however, the political ground would shift beneath members' feet. The Soviet launch of *Sputnik* on October 4, 1957, set off hysterics about Soviet supremacy in science and military technology. Imagine what it must have been like for citizens staring up into the night sky and seeing, for the first time, a satellite launched and maintained by the world's only other superpower and one, at that, that remained locked in nuclear escalation with the United States. A distant threat had found a way to watch us, to monitor our defenses, and to plot its aggressions. It was there for all to see, tracing the night sky. It stoked deep-seated fears that mere descriptions of Soviet designs had been unable to reach.

Sensing an opportunity, Eisenhower reframed the debate about education policy in terms of U.S. national security. Insisting that the nation meet this Soviet threat by building its own technical skills and human capital, Eisenhower managed to overcome the opposition within his own party that had killed every previous attempt to pass national education legislation.[5] With the National Defense Education Act, a four-year, $1 billion

2. *Congressional Record,* 1948, 80:2, 3290.
3. "Federal Education Aid Approved," *CQ Almanac 1958* (Washington, DC: Congressional Quarterly, 1959), http://library.cqpress.com/cqalmanac/cqal58-1341294.
4. For more, see Munger and Fenno (1962), who focus on the period from 1949 to 1961. Their analysis provides a more detailed discussion of the previous failures of various federal aid proposals introduced in the 1950s.
5. Major legislation involving federal education funding frequently has passed during wartime. Previous federal aid to education legislation tied to wars includes the Morrill Land Grant Act of 1862 (during the Civil War), the Smith Hughes Act (World War I), and the Lanham Act and G.I. Bill of Rights (World War II). For a more complete discussion, see "Federal Education Policy and the States, 1945–2004: A Brief Synopsis," originally published as part of the *States' Impact on Federal Education Policy Project* in

program focused on improving science education in the United States, the federal government finally secured its place in education policy. Absent the threat of war, it is difficult to see how this would have happened.

THE CASE FOR FEDERAL INVOLVEMENT IN PUBLIC EDUCATION

After World War II, a number of members of Congress recognized that only the federal government could address the challenges to public education posed by an aging infrastructure and demographic trends. During the Great Depression, birth rates had declined and capital for school construction had been limited. Subsequently, states and districts directed the few available resources toward more immediate projects supporting the war effort. As a result, very little school construction took place in the United States for almost two decades.[6] By 1945, existing school facilities were in poor repair and were wholly inadequate to meet demand.

With the postwar baby boom, the problem reached crisis levels. From 1945 to 1955, enrollments increased by almost 4 million elementary students per year, leaving local school districts scrambling for classroom space and, crucially, teachers.[7] During the war, private-sector jobs in manufacturing and industry had lured teachers away from public education, and after the war, teacher salaries were insufficient to lure them back.[8] Consequently, districts could not staff their schools, and teachers lacked serious training.

Many local school districts were ill equipped to address these challenges. Dependent on local property taxes for their revenues, districts could not expand their facilities or recruit an adequate number of quality teachers. Significant variation in states' support for students also contributed to large disparities in education levels among the states. Few states were getting ahead, and many were falling behind.[9] In the aftermath of

---

the New York State archives in January 2006, http://www.archives.nysed.gov/edpolicy /altformats/ed_background_overview_essay.pdf. See also Olson 1974.

6. Leonard 1956. For a more complete discussion of the classroom shortage and its implications, see Clowse 1981. See also "President Proposes Five-Year School Program," *CQ Almanac 1956* (Washington: Congressional Quarterly, 1957), http://library.cqpress .com/cqalmanac/cqal56-1348299.

7. Nona Brown, "Aid to Schools: The Problem and the Issue," *New York Times,* October 7, 1956, 195.

8. Summary based on "Aid to Schools," *CQ Almanac 1956* (Washington: Congressional Quarterly, 1957), http://library.cqpress.com/cqalmanac/cqal56-1349164; and "Federal Education Policy and the States, 1945–2004."

9. Munger and Fenno 1962, 14–18.

World War II, proponents of federal aid to education saw an opportunity to advance their case. Their early efforts, however, would falter, as opponents managed to tie their appeals to deeper and divisive debates about federal control, religion, and race.

INITIAL LEGISLATIVE EFFORTS, 1948–1954

In the 1948 presidential election, Harry Truman ran on a platform that included increased "general aid" to education. As part of his "fair deal," Truman envisioned a larger federal role in education, primarily through direct grants to states. Where charges of "communistic" federal involvement in local schools had derailed previous general aid proposals, a newly elected Truman hoped to allay concerns about local control and pave the way for increased federal funding of public education.[10] His efforts would ultimately founder, caught up in long-standing debates at the intersection of public governance and religion.

In 1948, the Senate passed a bill that would give states $300 million in education grants per year—a modest sum, but enough to lay a foundation for continued federal involvement in education. At the time Congressional debate focused primarily on whether the bill would allow parochial schools to receive federal money.[11] Although an amendment to bar federal funding to private schools failed decisively in the Senate, the conflict prevented the bill from clearing the House Education and Labor Committee. The following year, a similar bill passed the Senate, but House concerns about federal funds going to religious schools undermined support for the bill. This time around, Representative Graham Barden (D-NC) introduced a separate bill that would have restricted federal grants to tax-supported schools and prohibited any federal funds from going to religious or private schools. Barden's bill sparked a public confrontation between Roman Catholic leader Francis Cardinal Spellman and former First Lady Eleanor Roosevelt—a debate that ultimately proved to be the bill's undoing.[12]

The National Catholic Welfare Conference historically had opposed federal aid out of fear of growing secularism from greater federal control and competition from a better-financed public school system. Nevertheless, the classroom and teacher shortages had affected private schools al-

10. Ibid., 13–17. See also *CQ Almanac 1956*, 411.
11. "Federal Aid to Education," *CQ Almanac 1948* (Washington: Congressional Quarterly, 1949), http://library.cqpress.com/cqalmanac/cqal48-1408029.
12. Ibid. For a more complete discussion of the controversy between Cardinal Spellman and Mrs. Roosevelt, see Grant 1979.

most as much as they had affected public schools. Parochial schools also struggled to raise enough funds to repair classrooms and expand their facilities. Moreover, the Roman Catholic church and other private school administrators worried about the pressure that better public school facilities or increases in public school teacher salaries might place on private schools in an increasingly competitive education marketplace.[13] Hence, when Representative Barden introduced a measure that would exclude parochial schools from federal aid, Catholic leaders stood up in arms. Francis Cardinal Spellman attacked the plan as anti-Catholic and called Barden a "new apostle of bigotry." Cardinal Spellman also accused Eleanor Roosevelt of anti-Catholic bias when she wrote in her newspaper column that "we do not want to see public education connected with religious control of the schools."[14] In large part because of this opposition, the Barden bill never made it out of committee.

In the years ahead, proponents of federal aid to education continued to press their case. Legislators introduced amendments to "tidelands" oil bills that would redirect revenues raised from mineral leases to federal education grants. More than twenty submerged lands bills, most of them described as "compromises," were introduced during 1951. In every instance, these bills died in either the House or Senate. When Truman finally left office in 1953, he had not delivered on any of his promises to augment the size or scope of federal aid to public education.

EISENHOWER'S EARLY ATTEMPTS TO BREAK THE LOCAL IMPASSE, 1955–1957

After winning the 1952 presidential election, Dwight Eisenhower did not appear to be in any rush to address the nation's education problems. At the height of the Cardinal Spellman controversy, in fact, Eisenhower had publicly opposed Truman's federal aid proposals. Then the president of Columbia University, Eisenhower had written that "unless we are careful, even the great and necessary educational processes in our country will become yet another vehicle by which believers in paternalism, if not outright socialism, will gain still additional power for the central government."[15] During the 1952 presidential campaign, Eisenhower reiterated his concerns about federal control and funding to parochial schools and his opposition

13. Munger and Fenno 1962, 54–65.
14. Richard H. Parke, "Cardinal Calls Mrs. Roosevelt Anti-Catholic on School Bill," *New York Times*, July 23, 1949, 13.
15. Grant 1979, 2–3.

to general aid to education.[16] After assuming office as president, he insisted that the government should take no action with regard to federal aid to education until a full review of the situation had been made.

To facilitate this review, Eisenhower took two steps. First, he created a new cabinet-level department in 1953, the Department of Health, Education, and Welfare (HEW), to oversee the work of the existing federal Office of Education. Before the creation of HEW, the Office of Education had only limited powers to assist federal employees and their children and administer programs for veterans such as the G.I. Bill. Second, in his 1954 State of the Union address, Eisenhower asked local schools to report their needs regarding school construction and teacher salaries to the federal government.[17] He announced that these requests would be considered at the first-ever White House Conference on Education (WHCE) that would be conducted the following year.[18]

Eisenhower's decision to delay the WHCE until the following year drew criticism from both the National Education Association (NEA) and Democratic members of the Senate,[19] both of whom argued that the president was failing to provide the leadership needed to address an impending crisis. In 1954, the Senate considered a bill that would authorize $500 million in federal aid to the states for a two-year emergency school construction program. Although the bill did not come up for a vote, it provided an opportunity for interest groups to resurrect their lobbying efforts on Capitol Hill. On December 7, 1954, the House Education and Labor Special Subcommittee on Federal Aid for School Construction unanimously recommended that Congress appropriate money to help states expand school construction programs.[20] Chairman Carroll Kerns (R-PA) stated, "School construction is the answer to any phase of federal assistance to education." By Kerns' calculation, it would take at least $10 billion to meet the rising demand.[21]

In response to the growing calls for federal aid legislation, President Eisenhower announced in his 1955 State of the Union address that there were "grave educational problems" and an "unprecedented classroom

16. Martin 1998.
17. Eisenhower's 1954 State of the Union address, http://www.eisenhowermemorial.org/speeches/index.htm.
18. Ibid. See also "Aid to Schools," *CQ Almanac 1956.*
19. Clowse 1981. See also "Education Bill Voted: Senate Accepts White House Plan, Attacked as 'Trifling,'" *New York Times,* June 18, 1954, 3.
20. Summary based on "Aid to Schools," *CQ Almanac 1956.*
21. Ibid.

shortage."[22] By the time Eisenhower submitted his own plan on February 8, more than forty bills had been introduced in the 84th Congress.[23] When his bill made its way to the House and Senate, Eisenhower recognized that demographic trends justified some federal aid, but that "control and support" of education should continue to be a "state and local responsibility."[24] Eisenhower's plan focused primarily on the appropriation of $750 million for a three-year bond program, and it included another $200 million over three years for grants-in-aid to impoverished school districts deemed unable to undertake a bond program on their own.

The next day, Democrats in Congress quickly attacked the president's proposal as "government by gimmick" and an "empty hoax." According to Senator Matthew Neely (D-WV), "It would be as impossible to solve the nation's present educational problems in the manner recommended by the president as it would be to extinguish a city-wide conflagration with a squirt gun."[25] In fact, the president's proposal included the smallest net amount of federal funding out of all forty bills introduced. Even as he introduced his plan, Eisenhower insisted that a final solution on long-term federal funding should come only after the WHCE later that year.[26] Consequently, no federal aid bill—the president's or anyone else's—came to a floor vote in either chamber during 1955. Eisenhower had good reasons to proceed cautiously on the issue of federal aid to education. Truman's previous legislative attempts revealed just how intertwined federal aid to education had become with other complex and contentious issues on federalism and religion. And if that was not enough, federal aid to education was about to become entangled with one of the most divisive issues in American history: race.

After the Supreme Court's unanimous ruling in *Brown v. Board of Education of Topeka, Kansas* in 1954, federal aid could not support the construction of racially segregated schools. Declaring the principle of "equal educational opportunities," the court ruled that racially segregated schools were inherently unequal when maintained by the force of law or any other state action. Initially, this decision implied that any increase in federal aid would have to facilitate desegregation. In 1955, however, the

22. Eisenhower's 1955 State of the Union address, http://www.eisenhowermemorial.org/speeches/index.htm.

23. "President Proposes Five-Year School Program," *CQ Almanac 1956* (Washington: Congressional Quarterly, 1957), http://library.cqpress.com/cqalmanac/cqal56-1348299.

24. Ibid.

25. Ibid.

26. Leonard 1956.

court released a remedy-phase decision, *Brown II,* which required states and local school districts to eliminate segregationist statutes and pursue desegregation "with all deliberate speed."[27]

The issue of desegregation became a major topic of discussion at the WHCE a few months later. Proponents of federal aid worried that desegregation would put their entire agenda at risk. In an effort to inoculate federal aid to education from the politics of desegregation, these proponents advocated that desegregation efforts proceed only in accordance with local conditions. The official conference report stated, "The great social, psychological and organizational changes implicit in the recent decisions of the Supreme Court designed to abolish segregation in the public schools cannot be achieved with equal speed in every community."[28] Independently, Eisenhower had adopted this gradualist view as well. On July 6, 1955, Eisenhower declared that he "did not believe that anti-segregation restrictions should be written into school legislation" because segregation was a "separate problem."[29] The president further stated that the Supreme Court's most recent decision had specifically provided for gradual integration. By formally recognizing the *Brown II* decision, Eisenhower sought to separate the issue of federal aid to education legislation from that of segregation.

The WHCE, however, did not merely rationalize the president's prior policy positions. Indeed, the conference had a major impact on Eisenhower's evolving views on federal aid to education. Many supporters of federal aid argued that the White House had intended to use the conference to delay action, perhaps indefinitely. They accused the administration of filling the conference with like-minded conservatives, all but ensuring a final report that lent tepid support, if any, for federal aid. Citing inadequate representation of education groups, John Connors, then education director of the American Federation of Labor, argued that the WHCE was "stacked against the interest of school children."[30] However, an unexpected consensus quickly emerged at the conference: the federal government needed to do more to help the states. Virtually every one of the state and

27. Patterson 1996 provides a detailed discussion of *Brown*'s immediate ramifications and how national and local politics affected the implementation of the court's decisions.

28. "White House Conference on Education Report," April 1956, Greenwood Press, London.

29. "Folsom Renews School Aid Plea: Cites Eisenhower Attitude in Urging Bill Be Kept Free of Segregation Issue Prospective Floor Strategy," *New York Times,* June 25, 1956, 43.

30. "Aid to Schools," *CQ Almanac 1956.*

local conferences recognized the need for federal funding and requested massive support. The clear evidence of the demand for new facilities apparently convinced Eisenhower that the issue was more serious than he previously had believed.[31] Eisenhower later would declare that the WHCE had "dragged [him] into supporting" federal aid to education because it had demonstrated that school "conditions [were] deplorable."[32] While Eisenhower still had significant concerns about federal control, he came away from the conference willing to break with his own party and to recommend a major school construction initiative.

On January 12, 1956, Eisenhower announced his revised plan. Though similar in structure to his previous plan, it was vastly different in scale. Eisenhower's new proposal still included the provision for $750 million to support local bond programs. The new bill, however, increased the amount of federal grants-in-aid from $200 million over three years to $1.25 billion over five years. In many ways, Eisenhower's new proposal was quite similar to the leading Democratic plan that had been introduced by Congressman Augustine B. Kelley (D-PA) the previous year. The major discrepancies between the two bills were over the total size and timeline of the federal grants-in-aid. Eisenhower's plan included $1.25 billion over five years; the Kelley plan called for $1.6 billion over four years. The Kelley plan also decreased the amount of federal funds initially available for bond purchase to $300 million though it explicitly stated that subsequent allocations of up to an additional $450 million could be necessary. The other major provisions of the competing bills were quite similar.[33]

On July 5, 1956, the House rejected the Kelley bill by a 194–224 roll call vote. A civil rights amendment proved to be the bill's undoing. Introduced by Adam Clayton Powell (D-NY), the amendment effectively barred aid to states that operated racially segregated schools. Although Powell intended for his amendment to hasten racial desegregation in the South, its unintended consequence was to derail the entire federal aid program. In what has become the textbook case of strategic voting behavior,[34] ninety-six Republicans voted for the Powell amendment but against the bill. By voting for the amendment and ensuring its passage, these Republicans were able to turn the Democratic Party against itself. Although most southern Democrats could be counted on to vote for the Kelley bill strictly on its

31. Clowse 1981; "President Proposes Five-Year School Program," *CQ Almanac 1956*.
32. As quoted in Clowse 1981, 46, 149
33. "Aid to Schools," *CQ Almanac 1956*.
34. Riker 1986. For a contrary view, see Gilmour 2001.

merits, they could not vote for the civil rights rider. Because the two were linked, a vote for the Kelley bill became a vote for increasing the pace of desegregation. After seeing the disastrous results in the House, Senate Democrats chose not to move forward with their own version.

In 1957, the House again voted to kill a Democratic federal aid to education bill. In this case, Powell did not offer his segregation amendment. Instead, a Republican Congressman from New York, Stuyvesant Wainwright, did so. Wainwright had sponsored and introduced the two bills that embodied Eisenhower's education plan. Although Democratic leaders had convinced Powell not to reintroduce his controversial amendment, Wainwright knew that he could still split southern and northern Democrats, and thereby undermine support for the larger education initiative. On July 25, Wainwright's amendment passed.

The vote to kill the bill occurred just as it appeared that leading Democrats might be willing to support the president's plan.[35] Right after the Wainwright amendment passed, several Democratic leaders announced on the House floor that they would accept the administration's plan. Upon hearing of the possible compromise, Judge Howard Smith, a conservative Democrat from Virginia, introduced a motion to kill the bill. Supporters of school aid legislation unsuccessfully appealed to the president to make a last-minute effort on behalf of the bill. Eisenhower, however, refused to rally support from within his party for the three votes needed to continue debate and secure a vote on his bill.[36] The procedural move to kill the bill was adopted on a 208–203 split-party roll call vote, preventing the replacement amendment from coming to a floor vote.

Had he tried, Eisenhower might have been able to salvage his plan in the House. A majority of the president's own party had voted to kill the bill and denied themselves the opportunity to vote on the administration's preferred policy. These 111 Republican votes reflected widespread GOP opposition to federal school aid, particularly in the Midwest.[37] It seems plausible that the president could have brought around at least some of these members, but even if his bill cleared the House, Eisenhower still

35. "School Aid Loses Again," *New York Times*, July 27, 1957, 10; John D. Morris, "Democrats Blame President for School Aid Bill Defeat," *New York Times*, July 27, 1957, 1.

36. Morris, "Democrats Blame President"; Bess Furman, "Eisenhower's Aid Asked on Schools," *New York Times*, July 23, 1957, 19. For Eisenhower's comments in response, see his news conference on July 31, 1957, *Public Papers*, 1957, 575–576.

37. "Federal School Construction Aid Defeated," *CQ Almanac 1957* (Washington: Congressional Quarterly, 1958), http://library.cqpress.com/cqalmanac/cqal57-1345328.

would have had to muster the supermajority needed to pass the Senate. In 1956, concerns about federal control and segregation had prevented the Senate version of the president's plan from even making it to the floor. In 1957, prospects in the Senate appeared just as dim.

A NEW APPROACH

Shortly after this second legislative defeat, Eisenhower decided to abandon the fight on school construction. In a press conference, the president insisted that his "position was clear" but that "he had given the matter all the presidential consideration it deserved."[38] The president subsequently directed his advisers to scale back their education policy proposals. On October 3, 1957, the day before the launch of *Sputnik,* Sherman Adams informed State of the Union speechwriters that the president wanted to introduce "some school legislation—whatever its nature—but it need not anymore propose a large spending program for this purpose."[39]

The administration began considering several policy alternatives. A variety of legislative proposals were introduced or reconsidered in a number of policy areas, including foreign language training, vocational education, and financial aid for students. Proposals to increase college attendance gained particular traction. The President's Committee on Education Beyond High School, a follow-up to the WCHE, decried the "waste" of "talented but poor or unmotivated students" who did not attend college.[40] As a result, HEW assembled a task force on higher education to consider possible legislation.[41] The task force examined a number of ways that new federal legislation could improve college attendance and science output, focusing primarily on federal funding for college scholarships.

During 1957, at least twelve bills in the House and six in the Senate proposed various forms of federal aid to college students.[42] Congressman Carl Elliot (D-AL), chairman of the permanent Special Education subcommittee, began to work in close conjunction with HEW on the issues of scholarships and financial aid. Elliot planned hearings on what he perceived to be the nation's most valuable resource: its manpower. The nation's very survival, Elliot believed, crucially depended on the government's human capital investments. At the outset of the hearings, Elliot articulated his

38. Eisenhower news conference on July 31, 1957, *Public Papers,* 1957, 575–576.
39. Clowse 1981, 49.
40. Kerr-Tener 1987.
41. Ibid. See also Clowse 1981, 50–51.
42. "Federal School Construction Aid Defeated," *CQ Almanac 1957.*

intention "to get a real comparison between what Russia and our country are doing in these fields."[43] The Eisenhower administration supported Elliot's approach, especially its efforts to reframe the discussion of education as a national security concern, and to focus on college scholarships for talented but needy students. In the early fall of 1957, however, the political climate did not appear especially conducive to talk of education as a national security concern. That climate was about to change.

RESET: *SPUTNIK* NATIONALIZES THE DEBATE

On October 4, 1957, the Soviet Union launched the world's first orbiting satellite, *Sputnik*. The launch shook the American people to their core. No longer could the United States claim the mantle of scientific and technological superiority. When the Soviet Union launched a second satellite— *Sputnik II*—a month after the first, concerns about scientific dominance quickly transformed into genuine fears about American national security. Senator Henry Jackson (D-WA), the chairman of the Military Applications of Atomic Energy subcommittee, called the launch a "devastating blow to the United States' scientific, industrial and technical prestige in the world" and warned that the Soviets would be "throwing their weight around more than ever."[44] Other political leaders and intelligence analysts worried that the launch corroborated the Soviet Union's earlier claim that it had successfully fired an intercontinental ballistic missile.[45]

With the Soviet Union producing more than twice as many engineers per year as the United States, many viewed the launching of *Sputnik* as an education call to arms.[46] Educators beckoned the nation to "wake up to the dangers of educational neglect."[47] At its national conference attended by college presidents from over 400 institutions on October 10, the American Council on Education passed a resolution stating that the "Soviet satellite has shattered the nation's smug complacency about its schools and colleges."[48] The resolution argued that Americans "still considered

43. Ibid.
44. "Blow to U.S. Seen: Jackson Says Soviet Satellite Hurts Nation's Prestige," *New York Times,* October 6, 1957, 42.
45. Ibid. See also Robert K. Plumb, "The Missiles Race: Where the U.S. Stands Compared with Soviet; Soviet Missile," *New York Times,* November 10, 1957, 209.
46. "Text of Conclusions of the U.S. Report on Soviet Education," *New York Times,* November 11, 1957, 11.
47. Benjamin Fine, "Educators Upset by Soviet Stroke," *New York Times,* October 10, 1957, 11.
48. Ibid., 3.

education a luxury rather than a necessity" and called for "changes in America's education system" designed to improve science proficiency.[49] By the end of the month, virtually every state and regional education organization had issued statements calling for both local and federal action in the area of science education so that the United States might compete with the Soviet Union.[50]

For Eisenhower, the launching of *Sputnik* infused education reform with newfound urgency. In the first of two national addresses, the president argued that *Sputnik* had "real military significance" as it demonstrated that "Soviet expansionist aims have not changed." The president warned, "We could fall behind, unless we now face up to certain pressing requirements and set out to meet them at once."[51] The president then, for the first time, explicitly connected national security concerns to federal involvement in education: "According to my scientific friends, one of our greatest, and most glaring, deficiencies is the failure of us in this country to give high enough priority to scientific education and to the place of science in our national life."[52] Accordingly, Eisenhower announced the appointment of James Killian, then the president of the Massachusetts Institute of Technology, as the Special Assistant to the President for Science and Technology. The president subsequently indicated his intention to outline a program to restore America's scientific credibility and bolster its security.

Within a week, the administration released a federal policy paper that summarized the Soviet Union's aggressive academic investments and that called upon the nation to follow suit.[53] In a second television address on November 13, the president laid out many of the report's central findings and formally brought education to the forefront of his national security planning. He argued that Soviet advances in science and technology constituted the single greatest threat to U.S. national security: "[My scientific advisers] place this problem above all other immediate tasks of producing missiles and of developing new techniques in the

49. Ibid.

50. Ibid. See also "Eggheads Called Hope of Country," *New York Times,* October 26, 1957, 6; Austin C. Wehrwein, "Educators Urge High School Shift," *New York Times,* October 31, 1957, 33; Harold M. Schmeck, "Educators Urge Wakened Nation," *New York Times,* November 9, 1957, 2; "U.S. Satellite Lag Tied to Education," *New York Times,* November 9, 1957, 2.

51. "Radio and Television Address to the American People on Science in National Security," http://www.eisenhowermemorial.org/speeches/index.htm.

52. Ibid.

53. "Text of Conclusions of the U.S. Report on Soviet Education," *New York Times,* November 11, 1957, 11.

Armed Services."[54] Eisenhower then called for a new education program with dramatically greater ambitions than any previous proposal.
According to the president, the federal government needed to promote
consistent testing of students, resources for professional studies, additional laboratory facilities, fellowships and financial aid for promising
students, and incentives for more and better science teachers. Near the
conclusion of Eisenhower's address, aptly titled "Our Future Security,"
the president boldly stated, "This is National Education Week; it should
be National Education Year."[55]

After three years of failed attempts at school construction legislation,
members of the administration and supporters of federal aid saw *Sputnik*
as their opportunity to pass sweeping federal education legislation. The
crisis focused Americans on the threat posed by Soviet advancements in
science and technology, while also revealing deep deficiencies in their own
education system. In an effort to gather the nation's resolve, Secretary of
State John Dulles argued that although *Sputnik* constituted a short-term
"success" for the Soviets, its "mocking of the American people with its
'beep-beep' may go down in history as Mr. Kruschev's boomerang."[56]
According to Dulles, the satellite caused "a wave of mortification, anger,
and fresh determination to sweep the country" and increased Americans'
"willingness to make the kind of efforts and sacrifices necessary to win
that struggle."[57] More than that, though, it was the president who recognized political opportunity at hand. Before he had even introduced his
full education plan to Congress, Eisenhower told Secretary Folsom "anything you could hook on this defense situation would get by."[58] Suddenly,
it seemed, the president could abandon yesterday's piddling efforts to
support school construction and secure for the federal government a prominent and lasting role in public education.

THE NATIONAL DEFENSE EDUCATION ACT

Eisenhower used his 1958 State of the Union address to announce his
education initiative. Rather than offer a laundry list of reforms, as many
previous presidents had done, Eisenhower stated that he would be speaking

54. "Radio and Television Address to the American People on 'Our Future Security,'
November 13, 1957," http://www.eisenhowermemorial.org/speeches/index.htm.
55. Ibid.
56. "Text of Speech by Secretary Dulles and Transcript of Questions and Answers,"
New York Times, January 17, 1958, 4.
57. Ibid.
58. Clowse 1981, 523.

"only on matters bearing directly upon our security and peace."[59] Chief among such matters was education. In fact, education accounted for one pillar of a comprehensive eight-point plan for peace and security. According to Eisenhower, the United States needed to outdo the Soviets on their own terms, "outmatching them in military power, general technological advance, and specialized education and research."[60] To accomplish as much, the president argued, Congress needed to enact sweeping education legislation that would spur scientific achievement and provide incentives for teachers and higher education.

Later that month, on January 27, Eisenhower submitted to Congress a draft of what would become the National Defense Education Act. The president's four-year, $1.6 billion program included provisions for 10,000 college scholarships, expanded facilities and resources for science and mathematics teaching, improved counseling programs, foreign language teaching, fellowships for graduate study, and funding for the National Science Foundation.[61] These ideas were not new. Indeed, over the previous several years Congress had considered all the major provisions of the NDEA,[62] and every time Congress had rejected them.[63]

Within Congress, however, opposing forces continued to hold sway. Representative Cleveland Bailey (D-WV), chairman of the House Education and Labor General Education Subcommittee, said he intended to keep the bill within the subcommittee because of his concerns about desegregation and his irritation with Eisenhower's leadership during the 1957 school construction bill.[64] Other Democrats quickly introduced alternative measures in both the House and Senate. Lister Hill and twenty-six other Democrats introduced the leading proposal. The basic structure of Hill's bill appeared similar to Eisenhower's proposal, but it called for a far greater number of federal grants and science scholarships and had a total estimated cost of $3 billion. Carl Elliot (D-AL) introduced an identical bill in the House.

Worried about rising costs and federal controls, Republicans generally opposed Hill and Elliot's plan. Some within the president's party argued

59. Eisenhower's 1958 State of the Union address, http://www.eisenhowermemorial .org/speeches/index.htm.

60. "Radio and Television Address to the American People on 'Our Future Security': November 13, 1957."

61. "Federal Education Aid Approved," *CQ Almanac 1958* (Washington: Congressional Quarterly, 1959), http://library.cqpress.com/cqalmanac/cqal58-1341294.

62. Ibid.

63. Clowse 1981, 180.

64. Ibid.

that committing more than $1 billion in federal funds would unavoidably facilitate the federal government's eventual takeover of public education. Others worried that a large number of "communistic" federal scholarships would extend federal control to postsecondary education. After voicing his own opposition, House Minority Leader Joseph W. Martin (R-MA) said, "All education bills have difficulty in the House, and if this year is the exception, I'll be surprised."[65]

So Martin was surprised indeed—and he admitted as much on July 15—shortly after Eisenhower's bill passed the House Education and Labor Committee by a vote of 23 to 2. Martin then forecast that the bill would pass the House and "get a substantial majority." Although he said he had taken no poll, Martin recognized a "general sentiment" that the need to surpass the Soviets in science and technology "trumped other concerns"[66]—the very concerns about race, religion, and federal control, it bears emphasizing, that had derailed every previous attempt to enact federal education legislation.

The version of the bill that passed the House Education and Labor Committee authorized 23,000 new college scholarships per year, $220 million in federal loan funding to aid students, matching grants of $240 million over four years for states to purchase equipment to help teach science, language, and mathematics, $40 million for graduate student and teacher training, and $84 million for testing and guidance counselors. In a message sent to Stuyvesant Wainwright, Eisenhower claimed that HR 13247 was a "top-priority objective," but that he would prefer that the total number of scholarships be reduced to 10,000 and that they be administered on the basis of need. Several weeks later, Elliot announced that a bipartisan strategy group from the Special Education Subcommittee had agreed to support an amendment bringing the bill into line with the president's wishes. HR 13247 passed by a voice vote on August 8, but with it came two significant amendments. Walter Judd's (R-MN) amendment eliminated all federal scholarships and transferred the funds to a loan program for needy students. Powell's amendment, meanwhile, stipulated "that scholarships, loans and graduate fellowships must be awarded to students without discrimination based upon race, color, religion, national origin or sex."[67]

65. Ibid.
66. Bess Furman, "Passage Forecast on Education Aid," *New York Times,* July 3, 1958, 3.
67. "Federal Education Aid Approved," *CQ Almanac 1958.*

By a 62 to 26 roll call vote, the Senate passed its own version of the bill (S 4237), which reinstated the 23,000 federal scholarship provision stricken by the House. Differences between the two bills were then worked out in conference committee. On August 21, conferees agreed to a compromise that included the House provision on loans but eliminated Powell's nondiscrimination amendment. The compromise bill passed the Senate by a vote of 66 to 15 on August 21 and the House by a vote of 212 to 85 on August 23. Though some supporters of federal aid to education had hoped for a more sweeping law, most historians recognize the monumental importance of the NDEA. It established substantial new federal authority, significantly increased federal funding for education, and drastically enlarged the influence of HEW.[68] With recent Republican and Democratic presidents actively engaged in debates about various accountability provisions, charter school funds, and grants-in-aid, the precedential value of the NDEA persists to this day.

LESSONS

In most ways, the history of the federal government's entrance into education policy reaffirms the central arguments of the Policy Priority Model. For the better part of a decade, Congress considered repeated bills that would direct federal funds to local school districts. As long as the issue raised local concerns about race and/or religion, every one of these bills failed. It was not until the issue of education became linked to concerns about national security that a U.S. president could break through this impasse and enact major federal legislation on public schools. The launching of *Sputnik* fundamentally altered the context in which education initiatives were considered—in ways that distinctly advantaged the president. By arguing that Soviet successes in their space program affirmed the administration's assessments of the rival nation's scientific and technological superiority, Eisenhower found a way to direct federal funds to local school districts and reshape the education of students therein. Indeed, when *Sputnik* wrenched education from parochial considerations of race, religion, and local control, Eisenhower succeeded at last.

But there is a twist. When the breakthrough finally came, it came in a time of peace. To be sure, the possibility of war lingered in the background of these debates. In the aftermath of *Sputnik,* members of Congress reconsidered their prior positions on education not only because they worried

68. See, for example, Martin 1998, 7–12.

that war might erupt, but that if war occurred the United States would lose. All of this suggests that for presidential power to expand, actual troops fighting on foreign battlefields may not always be necessary. The mere threat of war may suffice. To the extent that all our previous empirical models coded this particular episode as a time of peace, they probably underestimate the true differences in members' voting behavior in times of full-blown war and genuine, robust peace.

7.2 *The Great Society and the 1965 Decision to Send Ground Troops into Vietnam*

The Great Society stands alongside Roosevelt's New Deal as the most significant collection of twentieth-century domestic reforms. Reflecting upon the first session of Johnson's Great Society Congress (the 89th), the *New York Times* concluded: "It is unquestionably one of the most glittering records of legislative accomplishment in history."[69] According to David Mayhew, more landmark enactments (forty-five) were passed during Johnson's administration than during any other presidency in the modern era. Of these, twenty-two were passed in 1964 and 1965, the peak years for Johnson's domestic agenda.[70]

Though Johnson enjoyed extraordinary legislative successes during these early years of his presidency, rising tensions in Southeast Asia soon commanded a substantial share of the president's attention. The war, of course, was not of Johnson's choosing: he had inherited an emergent crisis in Vietnam that the Kennedy administration had failed to resolve. Though he preferred to concentrate on the domestic reforms that constituted his Great Society, Johnson realized that the 1964 presidential campaign required him to attend—at least symbolically—to the spread of communism in Southeast Asia.

So as Johnson tallied a significant number of victories on domestic legislation in 1964 and 1965, he treaded carefully around the developments in Vietnam. Because many of his domestic policy priorities required support from conservative southern Democrats, who almost uniformly opposed the expansion of communism, the president felt that he needed to take a tough stance against North Vietnamese aggression. Simultaneously, Johnson recognized that waging a full-fledged war would provoke calls for massive

---

69. Editorial, *New York Times,* September 5, 1965.
70. Mayhew 1991.

spending cuts on domestic programs, thereby undercutting many of the domestic reforms to which he was so committed. The central political challenge facing the president was to do enough in Vietnam to keep southern Democrats on board with his domestic agenda while not doing so much that budgetary concerns came to the fore.

Johnson proceeded with his domestic priorities while escalating troop deployments to Vietnam. In doing so, however, he used the institutional advantages of the presidency to deceive the public about the nation's true involvement in Southeast Asia, fearing that support for his domestic programs would be rescinded if the public knew the true costs of the war. For the better part of four years, Johnson went to great lengths to downplay the full extent of U.S. military activities in Vietnam, insisting before Congress that U.S. policy had not changed and deliberately misleading the public about his intentions. At precisely the moment that Johnson could no longer deny that the United States was involved in a full-fledged war— namely, after the Tet Offensive in early 1968—Johnson declined to seek reelection in 1968.

This period of American history stands in rather odd juxtaposition to the arguments and evidence in this book. With the onset of the Vietnam War, we do not merely find a Congress perfectly willing to stand up against the president—a possibility that by itself, does not negate the Policy Priority Model. In this instance, we witness a president struggling mightily to escalate a military conflict (albeit only modestly) not so that he can enact policies that had previously eluded him, but rather to safeguard a set of domestic policy achievements that had already been enacted—and enacted, notably, during peace.

THE EMERGENT CRISIS IN VIETNAM

At the end of World War II, France sought to reestablish its colonial rule in Indochina. For the next several years, the Viet Minh, a Vietnamese nationalist group founded in 1941, launched an insurgent campaign against the French. The Viet Minh denounced French efforts at reconciliation, as inscribed in the 1949 Elysee Accords, and, with the ascension of Chairman Mao Zedong, they had a critical ally in Communist China. The Chinese provided the Viet Minh with a vast supply of weapons, which prompted the United States to back the French forces in southern Vietnam. By the spring of 1954, the Viet Minh had won decisive victories over the French in northern Vietnam, and the Geneva Accords signed in July that year established the 17th parallel as a temporary partition between the northern and southern regions, while providing for national elections in 1956 that would then unify the country.

From the vantage point of the United States, Vietnam constituted an emergent crisis with potentially vast regional implications. In a press conference on April 7, 1954, President Eisenhower articulated what came to be known as the "domino theory," which guided U.S. foreign policy in Southeast Asia for the next two decades. In response to a question about the strategic importance of Indochina, Eisenhower said, "You have broader considerations that might follow what you would call the 'falling domino' principle. You have a row of dominoes set up, you knock over the first one, and what will happen to the last one is the certainty that it will go over very quickly. So you could have a beginning of a disintegration that would have the most profound influences."[71] Concerned that the spread of communism into southern Vietnam would portend the fall of all of Southeast Asia to communism, President Eisenhower committed U.S. forces to the defense of South Vietnam in late 1954, shortly after French forces withdrew from the region. These early deployments, however, did little to reduce tensions in the region. By 1960, Communist insurgents had launched a series of successful guerilla attacks in South Vietnam, and Mao Zedong, sensing an opportunity to bolster his anti-imperialist credentials, lent increasing levels of support to the South Vietnamese rebel forces who would become known as the Viet Cong.

KENNEDY COMMITS TO VIETNAM — CAUTIOUSLY

When taking office in 1961, President Kennedy and his advisers recognized the deep challenges that came with crafting an effective Vietnam policy. That spring, Vice President Johnson flew to South Vietnam and issued a joint statement with President Ngo Dinh Diem that pledged U.S. support against what they called "unprovoked subversion and Communist terror."[72] Shortly thereafter, in a special address to Congress, Kennedy defined the crisis as a "contest of will and purpose as well as force and violence—a battle for minds and souls as well as lives and territory. And in that contest, we cannot stand aside." But while insisting that the United States stands "for the independence and equality of all nations,"

71. "The Row of Dominoes: Dwight D. Eisenhower Presidential Press Conference, April 7, 1954," http://www.vietnamwar.net/Eisenhower-2.htm.
72. "Joint Communique Issued at Saigon by the Vice President of the United States and the President of Viet-Nam," May 13, 1961, Department of State Bulletin, June 19, 1961, 956.

Kennedy also expressed reservations about how—and, more fundamentally, *whether*—the U.S. military should become more directly involved in the conflict. As he put it:

> There is no single simple policy which meets this challenge. Experience has taught us that no one nation has the power or the wisdom to solve all the problems of the world or manage its revolutionary tides—that extending our commitments does not always increase our security—that any initiative carries with it the risk of a temporary defeat—that nuclear weapons cannot prevent subversion—that no free people can be kept free without will and energy of their own.[73]

During his time in office, Kennedy frequently expressed U.S. sympathies with the plight of the South Vietnamese and denounced Communist aggression. His official policies, however, frustrated both hawks and doves within his administration. A 1961 white paper by the State Department entitled "A Threat to Peace: North Vietnam's Effort to Conquer South Vietnam" argued for, among other things, dramatic increases in military and financial support; other presidential advisers, however, called for the complete withdrawal of U.S. troops from the peninsula. Flouting both suggestions, Kennedy chose a middle option, in which he increased financial support for Diem while attaching a set of conditions to continued U.S. aid. By providing sufficient support the administration reasoned, South Vietnam would eventually prevail on its own.

Reports in late 1962 and early 1963 suggested that the challenges in Vietnam were more serious than the administration had believed. Senate Majority Leader Mike Mansfield (D-MT), on a visit to Saigon in December 1962, told President Kennedy that Diem was squandering U.S. financial aid. Michael V. Forrestal prepared a memo entitled "A Report on South Vietnam," delivered to Kennedy in February 1963, that concluded:

> Our overall judgment, in sum, is that we are probably winning, but certainly more slowly than we had hoped. At the rate it is now going the war will last longer than we would like, cost more in terms of both lives and money than we anticipated, and prolong the period in which a sudden and dramatic event could upset the gains already made.[74]

---

73. John F. Kennedy, "Special Message to the Congress on Urgent National Needs." May 25, 1961.

74. Michael Forrestal, 1963. "Memorandum to The President: A Report on South Vietnam." *The Pentagon Papers*, Gravel Edition. Vol. 2, 717–725.

In combination, these observations suggested that the current U.S. troop level would not break the impasse in Vietnam. To the extent that eventual success *was* possible, it would surely require years of sustained financial and military obligations.

At the same time, Kennedy believed that decreasing support for the South Vietnamese was not politically feasible. According to Ken O'Donnell, the president's appointments secretary and political adviser, Kennedy wanted to withdraw troops from Vietnam as early as March 1963.[75] In a subsequent conversation with Mansfield, Kennedy recognized the importance of withdrawing troops but insisted that he could not do so until after his reelection.[76] Similarly, when asked by his adviser Ted Sorenson whether he had considered reexamining U.S. foreign policy toward Vietnam, Kennedy indicated that "that's for the second term."[77] The decision to forge ahead was fraught with its own difficulties. As Langguth writes, "But to keep Americans fighting, and dying, in order to ensure his second term was not a decision to share widely. Kennedy would plug along instead with the unsatisfactory status quo until January 1965."[78]

Alas, Kennedy did not live to see the end of his first term, and with it, the end of U.S. involvement in South Vietnam. Instead, his successor Lyndon Johnson would inherit a military and political quagmire.

DEEPENING TROUBLES IN VIETNAM UNDER JOHNSON

The month before Kennedy's assassination in 1963, Diem himself was assassinated, leaving the South Vietnamese government at the brink of collapse. In mid-December 1963, Defense Secretary Robert McNamara reported that the situation in Saigon was "very disturbing" and that, barring substantial efforts to reverse the current trends, a "communist takeover of South Vietnam was likely."[79] Though the Johnson administration continued to direct financial aid and manpower support to the South Vietnam government, conditions only worsened. As Jeffrey Helsing wrote, "By the beginning of 1964, it was all the United States could do to keep the South Vietnamese government propped up and the communists at bay."[80] The junta that assumed power upon the removal of Diem

75. Bugliosi 2007, 1414; Langguth 2000, 208.
76. Langguth 2000, 208. See also O'Donnell and Powers 1972, 472.
77. Quoted in Langguth 2000, 209.
78. Ibid., 209.
79. Quoted in Helsing 2000, 22.
80. Ibid., 23.

quickly proved ineffectual; on January 29, 1964, with the complicity of the U.S. government, General Nguyen Khahn overthrew the junta and seized power.[81] Under Khahn, however, the problems for South Vietnam grew deeper still. As Herring noted, "military operations . . . had come to a complete standstill . . . The government's authority was nonexistent throughout much of the countryside [and] . . . the capital [Saigon] took on all the appearances of an armed camp."[82] When McNamara returned to South Vietnam in March 1964, he reported that the situation was "unquestionably worse" than it had been in the fall of 1963.[83]

In 1964, however, South Vietnam played a backseat role to domestic concerns. Johnson was convinced that his reelection prospects crucially depended on legislative achievements at home. Building upon the nation's prosperity, Johnson's vision of the Great Society—which included completing Kennedy's unfinished blueprint for a wide-ranging series of domestic and social reforms—would ensure the nation's greatness for years to come. To enact this vision, and especially to achieve the social reforms, Johnson needed the support of conservative southern Democrats.

Around the same time McNamara was reporting on the worsening situation in Vietnam, the joint chiefs of staff were proposing a series of graduated overt pressures against the North Vietnamese that included the initiation of air and ground operations. Yet Johnson and his advisers rejected the proposal because it would "raise a whole series of disagreeable questions"[84] that would "cause major disruptions at home, threatening Johnson's legislative program and his campaign for the presidency."[85] As he confessed to his national security adviser McGeorge Bundy, "[Vietnam] just worries the hell out of me. I don't see what we can ever hope to get out of there."[86]

Johnson's reluctance to enter into a full-blown war in Vietnam should not be confused with indifference to that nation's fate. To the contrary, Johnson and his advisers recognized that it was vitally important to "discourage any Soviet tendencies toward adventurism and encourage the nascent trend toward détente with the United States" and "continue to

81. Herring 2002, 133–134.

82. Ibid., 134.

83. Pentagon Papers 1971, 501; available at the National Archives, http://www.archives .gov/research/pentagon-papers/.

84. Herring 2002, 141.

85. Ibid., 138.

86. U.S. Department of State, Foreign Relations of the United States, 1964–68, volume 27, Mainland Southeast Asia: Regional Affairs, Washington, DC, document no. 53.

contain the presumably more aggressive and reckless Chinese."[87] For should the United States fail to fulfill its commitment to Vietnam, "our guarantees with regard to Berlin would lose their credibility"[88] and "there would be profound consequences everywhere."[89] Moreover, as Johnson told Doris Kearns Goodwin in 1970, "Everything I knew about history told me that if I got out of Vietnam and let Ho Chi Minh run through the streets of Saigon, then I'd be doing exactly what Chamberlin did in World War II. I'd be giving a big fat reward to aggression."[90]

A complete withdrawal, moreover, carried further costs at home. Johnson recognized that the fate of his most important domestic policy initiatives lay in the hands of southern Democrats who, he believed, would not sit quietly if the Communists triumphed in Vietnam. Showing weakness in Southeast Asia, Johnson feared, would rile southern conservatives and imperil the 1964 Civil Rights Act.[91] As the president lamented, "If I don't go in now and [the southern conservatives] show later that I should have, then they'll . . . push Vietnam up my ass every time."[92]

The central question for Johnson was to find some way of containing the conflict in Vietnam while continuing to advance his Great Society agenda. As long as he faced a reelection campaign, he noted, "The only thing I know to do is more of the same and do it more efficiently and effectively."[93] As George Herring noted, "fearing that large-scale involvement might jeopardize his chances of election in 1964 and threaten his beloved Great Society domestic programs, he temporized for over a year, expanding American assistance and increasing the number of advisers in hopes that a beefed-up version of his predecessor's policy might stave off disaster."[94] But, as we now know, it did not. While Johnson's chosen course took him through the 1964 elections, it did not deliver him from all-out war.

THE TONKIN GULF

One of the most well-known moments in the Vietnam conflict remains one of the most hotly debated. On August 2, 1964, the USS *Maddox* encoun-

87. Herring 2002, 137.
88. Quoted ibid., 115.
89. Quoted in Helsing 2000, 4.
90. Goodwin 1976, 196.
91. Herring 2002, 136.
92. Quoted in VanDeMark 1995, 60. For more on Johnson's concerns at the time, see Halberstam 1972, and Patterson 1996.
93. Goodwin 1976, 196.
94. Herring 2002, 131.

tered several North Vietnamese torpedo boats in the Gulf of Tonkin, just off the coast of North Vietnam. The *Maddox* fired upon the patrol boats, which responded in kind. Though Johnson was reportedly "enraged" upon hearing about the encounter, he did not retaliate.[95] Instead, the *Maddox* was instructed to remain in the Gulf, while the navy sent the destroyer *C. Turner Joy* for support. As Herring described it, "The United States may not have been seeking to provoke another attack, but it did not go out of its way to avoid one either."[96]

Two nights later, on August 4, the pair of destroyers reported being under attack. The ships claimed to have seen torpedoes and enemy searchlights, as well as sonar and radar contacts indicating enemy activity. When the president met with his advisers to discuss these reports, no one doubted their accuracy.[97] Secretary of State Dean Rusk characterized the attacks as "an act of war," and McNamara argued that "we cannot sit still as a nation and let them attack us on the high seas and get away with it."[98] The United States retaliated under Johnson's authorization, launching air strikes on naval sites in Vinh, which caused heavy damage to twenty-five torpedo boats and 90 percent of the oil storage facilities. Later that evening, Johnson addressed the nation. "As President and Commander in Chief," he began, "it is my duty to the American people to report that renewed hostile actions against United States ships on the high seas in the Gulf of Tonkin have today required me to order the military forces of the United States to take action in reply." Continuing, he asserted the necessity of retaliation:

> In the larger sense this new act of aggression, aimed directly at our own forces, again brings home to all of us in the United States the importance of the struggle for peace and security in Southeast Asia. Aggression by terror against the peaceful villagers of South Vietnam has now been joined by open aggression on the high seas against the United States of America.

95. Ibid., 142.
96. Ibid.
97. Subsequently, these reports have been called into question. James Stockdale, a navy pilot flying overhead that night, wrote, "I had the best seat in the house to watch that event, and our destroyers were just shooting at phantom targets—there were no PT boats there . . . There was nothing there but black water and American fire power" (Stockdale 1995, 98). As Johnson himself would later admit, "For all I know, our Navy was shooting at whales out there" (Herring 2002, 144).
98. Quoted in Herring 2002, 143.

The determination of all Americans to carry out our full commitment to the people and to the government of South Vietnam will be redoubled by this outrage. Yet our response, for the present, will be limited and fitting. We Americans know, although others appear to forget, the risks of spreading conflict. We still seek no wider war.[99]

Johnson then pushed for congressional authorization to take "all necessary measures to repel any armed attacks against the forces of the United States and to prevent further aggression." In so doing, Johnson immunized himself against criticism for failing to take stronger action against the North Vietnamese. But by limiting the actual retaliation to targeted strikes, Johnson also avoided the domestic challenges of waging all-out war. Members of Congress and the nation alike flocked to Johnson's side. Virtually overnight, his approval ratings increased from 42 to 72 percentage points.[100] On August 7, the Tonkin Gulf Resolution passed the House unanimously, and was opposed by only two members of the Senate. The president now had the formal authorization to escalate the conflict in Vietnam, but the better part of prudence convinced him to wait until after he won reelection.

CHOOSING NOT TO CHOOSE

On November 2, Johnson established an advisory group to chart a course in Vietnam. Upon winning reelection, however, his first order of business lay with his domestic agenda. Believing that the election results conferred a mandate—not just for him, but also for the newly elected Democratic supermajorities in both chambers of Congress—for the implementation of his Great Society policies, his domestic team worked furiously to propose a budget for fiscal year 1966. By prioritizing domestic affairs over Vietnam, Johnson recognized the possibility that war would undercut, rather than enhance, his ability to advance a domestic policy agenda at home. As Herring wrote, "Recognizing that even with his huge electoral mandate he would have only a brief honeymoon period to achieve his ambitious legislative goals, he was unwilling to permit the war to thwart his Great Society."[101]

Johnson continued to worry about southern conservatives' support for his programs. This time, his concern was that southern Democrats would

99. "Gulf of Tonkin Response," President Johnson's midnight television speech, August 4, 1964.
100. Herring 2002, 147.
101. Ibid., 151.

use the war to deny him his domestic goals. Rather than appearing "too weak" on Vietnam, as Halberstam described Johnson's earlier concerns, this time he wanted to avoid being seen as too aggressive. "They hate this stuff," Johnson said of conservatives' attitudes toward the Great Society. "They don't want to help the poor and the Negroes, but they're afraid to be against it at a time like this when there's all this prosperity. But the war—oh, they'll like the war." Plans of an escalation, therefore, "demanded absolute secrecy." [102]

In early December, consensus emerged about a two-phased bombing campaign against North Vietnam.[103] Johnson consented, authorizing an initial round of air strikes in Laos and a second round of bombing operations, which were to be accompanied by the deployment of a significant number of ground troops. But the president refused to make these plans public, and took further steps to prevent any possible leaks.[104] By concealing his foreign policy, Johnson made a distinctly political calculus meant to simultaneously protect American interests abroad and forestall any efforts to undo his domestic achievements.

A major escalation, it turned out, was just around the corner. On February 7, National Liberation Front units attacked the U.S. Army barracks at Pleiku, killing eight U.S. soldiers. The event served as a catalyst for a continuous bombing campaign and the introduction of 40,000 U.S. troops to secure the airfields, ports, and military infrastructure necessary to conduct the air campaign. Within seventy-two hours of the Pleiku attacks, Operation Flaming Dart had begun.

The air strikes continued long after the immediate retaliation against the National Liberation Front. Indeed, the bombing campaigns of Operation Flaming Dart shifted into a continuous program of air strikes against the North that became known as Operation Rolling Thunder. The administration continued to justify the air raids as a response to the Pleiku attacks and "emphatically denied any change of policy."[105] In truth, the bombings were gradually expanded through the spring of 1965, and "the air war quickly grew from a sporadic, halting effort into a regular, determined program."[106] These February events set the stage for Johnson's fateful decision to send ground troops in the summer of 1965.

102. Quoted in Langguth 2000, 328.
103. Kaiser 2000, 355.
104. McMaster 1997, 195.
105. Herring 2002, 154.
106. Ibid., 155.

THE GROUND WAR BEGINS

As spring gave way to summer, General William Westmoreland assumed control over American military operations in Vietnam. The political situation in South Vietnam worsened as yet another government—the fifth since the death of Diem—took charge in May. Recognizing the precarious political situation, Westmoreland and the joint chiefs of staff called for an increase of 150,000 troops. In so doing, General Earle Wheeler, chair of the joint chiefs, argued that Johnson "must take the fight to the enemy . . . No one ever won a battle sitting on his ass."[107] McNamara insisted that a rapid escalation would "stave off defeat in the short run and offer a good chance of producing a favorable settlement in the longer run."[108] All of Johnson's military advisers, however, also recognized that the war would be long and costly. According to the joint chiefs, winning the war would require 500,000 troops and five years.[109]

At the end of July, Johnson approved the deployment of 100,000 soldiers and authorized Westmoreland to "commit U.S. troops to combat independent of or in conjunction with [South Vietnamese] forces in any situation when . . . their use is necessary to strength the relative position of [South Vietnamese] forces."[110] Johnson called for the immediate deployment of half the troops, with the remaining 50,000 troops to be deployed before the year's end. The president further authorized an additional 100,000 troops for deployment in 1966. The Vietnam War had finally begun in earnest.

When Johnson convened his military advisers for a weeklong summit at the end of July, he was less concerned about what policy should actually be implemented than about how it should be presented to Congress and the American public. Indeed, after settling on a course of action on the first day, the discussion turned to "a new debate on tactics and above all on presentation to the country."[111] Heading these discussions was the issue of whether Johnson should disclose the full extent of the forthcoming escalation. Some of his advisers, including McNamara, urged Johnson to make it clear that American combat forces were now committed to the efforts

---

107. Quoted in Neustadt and May 1988, 78.
108. Quoted in Johnson 1971, 145–146.
109. Helsing 2000, 163.
110. Pentagon Papers 1971, 412.
111. William Bundy, unpublished manuscript, chapter 27, 33. LBJ Presidential Library, Austin, TX.

in Vietnam and that he had adopted "a major change in U.S. policy."[112] General Wheeler similarly argued that "we need to make this a clear and somber matter—that [the war] will not be quick—no single action will bring victory,"[113] while George Ball cast the situation in even starker terms, insisting that "we need to be damn serious with the American public."[114]

Others within the administration worried about the domestic political consequences of such transparency. Assistant Secretary of State Harlan Cleveland argued that "a doubling of our forces in Vietnam does not, it seems to me, need to be played as a major policy change,"[115] and McGeorge Bundy emphasized that "much is to be said for playing this low-key."[116] Johnson, meanwhile, remained deeply concerned about the state of affairs within Congress. In particular, he worried that that by rapidly escalating troop levels in Vietnam, "that bitch of a war would destroy the woman [he] really loved—the Great Society."[117] Some components of his Great Society programs had yet to be enacted into law, and others still required funding. Rather than disclose the full extent of the planned military escalation and thereby jeopardize his social reforms, Johnson sought to defer financing decisions until the following year, at which point troops would already be in the field and Congress would have little choice but to support them. As Bundy later admitted:

> Johnson knew his Congress, and knew that the practical majority he held in 1965 was a precarious one. Once the Congress got itself involved in direct responsibility for the Vietnam War, conservatives would move from sufferance to opposition and to harsh cutting of domestic funds, and moderates from unstinting support to sympathy for the economy. The result, over time, would be to make the program ineffective.[118]

The president thus rebuffed McNamara's request that a national state of emergency be announced and an increase in taxes to fund the war be requested, as well as the joint chiefs' request for the full mobilization of the

112. Valenti's notes on July 21, 1965, meeting. Foreign Relations of the United States, 1964–1968, Volume III, Vietnam June-December 1965, 76. Notes of meeting, http://webdoc.s4b.gwdg.de/ebook/p/2005/dep_of_state/www/about-state/history/vol_iii/070.htm.
113. Quoted in Helsing 2000, 165; Hammond 1996, 183.
114. Ibid.
115. July 22, 1965, memo to Dean Rusk from Harlan Cleveland, quoted in Hammond 1996.
116. Quoted in Helsing 2000, 174.
117. Goodwin 1976, 251.
118. Quoted in Helsing 2002, 171.

reserves. Instead, the president ordered his staff to implement his military decisions in a "low-keyed manner" in the hopes of avoiding "undue concern and excitement in the Congress and in domestic public opinion."[119]

Rather than announce the escalation during a prime-time address, Johnson held a routine noontime press conference on July 28, in which he misled the American people and Congress about the full extent of military activities in Vietnam. Johnson said simply that he had increased military forces by 50,000 soldiers, failing to acknowledge that 50,000 more troops would be en route to Southeast Asia before the end of 1965, and that another 100,000 would arrive in 1966. When meeting with congressional leaders the day before the announcement, Johnson insisted that there was no change in policy.[120]

For Johnson, the way in which the escalation was presented to Congress and the American people was at least as important as the escalation itself. Johnson's low-key strategy, as Helsing described it, "was a direct result of his desire to maintain prosperity, contain communism, and create a Great Society. He could not have the latter without ensuring the first two."[121] Vietnam and the Great Society, Johnson believed, were inextricably linked. As he later recalled, "I knew the day it exploded into a major debate on the war, that day would be the beginning of the end of the Great Society."[122]

Johnson pursued this strategy for as long as he could. But as casualties mounted and media reports from Vietnam steadily made their way back home, it became increasingly difficult for him to deny the true extent of the war efforts. After the Tet Offensive in early 1968, Johnson had no choice but to come clean and admit that the United States was engaged in a full-blown war, and one that he would not see to the end.

LESSONS

Vietnam hung like a dark cloud over Johnson's tenure in office. The president feared being labeled "soft" on communism, particularly in light of Truman's failure to keep China out of Communist hands in 1949. Johnson, further, had a deep commitment to containment and the fight against communism, yet it was unclear to what extent victory in Vietnam was even possible. For Johnson, these costs risked compromising the most important

119. Herring 2002, 166.
120. Helsing 2000, 177.
121. Ibid., 9.
122. Quoted in Goodwin 1976, 283.

tenets of his Great Society programs. As one historian wrote, "Lyndon Johnson's greatest fault as a political leader was that he chose not to choose between the Great Society and the war in Vietnam."[123]

Johnson chose not to choose precisely because he believed that the Vietnam War would attenuate—not augment—his influence over domestic policy. The many domestic legislative accomplishments that made up his Great Society were accomplished *in spite of,* not because of, the war he waged in Vietnam, and Johnson hesitated to address the Vietnam conflict in a serious way because he firmly believed that doing so would undermine congressional support for his domestic initiatives. Furthermore, once Johnson had committed the U.S. military to a course of action, he refused to disclose the full extent of U.S. military activities in Southeast Asia precisely because he believed that Congress would rescind its support for the Great Society.

In this way, the Vietnam case counters the central claim of this book. Johnson did not realize increased policy success with the beginning of war, but rather sought to delay (and then failed to disclose) the onset of war so that his domestic influence would not be diminished. We already have recognized the possibility of heterogeneous effects of war on presidential influence. This case study suggests that rather than running from positive to null, the effects may occasionally reach into the negative. But this case also suggests that the institutional advantages of the presidency— and specifically, the president's informational advantages with respect to military operations—may allow the president to both issue and then frame decisions about war and peace. Wars, after all, are not merely waged: they are fashioned and refashioned, often in ways that suit the president's political interests. Thus, to the extent that our earlier chapters found mixed evidence of the expansion of Johnson's policy success during the Vietnam War, our results do not take stock of the ways in which such institutional advantages enabled Johnson to achieve policy success while denying the existence of a wartime state.

7.3 *Bush's Wartime Effort to Reform Social Security*

Fresh off his reelection in 2004, George W. Bush launched the most ambitious domestic policy reform of his presidency: the reformation of Social Security. With two wars ongoing, Republican seat gains in recent elections,

123. Berman 1982, 150.

a series of successful domestic policy achievements in his first term, and buoyed by his reelection victory, Bush pressed forward on his domestic agenda. But despite a massive public relations campaign, Bush failed to gain traction in either chamber of Congress. Indeed, even ideologically conservative legislators who had initially supported Bush's proposal ultimately refused to rally behind the president.

Why did the president seek to reform the single most popular domestic policy program? And with all that he had going in his favor, why did he fail? The answers to both questions relate in no small part to the national and local implications of Social Security policy reform. Bush pursued reform on this politically sensitive issue because he viewed—correctly, by all indications—the Iraq and Afghanistan wars, not to mention the more nebulous war on terror, as accentuating the importance of national policy considerations. Further, he sought to link his domestic reform proposal to national policy outcomes by invoking the same rhetoric that characterized the ongoing wars in the Middle East—that of a unifying national threat. But Bush was unable to effectively link his domestic agenda to a national threat in the eyes of the nation, as Social Security retained deep local moorings that were not easily dislodged, even during war. Recognizing the electoral costs of standing with the president, legislators withdrew their support.

Bush's miscalculation was not in recognizing that his wars nationalized politics, nor was it in perceiving that the nationalization of politics augured well for his domestic policy agenda. Rather, Bush failed to appreciate the depth of opposition to any policy reform that threatened the continuing flow of Social Security benefits. The president most likely could have reformed some other domestic policy, but by choosing Social Security he overreached.

BUSH INTRODUCES SOCIAL SECURITY REFORM

In 2005, Bush designated Social Security reform as his top domestic priority. His interest in Social Security was not impulsive. As early as 1978, Bush had called for partial privatization of the Social Security system,[124] and in the 2000 presidential election Bush reiterated his view that "we should trust Americans by giving them the option of investing part of their

124. William Galston, "Why President Bush's 2005 Social Security Initiative Failed, and What It Means for the Future of the Program," *NYU Wagner,* September 2007.

Social Security contributions in private accounts."[125] The president again mentioned the topic in the 2004 State of the Union Address and throughout the campaign season that followed.

Rather than tinker at the margins, Bush sought to reform the very structure of Social Security. Under the existing "pay-as-you-go" system, workers beneath the established retirement age paid a Social Security tax that directly funded retirees. Under Bush's scheme, citizens under the age of 55 at first (this age cutoff would fade away over time) could invest a portion of their Social Security savings into stocks and bonds. Upon retirement, these citizens would claim the money resulting from their investments. Because retirees were still slated to receive their benefits in the existing system, either additional funds would need to be raised, or benefits would need to be reduced.

Fully cognizant that his plan was both ambitious and politically divisive, the president waited for a more conducive political climate to pursue his goals. To advance his domestic policy agenda, he would need money, voter support, and a large number of Republican seats within Congress. To get these, he would need to focus the country on a unifying national threat.

On the heels of his reelection in 2004, Bush believed that the time was right to make his move. In the two previous elections, Republicans had strengthened their hold in Congress. In 2002, Republicans jumped from 221 to 229 seats in the House of Representatives, and from 49 to 51 seats in the Senate—a rather extraordinary achievement given the historical tendency for the president's party to lose seats in midterm elections. Then, in the midst of a second war, this one in Iraq, Bush enjoyed a successful reelection campaign in which he won a majority of the popular vote— something he had failed to do in the 2000 presidential election. Meanwhile, Republicans had made further gains in Congress, securing a total of 232 seats in the House and 55 seats in the Senate. With two wars in progress and Republican victories in consecutive general elections, Bush thought that his political strength was at an all-time high. As he put it just after the 2004 election, "I earned capital in this campaign, political capital, and now I intend to spend it."[126]

---

125. "Bush for President" announcement, July 12, 1999. http://www.4president.org /speeches/2000/georgewbush2000announcement.htm.

126. Press conference, November 4, 2004. Richard W. Stevenson, "Confident Bush Outlines Ambitious Plans for 2nd Term," *New York Times*, Nov. 5, 2004. http://wwwnytimes .com/2004/11/05/politics/campaign/05Bush.html?_r=0.

Bush made Social Security reform the centerpiece of his 2005 State of the Union Address. He devoted more time to this subject—nearly a quarter of his entire speech—than to any other domestic policy.[127] And that was only the beginning. Over the next four months, Bush delivered more than fifty speeches across the country, laying out his plan for reform.

The president did his best to focus the nation—the electorate and politicians alike—on national policy objectives. During his speeches on domestic policy reform, he invariably began by referencing the ongoing conflicts in Afghanistan and Iraq. In the State of the Union, the only issue to receive more time than Social Security reform was the Middle East. Again and again the president referenced the looming threat of terrorism, backed by "radicalism and ideologies of murder."[128] At the same time, the president made much of the recent Iraqi election for a new Transitional National Assembly, in which "millions of citizens went to the polls and elected 275 men and women to represent them."[129] With these twin themes of fear and hope, the president heralded the importance of national, if not global, challenges.

References to war were not limited to the State of the Union address. On his campaign to reform Social Security, Bush regularly opened town hall meetings and question-and-answer sessions by reminding the audience of the foreign threats that the nation faced. On February 3, for example, he began with these remarks:

> Before we talk about Social Security, I do want to talk a little bit about the amazing times we're living in. Just think about what has happened in the last four months. There was an election in Afghanistan. Millions— millions of people voted for a leader, for a President for the first time in 5,000 years . . . It wasn't all that long ago that the Taliban was providing safe haven to al Qaida in Afghanistan. And , and that's where they plotted and trained. That's why we went in, to rout them out . . . And you saw last Sunday some incredibly brave people in Iraq defy the terrorists and cast their ballots by the millions.[130]

127. State of the Union address, February 2, 2005. http://www.washingtonpost.com/wp-srv/politics/transcripts/bushtext_020205.html.

128. Ibid.

129. Ibid.

130. Remarks in a Discussion on Strengthening Social Security and a Question-and-Answer Session in Great Falls, Montana, February 3, 2005, http://www.ssa.gov/history/gwbushstmts5.html#02032005.

On March 18, his discussion began similarly:

> Before we get to Social Security, I want to say a couple of other points. I want to thank the members of the United States military and those who support the military . . . One of the most amazing events is when over eight million Iraqis, in complete defiance of people who were trying to prevent them from going to the polls by creating incredible fear—they said, "You're not going to stop us. We long to be free." And they went to the polls sending a clear signal.[131]

By reminding his audience of foreign concerns—both the struggles and successes—Bush sought to focus the country's attention on national goals, hoping that it would remain there when the discussion turned to Social Security.

When lobbying Congress, the president again tried to draw attention to national goals by portraying Social Security reform as a necessary solution to a grave and imminent national threat—a threat that would require a unified national front. He did this by portraying the current Social Security policy as in a state of crisis. When introducing the subject in the State of the Union, he began by saying that "the system [of Social Security] is headed toward bankruptcy. And so we must join together to strengthen and save Social Security."[132] He reiterated this point throughout the coming months, repeatedly noting that "we got a problem in Social Security," as the system was not solvent, and all Americans would lose Social Security coverage sometime between 2018 and 2042.[133] In these ways, Bush attempted to unify public attention on national objectives and threats to the long term solvency of Social Security.

A FAILED WARTIME BID

Ultimately, Bush failed to reform Social Security. Despite the president's best efforts, his proposal made little headway. Neither the House nor Senate so much as voted on the president's proposal. By the fall, the president abandoned the initiative entirely.

This policy failure can be traced to two primary causes. First, notwithstanding his orchestrated public appeals, Bush failed to convince the

---

131. "Remarks in a Discussion on Strengthening Social Security in Pensacola," Florida, March 18, 2005, http://www.ssa.gov/history/gwbushstmts5.html#03182005.
132. State of the Union address, February 2, 2005.
133. "Remarks in a Discussion on Strengthening Social Security in Pensacola," Florida, March 18, 2005.

country that his Social Security reform was linked to an imminent national crisis. Polls conducted by the *Washington Post* and Gallup indicated that only 25 and 18 percent, respectively, of respondents viewed Social Security as "in crisis" in December 2004. These numbers only declined during Bush's domestic policy push.[134]

Moreover, even those who believed that Social Security stood on the brink of bankruptcy remained unconvinced that Bush's proposed reforms would solve the crisis. The crux of the Social Security system's problem was its long-running solvency, for which the most controversial elements of Bush's proposal—partial privatization—offered no remedy. At best, private accounts would function alongside other fiscal reforms. The only real solutions to the potential bankruptcy of Social Security involved lowering benefits to retirees, raising the age at which one received benefits, or raising taxes. Recognizing the unpopularity of these options, Bush shied away from them.[135] After evading the issue for months, even Bush admitted in mid-March that "personal accounts do not solve the issue [of solvency]."[136]

In actuality, partial privatization might have exacerbated the system's fiscal woes. Private accounts, after all, would have required advance-funding to supplement the current pay-as-you-go system. Introducing this advance-funding without reducing benefits to current retirees would result in substantial short-run transition costs. And therein lay the biggest obstacle to the proposed advance-fund retirement system: the political costs preceded the political benefits by decades.[137] As Douglas Arnold argued, such a system "deliver[s] no benefits in the near term for which politicians can claim credit."[138]

Social Security also had deep local connections that even war could not fray. The privatization program was politically divisive, saturated in interest group politics, and sensitive to citizens on an individual level—everyone wanted to know with certainty that in retirement they would secure the benefits owed them. Where support for reform existed, it was to be found almost exclusively among Republicans. Additionally, the American Asso-

134. "Bush Failing in Social Security Push," Pew Research Center, March 2, 2005, http://people-press.org/report/238/bush-failing-in-social-security-push.
135. Polling supported this belief. The majority of the public opposed each of these three measures. A fourth solution—just increasing the tax on the rich—did receive popular support, but Bush refused to consider this measure.
136. William Galston, "Why President Bush's 2005 Social Security Initiative Failed, And What It Means For The Future Of The Program." *NYU Wagner*, September 2007, 5.
137. Ibid.
138. Arnold 1998, 220.

ciation of Retired Persons (AARP)—a highly active interest group, both in terms of campaign contributions and voter mobilization—staunchly opposed any form of privatization and stood poised to run campaigns against anyone who endorsed reform.

Business-as-usual politics prevailed, and business-as-usual politics did not favor Social Security reform. Due to the advance-fund retirement system's need for an estimated trillion dollars in additional revenue, legislators equated the reform with political suicide. As Kirk O'Donnel, longtime aid to Tip O'Neil, had put it some decades prior, "Social Security is the third rail of American politics. Touch it, you're dead."[139] Members of Congress realized they would have to sell their states and districts on a tax increase, with any potential payoff being decades away. For legislators concerned with immediate elections supporting such a reform simply was not an option.

A declining economy left many Americans worried about their retirement funds, and partial privatization meant transferring money into inherently risky stocks and bonds. When voters learned that privatization entailed significantly lower guaranteed benefits for all but the lowest income citizens, approval for Bush's reform dropped even further. Senator Max Baucus (D-MT) voiced this concern in late April: "Remember, when we talk about private accounts, we're talking about carve-outs, taking away from Social Security, not add-ons . . . It's such a bad idea." Senate Finance Committee Chairman Chuck Grassley (R-IA), himself an early advocate of Bush's proposal, acknowledged that out of the eleven Republicans on the Finance Committee, only five or six supported Bush's proposal. Grassley further noted that, due to the need to either raise taxes or reduce benefits, "none of the 535 members of Congress, including all 100 senators really want to deal with Social Security."[140] Even securing agreement on elements of Social Security reform not closely related to the president's proposal (such as solutions to the impending bankruptcy) proved difficult, as members of the Finance Committee boycotted the meetings.[141]

Legislators recognized that their constituents were far more concerned with tax raises or benefit reductions than they were with potential long-term solvency issues. And this, ultimately, proved to be the president's

139. As quoted in William Safire, "On Language: Third Rail," *New York Times,* February 18, 2007.

140. "The Senate Finance Committee Holds Hearings on Social Security Reform," PBS Online News Hour, April 26, 2005.

141. "Social Security 'consensus' seen," *Washington Times,* June 28, 2005.

undoing. Demonstrating little penchant for either increasing taxes or reducing benefits, citizens continued to view Social Security in strictly individualistic terms. Notwithstanding two wars and lingering fears about terrorism, people's concerns about their personal welfare trumped any considerations about the long-term viability of Social Security.[142]

Not coincidentally, for the president the Iraq war was rapidly turning from a political asset into a liability. After some promising signs in early 2005, hopes for a withdrawal of U.S. troops disappeared in May, Iraq's bloodiest month since the initial U.S. invasion in 2003. In that month, over 700 Iraqi civilians died as well as 79 U.S. soldiers. Later that summer, the Bush administration would admit that "what we expected to achieve [a model new democracy, a self-supporting oil industry, or a society in which the majority of people are free from serious security threats] was never realistic given the timetable or what unfolded on the ground."[143]

Opponents of Social Security reform sought to exploit doubts about Bush's handling of the Iraq war by portraying the president as untrustworthy and incompetent in both foreign and domestic policy. *New York Times* columnist and perennial Bush critic Paul Krugman argued as follows: "The campaign for privatization provided an object lesson in how the administration sells its policies: by misrepresenting its goals, lying about the facts and abusing its control of government agencies. These were the same tactics used to sell both tax cuts and the Iraq war."[144] Or as a prominent MoveOn.org advertisement put it, "First George Bush said Saddam Hussein had weapons of mass destruction and a 'mushroom cloud' was imminent . . . Now George Bush is misleading us about Social Security."[145]

For all intents and purposes, the proposal was dead by May 2005. At that time, House Majority Whip Roy Blunt released the list of "priority legislation" on the post-Memorial Day calendar, in which "social security reform was notably absent."[146] Other advocates of the president's pro-

142. Jackie Calmes, "How a Victorious Bush Fumbled Plan to Revamp Social Security," *Wall Street Journal,* October 20, 2005.

143. Robin Wright and Ellen Knickmeyer, "U.S. Lowers Sights On What Can Be Achieved in Iraq; Administration Is Shedding 'Unreality' That Dominated Invasion, Official Says," *Washington Post,* August 14, 2005.

144. Paul Krugman, "Deficits and Deceit," *New York Times,* March 4, 2005.

145. See www.moveon.org/press/pdfs/pro20105.pdf.

146. Patrick O'Connor, "Social Security in Limbo," *The Hill,* June 1, 2005, http://archive.truthout.org/article/social-security-limbo.

posal simply clammed up. Representative Paul Ryan (R-WI) and Senator John Sununu (R-NH), who had reintroduced variants of the president's proposal in their respective chambers as late as April,[147] said precious little about the issue thereafter. Perhaps most telling, Republicans who had previously indicated that they would support Social Security reform abandoned the president's proposal altogether. Senator Lindsey Graham (R-SC), who had campaigned in 2002 to privatize Social Security, withdrew his support in April 2005, stating that Bush's proposal was fiscally irresponsible.[148] After initially supporting Bush's proposal outright, Senator Jim DeMint (R-SC) backed off from this position and proposed a much more moderate version of the bill in July 2005.[149] By October, Bush's own press secretary admitted defeat. As Scott McClellan recognized in a press conference, "There seems to be a diminished appetite in the short term. But I'm going to remind people that there is a long-term issue that we must solve. When the appetite to address it—you know, that's going to be up to the members of Congress."[150] Until then, though, the president would abandon the fight.

LESSONS

Bush's attempt at Social Security reform in 2005 reveals two important themes that run through this book. First, war has the potential to expand presidential power, and it does this by unifying the country—the electorate and legislators alike—around national objectives. It was this insight, after all, that convinced Bush to pursue Social Security reform in the first place. Absent Republican seat gains in Congress and the persistence of war abroad, it is not clear that Bush would have even attempted to reform Social Security. But when he did, he continually referenced these ongoing wars, just as concerns about foreign threats imbued his rhetoric. The president did everything he could to fix the public's attention on national policy imperatives and, by implication, to temper their more parochial, individualistic concerns.

147. "Ryan and Sununu Reintroduce Reform Bill," Cato Institute, April 27, 2005, http://www.socialsecurity.org/daily/04-27-05.html.

148. Geoff Earle, "Swing Conservative," *Washington Monthly,* April 2005.

149. Jackie Calmes, "How a Victorious Bush Fumbled Plan to Revamp Social Security," *Wall Street Journal,* October 20, 2005.

150. Press briefing with Scott McClellan. Oct. 5, 2005, www.presidency.ucsb.edu/ws/index.php?pid=73160.

Just as important, though, this case illustrates some of the limits to presidential influence during war. Issues that require tax increases or benefit cuts—as Social Security reform would have—are always difficult to sell to reelection-seeking legislators, particularly when the potential benefits of such reforms are delayed. Though war does increase the president's bargaining power, it does not give him free rein to implement any policy he desires. With Social Security, Bush confronted a basic truth about our system of checks and balances: power, even presidential power during war, is always limited; at any moment some policy fights simply cannot be won.

7.4 *Final Remarks*

The cases in this chapter underscore at least two limits of the Policy Priority Model itself and its application to wartime politics at home. First, having registered extraordinary legislative achievements in peace, presidents cannot automatically expect even greater achievements during war. Quite the opposite, in fact. For reasons that the Policy Priority Model does not account for—that is, budget trade-offs between foreign and domestic policy—wars may imperil past domestic policy achievements. This is precisely the story of Johnson's steady and largely understated escalation of the Vietnam War between 1965 and 1968. Having enacted landmark legislation in 1964 and 1965 with the support of Democratic supermajorities in the House and Senate, Johnson worried greatly about the implications of a full-blown war in Southeast Asia for his Great Society—with cause, it turns out. For at precisely the moment that the public caught wind of the size of the Vietnam War in early 1968, Johnson withdrew from consideration for the Democratic presidential nomination.

The second point relates to the gains a president can reasonably expect from war. Just because the nation is at war, members of Congress need not accede to presidential demands, and certainly not to those that would revamp domestic policies that enjoy widespread public support. Two ongoing wars and a recent reelection to boot did not deliver the influence needed for Bush to tackle Social Security reform in 2005. Despite his repeated efforts to invoke the Iraq and Afghanistan wars and to cast entitlement reform in terms of national security, Bush ultimately failed to overhaul Social Security. In this textbook case of overreach, we witnessed the appeals of a wartime president falling on deaf ears around the nation and, more crucially perhaps, on Capitol Hill.

If Bush's experience tempers our assessment of war's influence, Eisenhower's amply resuscitates it. Eisenhower leveraged the mere *threat* of war to pass sweeping education legislation. And with military conflict becoming a near constant presence in an age of terrorist threats, foreign occupation, and democratization within the Middle East, future presidents may have an even deeper grab bag of opportunities to nationalize domestic political reform.

PART IV

Conclusion

CHAPTER 8

Summaries, Speculations, and Extensions

On a basic level, the findings presented in this book provide rather broad support for a common view about American governance: presidential power predictably and reliably expands during times of war, and then recedes as the nation returns to peace. Nearly all our empirical chapters present supporting evidence on this score. Presidential budget requests are honored to a greater degree when the nation is at war, members of Congress compile voting records that better reflect the president's preferences during war than during peace, and presidents are able to use the specter of war to achieve significant legislative victories that otherwise would elude them. Moreover, the effects of war do *not* appear to be concentrated among foreign policy initiatives. Rather, during war presidents obtain a heightened degree of success in both foreign and domestic affairs; and to the extent that differences are observed, evidence of a wartime effect is greater in domestic than in foreign policy.

Importantly, though, all wars do not affect presidential success in Congress equally. And these results, too, are rather consistent across the various empirical chapters. Two wars—World War II and the post-9/11 wars—yielded especially large increases in presidential influence. During these wars, presidents Roosevelt and Bush had greater success in passing their budgets, just as members of Congress compiled legislative voting records that more closely resembled the president's preferences. As the case studies in Chapter 6 highlight, Roosevelt leveraged the war to stave off more restrictive labor bills that threatened to fracture his domestic political coalition, just as Bush instituted immigration reforms that had been the subject of considerable opposition within Congress before 9/11.

Other major modern wars, however, did not have nearly as large an impact on presidential-congressional relations. During the Korean War, Truman's budget proposals were no more successful than his peacetime budget requests; nor do we find consistent evidence that the Korean War yielded a Congress more willing to vote in ways that reflected Truman's ideological preferences, at least not at the war's outset. We observed similar results for the Vietnam War, when presidential budget requests were marginally more successful, while congressional roll call votes proved no more (and perhaps less) consistent with the president's ideological orientation. Finally, during the Persian Gulf War, neither Bush's lone wartime budget request nor his broader legislative agenda received an especially accommodating hearing in Congress.

What might explain the heterogeneous effects of war on presidential influence? Here, our task turns to theory. For in addition to investigating *whether* wars increase presidential power, we scrutinize *why* members of Congress might be more willing to support the president during war than during peace. The Policy Priority Model generates unambiguous predictions about the conditions under which the president realizes heightened degrees of success. In particular, the model demonstrates that members of Congress will enact policies that more closely reflect presidential preferences when they assign greater importance to the national vis-à-vis local implications of public policy. Among the various classes of events that might alter the criteria that members use to evaluate public policy, we maintain, wars rank among the most robust. Hence, it is because wars change *how* members of Congress think about policies generally that wars alter *what* members think about specific policy alternatives. Moreover, and this is crucial, wars do so in ways that increase the chances that members will favor policy instruments that generate outcomes that better reflect the president's wishes.

World War II and the post-9/11 wars augmented presidential influence because they so profoundly increased the significance of national outcomes. The Korean, Vietnam, and Persian Gulf wars, by contrast, did relatively little to persuade members of Congress to privilege national considerations over local ones—and, as a consequence, presidents during these wars did not enjoy nearly as much influence over the appropriations or legislative processes. This is not to say that these wars were unimportant or inconsequential in some absolute sense. It is merely to recognize that with respect to presidential power, the subject of this book's study, they pale in comparison to World War II and the post-9/11 wars.

Importantly, the pattern of findings we observe stands in stark contrast to other competing explanations for the relevance of war to interbranch bargaining. For instance, a fair bit of existing research suggests that public support for war, and for the president in particular, declines as casualties mount. To the extent that congressional voting records reflect such public sentiments, we would expect presidential influence to wane as wartime casualties increase. By this standard, presidential power would have expanded most during the Persian Gulf War, and least during World War II. On the other hand, if increased support for the president is a function of a war's domestic mobilization efforts, we would expect to see evidence of increased presidential power only in World War II. By yet another account, if presidents wield increased influence during wartime when a large proportion of Congress is composed of the president's copartisans, World War II and the Korean and Vietnam wars should have produced the largest effects. Finally, if wartime success is contingent upon the public rallying behind the president, then the largest effects, by far, should appear in the post-9/11 wars. Though not grounded in clear theory, these alternative explanations obviously yield very different sets of predictions from the Policy Priority Model about the heterogeneous impacts of war. None, though, provide a better accounting for our empirical results.

Our empirical findings also allow us to distinguish among competing mechanisms that appear within the Policy Priority Model itself. Recall that in the model presidential success increases in both the importance the legislator assigns to national outcomes and in the uncertainty of the policy-making environment. Wars plausibly generate both of these effects, but they do so to different degrees in different policy domains. Because members of Congress already tend to evaluate foreign policy primarily on the basis of the national outcomes, wars may have a greater impact on their assessments of domestic policies. Foreign wars undeniably increase the uncertainty of foreign policy outcomes more than domestic ones. The fact that our empirical findings demonstrate that war's impact not only extends to but is particularly pronounced in domestic policy gives further credence to our preferred explanation.

These findings, of course, are fraught with normative implications, at least some of which are salutary. Indeed, they provide some comfort to critics of how we, as a nation, go to war. Deference to the commander in chief, we argue, arises not because members of Congress are intent upon skirting their constitutional obligations in matters involving war in order to avoid blame or responsibility. Rather, congressional deference derives from a propensity of politicians to assign less credence to parochial considerations and more to national ones during times of war, and out of a further recognition that the president has superior information on the national implications of public policy. To the extent that we want Congress to pay more attention to our collective fate as a nation and less to the private, local considerations that do so much to divide us, then war—or more exactly, war's effect on public policy making—is not altogether bad.

Before we all rush out to celebrate this state of affairs, we need to recognize other, more troubling implications of our theory and findings. Two, in our view, stand out. First, precisely because expertise yields influence, presidents have powerful incentives to jealously guard their own. Though members of Congress will extract what information they can, the president cannot be expected to heartily comply. Why should he? Sharing information only weakens his bargaining leverage and leads to the enactment of policies with which he disagrees. More disconcerting still, our theory and findings reveal powerful motivations for presidents to take the nation to war when military action is a plausible course of action; when it is not, he may at least invoke the rhetoric of war when delving into policy domains. Thus, it is no surprise that, with the exception of the 1980s, this country has waged a major war at some point in each of the last eight decades. Literally hundreds of smaller military ventures have been waged, and domestic debates about a wide range of policy matters—from drugs to foreign aid to health care—are regularly infused with the language of war. War, as both fact and metaphor, provides a powerful mechanism for presidents to shift policy debates onto more profitable grounds.

8.1 *Holes and Extensions*

This book makes an important shift in the way we study war and presidential power—one away from grand narratives and loose evidence and toward careful theorizing and rigorous empirics. The theory and evidence offered here, however, certainly do not represent all that can be done, but merely provide a starting point for the renewed study of this longstanding issue in American politics. And from where we sit, a great deal more work remains.

EMPIRICAL

Though the findings in this book broadly support our theory, there remain some empirical curiosities that are not fully explained. In Chapter 5, for instance, our estimates of the effects of the Korean and Persian Gulf wars are inconsistent across chambers. In both instances we find evidence of increased accommodation to the president's preferences among members of the House, but not in the Senate. It is not immediately obvious why such differences should emerge. It is possible that members of the Senate are, on average, more insulated from the effects of war, perhaps because of their longer terms in office and staggered election cycles. Such an explanation, though, is admittedly post hoc. Moreover, it does not easily account for the fact that we find significant changes in the voting habits of members of both the House and Senate in both World War II and Afghanistan.

Another curiosity concerns the differences between the transitions from peace to war and from war to peace. We find consistent evidence that the end of nearly all of our wars—the one exception being the Persian Gulf War—yielded congresses that were less willing to vote with the president then in office. At the outbreak of war, meanwhile, members' voting habits more closely aligned with only Roosevelt's and Bush's underlying ideologies. Consistent with our theory, local concerns may have promptly come to the fore at the end of all our wars, while they faded to the background at the outset of only two. Perhaps. Without further investigation, we are reluctant to dismiss the possibility that there are important distinctions between the escalations and de-escalations of foreign conflict to which neither our theory nor our characterization of modern wars speaks.

Beyond matters of interpretation, there also remain important areas of continued empirical study. Our main empirical tests, after all, look at either policy outcomes or the voting habits of all members of Congress. Future work should do more to distinguish the variable impact of war within Congress. Nothing about the Policy Priority Model, after all, precludes the possibility of heterogeneous wartime effects among members of Congress. If, for instance, members only reconsider the criteria by which they evaluate policy alternatives when they support the broader aims of a war effort, then evidence of wartime changes in voting behavior should be confined to this subset of the House and Senate. Similarly, if members face particularly strong pressures to deliver constituency benefits during election years, then the effects of war may vary for the subset of Senators who face reelection relative to those who can count on remaining in office for a longer period of time. Surely other possibilities exist, which we hope scholars will explore.

Future empirical work might investigate whether events beyond war might augment the salience of national outcomes, thereby bolstering presidential influence. When looking for such events and such influence, scholars should remain attuned to the possibility that the effects will be more localized than those observed for large-scale military ventures. We found no evidence, for instance, that smaller military ventures in the 1990s, presidential scandals, or the Iran hostage crisis altered members' general voting behavior. Nor did we observe any indication that the launching of

Sputnik altered the president's influence over any policy domain other than education. One can well imagine that the effects of economic crises might be confined to economic policy, in much the same way that concerns about international drug trade might augment the president's influence over just drug policy.

While entertaining the possibilities that events other than war change legislators' evaluations of the importance of local and national outcomes, scholars might consider an interesting corollary to our central argument: as politics become more localized, congressional support for the president should decline. Hence, when a legislator finds cause to prioritize local over national outcomes—imagine, for instance, the sectional pressures members of Congress face when their district or state has just experienced a massive flood or a deadly crime spree—she will appear less supportive of the president.

Finally, and perhaps most obviously, these empirical investigations should look beyond the case of Washington, D.C. For instance, the model might be profitably applied to bargaining arrangements between state legislators and governors, or to those between legislatures and executives abroad that operate in systems of government that are broadly consistent with the Policy Priority Model. Cast in such general terms, the model may offer insights into executive-legislative deliberations in a wide array of political contexts. We see no reason why its insights should uniquely apply to the U.S. president and Congress.

THEORETICAL

In addition to continued empirical scrutiny, the Policy Priority Model invites a variety of theoretical extensions. As a simplifying assumption, we set the mappings of policies into local and national outcomes to be positively correlated with one another. Future work might allow for these processes to be negatively correlated, and then to estimate comparative statics on the extent of correlation. In so doing, we might gain insight into the variable willingness of those members of Congress from districts that constitute microcosms of the country as a whole to support the president as compared with those members who represent outlying jurisdictions.

As we have already noted, the Policy Priority Model presents a rather anemic presidency, one whose capacity to influence public policy is restricted entirely to proposal making. Future work ought to incorporate some of the other tools available to the president, some of which are enshrined in the Constitution (e.g., the veto) and others of which are the joint product of presidential initiative and congressional delegation (e.g., the opportunity to forego the legislative process and set policy unilaterally). Although these richer models can be expected to yield heightened assessments of presidential influence, it remains to be seen whether they materially alter our assessments of the marginal impact of war on presidential bargaining success. Additionally, these models may profitably enhance our understanding not only of the effect of war on public policy, but also of its effects on the strategies presidents employ to advance their policy interests.

The Policy Priority Model might also benefit from some technical refinements and extensions. Scholars with a deeper understanding of mathematics than us might consider alternative mapping functions from policies into outcomes—and with them, alternative solution concepts. For instance, scholars might examine whether our core predictions hold when the mapping functions are characterized as Brownian motions, as in Steve Callander's work. In this setup, when players become experts they learn something about the translation of policies into outcomes, rather than insulating themselves from exogenous shocks; hence, rather than solving for subgame perfection, the analyst would identify conditions that support perfect Bayesian equilibria.

Finally, scholars would do well to investigate the conditions under which multiple members of Congress, as opposed to a single representative member, invest in expertise about the intermittently discrete and overlapping mapping processes of policies into national and local outcomes. Clearly, a substantial amount of existing scholarship already explores the ways in which congressional committees help solve the basic informational problems faced by Congress as a whole. What remains unclear is how committees, or any other congressional institution, affect the president's calculus about whether to acquire expertise, and whether, in turn, the existence of such institutions in any way alters our predictions about war and presidential success.

OTHER TOPICS ON WAR AND PRESIDENTIAL POWER

The most expansive opportunities for continued research lie beyond the kinds of congressional vote-switching analyses we conduct here. Opportunities for presidential influence, after all, extend well beyond the formal lawmaking process. For all intents and purposes, the empirical and formal literatures in American politics have paid barely any mind to questions about the broader relationships between war and presidential power.

How do wars influence trends in domestic unilateral policy making (e.g., the issuance of executive orders, proclamations, national security directives), signing statements, and foreign policy making (whether by treaty or executive agreement)? Does Congress tend to delegate broader powers to the president during war? And if so, do these powers extend beyond military matters? When issuing emergency legislation, does Congress facilitate the exercise of presidential power long after a particular crisis has passed and in domains that only tangentially relate to the crisis itself? How do wars affect both the design of and presidential control over the federal bureaucracy?

The questions, of course, do not end with Congress. Are judges and justices less likely to hear challenges to executive authority during war? When they do consider such cases, are judges and justices any more likely to side with the president? And what of bureaucrats? In the advice they give and the actions they take, do bureaucrats more closely attend to the president's policy wishes in war than in peace?

To be sure, a handful of empirical studies do investigate these issues.[1] None, however, are grounded in deep theory. The preponderance of scholarship on these topics, like that on congressional voting behavior as summarized in Chapter 1, consists of sweeping historical narratives and normatively driven legal studies. On a broad array of questions involving war and separations of powers generally, and presidential power in particular, the field cries out for theoretical and empirical advancement.

8.2 *The Future of War*

As we finish this book, tens of thousands of U.S. troops remain engaged in a ten-year struggle in Afghanistan. Though Obama has delivered on his promise to draw down in Iraq, thousands of troops remain there as well. The United States recently joined NATO forces to assist in the democratization movement in Libya—a military campaign that remains ongoing. More recently still, an elite group of Navy SEALs entered Pakistan undetected, descended into a private compound in Abbottabad, and killed Osama bin Laden, the chief architect and financial supporter of the September 11 attacks. From all sides of the political spectrum, the dominant messages have communicated both jubilation and vigilance, for the death of one man does

---

1. For summaries of these literatures, see Howell and Johnson 2009, and Howell 2011.

not stamp out the larger "war on terror." Meanwhile, Iran moves forward on its nuclear weapons program, North Korea's foreign policy is as erratic as ever, the Israeli-Palestinian conflict continues to confound every international negotiator, and on and on.

In such a world, what would it mean for peace to return? What is the equivalent of V-J Day in the wars against terrorism, the Taliban in Afghanistan, or the more extreme elements in Iran? When it occurs, will it be accompanied by ticker-tape parades, iconic images of swooning women welcoming home the nation's soldiers, and a sense that now, at last, we can return to the distinctly local concerns of our communities, families, and homes?

War has rooted deeply into the nation's conscious. It may well have become a permanent fixture on the political landscape. Distinctions between states of war and peace have always been subject to interpretation, particularly given the steady escalations and de-escalations that characterize modern warfare. In the contemporary world, though, such distinctions may have become blurred beyond recognition.

In some senses, the notion that war is exceptional to politics has always been mistaken, but it has especially been so in the post–World War II era. A variety of forces, however, have conspired to make war a mainstay of American politics. Three, to our minds, stand above all others. The first concerns the web of relationships that typically fall under the rubric of globalization. It is difficult to even conceive of many events abroad that do not, in one way or another, affect the United States. Our interests are too far reaching, and our dependencies too great, to ignore any region of the world. Goings on that once could be written off as someone else's problem—civil wars, regional instabilities, humanitarian crises, border disputes, assassination attempts—have very much become our own. Though politicians disagree vehemently about the proper response to such crises, all within the mainstream of American politics concede that lapsing into isolationism is simply unacceptable.

The second force—or more accurately, the second fact—about contemporary politics is the U.S. hegemony in the international arena. Whether by reference to its economic productivity, military might, cultural dominance, or political influence, the United States is unrivaled. To be sure, ongoing debate persists about whether the future of the American "empire" is one of ascendance or decline. But historians and political analysts broadly agree that for at least the foreseeable future, the United States will remain if not the only superpower, then one of a handful. Given its hegemonic status, the United States operates at the very center of international politics, commanding the attention of every foreign state and international organization, and often dictating the range of acceptable responses to regional crises.

Finally, there is the nature of contemporary threats to U.S. security. Rarely does the United States square off against a foreign combatant, its soldiers lined up against ours, successive rounds of fire exchanged, leading irrevocably to a decisive ending. Rather, battles are episodic and unanticipated, with the enemy striking and then abruptly fading back into civilian populations. Today, the enemy's primary objective is to outlast the United States, not defeat it—to undermine its will, not conquer its armies.

The identity of foreign combatants, too, has changed. Nowhere is this truer than in the ongoing military campaign against terrorism. Though terrorist organizations may receive various forms of support from nation states, they also retain considerable autonomy from them. Terrorist organizations are highly decentralized, consisting of independent cells that may not even know of one another, following leaders who are eminently replaceable. As a consequence, it is difficult to see how either the structure of existing international organizations or the content of existing international law can meaningfully resolve conflicts involving these nonstate actors. Nor can the United States do it alone, sitting down with these organizations, deliberating over its differences with them, then signing a peace accord that sets matters right once and for all. If terrorist organizations cannot be eradicated or pacified, then true peace may prove elusive. The closest approximation instead may be the containment of terrorist threats achieved through continual monitoring and steadfast military preparedness.

8.3 *A Future for the Policy Priority Model*

All of this portends an even more influential presidency in the twenty-first century than the one that came of age in the twentieth. With war always in the discussion, the baseline for evaluating the importance of local qua national outcomes clearly has shifted. Indeed, to the extent that any organized groups are arguing on behalf of local interests—the Tea Party might be one such example—they are pushing greater state and municipal government autonomy rather than the fortification of constituency ties to members of Congress. To the extent that presidents retain clear informational advantages about the mapping of policies onto outcomes—and in the near term, at least, there is every reason to expect that they will—the nationalization of American politics augurs well for the president's policy agenda.

Change, when it occurs, may take the form of a reduction in members' assessments of the importance of national outcomes. And rather than foreign wars generating short-term spikes in presidential influence, the impetus for change may come from quintessentially regional crises like storms and oil spills devastating coastal cities and communities, tornadoes wiping out southern towns, manufacturing plants closing and the accompanying dislocation of their workers, or springtime frosts devastating whole crops. So as to appear responsive to these kinds of distinctly local exigencies, members of Congress may temporarily downgrade the importance of national outcomes, and in so doing stand in the way of the president's policy agenda.

Over the longer term, one should not count Congress out. For starters, with the normalization of military activities abroad may come a change in the psychology of war itself. As citizens learn to live with war, their attention may return to the local, private, and parochial interests. In turn, these citizens may demand that their elected representatives in Congress privilege local outcomes once again.

Alternatively, large shifts in the importance of national outcomes may induce what amounts to a change in equilibria in the Policy Priority Model. Congress may eventually see fit to incur the costs of acquiring expertise about the mappings of policies onto both local *and* national outcomes. Should it do so, then the basis for expecting that marginal alterations in the importance of national outcomes will increase presidential success promptly dissipates.

For the foreseeable future, however, the increase in wartime activities— buttressed by globalization trends, the obligations and expectations that accompany international hegemony, and the particular brand of adversaries faced by our military—bodes well for the president's policy agenda at home. The normalization of war will take time. Even if it is achieved, presidents will retain plenty of opportunities to underscore the importance of foreign military conflicts for the American public. Meanwhile, for legislators to acquire expertise about national outcomes requires a great deal more than the Policy Priority Model suggests. Rather than paying a one-time fixed cost, successive generations of members will have to coordinate with one another in the construction of bureaucratic institutions that rival those within the executive branch.

Presidential power is now and always shall be contested. But as long as war looms large in the American conscience, presidents will have an important advantage in their dealings with Congress.

PART V

Appendixes

APPENDIX A

Technical Details, Chapter 2

THEOREM 1

For sufficiently large c_1^L and sufficiently small c_2^L and c_1^P, an equilibrium exists wherein the President acquires expertise on only national outcomes and proposes a policy that produces either his ideal national outcome or, under select circumstances, the Legislator's. The Legislator then acquires expertise on only local outcomes and enacts a policy that is either closer to her ideal point (in the case when the President proposes the policy that produces his ideal point) or perfectly matches the President's proposal (in the case when the President proposes her ideal point).

PROOF

In this equilibrium, the strategies are as follows:

$$S_P = \left(A_1, p^P = \frac{x_1^P}{\mu_1} \right)$$

$$S_L = \begin{cases} \left(A_2, p^L = \dfrac{\dfrac{1}{3}\lambda k_1^2 \dfrac{x_1^P}{\mu_1}}{\lambda \mu_1^2 + \dfrac{1}{3}\lambda k_1^2 + \mu_2^2} \right) & \text{if } S_P = \left(A_1, p^P \le \dfrac{x_1^P}{\mu_1} \right) \\[2em] (A_2, p^L = 0) & \text{if } S_P = \left(A_1, p^P > \dfrac{x_1^P}{\mu_1} \right) \\[1.5em] (A_2, p^L = 0) & \text{if } S_P = \left(A_2, p^P \le \dfrac{x_1^P}{\mu_1} \right) \\[1.5em] (A_2, p^L = 0) & \text{if } S_P = \left(A_2, p^P > \dfrac{x_1^P}{\mu_1} \right) \\[1.5em] \left(A_2, p^L = \dfrac{\dfrac{1}{3}\lambda k_1^2 \dfrac{x_1^P}{\mu_1}}{\lambda \mu_1^2 + \dfrac{1}{3}\lambda k_1^2 + \mu_2^2} \right) & \text{if } S_P = \left(B, p^P \le \dfrac{x_1^P}{\mu_1} \right) \\[2em] (A_2, p^L = 0) & \text{if } S_P = \left(B, p^P > \dfrac{x_1^P}{\mu_1} \right) \\[1.5em] (A_2, p^L = 0) & \text{if } S_P = \left(\varnothing, p^P \le \dfrac{x_1^P}{\mu_1} \right) \\[1.5em] (A_2, p^L = 0) & \text{if } S_P = \left(\varnothing, p^P > \dfrac{x_1^P}{\mu_1} \right) \end{cases}$$

Both P and L must be best-responding to the other player's strategies. Solving by backward induction, we begin by calculating the optimal policy p^L that L will enact. This is done by choosing p^L to maximize $\mathbb{E}(U_L)$ conditional on S_P and S_L ($\max_{p^L}\mathbb{E}(U_L(p^L|S_P, S_L))$). Note that $\mathbb{E}(x_j) = \mathbb{E}(\psi_j(p^i))$, and variations in ψ_j will lead the utility function to take different forms in different subgames. On the equilibrium path, for instance, $\mathbb{E}(U_L) = \lambda[-(\mu_1 p^L + (p^P - p^L)z_1)^2] - (\mu_2 p^L)^2 = -\lambda(\mu_1 p^L)^2 - \lambda(p^P - p^L)^2\left(\dfrac{k_1^2}{3}\right) - (\mu_2 p^L)^2$.

We then plug this value of $(p^L)^*$ into $\mathbb{E}(U_L)$, and we compare the expected utilities across the four actions available to L in each subgame. There are four subgames to consider (we omit the four subgames in which P proposes a policy greater than that which would induce his ideal national outcome, as those subgames are equivalent to the fourth case shown below).

Case 1: $S_P = (A_1, p^p)$

(a) $EU_L(S_L = A_1, p^L) = -\lambda \mu_1^2 (p^L)^2 - (\mu_2 p^L)^2 - \dfrac{k_2^2}{3} - c_1^L$

$\Rightarrow (p^L)* = 0$

$\Rightarrow EU_L(\cdot) = -\dfrac{k_1^2}{3} - c_1^L$

(b) $EU_L(S_L = (A_2, p^L)) = \lambda \left[-(\mu_1 p^L)^2 - \left(\dfrac{x_1^P}{\mu_1} - p^L \right)^2 \dfrac{k^2}{3} \right] - (\mu_2 p^L)^2 - c_2^L$

$\Rightarrow (p^L)* = \dfrac{\dfrac{1}{3} \lambda k_1^2 \dfrac{x_1^p}{\mu_1}}{\lambda \mu_1^2 + \dfrac{1}{3} \lambda k_1^2 + \mu_2^2}$

$\Rightarrow EU_L(\cdot) = \lambda \left[-\left(\mu_1 \left(\dfrac{\dfrac{1}{3} \lambda k_1^2 \dfrac{x_1^p}{\mu_1}}{\lambda \mu_1^2 + \dfrac{1}{3} \lambda k_1^2 + \mu_2^2} \right) \right)^2 \right.$

$\left. -\left(\dfrac{x_1^P}{\mu_1} - \left(\dfrac{\dfrac{1}{3} \lambda k_1^2 \dfrac{x_1^p}{\mu_1}}{\lambda \mu_1^2 + \dfrac{1}{3} \lambda k_1^2 + \mu_2^2} \right) \right)^2 \dfrac{k^2}{3} \right.$

$\left. -\left(\mu_2 \left(\dfrac{\dfrac{1}{3} \lambda k_1^2 \dfrac{x_1^p}{\mu_1}}{\lambda \mu_1^2 + \dfrac{1}{3} \lambda k_1^2 + \mu_2^2} \right) \right)^2 \right] - c_2^L$

(c) $EU_L(S_L = B, p^L) = \lambda(-\mu_1 p^L)^2 - (\mu_2 p^L)^2 - c_1^L - c_2^L$

$\Rightarrow (p^L)* = 0$

$\Rightarrow EU_L(\cdot) = -c_1^L - c_2^L$

(d) $EU_L(S_L = \varnothing, p^L) = \lambda \left[-(\mu_1 p^L)^2 - \left(\dfrac{x_1^P}{\mu_1} - p^L \right)^2 \dfrac{k^2}{3} \right] - (\mu_1 p^L)^2 - \dfrac{k^2}{3}$

$$\Rightarrow (p^L)^* = \frac{\dfrac{1}{3}\lambda k_1^2 \dfrac{x_1^p}{\mu_1}}{\lambda\mu_1^2 + \dfrac{1}{3}\lambda k_1^2 + \mu_2^2}$$

$$\Rightarrow EU_L(\cdot) = \lambda \left[-\left(\mu_1 \left(\frac{\dfrac{1}{3}\lambda k_1^2 \dfrac{x_1^p}{\mu_1}}{\lambda\mu_1^2 + \dfrac{1}{3}\lambda k_1^2 + \mu_2^2} \right) \right)^2 \right.$$

$$-\left(\frac{x_1^p}{\mu_1} - \left(\frac{\dfrac{1}{3}\lambda k_1^2 \dfrac{x_1^p}{\mu_1}}{\lambda\mu_1^2 + \dfrac{1}{3}\lambda k_1^2 + \mu_2^2} \right) \right)^2 \frac{k^2}{3} \right].$$

$$-\left(\mu_1 \left(\frac{\dfrac{1}{3}\lambda k_1^2 \dfrac{x_1^p}{\mu_1}}{\lambda\mu_1^2 + \dfrac{1}{3}\lambda k_1^2 + \mu_2^2} \right) \right)^2 - \frac{k^2}{3}$$

In this subgame, (b) is preferred to (a) if

$$c_1^L > \lambda \left[\left(\mu_1 \left(\frac{\dfrac{1}{3}\lambda k_1^2 \dfrac{x_1^p}{\mu_1}}{\lambda\mu_1^2 + \dfrac{1}{3}\lambda k_1^2 + \mu_2^2} \right) \right)^2 + \left(\frac{x_1^p}{\mu_1} - \left(\frac{\dfrac{1}{3}\lambda k_1^2 \dfrac{x_1^p}{\mu_1}}{\lambda\mu_1^2 + \dfrac{1}{3}\lambda k_1^2 + \mu_2^2} \right) \right)^2 \frac{k^2}{3} \right]$$

$$+ \left(\mu_2 \left(\frac{\dfrac{1}{3}\lambda k_1^2 \dfrac{x_1^p}{\mu_1}}{\lambda\mu_1^2 + \dfrac{1}{3}\lambda k_1^2 + \mu_2^2} \right) \right)^2 + c_2^L - \frac{k_1^2}{3}.$$

And (b) is preferred to (c) if

$$c_1^L > \lambda \left[\left(\mu_1 \left(\frac{\frac{1}{3}\lambda k_1^2 \frac{x_1^P}{\mu_1}}{\lambda \mu_1^2 + \frac{1}{3}\lambda k_1^2 + \mu_2^2} \right) \right)^2 + \left(\frac{x_1^P}{\mu_1} - \left(\frac{\frac{1}{3}\lambda k_1^2 \frac{x_1^P}{\mu_1}}{\lambda \mu_1^2 + \frac{1}{3}\lambda k_1^2 + \mu_2^2} \right) \right)^2 \frac{k^2}{3} \right]$$

$$+ \left(\mu_2 \left(\frac{\frac{1}{3}\lambda k_1^2 \frac{x_1^P}{\mu_1}}{\lambda \mu_1^2 + \frac{1}{3}\lambda k_1^2 + \mu_2^2} \right) \right)^2 .$$

And (b) is preferred to (d) if $c_2^L < \dfrac{k^2}{3}$.

Case 2: $S_P = (A_2, p^p)$

(a) $EU_L(S_L = A_1, p^L) = -\lambda(\mu_1 p^L)^2 - (\mu_2 p^L)^2 - \left(\dfrac{x_1^P}{\mu_1} - p^L \right)^2 \dfrac{k_2^2}{3} - c_1^L$

$$\Rightarrow (p^L)^* = \frac{\frac{1}{3}p^P k_2^2}{\lambda \mu_1^2 + \frac{1}{3}k_2^2 + \mu_2^2}$$

$$\Rightarrow EU_L(\cdot) = -\lambda \left[\mu_1 \left(\frac{\frac{1}{3}\frac{x_1^P}{\mu_1} k_2^2}{\lambda \mu_1^2 + \frac{1}{3}k_2^2 + \mu_2^2} \right) \right]^2 - \left[\mu_2 \left(\frac{\frac{1}{3}\frac{x_1^P}{\mu_1} k_2^2}{\lambda \mu_1^2 + \frac{1}{3}k_2^2 + \mu_2^2} \right) \right]^2$$

$$- \left(\frac{x_1^P}{\mu_1} - \left(\frac{\frac{1}{3}\frac{x_1^P}{\mu_1} k_2^2}{\lambda \mu_1^2 + \frac{1}{3}k_2^2 + \mu_2^2} \right) \right)^2 \frac{k_2^2}{3} - c_1^L$$

(b) $EU_L(S_L = A_2, p^L) = -\lambda(\mu_1 p^L)^2 - \lambda \dfrac{k_1^2}{3} - (\mu_2 p^L)^2 - c_2^L$

$$\Rightarrow (p^L)^* = 0$$

$$\Rightarrow EU_L(\cdot) = -\lambda \frac{k_1^2}{3} - c_2^L$$

(c) $EU_L(S_L = B, p^L) = -\lambda(\mu_1 p^L)^2 + (\mu_2 p^L)^2 - c_1^L - c_2^L$

$$\Rightarrow (p^L)^* = 0$$

$$\Rightarrow EU_L(\cdot) = -c_1^L - c_2^L$$

(d) $EU_L(S_L = \varnothing, p^L) = -\lambda(\mu_1 p^L)^2 - \lambda\dfrac{k_1^2}{3} - (\mu_2 p^L)^2 - (p^P - p^L)^2 \dfrac{k_2^2}{3}$

$$\Rightarrow (p^L)^* = \frac{\dfrac{1}{3}p^P k_2^2}{\lambda\mu_1^2 + \dfrac{1}{3}k_2^2 + \mu_2^2}$$

$$\Rightarrow EU_L(\cdot) = -\lambda\left(\mu_1 \left(\frac{\dfrac{1}{3}\dfrac{x_1^P}{\mu_1}k_2^2}{\lambda\mu_1^2 + \dfrac{1}{3}k_2^2 + \mu_2^2}\right)\right)^2$$

$$-\lambda\dfrac{k_1^2}{3} - \left(\mu_2 \left(\frac{\dfrac{1}{3}\dfrac{x_1^P}{\mu_1}k_2^2}{\lambda\mu_1^2 + \dfrac{1}{3}k_2^2 + \mu_2^2}\right)\right)^2$$

$$-\left(\frac{x_1^P}{\mu_1} - \left(\frac{\dfrac{1}{3}\dfrac{x_1^P}{\mu_1}k_2^2}{\lambda\mu_1^2 + \dfrac{1}{3}k_2^2 + \mu_2^2}\right)\right)^2 \dfrac{k_2^2}{3}$$

In this subgame, (b) is preferred to (a) if

$$c_1^L > -\lambda\left(\mu_1\left(\frac{\dfrac{1}{3}\dfrac{x_1^P}{\mu_1}k_2^2}{\lambda\mu_1^2 + \dfrac{1}{3}k_2^2 + \mu_2^2}\right)\right)^2 - \left(\mu_2\left(\frac{\dfrac{1}{3}\dfrac{x_1^P}{\mu_1}k_2^2}{\lambda\mu_1^2 + \dfrac{1}{3}k_2^2 + \mu_2^2}\right)\right)^2$$

$$-\left(\frac{x_1^P}{\mu_1} - \left(\frac{\dfrac{1}{3}\dfrac{x_1^P}{\mu_1}k_2^2}{\lambda\mu_1^2 + \dfrac{1}{3}k_2^2 + \mu_2^2}\right)\right)^2 \dfrac{k_2^2}{3} + \lambda\dfrac{k_1^2}{3} + c_2^L.$$

And (b) is preferred to (c) if $c_1^L > \lambda\dfrac{k_1^2}{3}$. And (b) is preferred to (d) if

$$c_2^L < \lambda \left(\mu_1 \left(\frac{\frac{1}{3} \frac{x_1^P}{\mu_1} k_2^2}{\lambda \mu_1^2 + \frac{1}{3} k_2^2 + \mu_2^2} \right) \right)^2 + \lambda \frac{k_1^2}{3} + \left(\mu_2 \left(\frac{\frac{1}{3} \frac{x_1^P}{\mu_1} k_2^2}{\lambda \mu_1^2 + \frac{1}{3} k_2^2 + \mu_2^2} \right) \right)^2$$

$$+ \left(\frac{x_1^P}{\mu_1} - \left(\frac{\frac{1}{3} \frac{x_1^P}{\mu_1} k_2^2}{\lambda \mu_1^2 + \frac{1}{3} k_2^2 + \mu_2^2} \right) \right)^2 \frac{k_2^2}{3} - \lambda \frac{k_1^2}{3}.$$

Case 3: $S_P = (B, p^P)$

(a) $EU_L(S_L = A_1, p^L) = -\lambda(\mu_1 p^L)^2 - (\mu_2 p^L)^2 - \left(\frac{x_1^P}{\mu_1} - p^L \right)^2 \frac{k_2^2}{3} - c_1^L$

$$\Rightarrow (p^L)^* = \frac{\frac{1}{3} p^P k_2^2}{\lambda \mu_1^2 + \frac{1}{3} k_2^2 + \mu_2^2}$$

$$\Rightarrow EU_L(\cdot) = -\lambda \left(\mu_1 \left(\frac{\frac{1}{3} p^P k_2^2}{\lambda \mu_1^2 + \frac{1}{3} k_2^2 + \mu_2^2} \right) \right)^2 - \left(\mu_2 \left(\frac{\frac{1}{3} p^P k_2^2}{\lambda \mu_1^2 + \frac{1}{3} k_2^2 + \mu_2^2} \right) \right)^2$$

$$- \left(\frac{x_1^P}{\mu_1} - \left(\frac{\frac{1}{3} p^P k_2^2}{\lambda \mu_1^2 + \frac{1}{3} k_2^2 + \mu_2^2} \right) \right)^2 \frac{k_2^2}{3} - c_1^L$$

(b) $EU_L(S_L = A_2, p^L) = -\lambda(\mu_1 p^L)^2 - \lambda \left(\frac{x_1^P}{\mu_1} - p^L \right)^2 \frac{k_1^2}{3} - (\mu_2 p^L)^2 - c_2^L$

$$\Rightarrow (p^L)^* = \frac{\frac{1}{3} \lambda k_2^2 \frac{x_1^P}{\mu_1}}{\lambda \mu_1^2 + \frac{1}{3} \lambda k_1^2 + \mu_2^2}$$

$$\Rightarrow EU_L(\cdot) = -\lambda\left[\left[\left(\mu_1\left(\dfrac{\tfrac{1}{3}\lambda k_1^2 \dfrac{x_1^P}{\mu_1}}{\lambda\mu_1^2 + \tfrac{1}{3}\lambda k_1^2 + \mu_2^2}\right)\right)^2 - \lambda\left(\dfrac{x_1^P}{\mu_1} - \left(\dfrac{\tfrac{1}{3}\lambda k_1^2 \dfrac{x_1^P}{\mu_1}}{\lambda\mu_1^2 + \tfrac{1}{3}\lambda k_1^2 + \mu_2^2}\right)\right)^2 \dfrac{k_1^2}{3}\right]$$

$$-\left(\mu_2\left(\dfrac{\tfrac{1}{3}\lambda k_1^2 \dfrac{x_1^P}{\mu_1}}{\lambda\mu_1^2 + \tfrac{1}{3}\lambda k_1^2 + \mu_2^2}\right)\right)^2 - c_2^L$$

(c) $EU_L(S_L = B, p^L) = -\lambda\left(\mu_1 p^L\right)^2 - \left(\mu_2 p^L\right)^2 - c_1^L - c_2^L$

$$\Rightarrow (p^L)^* = 0$$

$$\Rightarrow EU_L(\cdot) = -c_1^L - c_2^L$$

(d) $EU_L(S_L = \varnothing, p^L) = -\lambda(\mu_1 p^L)^2 - \lambda\left(\dfrac{x_1^P}{\mu_1} - p^L\right)^2 \dfrac{k_1^2}{3} - (\mu_2 p^L)^2 - \left(\dfrac{x_1^P}{\mu_1} - p^L\right)\dfrac{k_2^2}{3}$

$$\Rightarrow (p^L)^* = \dfrac{\tfrac{1}{3}p^P\left(\lambda k_1^2 + k_2^2\right)}{\lambda\mu_1^2 + \mu_2^2 + \tfrac{1}{3}\left(\lambda k_1^2 + k_2^2\right)}$$

$$\Rightarrow EU_L(\cdot) = -\lambda\left(\mu_1\left(\dfrac{\tfrac{1}{3}p^P\left(\lambda k_1^2 + k_2^2\right)}{\lambda\mu_1^2 + \mu_2^2 + \tfrac{1}{3}\left(\lambda k_1^2 + k_2^2\right)}\right)\right)^2$$

$$-\lambda\left(\dfrac{x_1^P}{\mu_1} - \left(\dfrac{\tfrac{1}{3}p^P\left(\lambda k_1^2 + k_2^2\right)}{\lambda\mu_1^2 + \mu_2^2 + \tfrac{1}{3}\left(\lambda k_1^2 + k_2^2\right)}\right)\right)^2 \dfrac{k_1^2}{3}$$

$$-\left(\mu_2\left(\dfrac{\tfrac{1}{3}p^P\left(\lambda k_1^2 + k_2^2\right)}{\lambda\mu_1^2 + \mu_2^2 + \tfrac{1}{3}\left(\lambda k_1^2 + k_2^2\right)}\right)\right)^2 - \left(\dfrac{x_1^P}{\mu_1} - \left(\dfrac{\tfrac{1}{3}p^P\left(\lambda k_1^2 + k_2^2\right)}{\lambda\mu_1^2 + \mu_2^2 + \tfrac{1}{3}\left(\lambda k_1^2 + k_2^2\right)}\right)\right)\dfrac{k_2^2}{3}$$

$$\left(\dfrac{\tfrac{1}{3}p^P\left(\lambda k_1^2 + k_2^2\right)}{\lambda\mu_1^2 + \mu_2^2 + \tfrac{1}{3}\left(\lambda k_1^2 + k_2^2\right)}\right)^2 - \left(\dfrac{x_1^P}{\mu_1} - \left(\dfrac{\tfrac{1}{3}p^P\left(\lambda k_1^2 + k_2^2\right)}{\lambda\mu_1^2 + \mu_2^2 + \tfrac{1}{3}\left(\lambda k_1^2 + k_2^2\right)}\right)\right)^2 \dfrac{k_2^2}{3}$$

In this subgame, (b) is preferred to (a) if

$$
c_1^L > \lambda \left(\mu_1 \left(\frac{\frac{1}{3}\lambda k_1^2 \frac{x_1^P}{\mu_1}}{\lambda \mu_1^2 + \frac{1}{3}\lambda k_1^2 + \mu_2^2} \right) \right)^2 + \lambda \left(\frac{x_1^P}{\mu_1} - \left(\frac{\frac{1}{3}\lambda k_1^2 \frac{x_1^P}{\mu_1}}{\lambda \mu_1^2 + \frac{1}{3}\lambda k_1^2 + \mu_2^2} \right) \right)^2 \frac{k_1^2}{3}
$$

$$
+ \left(\mu_2 \left(\frac{\frac{1}{3}\lambda k_1^2 \frac{x_1^P}{\mu_1}}{\lambda \mu_1^2 + \frac{1}{3}\lambda k_1^2 + \mu_2^2} \right) \right)^2 + c_2^L - \lambda \left(\mu_1 \left(\frac{\frac{1}{3}p^P k_2^2}{\lambda \mu_1^2 + \frac{1}{3}k_2^2 + \mu_2^2} \right) \right)^2
$$

$$
- \left(\mu_2 \left(\frac{\frac{1}{3}p^P k_2^2}{\lambda \mu_1^2 + \frac{1}{3}k_2^2 + \mu_2^2} \right) \right)^2 - \left(\frac{x_1^P}{\mu_1} - \left(\frac{\frac{1}{3}p^P k_2^2}{\lambda \mu_1^2 + \frac{1}{3}k_2^2 + \mu_2^2} \right) \right)^2 \frac{k_2^2}{3}.
$$

And (b) is preferred to (c) if

$$
c_1^L > \lambda \left(\mu_1 \left(\frac{\frac{1}{3}\lambda k_1^2 \frac{x_1^P}{\mu_1}}{\lambda \mu_1^2 + \frac{1}{3}\lambda k_1^2 + \mu_2^2} \right) \right)^2 + \lambda \left(\frac{x_1^P}{\mu_1} - \left(\frac{\frac{1}{3}\lambda k_1^2 \cdot \frac{x_1^P}{\mu_1}}{\lambda \mu_1^2 + \frac{1}{3}\lambda k_1^2 + \mu_2^2} \right) \right)^2 \frac{k_1^2}{3}
$$

$$
+ \left(\mu_2 \left(\frac{\frac{1}{3}\lambda k_1^2 \frac{x_1^P}{\mu_1}}{\lambda \mu_1^2 + \frac{1}{3}\lambda k_1^2 + \mu_2^2} \right) \right)^2.
$$

And (b) is preferred to (d) if

$$
c_2^L > \lambda \left(\mu_1 \left(\frac{\frac{1}{3}p^P \left(\lambda k_1^2 + k_2^2 \right)}{\lambda \mu_1^2 + \mu_2^2 + \frac{1}{3}\left(\lambda k_1^2 + k_2^2 \right)} \right) \right)^2 + \lambda \left(\frac{x_1^P}{\mu_1} - \left(\frac{\frac{1}{3}p^P \left(\lambda k_1^2 + k_2^2 \right)}{\lambda \mu_1^2 + \mu_2^2 + \frac{1}{3}\left(\lambda k_1^2 + k_2^2 \right)} \right) \right)^2 \frac{k_1^2}{3}
$$

$$
+ \left(\mu_2 \left(\frac{\frac{1}{3}p^P \left(\lambda k_1^2 + k_2^2 \right)}{\lambda \mu_1^2 + \mu_2^2 + \frac{1}{3}\left(\lambda k_1^2 + k_2^2 \right)} \right) \right)^2 + \left(\frac{x_1^P}{\mu_1} - \left(\frac{\frac{1}{3}p^P \left(\lambda k_1^2 + k_2^2 \right)}{\lambda \mu_1^2 + \mu_2^2 + \frac{1}{3}\left(\lambda k_1^2 + k_2^2 \right)} \right) \right)^2 \frac{k_2^2}{3}.
$$

$$
- \lambda (\mu_1 p^L)^2 - \lambda \left(\frac{x_1^P}{\mu_1} - p^L \right)^2 \frac{k_2^2}{3} - (\mu_2 p^L)
$$

Case 4: $S_p = (\varnothing, p^p)$

(a) $EU_L(S_L = A_1, p^L) = -\lambda(\mu_1 p^L)^2 - (\mu_2 p^L)^2 - \dfrac{k_2^2}{3} - c_1^L$

$\Rightarrow (p^L)^* = 0$

$\Rightarrow EU_L(\cdot) = -\dfrac{k_2^2}{3} - c_1^L$

(b) $EU_L(S_L = A_2, p^L) = -\lambda(\mu_1 p^L)^2 - \dfrac{\lambda k_1^2}{3} - (\mu_2 p^L)^2 - c_2^L$

$\Rightarrow (p^L)^* = 0$

$EU_L(\cdot) = -\dfrac{\lambda k_1^2}{3} - c_2^L$

(c) $EU_L(S_L = B, p^L) = -\lambda(\mu_1 p^L)^2 + (\mu_2 p^L)^2 - c_1^L - c_2^L$

$\Rightarrow (p^L)^* = 0$

$\Rightarrow EU_L(\cdot) = -c_1^L - c_2^L$

(d) $EU_L(S_L = \varnothing, p^L) = -\lambda(\mu_1 p^L)^2 - \lambda\dfrac{k_1^2}{3} - (\mu_2 p^L)^2 - \dfrac{k_2^2}{3}$

$\Rightarrow (p^L)^* = 0$

$\Rightarrow EU_L(\cdot) = -\dfrac{\lambda k_1^2}{3} - \dfrac{k_2^2}{3}$

In this subgame, (b) is preferred to (a) if $c_1^L > \dfrac{\lambda k_1^2}{3} - \dfrac{k_2^2}{3} + c_2^L$; and (b) is preferred to (c) if $c_1^L > \dfrac{\lambda k_1^2}{3}$; and (b) is preferred to (d) if $c_2^L > \dfrac{k_2^2}{3}$. Thus, for sufficiently large c_1^L and sufficiently small c_2^L, L's optimal strategy is defined as previously shown.

Moving backward up the game tree, we compare the expected utilities for the President (EU_P) available at each of his possible actions. P always prefers a strategy that includes A_1 to one that includes B, and a strategy that includes $\varnothing$ to A_2. Further, as long as $(x_1^P)^2 \geq \left(x_1^P - \mu_1 \left(\dfrac{\lambda z p^P}{\lambda(\mu_1^2 + z) + \mu_2^2} \right) - \left(p^P - \left(\dfrac{\lambda z p^P}{\lambda(\mu_1^2 + z) + \mu_2^2} \right) \right) z \right)^2$, any strategy in which $p^P \neq \dfrac{x_1^P}{\mu_1}$ is dominated by one where $p^P = \dfrac{x_1^P}{\mu_1}$. Therefore, we need only to show that

$$EU_P\left(S_P = \left(A_1, p^P = \dfrac{x_1^P}{\mu_1} \,|\, S_L \right) \right) > EU_P\left(S_L = \left(\varnothing, p^P = \dfrac{x_1^P}{\mu_1} \,|\, S_L \right) \right).$$

This requires

$$-(x_1^P)^2\left(1-\frac{\frac{1}{3}\lambda k_1^2}{\lambda\mu_1^2+\frac{1}{3}\lambda k_1^2+\mu_2^2}\right)^2-c_1^P>-(x_1^P)^2$$

$$\Rightarrow(x_1^P)^2\left(1-\left(1-\frac{\frac{1}{3}\lambda k_1^2}{\lambda\mu_1^2+\frac{1}{3}\lambda k_1^2+\mu_2^2}\right)^2\right)>c_1^P$$

$$\Rightarrow(x_1^P)^2\left(\frac{\frac{1}{3}\lambda k_1^2}{\lambda\mu_1^2+\frac{1}{3}\lambda k_1^2+\mu_2^2}\right)\left(2-\frac{\frac{1}{3}\lambda k_1^2}{\lambda\mu_1^2+\frac{1}{3}\lambda k_1^2+\mu_2^2}\right)>c_1^P.$$

If $(x_1^P)^2<\left(x_1^P-\mu_1\left(\frac{\lambda z p^P}{\lambda(\mu_1^2+z)+\mu_2^2}\right)-\left(p^P-\left(\frac{\lambda z p^P}{\lambda(\mu_1^2+z)+\mu_2^2}\right)\right)z\right)^2$, then
the President proposes the policy that produces the Legislator's ideal
outcome. Therefore, we need only show that $EU_P\left(S_P=\left(A_1,p^P=0\,|\,S_L\right)\right)>$
$EU_P\left(S_L=\left(\varnothing,p^P=0\,|\,S_L\right)\right)$. This requires that $-(x_1^P)^2-c_1^P>-(x_1^P)^2-\frac{1}{3}k_1^2$
$\Rightarrow\frac{1}{3}k_1^2>c_1^P$.

Thus, for sufficiently small c_1^P and c_2^L and sufficiently large c_1^P, the strategies we have listed form an equilibrium.

THEOREM 2

The following five comparative statics hold on presidential proposal power
(Θ^*) whenever the President proposes the policy that produces his ideal
outcome:

1. $\dfrac{\partial\Theta^*}{\partial\mu_1}\le0$ if $k_1^2\le\dfrac{3\lambda^2\mu_1^4+6\lambda\mu_1^2\mu_2^2+3\mu_2^4}{\lambda^2\mu_1^2-\lambda\mu_2^2}.$

2. $\dfrac{\partial\Theta^*}{\partial\mu_2}\ge0\ \forall\mu_2.$

3. $\dfrac{\partial\Theta^*}{\partial x_1^P}\ge0\ \forall x_1^P.$

4. $\dfrac{\partial\Theta^*}{\partial\lambda_1}\ge0\ \forall k_1.$

5. $\dfrac{\partial\Theta^*}{\partial\lambda}\le0\ \forall\lambda.$

PROOF

$$(p^L)^* = \frac{\frac{1}{3}k_1^2 \lambda p^P}{\lambda \mu_1^2 + \frac{1}{3}k_1^2 \lambda + \mu_2^2} = \frac{\frac{1}{3}k_1^2 \lambda \frac{x_1^P}{\mu_1}}{\lambda \mu_1^2 + \frac{1}{3}k_1^2 \lambda + \mu_2^2} = \frac{\frac{1}{3}k_1^2 \frac{x_1^P}{\mu_1}}{\mu_1^2 + \frac{1}{3}k_1^2 + \frac{\mu_2^2}{\lambda}}$$

$$\Theta^* = \frac{x_1^P}{\mu_1} - \frac{\frac{1}{3}k_1^2 \frac{x_1^P}{\mu_1}}{\mu_1^2 + \frac{1}{3}k_1^2 + \frac{\mu_2^2}{\lambda}} = \frac{(3\lambda \mu_1^2 + 3\mu_2^2)x_1^P}{\mu_1(3\lambda \mu_1^2 + \lambda k_1^2 + 3\mu_2^2)}$$

1. $\dfrac{\partial \Theta^*}{\partial \mu_1} = \dfrac{(6\lambda \mu_1 x_1^P)(3\lambda \mu_1^3 + \lambda \mu_1 k_1^2 + 3\mu_1 \mu_2^2) - (9\lambda \mu_1^2 + \lambda k_1^2 + 3\mu_2^2)(3\lambda \mu_1^2 x_1^P + 3\mu_2^2 x_1^P)}{\left[\mu_1(3\lambda \mu_1^2 + \lambda k_1^2 + 3\mu_2^2)\right]^2} < 0$

$\Rightarrow 6\lambda^2 \mu_1^4 + 2\lambda^2 \mu_1^2 k_1^2 + 6\lambda \mu_1^2 \mu_2^2 < 9\lambda^2 \mu_1^4 + 9\lambda \mu_1^2 \mu_2^2 + \lambda^2 \mu_2^2 k_1^2 + 3\lambda \mu_1^2 \mu_2^2 + 3\mu_2^4$

$\Rightarrow k_1^2(\lambda^2 \mu_1^2 - \lambda \mu_2^2) < 3\lambda^2 \mu_1^4 + 6\lambda \mu_1^2 \mu_2^2 + 3\mu_2^4$

$\Rightarrow k_1^2 < \dfrac{3\lambda^2 \mu_1^4 + 6\lambda \mu_1^2 \mu_2^2 + 3\mu_2^4}{\lambda^2 \mu_1^2 - \lambda \mu_2^2}$

2. $\dfrac{\partial \Theta^*}{\partial \mu_2} = \left(\dfrac{x_1^P}{\mu_1}\right) - \dfrac{(-2\mu_2)\left(\frac{1}{3}k_1^2 \lambda \frac{x_1^P}{\mu_1}\right)}{\left(\lambda \mu_1^2 + \frac{1}{3}\lambda k_1^2 + \mu_2^2\right)^2} > 0 \ \forall \mu_2$

3. $\dfrac{\partial \Theta^*}{\partial x_1^P} = \dfrac{(3\lambda \mu_1^2 + 3\mu_2^2)}{\mu_1(3\lambda \mu_1^2 + \lambda k_1^2 + 3\mu_2^2)} > 0 \ \forall x_1^P$

4. $\dfrac{\partial \Theta^*}{\partial k_1} = \left(\dfrac{x_1^P}{\mu_1}\right) - \dfrac{\left(\frac{1}{3}\lambda \frac{x_1^P}{\mu_1}\right)\left(\lambda \mu_1^2 + \frac{1}{3}k_1^2 \lambda + \mu_2^2\right) - \left(\frac{1}{3}\lambda\right)\left(\frac{1}{3}k_1^2 \lambda \frac{x_1^P}{\mu_1}\right)}{\left(\lambda \mu_1^2 + \frac{1}{3}\lambda k_1^2 + \mu_2^2\right)^2} < 0 \ \forall k_1$

5. $\dfrac{\partial \Theta^*}{\partial \lambda} = \left(\dfrac{x_1^P}{\mu_1}\right) - \dfrac{\left(\frac{1}{3}k_1^2 \frac{x_1^P}{\mu_1}\right)\left(\lambda \mu_1^2 + \frac{1}{3}k_1^2 \lambda + \mu_2^2\right) - \left(\mu_1^2 + \frac{1}{3}k_1^2\right)\left(\frac{1}{3}k_1^2 \lambda \frac{x_1^P}{\mu_1}\right)}{\left(\lambda \mu_1^2 + \frac{1}{3}\lambda k_1^2 + \mu_2^2\right)^2} < 0 \ \forall \lambda$

These comparative statics involving μ_1, μ_2, k_1, and λ are true as long as the inequality identified in Theorem 1 holds. If the inequality does not hold, then the President capitulates to the Legislator's ideal policy. In this case, it follows that changes in any of these four parameters do not result in changes in Θ^*.

The comparative statics involving x_1^P identified in Theorem 2 hold when the inequality identified in Theorem 1 is true. In the knife-edge case where the President's ideal policy becomes sufficiently close to the Legislator's ideal policy, the inequality switches, and the President shifts his proposal from a policy inducing his ideal national outcome to one inducing the Legislator's preferred outcome. In this case, Θ^* increases in a step function. Once in the range where the inequality in Theorem 1 is false, it is again true that Θ^* is strictly decreasing in x_1^P.

THEOREM 3

For sufficiently small c_1^L and c_2^L, an equilibrium exists wherein the President acquires no expertise and proposes the policy that produces his ideal national outcome, and the Legislator acquires expertise on both national and local outcomes and enacts a policy.

PROOF

In this equilibrium, the strategies are as follows:

$$S_P = \left(\varnothing, p^P = \frac{x_1^P}{\mu_1} \right)$$
$$S_L = (B, p^L = 0)$$

As in Theorem 1, both P and L must be best-responding to the other player's strategies. Solving by backward induction, recall that L's optimal policy, conditional on L acquiring expertise on both national and local outcomes, will always be $p^L = 0$. Moreover, L's optimal policy p^L, and resulting expected utility, will always be the same as specified in the four cases identified in Theorem 1. Therefore, for L to be best-responding, action (c) must provide the highest expected utility to L in each of the four cases.

Case 1: $S_P = (A_1, p^P)$

In this subgame, (c) is preferred to (a) if $c_2^L < \dfrac{1}{3}k_2^2$. And (c) is preferred to (b) if

$$
c_1^L < \lambda \left[\left(\mu_1 \left(\frac{\frac{1}{3}\lambda k_1^2 \frac{x_1^P}{\mu_1}}{\lambda \mu_1^2 + \frac{1}{3}\lambda k_1^2 + \mu_2^2} \right) \right)^2 + \left(\frac{x_1^P}{\mu_1} - \left(\frac{\frac{1}{3}\lambda k_1^2 \frac{x_1^P}{\mu_1}}{\lambda \mu_1^2 + \frac{1}{3}\lambda k_1^2 + \mu_2^2} \right) \right)^2 \frac{k^2}{3} \right]
$$

$$
+ \left(\mu_2 \left(\frac{\frac{1}{3}\lambda k_1^2 \frac{x_1^P}{\mu_1}}{\lambda \mu_1^2 + \frac{1}{3}\lambda k_1^2 + \mu_2^2} \right) \right)^2 .
$$

And (c) is preferred to (d) if

$$
c_1^L + c_2^L < \lambda \left[\left(\mu_1 \left(\frac{\frac{1}{3}\lambda k_1^2 \frac{x_1^P}{\mu_1}}{\lambda \mu_1^2 + \frac{1}{3}\lambda k_1^2 + \mu_2^2} \right) \right)^2 + \left(\frac{x_1^P}{\mu_1} - \left(\frac{\frac{1}{3}\lambda k_1^2 \frac{x_1^P}{\mu_1}}{\lambda \mu_1^2 + \frac{1}{3}\lambda k_1^2 + \mu_2^2} \right) \right)^2 \frac{k_1^2}{3} \right]
$$

$$
+ \left(\mu_2 \left(\frac{\frac{1}{3}\lambda k_1^2 \frac{x_1^P}{\mu_1}}{\lambda \mu_1^2 + \frac{1}{3}\lambda k_1^2 + \mu_2^2} \right) \right)^2 + \frac{k_2^2}{3}
$$

Case 2: $S_P = (A_2, p^P)$

In this subgame, (c) is preferred to (a) if

$$
c_2^L < \lambda \left[\mu_1 \left(\frac{\frac{1}{3}\frac{x_1^P}{\mu_1}k_2^2}{\lambda \mu_1^2 + \frac{1}{3}k_2^2 + \mu_2^2} \right) \right]^2 + \mu_2 \left(\frac{\frac{1}{3}\frac{x_1^P}{\mu_1}k_2^2}{\lambda \mu_1^2 + \frac{1}{3}k_2^2 + \mu_2^2} \right) \Bigg)^2
$$

$$
+ \left(\frac{x_1^P}{\mu_1} - \left(\frac{\frac{1}{3}\frac{x_1^P}{\mu_1}k_2^2}{\lambda \mu_1^2 + \frac{1}{3}k_2^2 + \mu_2^2} \right) \right)^2 \frac{k_2^2}{3} .
$$

And (c) is preferred to (b) if $c_1^L < \lambda \dfrac{k_2^2}{3}$. And (c) is preferred to (d) if

$$c_1^L + c_2^L < \lambda \left(\mu_1 \left(\frac{\frac{1}{3}\frac{x_1^P}{\mu_1}k_2^2}{\lambda\mu_1^2 + \frac{1}{3}k_2^2 + \mu_2^2} \right) \right)^2 + \lambda\frac{k_1^2}{3} + \left(\mu_2 \left(\frac{\frac{1}{3}\frac{x_1^P}{\mu_1}k_2^2}{\lambda\mu_1^2 + \frac{1}{3}k_2^2 + \mu_2^2} \right) \right)^2$$

$$+ \left(\frac{x_1^P}{\mu_1} - \left(\frac{\frac{1}{3}\frac{x_1^P}{\mu_1}k_2^2}{\lambda\mu_1^2 + \frac{1}{3}k_2^2 + \mu_2^2} \right) \right)^2 \frac{k_2^2}{3}.$$

Case 3: $S_P = (B, p^p)$

In this subgame, (c) is preferred to (a) if

$$c_2^L < \lambda \left(\mu_1 \left(\frac{\frac{1}{3}\frac{x_1^P}{\mu_1}k_2^2}{\lambda\mu_1^2 + \frac{1}{3}k_2^2 + \mu_2^2} \right) \right)^2 + \left(\mu_2 \left(\frac{\frac{1}{3}\frac{x_1^P}{\mu_1}k_2^2}{\lambda\mu_1^2 + \frac{1}{3}k_2^2 + \mu_2^2} \right) \right)$$

$$+ \left(\frac{x_1^P}{\mu_1} - \left(\frac{\frac{1}{3}\frac{x_1^P}{\mu_1}k_2^2}{\lambda\mu_1^2 + \frac{1}{3}k_2^2 + \mu_2^2} \right) \right)^2 \frac{k_2^2}{3}.$$

And (c) is preferred to (b) if

$$c_1^L < \lambda \left(\mu_1 \left(\frac{\frac{1}{3}\lambda k_1^2 \frac{x_1^P}{\mu_1}}{\lambda\mu_1^2 + \frac{1}{3}\lambda k_1^2 + \mu_2^2} \right) \right)^2 + \lambda \left(\frac{x_1^P}{\mu_1} - \left(\frac{\frac{1}{3}\lambda k_1^2 \frac{x_1^P}{\mu_1}}{\lambda\mu_1^2 + \frac{1}{3}\lambda k_1^2 + \mu_2^2} \right) \right)^2 \frac{k_1^2}{3}$$

$$+ \left(\mu_2 \left(\frac{\frac{1}{3}\lambda k_1^2 \frac{x_1^P}{\mu_1}}{\lambda\mu_1^2 + \frac{1}{3}\lambda k_1^2 + \mu_2^2} \right) \right)^2.$$

And (c) is preferred to (d) if

$$c_1^L + c_2^L < \lambda \left[\mu_1 \left(\frac{\frac{1}{3}p^P(\lambda k_1^2 + k_2^2)}{\lambda \mu_1^2 + \mu_2^2 + \frac{1}{3}(\lambda k_1^2 + k_2^2)} \right) \right]^2$$

$$+ \lambda \left[\frac{x_1^P}{\mu_1} - \left(\frac{\frac{1}{3}p^P(\lambda k_1^2 + k_2^2)}{\lambda \mu_1^2 + \mu_2^2 + \frac{1}{3}(\lambda k_1^2 + k_2^2)} \right) \right]^2 \frac{k_1^2}{3}$$

$$+ \left[\mu_2 \left(\frac{\frac{1}{3}p^P(\lambda k_1^2 + k_2^2)}{\lambda \mu_1^2 + \mu_2^2 + \frac{1}{3}(\lambda k_1^2 + k_2^2)} \right) \right]$$

Case 4: $S_P = (\emptyset, p^p)$

In this subgame, (c) is preferred to (a) if $c_2^L < \frac{k_2^2}{3}$. And (c) is preferred to (b) if $c_1^L < \frac{\lambda k_1^2}{3}$. And (c) is preferred to (d) if $c_1^L + c_2^L < \frac{\lambda k_1^2}{3} + \frac{k_2^2}{3}$. Thus, for sufficiently small c_1^L and c_2^L, L's optimal strategy is $S_L = (B, p^L = 0)$.

Moving backward up the game tree, we compare the expected utilities for the president available at each of his possible actions. Because, in equilibrium, L is acquiring expertise on both national and local outcomes, she will not condition her strategy on the President's expertise or proposal p^P. Therefore, P will never acquire expertise on either mapping function, as doing so would impose a cost of c_1^P or c_2^P and provide no expected utility benefit. Further, any proposal p^P will be ignored by L, so all values of p^P are equally appealing to P. So $S_P = \left(\emptyset, p^P = \frac{x_1^P}{\mu_1} \right)$ is a best-response for P, given L's strategy. Thus, for sufficiently small c_1^L and c_2^L, the strategies listed above form an equilibrium.

THEOREM 4

In the equilibrium identified in Theorem 3, the following five comparative statics hold on presidential proposal power (Θ^*):

1. $\dfrac{\partial \Theta^*}{\partial \mu_1} \leq 0 \ \forall \mu_1$

2. $\dfrac{\partial \Theta^*}{\partial \mu_2} \geq 0 \ \forall \mu_2$

3. $\dfrac{\partial \Theta^*}{\partial x_1^P} \geq 0 \;\; \forall x_1^P.$

4. $\dfrac{\partial \Theta^*}{\partial k_1} = 0 \;\; \forall k_1$

5. $\dfrac{\partial \Theta^*}{\partial \lambda} = 0 \;\; \forall \lambda.$

PROOF

$$(p^L)^* = 0$$

$$\Theta^* = \frac{x_1^P}{\mu_1} - 0 = \frac{x_1^P}{\mu_1}.$$

Because Θ^* is only a function of x_1^P and μ_1, the comparative statics on all other parameters must be zero. It can be clearly seen that Θ^* is increasing in x_1^P and decreasing in μ_1.

APPENDIX B

Alternative Bridging Criteria, Chapter 5

In lieu of interest groups, we rely upon individual members of Congress. From the outset, we acknowledge that this approach is fraught with dangers. For starters, we must assume that at least some members of Congress do not change their voting behavior when the nation enters or exits war. Should every member of Congress shift by a common unit, this bridging criterion will necessarily recover estimates indicating that peace and wartime votes are identical. Should we select the wrong member of Congress, it is possible to generate estimates of ideal point changes that are completely wrong. If in the 107th Congress, for instance, we select as bridge actors the Democratic and Republican Senators who in fact shifted the most in the conservative direction, our analysis for all other members will falsely reveal modest shifts in the liberal direction.

To select members of Congress whose voting behavior is likely to be least affected by war, we apply two different decision rules. The first draws on our analysis of the 107th Congress, wherein we found that the war had a larger impact on Democrats representing jurisdictions where Bush performed well in 2000 and on Republicans representing jurisdictions where Bush performed poorly. To wit, in World War II and the Korean War we select (data permitting) the member of the president's party from the state or district in which the president performed the best in the most recent presidential election, and the member of the opposition party from the state or district in which the president fared the worst.[1]

As a second decision rule, we focus on those members who exhibit high levels of ideological stability—members, we suggest, who are demonstrably less likely to adjust their voting behavior in response to war, presidential appeals, or anything else. To identify these individuals, we estimated

1. House elections data were generously provided by Gary Jacobson. Data on district-level presidential returns are not available until the 1952 election, so we do not use this bridging criterion for House members in World War II or the beginning of the Korean War.

member ideal points for the entire set of roll calls that span peace and wartime periods. The Bayesian credible intervals associated with each member's ideal points provide information about the ideological stability of his or her voting record. Members with larger intervals, ceteris paribus, can be said to vote less ideologically consistently, and members with smaller intervals vote more consistently.

We cannot simply select as our bridge actors the Democrat and Republican with the smallest credible interval. These intervals, after all, also reflect each member's location within the larger distribution of ideal point estimates. Centrist legislators tend to have very precisely estimated ideal points, because there are many cutting lines that separate them from other centrists. It is more difficult to know exactly how extreme a very conservative or liberal member is, however, because there are fewer cutpoints between them and other like-minded legislators. We therefore regress the estimated credible intervals on a polynomial expression of their associated ideal points, and then we recover the residuals. Members with the largest negative residuals, we suggest, vote most consistently given their location in the ideological distribution, whereas those with the largest positive residual vote least consistently given their location.[2] Members of the former group qualify as plausible bridges. Because the differences in the size of the residuals are quite small, and because we do not want to make strong claims about the accuracy of the regression's specification, we select as bridges the three Democratic and three Republican members with the largest negative residuals. We then calculate the aggregate shift in chamber ideal points using each of their nine combinations, and we report the results from the pair that yields the median mean shift.

Recall that in our analysis of the 107th Congress, party leadership constituted another significant predictor of members' voting shifts. Particularly among Republicans, party leaders moved significantly further in the conservative direction after the outbreak of war than did rank-and-file members. Hence, for both decision rules we consider only members who are not party leaders. As a practical consideration, we further limit our selection of Democratic bridge actors to non-southerners so as to ensure adequate coverage of the liberal and conservative regions of the (assumed) unidimensional continuum.

2. This approach is similar in spirit to Lauderdale 2010, who develops a Bayesian heteroskedastic ideal point estimator to directly model the legislator-specific variances that describe the extent to which legislators' voting behavior is not conditioned on the primary liberal-conservative dimension.

Table A.B1 ASSESSING MEMBER BRIDGES

Congress and Chamber	Expected Direction	Interest Group Results	Presidential Vote Share Criterion	Regression Residuals Criterion	Reverse Presidential Vote Share	Reverse Regression Residuals
107th House	Conservative (+)	+0.54	+0.06	+0.15	−0.16	−0.01
107th Senate	Conservative (+)	+0.69	+0.10	+0.00	−0.01	−0.08

Note: Cell entries reflect the mean shifts in chamber ideal point estimates. Entries in bold indicate statistical significance at $p < .05$ or lower, using one-tailed t-tests. Entries in the first three columns of results test the hypothesis that shifts in the expected direction (second column) are observed, and the entries in the two rightmost columns test the hypothesis that shifts opposite those expected are observed.

As an initial check on both decision rules, we replicated the analysis for the Afghanistan war, in which interest group positions are available to anchor our analyses. In all four cases, these two decision rules yield results that are consistent with those generated from interest group bridges. These results are displayed in Table A.B1.

As a further check, we again replicated the analyses for the Afghanistan war, but this time we selected those individuals who, under the two decision rules, we would expect to be the worst possible bridges. Thus, under the first decision rule, we selected the individual from the president's party who represented the district or state where the president performed least well in the previous election, and the individual from the opposition party where the president performed best. Under the second decision rule, we selected those individuals from both parties with the largest positive residuals. If our decision rules do a reasonable job of distinguishing members whose voting patterns are more and less resilient to war, then these "reverse bridges" should generate very different results from the more reliable estimates based upon interest group bridges. And so they do. In all four cases, as Table A.B1 shows, we found shifts in the opposite direction from those observed in the interest group bridges. Further, two of these cases show statistically significant movement in the direction opposite from what we find using the interest group bridges. Together, these two cross validations suggest that we have a plausible basis for examining the impact of earlier wars across a variety of legislation.

APPENDIX C

Summary Tables, Chapter 5

The tables that follow report summary statistics for each of the analyses conducted in Chapter 6. Positive entries indicate shifts in the conservative direction upon the beginning of war. They cannot be meaningfully compared across chambers or bridging criteria. Entries in *italics* indicate statistical significance at $P < .10$ or lower, and **bold** entries indicate statistical significance at $P < .01$ or lower. Other table entries follow the guidelines listed below.

Column Entry	Notes
Mean Shift	Reports the mean differences between roll call voting behavior during war and peace. Statistical significance is assessed using one-tailed t-tests.
Median Shift	Reports the differences in chamber medians between roll call voting behavior before and during war. Statistical significance is assessed using one-tailed Wilcoxon signed-rank tests.
(N) Total	Number of legislators.
(N) Significant	Number of legislators whose peacetime and wartime roll call voting records are statistically different at $p < .01$.
(N) Expected Direction	Number of significant shifts in the expected direction. If bold, then conditional probability of observing this many shifts is statistically significant at $p < .01$. If italicized, then significant at $p < .10$.
Abbreviation	Full Name
ACA	Americans for Constitutional Action
ACU	American Conservative Union
ADA	Americans for Democratic Action
AFL-CIO	American Federal of Labor and Congress of Industrial Organizations

Table A.C1. ENTRY INTO WAR IN AFGHANISTAN: 107TH CONGRESS

Chamber	Expected Direction	Bridge Criteria	Bridge Actors (Conservative, Liberal)	Mean Shift	Median Shift	(N) Total	(N) Significant	(N) Expected Direction
House	Conservative (+)	Interest groups	ACU, ADA	+0.54	+1.28	430	362	323
House	Conservative (+)	Interest groups	ACU, AFL-CIO	+0.69	+1.01	430	423	423
House	Conservative (+)	Presidential vote share	Hansen, Serrano	−0.06	+0.25	430	377	248
House	Conservative (+)	Ideological consistency	Miller, McDermott	+0.15	+0.28	430	375	322
Senate	Conservative (+)	Interest groups	ACU, ADA	+1.21	−1.26	100	99	99
Senate	Conservative (+)	Interest groups	ACU, AFL-CIO	+1.08	+1.05	100	90	86
Senate	Conservative (+)	Presidential vote share	Hatch, Reed	+0.10	−0.01	100	88	62
Senate	Conservative (+)	Ideological consistency	Gramm, Durbin	+0.00	−0.08	100	83	29
House (Domestic)	Conservative (+)	Interest groups	ACU, ADA	+0.45	+0.56	430	131	131
House (Domestic)	Conservative (+)	Presidential vote share	Hansen, Serrano	+0.16	+0.25	430	119	113
House (Domestic)	Conservative (+)	Ideological consistency	Miller, McDermott	+0.23	+0.26	430	210	203
Senate (Domestic)	Conservative (+)	Interest groups	ACU, ADA	+1.78	+1.93	100	95	95
Senate (Domestic)	Conservative (+)	Presidential vote share	Hatch, Reed	+0.17	+0.31	100	39	33
Senate (Domestic)	Conservative (+)	Ideological consistency	Gramm, Durbin	+0.03	+0.16	100	34	19
House (Foreign)	Conservative (+)	Presidential vote share	Hansen, Serrano	−0.14	−0.01	430	28	3
House (Foreign)	Conservative (+)	Ideological consistency	Miller, McDermott	+0.02	+0.09	430	7	4
Senate (Foreign)	Conservative (+)	Presidential vote share	Hatch, Reed	+0.59	−0.02	100	14	14
Senate (Foreign)	Conservative (+)	Ideological consistency	Gramm, Durbin	−0.13	−0.39	100	4	0

Table A.C2. ENTRY INTO WORLD WAR II: 77TH CONGRESS

Chamber	Expected Direction	Bridge Criteria	Bridge Actors (Conservative, Liberal)	Mean Shift	Median Shift	(N) Total	(N) Significant	(N) Expected Direction
House	Liberal (–)	Ideological consistency	Taber, May	**–1.60**	**–1.32**	424	280	**263**
Senate	Liberal (–)	Presidential vote share	Gurney, Hayden	**–0.25**	**–0.19**	95	74	44
Senate	Liberal (–)	Ideological consistency	Wiley, Green	**–0.31**	**–0.41**	95	85	**53**
House (Domestic)	Liberal (–)	Ideological consistency	Taber, May	**–4.21**	**–4.15**	424	402	**321**
Senate (Domestic)	Liberal (–)	Presidential vote share	Gurney, Hayden	–0.04	–0.05	95	0	0
Senate (Domestic)	Liberal (–)	Ideological consistency	Wiley, Green	+0.57	+0.67	95	74	29
House (Foreign)	Liberal (–)	Ideological consistency	Taber, May	**–1.53**	**–1.58**	424	335	**322**
Senate (Foreign)	Liberal (–)	Presidential vote share	Gurney, Hayden	–0.01	–0.01	95	0	0
Senate (Foreign)	Liberal (–)	Ideological consistency	Wiley, Green	**–0.34**	**–0.45**	95	52	**41**

Table A.C3. EXIT FROM WORLD WAR II: 79TH CONGRESS

Chamber	Expected Direction	Bridge Criteria	Bridge Actors (Conservative, Liberal)	Mean Shift	Median Shift	(N) Total	(N) Significant	(N) Expected Direction
House	Conservative (+)	Ideological consistency	Winter, Dawson	+0.16	+0.32	430	228	**137**
Senate	Conservative (+)	Presidential vote share	Capper, E. Thomas	+0.03	+0.33	90	64	35
Senate	Conservative (+)	Ideological consistency	Hickenlooper, McFarland	+0.12	+0.43	90	63	**40**
House (Domestic)	Conservative (+)	Ideological consistency	Winter, Dawson	+0.30	+0.38	430	157	**141**
Senate (Domestic)	Conservative (+)	Presidential vote share	Capper, E. Thomas	+0.17	+0.26	90	28	**21**
Senate (Domestic)	Conservative (+)	Ideological consistency	Hickenlooper, McFarland	+0.22	+0.29	90	42	26
House (Foreign)	Conservative (+)	Ideological consistency	Winter, Dawson	−0.09	−0.07	430	140	25
Senate (Foreign)	Conservative (+)	Presidential vote share	Capper, E. Thomas	−0.56	−0.56	90	43	1
Senate (Foreign)	Conservative (+)	Ideological consistency	Hickenlooper, McFarland	+0.23	+0.25	90	31	**23**

Table A.C4. ENTRY INTO KOREAN WAR: 81ST CONGRESS

Chamber	Expected Direction	Bridge Criteria	Bridge Actors (Conservative, Liberal)	Mean Shift	Median Shift	(N) Total	(N) Significant	(N) Expected Direction
House	Liberal (−)	Ideological consistency	Scrivner, Carroll	**−0.50**	**−0.84**	428	360	**286**
Senate	Liberal (−)	Presidential vote share	Aiken, J. W. Thomas	+0.18	+0.10	92	85	34
Senate	Liberal (−)	Ideological consistency	Butler, Neely	+0.12	+0.02	92	74	30
House (Domestic)	Liberal (−)	Ideological consistency	Scrivner, Carroll	**−0.26**	**−0.34**	428	162	**116**
Senate (Domestic)	Liberal (−)	Presidential vote share	Aiken, J. W. Thomas	**−9.25**	**−8.19**	92	90	**63**
Senate (Domestic)	Liberal (−)	Ideological consistency	Butler, Neely	**−0.26**	**−0.38**	92	71	**50**
House (Foreign)	Liberal (−)	Ideological consistency	Scrivner, Carroll	−0.03	−0.04	428	95	41
Senate (Foreign)	Liberal (−)	Presidential vote share	Aiken, J. W. Thomas	+0.14	+0.17	92	69	30
Senate (Foreign)	Liberal (−)	Ideological consistency	Butler, Neely	+0.20	+0.11	92	50	12

Table A.C5. EXIT FROM KOREAN WAR: 83RD CONGRESS

Chamber	Expected Direction	Bridge Criteria	Bridge Actors (Conservative, Liberal)	Mean Shift	Median Shift	(N) Total	(N) Significant	(N) Expected Direction
House	Liberal (−)	Presidential vote share	W. Smith, Powell	**−0.15**	**−0.14**	429	280	**200**
House	Liberal (−)	Ideological consistency	Javits, Eberharter	**−0.55**	**−0.58**	429	324	**306**
Senate	Liberal (−)	Presidential vote share	Aiken, Kilgore	**−0.38**	**−0.39**	92	81	**76**
Senate	Liberal (−)	Ideological consistency	Bennett, Hayden	**−0.28**	**−0.27**	92	82	*48*
House (Domestic)	Liberal (−)	Presidential vote share	W. Smith, Powell	+0.35	+0.19	429	283	136
House (Domestic)	Liberal (−)	Ideological consistency	Javits, Eberharter	**−2.54**	**−2.56**	429	0	0
Senate (Domestic)	Liberal (−)	Presidential vote share	Aiken, Kilgore	**−0.40**	**−0.66**	92	71	**53**
Senate (Domestic)	Liberal (−)	Ideological consistency	Bennett, Hayden	−0.14	−0.33	92	58	**40**
House (Foreign)	Liberal (−)	Presidential vote share	W. Smith, Powell	+0.98	+0.95	429	0	0
House (Foreign)	Liberal (−)	Ideological consistency	Javits, Eberharter	**−0.90**	**−0.86**	429	0	0
Senate (Foreign)	Liberal (−)	Presidential vote share	Aiken, Kilgore	+0.07	−0.02	92	55	15
Senate (Foreign)	Liberal (−)	Ideological consistency	Bennett, Hayden	+0.41	−0.87	92	64	*41*

Table A.C6. ENTRY INTO VIETNAM WAR: 88TH AND 89TH CONGRESSES

Chamber	Expected Direction	Bridge Criteria	Bridge Actors (Conservative, Liberal)	Mean Shift	Median Shift	(N) Total	(N) Significant	(N) Expected Direction
House	Liberal (−)	Interest groups	ACA, ADA	+0.35	+0.38	341	273	17
House	Liberal (−)	Presidential vote share	Utt, Powell	+0.34	+0.38	341	300	37
House	Liberal (−)	Ideological consistency	Halpern, Perkins	+0.47	+0.53	341	10	1
Senate	Liberal (−)	Interest groups	ACA, ADA	+0.28	+0.42	90	66	26
Senate	Liberal (−)	Presidential vote share	Jordan, Pell	**−0.30**	**−0.05**	90	81	43
Senate	Liberal (−)	Ideological consistency	Curtis, Jackson	−0.23	−0.01	90	81	44
House	Liberal (−)	Interest groups	ACA, ADA	+0.39	+0.27	341	8	0
House	Liberal (−)	Presidential vote share	Utt, Powell	+0.59	+0.42	341	196	1
House	Liberal (−)	Ideological consistency	Halpern, Perkins	+0.08	−0.19	341	0	0
Senate (Domestic)	Liberal (−)	Interest groups	ACA, ADA	*−0.14*	*−0.08*	90	0	0
Senate (Domestic)	Liberal (−)	Presidential vote share	Jordan, Pell	−0.03	+0.01	90	64	*38*
Senate (Domestic)	Liberal (−)	Ideological consistency	Curtis, Jackson	−0.03	+0.02	90	56	31
House (Foreign)	Liberal (−)	Presidential vote share	Utt, Powell	+0.17	+0.20	341	56	31
House (Foreign)	Liberal (−)	Ideological consistency	Halpern, Perkins	+1.72	+2.23	341	187	24
Senate (Foreign)	Liberal (−)	Presidential vote share	Jordan, Pell	**−0.35**	**−0.40**	90	31	**23**
Senate (Foreign)	Liberal (−)	Ideological consistency	Curtis, Jackson	+0.33	+0.30	90	28	4

Table A.C7. EXIT FROM VIETNAM WAR: 92ND AND 93RD CONGRESSES

Chamber	Expected Direction	Bridge Criteria	Bridge Actors (Conservative, Liberal)	Mean Shift	Median Shift	(N) Total	(N) Significant	(N) Expected Direction
House	Liberal (−)	Interest groups	ACU, ADA	−0.03	−0.02	359	150	86
House	Liberal (−)	Presidential vote share	Camp, Conyers	−0.14	−0.07	359	311	220
House	Liberal (−)	Ideological consistency	Snyder, Mitchell	−0.06	−0.01	359	281	178
Senate	Liberal (−)	Interest groups	ACU, ADA	−0.45	−0.59	87	67	65
Senate	Liberal (−)	Presidential vote share	Bellmon, Kennedy	+0.11	−0.11	87	76	37
Senate	Liberal (−)	Ideological consistency	Curtis, Stevenson	−0.20	−0.37	87	75	63
House (Domestic)	Liberal (−)	Interest groups	ACU, ADA	+0.02	+0.02	359	1	0
House (Domestic)	Liberal (−)	Presidential vote share	Camp, Conyers	−1.08	−0.93	359	296	285
House (Domestic)	Liberal (−)	Ideological consistency	Snyder, Mitchell	−0.17	−0.14	359	110	99
Senate (Domestic)	Liberal (−)	Interest groups	ACU, ADA	+0.42	+0.30	87	0	0
Senate (Domestic)	Liberal (−)	Presidential vote share	Bellmon, Kennedy	−0.13	−0.24	87	43	32
Senate (Domestic)	Liberal (−)	Ideological consistency	Curtis, Stevenson	−0.17	−0.27	87	45	40
House (Foreign)	Liberal (−)	Presidential vote share	Camp, Conyers	−0.50	−0.44	359	100	100
House (Foreign)	Liberal (−)	Ideological consistency	Snyder, Mitchell	+0.06	+0.17	359	42	16
Senate (Foreign)	Liberal (−)	Presidential vote share	Bellmon, Kennedy	+0.06	−0.17	87	40	25
Senate (Foreign)	Liberal (−)	Ideological consistency	Curtis, Stevenson	−0.37	−0.50	87	45	44

Table A.C8. ENTRY INTO PERSIAN GULF WAR: 101ST AND 102ND CONGRESSES

Chamber	Expected Direction	Bridge Criteria	Bridge Actors (Conservative, Liberal)	Mean Shift	Median Shift	(N) Total	(N) Significant	(N) Expected Direction
House	Conservative (+)	Presidential vote share	Dannemeyer, Hayes	+0.36	+0.40	390	273	239
House	Conservative (+)	Ideological consistency	Green, Jontz	−0.02	+0.02	390	271	122
Senate	Conservative (+)	Presidential vote share	Garn, Pell	−0.15	−0.21	95	49	21
Senate	Conservative (+)	Ideological consistency	Jeffords, Kennedy	−0.27	−0.39	95	27	3
House (Domestic)	Conservative (+)	Presidential vote share	Dannemeyer, Hayes	+0.10	+0.21	390	345	148
House (Domestic)	Conservative (+)	Ideological consistency	Green, Jontz	+0.09	+0.18	390	311	176
Senate (Domestic)	Conservative (+)	Presidential vote share	Garn, Pell	−0.48	−0.86	95	74	26
Senate (Domestic)	Conservative (+)	Ideological consistency	Jeffords, Kennedy	−0.73	−1.14	95	84	35

Table A.C9. EXIT FROM PERSIAN GULF WAR: 102ND CONGRESS

Chamber	Expected Direction	Bridge Criteria	Bridge Actors (Conservative, Liberal)	Mean Shift	Median Shift	(N) Total	(N) Significant	(N) Expected Direction
House	Liberal (−)	Presidential vote share	Dannemeyer, Hayes	**−0.30**	**−0.52**	390	303	**273**
House	Liberal (−)	Ideological consistency	Green, Jontz	**−0.08**	**−0.22**	390	317	**174**
Senate	Liberal (−)	Presidential vote share	Garn, Pell	+0.27	+0.23	95	52	18
Senate	Liberal (−)	Ideological consistency	Jeffords, Kennedy	+0.27	+0.31	95	31	4
House (Domestic)	Liberal (−)	Presidential vote share	Dannemeyer, Hayes	**−0.13**	**−0.18**	390	45	**31**
House (Domestic)	Liberal (−)	Ideological consistency	Green, Jontz	+0.34	+0.22	390	163	73
Senate (Domestic)	Liberal (−)	Presidential vote share	Garn, Pell	+0.49	+0.69	95	14	0
Senate (Domestic)	Liberal (−)	Ideological consistency	Jeffords, Kennedy	+0.17	+0.31	95	11	4

Table A.C10. ENTRY INTO WORLD WAR I: 64TH AND 65TH CONGRESSES

Chamber	Expected Direction	Bridge Criteria	Bridge Actors (Conservative, Liberal)	Mean Shift	Median Shift	(N) Total	(N) Significant	(N) Expected Direction
House	Liberal (−)	Ideological consistency	Schall, Gallagher	+0.02	+0.03	352	288	155
Senate	Liberal (−)	Presidential vote share	LaFollette, Chamberlain	**−0.45**	**−0.05**	80	71	41
Senate	Liberal (−)	Ideological consistency	Poindexter, Shafroth	−0.13	**−0.20**	80	52	32

Table A.C11. EXIT FROM WORLD WAR I: 65TH AND 66TH CONGRESSES

Chamber	Expected Direction	Bridge Criteria	Bridge Actors (Conservative, Liberal)	Mean Shift	Median Shift	(N) Total	(N) Significant	(N) Expected Direction
House	Conservative (+)	Ideological consistency	Morgan, Gallagher	+0.00	−0.28	330	254	91
Senate	Conservative (+)	Presidential vote share	Nelson, Chamberlain	+0.11	+0.23	83	52	26
Senate	Conservative (+)	Ideological consistency	Poindexter, Thomas	+0.20	+0.19	83	79	42

APPENDIX D

Robustness Checks, Chapter 5

D.1 ALTERNATIVE ESTIMATION PROCEDURES

The main findings for the 107th Congress do not appear to be especially sensitive to the particular estimation procedure that we employ. Recall that in our approach we obtain estimates of members' voting records during peace and war using two separate roll call matrices—one containing all roll call votes from the beginning of the 107th Congress through October 6, 2001, and the second containing roll call votes that occurred on or after October 7, 2001. The estimates for the American Conservative Union (ACU) and the Americans for Democratic Action (ADA) are used to postprocess legislators' ideal point estimates and thereby generate comparable estimates across the two time periods. As another check on the validity of our results, we replicate the approach found in Bailey (2007) and Shor et al. (2010) while continuing to use the ADA and ACU as our bridge actors. Specifically, we create one roll call matrix for each chamber, in which each legislator's voting record is split over two rows. One row contains her prewar roll call votes, and the other contains her voting record after the war had begun. Each of our interest group bridges, meanwhile, appears in just one row of the data matrix, thereby providing the needed "glue" to facilitate comparable peacetime and wartime estimates.

The results, which appear in Figure A.D1, appear broadly consistent with those already reported. We continue to observe substantial shifts in the conservative direction in both chambers of Congress. The mean shifts in the House and Senate are +0.26 and +0.50 respectively. The magnitude of these shifts cannot be compared to those recovered from our own estimation procedure. In both cases, however, they are statistically significant.

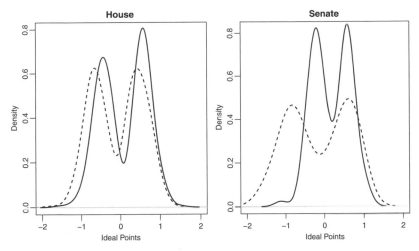

Figure A.D1. SHIFTS IN VOTING BEHAVIOR IN THE 107TH CONGRESS USING AN ALTERNATIVE ESTIMATING PROCEDURE.

Plots show the distribution of ideal points in the 107th Congress before and after the beginning of the war in Afghanistan. Dashed lines reflect the distribution of ideal points before the war in Afghanistan began, and the solid lines reflect the distribution of ideal points after the war began. The American Conservative Union (ACU) and Americans for Democratic Action (ADA) were used to bridge the two time periods. The mean shift in the House upon the beginning of war is +0.26, and the mean shift in the Senate is +0.50.

D.2 ALTERNATIVE INTEREST GROUP BRIDGES

Our primary estimation strategy hinges upon the assumption that interest groups, more so than most other political actors, are unlikely to adjust their positions on pending legislation in ways that correspond with the presence or absence of war. Our use of interest groups to evaluate voting behavior in the 107th Congress would be problematic if one (or both) of the interest groups shifted to the ideological left because it would falsely reveal shifts in member voting records in the conservative direction.[1] It is improbable that the ACU would demonstrate more liberal voting behavior after war than before war, but this could be a concern with the ADA. Thus, we replicate our analysis, but this time substitute positions taken by

---

1. On the other hand, if one or both interest groups took more conservative positions during war than they did before the war, the magnitude of the shifts we observe *under-state* the extent to which members of Congress voted in accordance with the president's preferences once the war began.

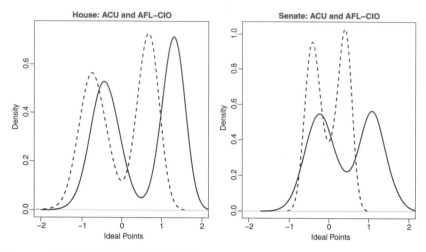

Figure A.D2. ALTERNATIVE INTEREST GROUP BRIDGES.

Plots show the distribution of ideal points in the 107th Congress before and after the beginning of the war in Afghanistan using the American Conservative Union (ACU) and the American Federation of Labor and Congress of Industrial Organizations (AFL-CIO) to link the two time periods. The results are nearly identical to those obtained using the Americans for Democratic Action (ADA) in place of the AFL-CIO, which suggests that they are not driven by strategic behavior by interest groups. Dashed lines reflect the distribution of ideal points before the war in Afghanistan began, and the solid lines reflect the distribution of ideal points after the war began.

the American Federation of Labor and Congress of Industrial Organizations (AFL-CIO) for those taken by the ADA.

As Figure A.D2 shows, we again find that members of Congress had more conservative wartime voting records. Furthermore, the magnitude of the aggregate shifts appears to be greater in both chambers when the AFL-CIO is substituted for the ADA; an even greater number of members of both the House and Senate exhibited significantly more conservative records in the postwar period. This improves our confidence in the use of the ACU and ADA as bridge actors, and indicates that our findings for the 107th Congress are robust to the choice of bridges.

We also obtain similar substantive results when we use more than two interest groups as our bridges. The results of supplementing the ACU and ADA with the AFL-CIO, the American Civil Liberties Union (ACLU), the League of Conservation Voters (LCV), and the Public Interest Research Group (PIRG) in both chambers appear in Figure A.D3.[2] We

2. These constitute the complete set of available interest groups that selected sufficient numbers of key votes to serve as bridges in both chambers in the 107th Congress.

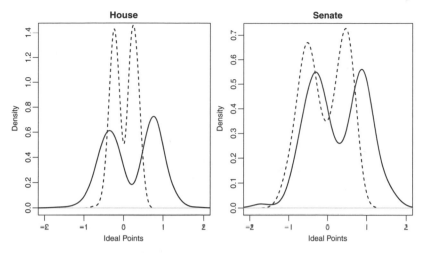

Figure A.D3. SHIFTS IN VOTING BEHAVIOR IN THE 107TH CONGRESS USING SIX BRIDGE ACTORS.

Plots show the distribution of ideal points in the 107th Congress before and after the beginning of the war in Afghanistan. Dashed lines reflect the distribution of ideal points before
the war in Afghanistan began, and the solid lines reflect the distribution of ideal points
after the war began. In both chambers, the American Civil Liberties Union (ACLU),
American Conservative Union (ACU), Americans for Democratic Action (ADA), American Federation of Labor and Congress of Industrial Organizations (AFL-CIO), League
of Conservation Voters (LCV), and Public Interest Research Group (PIRG) are used to
link the two time periods. The mean shift in the House at the beginning of war is +0.49, and
the mean shift in the Senate is +0.58.

now observe mean shifts of +0.49 and +0.58 in the House and Senate,
respectively.

Though we recover similar results, for several reasons we are reluctant
to rely upon a broader population of interest groups as our bridge actors.
For starters, we have concerns about the underlying dimension along
which we are attempting to place legislators. Unlike the ACU and the
ADA, most interest groups, with the possible exception of PIRG, focus on
a rather narrow set of policy interests. The LCV, for instance, focuses on
environmental issues, and the ACLU is nearly exclusively concerned with
civil liberties concerns. Throughout Chapter 5, we assume that legislators'
voting records can be characterized by a single ideological dimension that
broadly defines the liberal-conservative spectrum. It is less clear, however,
that such an assumption appropriately extends to single-issue interest

When also using the National Farmers Union (NFU) and National Right to Life Council
(NRLC), which are only available for the House, we again observe significant shifts in
the conservative direction.

groups, whose policy positions on the ideological dimension of interest are not well explained by the spatial logic of legislative behavior.

Moreover, should we look beyond the ADA and ACU, we must continually draw on a different collection of interest groups across chambers and wars. Data for most of these single-issue interest groups are available for shorter periods of time; when the group data are available, we find that these interest groups tend to take positions on a much smaller number of bills—typically on the order of 50 percent fewer. These facts have two related consequences. First, by changing the composition of our reference group, we further complicate efforts to broadly compare the impact of different wars on members' voting behavior in the House and Senate, a problem that becomes full-blown when we distinguish foreign and domestic policies. Second, because the vast majority of issue-specific interest groups focus on a small number of domestic policies, for purely practical reasons we cannot use them when estimating changes in legislators' voting behavior on foreign policy initiatives. By contrast, both the ADA and ACU take a sufficient number of positions to serve as bridges for both domestic and foreign policies. For those wars in which interest group positions are simply not available, we rely on legislators whose voting records, by our stipulation alone, are likely to remain stable across peace and war to serve as our bridges. Assuming our criteria for selecting these legislators are sound—and we note in the text a variety of reasons for believing otherwise—these bridges also permit comparisons of changes in voting records within foreign and domestic policy domains.

D.3 CHANGES IN THE AGENDA

Though the available evidence supports the contention that the voting records of members of Congress shifted in the ideological direction of the president when the nation waged war against Afghanistan, such movement is observationally equivalent to a shift in the agenda in the opposite direction. These concerns, if realized, present problems for our results in many of the same ways as we discussed earlier regarding the stability of interest group position taking. A moderate legislator may appear to have become more conservative, for instance, either because she indeed voted more conservatively or because the agenda became more liberal. To ensure that our findings are not an artifact of agenda changes, we conducted two supplementary analyses.

First, recall that on May 24, 2001, Senator James Jeffords of Vermont switched his party affiliation from Republican to Independent and announced he would caucus with the Democrats. Before his switch, Democrats and Republicans had a 50–50 split in the Senate. After the switch, Democrats had sole control of the Senate, 50–49, with Jeffords the lone Independent. This change in leadership may have affected the agenda on which Senators voted. It may also have affected the House agenda, as House leaders may have changed their expectations about what they could get through the Senate.

To account for this change in majority party, we replicate the original analysis with the full set of wartime roll call data, but we limit the peacetime roll call data to the period after Jeffords switched his party affiliation. Our substantive findings remain unchanged, as Figure A.D4 illustrates. With the outbreak of the war in Afghanistan, we continue to see the House Republicans and the Democratic and Republican Senators lurching to the right. Thus, to the extent that congressional agendas are a function of party control, we find no evidence that changes in the agenda are responsible for the findings we have described.

As a further check, we examine the distribution of estimated cutpoints for roll call votes in the 107th Congress. The cutpoints indicate where

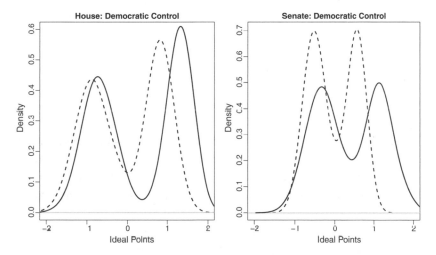

Figure A.D4. ACCOUNTING FOR PARTISAN CONTROL OF CONGRESS.

Plots show the distribution of ideal points in the 107th Congress before and after the beginning of the war in Afghanistan. Prewar votes are limited to the period after the Democrats gained control of the Senate following Senator James Jeffords's defection from the Republicans on May 22, 2001. The American Conservative Union (ACU) and Americans for Democratic Action (ADA) are used to link the prewar and postwar periods. Dashed lines reflect the distribution of ideal points before the war in Afghanistan began, and the solid lines reflect the distribution of ideal points after the war began.

the separation occurs between supporters and opponents of a bill. For instance, in a 100-member legislature in which sixty liberal members vote for a bill and forty conservative members vote against it, the cutpoint is located between the least liberal legislator who voted for the bill and the least conservative member who voted against it. In a legislature controlled by Democrats with ideal points with mean zero, the cutpoints on most bills are likely to be located on the right (conservative) side of zero; in a legislature controlled by Republicans, most cutpoints are likely to fall on the left (liberal) side of zero.

We calculate cutpoints using the item parameters that are generated simultaneously with legislator ideal points.[3] As discussed previously, β_j is the item-discrimination parameter that indicates how well vote j distinguishes between liberals and conservatives, and α_j provides an indication of the ideological location of the proposal (similar to an intercept term). Cutpoints are calculated by dividing the location parameter by the discrimination parameter. Roll call votes that are unanimous or extremely lopsided do not provide any information about member ideal points because every member (or virtually every member) votes in the same way. Such uninformative votes have discrimination parameters very close to zero, resulting in cutpoints that go to infinity in the limit. Consequently, we drop all roll calls for which the discrimination parameter is indistinguishable from zero.

Figure A.D5 displays the distribution of cutpoints in the House and Senate. The dashed lines indicate the distribution of cutpoints before Jeffords switched his party affiliation, the dotted lines indicate the distribution of cutpoints after the Jeffords switch but before the onset of war, and the solid lines indicate the distribution of cutpoints during the war. According to the logic we have outlined, cutpoints should be more conservative after the Jeffords switch than when control of the Senate was shared. Should we see cutpoints on the right side of zero once the war had begun, we have reason to suspect that the shifts in voting behavior that we observe in our analyses are artifacts of shifts in the agenda.

Across the three time periods, the median House cutpoints all fall just to the left of zero. The distribution of post–Jeffords switch cutpoints is flatter than observed before the Jeffords switch. But the distribution of the cutpoints immediately before and after the outbreak of war are indistinguishable from one another, suggesting that an agenda change is

3. See Krehbiel et al. 2005 for a similar analysis of legislative cutpoints.

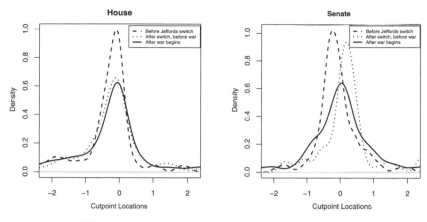

Figure A.D5. AGENDA CHANGES IN THE 107TH CONGRESS.

Cutpoint densities reported during three periods of the 107th Congress illustrate before the Jeffords switch (dashed), after the Jeffords switch but before the war (dots), and after the war's commencement (solid). Cutpoints reflect the position in ideological space that separates members who voted for a particular bill from those who voted against it. Cutpoints to the right of the midpoint indicate agenda control by liberals, and cutpoints to the left indicate agenda control by conservatives.

not responsible for the observed conservative shift in the voting records of House members.

In the Senate, we do observe changes in the cutpoint distributions. The cutpoints before the Jeffords switch were more conservative than those after the switch but before the war, indicating that the agenda indeed shifted to the left after the Democrats gained control of the Senate. Once the war began, however, the cutpoints shifted in the liberal direction, indicating that Democrats put forth a more conservative agenda once the war began. This fact suggests that comparisons of peace and wartime ideal point estimates based upon roll calls that occurred after the Jeffords switch understate the extent to which senators voted more conservatively once the Afghanistan war began.

In tandem, the analyses of the item cutpoints in the House and Senate greatly boost our confidence in our findings. If we had observed a significant shift in the agenda in the liberal direction, we would have reason to believe that the observed conservative shifts in the ideal point estimates are driven by changes in the agenda, which are observationally equivalent phenomena. We are less concerned about conservative shifts in the agenda; to the extent that evidence of this exists, we have reason to believe that the recovered shifts in ideal points *understate* the true magnitude of

the shifts in voting behavior. Nevertheless, we see no evidence of significant agenda shifts in the House, and evidence of a modest shift in the conservative direction in the Senate. However, the wartime Senate agenda is
not as conservative as the peacetime agenda when Republicans controlled
the chamber before the Jeffords switch, thus providing additional support
for the main findings.

Finally, we consider the possibility that the kinds of policy items on the
congressional wartime agenda are altogether different from those on the
peacetime agenda. The onset of war, for example, could focus Congress's
attention on issues related to foreign policy and national security and away
from domestic concerns such as employment and education policy. Should
this be the case, it is possible that the changes in the substantive content
of the agenda—rather than changes in individual voting behavior—are
responsible for the shifts we report in Chapter 5.

Table A.D1 shows the distribution of roll call votes across issue areas
during the 107th House of Representatives. The wartime congressional
agenda did include more legislation related to national defense and foreign
affairs, but domestic policy did not simply fade into the background. Purely
domestic policies constituted approximately the same percentage of the
legislative agenda during the war as they did before the war began. Thus,
as Table A.D1 shows, war did not dramatically reshape the policy content
of the congressional agenda. This provides additional confirmation that
our results for the 107th Congress are due to shifts in the way individual
legislators voted on legislation that coincided with the presence of war.

Table A.D1. ROLL CALL VOTES BY ISSUE TYPE

Issue Category	Before War Begins (%)	After War Begins (%)
Symbolic, Internal, and Procedural	18.06	19.21
Appropriations	27.50**	15.40
Defense	3.33	6.35
Foreign Policy	9.17*	14.76
Economy, Taxes, and Budget	15.56	13.81
Energy and Environment	6.11**	2.54
Government Operations, Civil Rights, and Justice	3.06**	9.05
Welfare and Human Services	9.17	7.62
Miscellaneous Domestic	8.06	11.27

Note: Entries in each column are the percentage of bills in each period that fall under the row cat-
egory. Data source: David W. Rodhe, Roll Call Voting Data for the United States House of Representatives, 1953–2004. Compiled by the Political Institutions and Public Choice Program, Michigan
State University, East Lansing, MI, 2004.
*differences in two columns are significant at $p<.05$, two-tailed test, **$p<.01$.

D.4 SUBSETS OF ROLL CALL VOTES

We recognize that the observed effects of war on members' voting behavior might be confined to particular types of votes. The shifts observed in the figures above, for instance, might be driven primarily by changes in the ways members vote on purely procedural and/or symbolic items, while members record more consistent voting records on more substantively significant issues.

To explore these possibilities, we reestimate members' ideal points on the basis of various subsets of roll calls, and again use the interest groups as bridge actors. We distinguish substantive and significant votes in several ways. First, we consider the subset of bills that received coverage in the *New York Times* and/or *Wall Street Journal*. Second, we restrict the sample to include only "strategically significant" bills by use of a measure of closeness that accounts for different passage thresholds.[4] We restrict the sample to bills with competitiveness ratings of .90 and higher.

Though the magnitude of the shifts attenuates slightly, in every instance but one these different subsets of roll calls yield evidence of large wartime shifts in the conservative direction. These findings suggest that while members of Congress granted solid support to the president on matters related to the conduct of military activities in Afghanistan, this support extended well beyond the realm of purely symbolic gestures of national unity.[5] Indeed, the sole instance where differences between war and peacetime votes were not found was on the subset of House bills that received prominent newspaper coverage. It is quite possible that on this subset of highly visible bills, House members held firm to their prewar voting habits. For two reasons, though, we are reluctant to make too much of this finding: first, senators did reveal significant movement to the ideological right on this class of bills; second, these estimates are based on a much smaller number of actual votes (103 in total, of which interest groups took positions on just 26) than those observed for the other subsets that we analyzed.

D.5 DEFINING THE BEGINNING OF WAR

In selecting the dates that mark the beginnings and ends of wars, we follow Epstein et al. (2005). Beginnings are defined by major U.S. troop

---

4. These data come from Krehbiel and Woon 2005.
5 As we explained earlier, there are too few interest group positions on foreign policy issues to reliably use them to scale our estimates.

deployments, not by the underlying events the precipitated the deployments. Hence, in the 107th Congress, October 7, 2001 (when the Afghanistan war began), marks the beginning of war. We recognize, though, that members' changing voting behavior may not have coincided perfectly with the outbreak of war. For instance, members may have lurched to the right in the immediate aftermath of the 9/11 terrorist attacks. Alternatively, the members' shift to the ideological right may have occurred later in the war. Finally, and perhaps most importantly, we must consider the possibility that factors having nothing to do with the war precipitated the observed shift to the ideological right.

To explore these possibilities, we estimate members' ideal points using arbitrary dates during 2001 to distinguish "treatment" and "control" conditions—specifically, the 1st and 15th of every month between May and November 2001. We then estimate the magnitude of the observed shifts for each set of estimates in the House and Senate. If members moved to the ideological right immediately after 9/11 and then held firmly to their new positions, we should see a steady increase in the size of the estimated shifts between May 1 and September 11, and a decrease thereafter. If members either delayed their move to the right until later in the war or continued to edge farther to the ideological right throughout the duration of the time series, then we should see a steady increase in the size of the estimated shifts over time. And finally, if prewar factors having nothing to do with the terrorist attacks or the subsequent military intervention into Afghanistan induced this ideological shift, then the distributions should peak before 9/11 and decline thereafter.

Figure A.D6 presents the results. From the very start of the time series, shifts in the conservative direction are observed. This is to be expected, given that the votes before May 1 all occurred during peace, while those held thereafter occurred in periods of both peace and war. More revealing, then, are the trends in the distributions over time. In the House they steadily increase over the entire period, while in the Senate they peaked and then subsequently declined in October and November. These data do not allow us to discern whether different members moved just once though at different times, or whether members moved together but repeatedly during this period. However, the findings do support two conclusions: first, that factors unrelated to the war are probably not responsible for members' changes in voting behavior; and second, that members continued to tack to the right of the ideological continuum in the weeks and months that followed the 9/11 attacks.

House

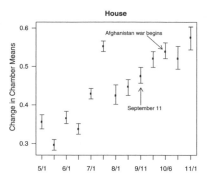

Senate

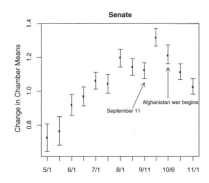

Figure A.D6. CHANGES IN VOTING BEHAVIOR OVER THE COURSE OF THE 107TH CONGRESS.

Plots display mean shifts in chamber voting behavior, splitting roll data for the 107th Congress at each of the dates in 2001 listed along the x-axes. Larger positive shifts indicate larger movements in the conservative direction. The error bars represent the 95% confidence intervals around the differences in means.

D.6 RISING CONSERVATISM AND WAR

It also is possible that the shifts observed after the outbreak of the war in Afghanistan had less to do with the president per se and more to do with a rising conservatism evoked by war. We investigate changes in voting behavior in another legislative body around the time of the Afghanistan war. The California legislature furnished numerous roll call votes in the 2001–2002 session, on which high-profile liberal and conservative interest groups (the California League of Conservation Voters and Chamber of Commerce, respectively) took public positions, and it was engaged with bargaining with a Democratic executive (Gov. Gray Davis) then under its watch.[6]

The findings are striking, as Figure A.D7 demonstrates. Rather than observing a shift in the conservative direction in the aftermath of the war in Afghanistan, members of the California assembly revealed strikingly more liberal voting records. Shifts in estimated mean ideal points were −0.55 and −0.66 in the California Assembly and Senate, respectively. Showing that wars have a comparable effect on legislative support for governors as they do for presidents (as this one data point suggests) goes well beyond the scope of this study, but the findings from California weigh

6. Roll call data for the California legislature were compiled by Jeff Lewis and are available at http://adric.sscnet.ucla.edu/california. Legislative scorecards for the League of Conservation Voters and Chamber of Commerce can be found at http://www.ecovote.org/scorecard and http://www.calchamber.com/GovernmentRelations/AdvocacyResources/Pages/LegislatorVoteRecord.aspx, respectively.

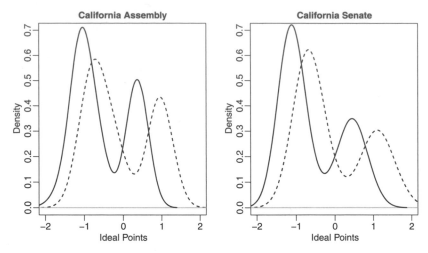

Figure A.D7. CHANGES IN VOTING BEHAVIOR IN THE CALIFORNIA LEGISLATURE.

Dashed lines reflect the distribution of ideal points for roll call votes cast in the California legislature before the beginning of the war in Afghanistan, and the solid lines reflect the distribution of ideal points for votes cast after the beginning of the war. The Chamber of Commerce and the League of Conservation Voters were used to link the two time periods.

against the notion that the war in Afghanistan evoked a uniform and widespread conservative reaction that had little to do with the president.

D.7 PLACEBO TESTS

The beginnings of World War II and the Afghanistan war, for which we obtain the most robust evidence of congressional accommodation to the president upon the commencement of war, both occurred near the end of new congressional terms. It is possible that the trends we observe in the 77th and 107th Congresses have nothing to do with the outbreak of war per se, but rather represent typical changes in the voting habits of members over the course of a congressional term. To investigate this possibility, we generate ideal points for the first and second sessions of three congresses during which no major military actions occurred: the 95th (Carter), 99th (Reagan), and 103rd (Clinton). We select these congresses and presidents because the first years of the Kennedy, Reagan, and George H. W. Bush terms presented military and foreign policy challenges related to the Cold War, and President Ford assumed the presidency just months before the end of the 93rd Congress in the wake of Nixon's resignation, so these may not serve as ideal "control" conditions. To ensure the comparability of

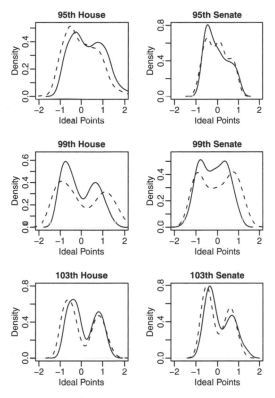

Figure A.D8. PLACEBO TESTS.

Plots contain the distribution of ideal points estimated during the first (dashed lines) and second (solid lines) sessions of the 95th (1977–78), 99th (1985–86), and 103rd (1993–94) congresses. The American Conservative Union (ACU) and Americans for Democratic Action (ADA) are the bridge actors used to link the sessions.

members' estimated ideal points in these placebo tests, we again rely upon the ADA and ACU as bridges.

The results look quite different from those observed in the 77th and 107th Congresses, as Figure A.D8 illustrates. In the 95th House, member ideal points shifted slightly to the right (in the conservative direction) during the second session, while there were no significant differences in the Senate. Things look much the same in the 99th Congress. Though there appears to be much less variance in House member ideal points during the second session than in the first, the means and medians for each session indicate little aggregate movement. In the 99th Senate, meanwhile, there is clearer evidence of an ideological shift to the left. Note, however, that this is away from, rather than toward, the ideological position of the president

(Reagan). These patterns also hold for the 103rd Congress, where we see more systematic evidence of shifting voting behavior, though in both chambers it occurs in the conservative direction, away from President Clinton.

Taken together, these findings provide little evidence of systematic shifts in legislator voting records over the course of a single congress. To the extent that aggregate changes are observed, the movement occurs in the direction opposite the ideological position of the president—a finding that may reflect member posturing in anticipation of midterm losses for the president's party. Were this pattern to hold for the 77th Congress, members would have more conservative voting records after the outbreak of war, and members of the 107th Congress would have more liberal voting records. All of the evidence, however, suggests that just the opposite occurred.

BIBLIOGRAPHY

Ackerman, Bruce A. 2006. *Before the Next Attack: Preserving Civil Liberties in an Age of Terrorism*. New Haven, CT: Yale University Press.

Aidlin, Joseph W. 1942. "The Constitutionality of the 1942 Price Control Act." *California Law Review* 30:648–654.

Arnold, R. Douglas. 1998. "The Politics of Reforming Social Security." *Political Science Quarterly* 113:219–225.

Asher, Herbert B., and Herbert F. Weisberg. 1978. "Voting Change in Congress: Some Dynamic Perspectives on an Evolutionary Process." *American Journal of Political Science* 22:391–425.

Austen-Smith, David. 1990. "Information Transmission in Debate." *American Journal of Political Science* 34:124–152.

Bafumi, Joseph, Andrew Gelman, David K. Park, and Noah Kaplan. 2005. "Practical Issues in Implementing and Understanding Bayesian Ideal Point Estimation." *Political Analysis* 13:171–187.

Bailey, Michael. 2007. "Comparable Preference Estimates across Time and Institutions for the Court, Congress and Presidency." *American Journal of Political Science* 51:433–448.

Bailey, Michael, and Kelly Chang. 2001. "Ideal Point Estimation with a Small Number of Votes: A Random-Effects Approach." *Political Analysis* 9:192–210.

Bank, Steven, Kirk Stark, and Joseph Thorndike. 2008. *War and Taxes*. Washington, DC: Urban Institute.

Battaglini, Marco, and Stephen Coate. 2008. "Pareto Efficient Income Taxation with Stochastic Abilities." *Journal of Public Economics* 92:844–868.

Bensel, Richard. 1990. *Yankee Leviathan: The Origins of Central State Authority in America, 1859–1877*. New York: Cambridge University Press.

Berinsky, Adam J. 2009. *In Time of War: Understanding Public Opinion, From World War II to Iraq*. Chicago: University of Chicago Press.

Berman, Larry. 1982. *Planning a Tragedy: The Americanization of the War in Vietnam*. New York: W.W. Norton.

Bernstein, Irving. 1969. *The Turbulent Years: A History of the American Worker*. Boston: Houghton Mifflin.

Bernstein, Michael A. 1987. *The Great Depression: Delayed Recovery and Economic Change in America, 1929–1939*. Cambridge: Cambridge University Press.

Berry, Christopher R., Barry Burden, and William G. Howell. 2010. "The President and the Distribution of Federal Spending." *American Political Science Review* 104:783–799.

Blumer, Herbert. 1943. "Morale." In *American Society in Wartime,* edited by William F. Ogburn, 207–231. Chicago: University of Chicago Press.

Bodnar, John. 1992. *Remaking America: Public Memory, Commemoration, and Patriotism in the Twentieth Century.* Princeton, NJ: Princeton University Press.

Bond, Jon R., and Richard Fleisher. 1990. *The President in the Legislative Arena.* Chicago: University of Chicago.

Brinkley, Alan. 1995. *The End of Reform: New Deal Liberalism in Recession and War.* New York: Vintage Books.

Brody, Richard A. 1991. *Assessing the President: The Media, Elite Opinion, and Public Support.* Palo Alto, CA: Stanford University Press.

Bryce, James. 1995 [1888]. *The American Commonwealth.* 2 vols. Indianapolis: Liberty Fund.

Bugliosi, Vincent. 2007. *Reclaiming History: The Assassination of President John F. Kennedy.* New York: W.W. Norton.

Burns, James MacGregor. 1970. *Roosevelt: Soldier of Freedom 1940–1945.* New York: Harcourt, Brace, Jovanovich.

Callander, Steven. 2008. "A Theory of Policy Expertise." *Quarterly Journal of Political Science* 3:123–140.

Canes-Wrone, Brandice. 2005. *Who Leads Whom?* Chicago: University of Chicago Press.

Canes-Wrone, Brandice, William G. Howell, and David E. Lewis. 2008. "Toward a Broader Understanding of Presidential Power: A Reevaluation of the Two Presidencies Thesis." *Journal of Politics* 70:1–16.

Cantril, Hadley, ed. 1951. *Public Opinion, 1935–1946.* Princeton, NJ: Princeton University Press.

Carmines, Edward G., and James A. Stimson. 1989. *Issue Evolution: Race and the Transformation of American Politics.* Princeton, NJ: Princeton University Press.

Carson, Jamie, Michael Crespin, Jeffrey Jenkins, and Ryan Vander Wielen. 2004. "Shirking in the Contemporary Congress: A Reappraisal." *Political Analysis* 12:176–179.

Clark, Tom. 2006. "Judicial Decision-Making during Wartime." *Journal of Empirical Legal Studies* 3:397–419.

Clinton, Joshua. 2007. "Lawmaking and Roll Calls," *Journal of Politics,* 69:455–467.

Clinton, Joshua, Simon Jackman, and Doug Rivers. 2004. "The Statistical Analysis of Roll Call Voting: A Unified Approach." *American Political Science Review* 98:355–370.

Clinton, Joshua, and David Lewis. 2008. "Expert Opinion, Agency Characteristics, and Agency Preferences." *Political Analysis* 16:3–20.

Clowse, Barbara Barksdale. 1981. *Brainpower for the Cold War: The Sputnik Crisis and National Defense Education Act of 1958.* Westport, CT: Greenwood Press.

Cohen, Jeffrey. 1982. "The Impact of the Modern Presidency on Presidential Success in the U.S. Congress." *Legislative Studies Quarterly* 7:515–532.

Corwin, Edward. 1917. "War, the Constitution Moulder." *New Republic,* June 9, 153–155.

———. 1947. *Total War and the Constitution.* New York: Alfred A. Knopf.

———. 1956. "Woodrow Wilson and the Presidency." *Virginia Law Review* 43:761–783.

———. 1957 [1945]. *The President, Office, and Powers, 1787–1957: History and Analysis of Practice and Opinion.* 4th rev. ed. New York: New York University Press.

Crawford, Vincent, and Joel Sobel. 1982. "Strategic Information Transmission." *Econometrica* 50:1431–1451.

Crenson, Matthew A., and Benjamin Ginsberg. 2007. *Presidential Power: Unchecked and Unbalanced.* New York: W.W. Norton.

Dubofsky, Warren and Melvyn Van Tine. 1977. *John L. Lewis: A Biography.* New York: Quadrangle/New York Times Book Co.

Dudziak, Mary L. 2012. *Wartime: An Idea, Its History, Its Consequences.* New York: Oxford Universiy Press.

Edwards, George C., III. 1989. *At the Margins: Presidential Leadership of Congress.* New Haven, CT: Yale University Press.

Epstein, Lee, Daniel Ho, Gary King, and Jeffrey Segal. 2005. "The Supreme Court during Crisis: How Wars Affect Only Non-War Cases." *New York University Law Review* 80:1–116.

Fatovic, Clement. 2009. *Outside the Law: Emergency and Executive Power.* Baltimore: Johns Hopkins University Press.

Ferejohn, John, and Keith Krehbiel. 1987. "The Budget Process and the Size of the Budget." *American Journal of Political Science* 31:296–320.

Fisher, Louis. 2000. *Congressional Abdication on War and Spending.* College Station: Texas A&M University Press.

———. 2004. *Presidential War Power.* 2nd ed. Lawrence: University of Kansas Press.

———. 2008. *The Constitution and 9/11: Recurring Threats to Americas Freedoms.* Lawrence: University Press of Kansas.

Fletcher, George P. 2002. *Romantics at War: Glory and Guilt in the Age of Terrorism.* Princeton, NJ: Princeton University Press.

Ford, Henry Jones. 1898. *The Rise and Growth of American Politics.* New York: Macmillan.

Fowler, Linda. 1982. "How Interest Groups Select Issues for Rating Voting Records on members of the U.S. Congress." *Legislative Studies Quarterly* 7:401–413.

Fraser, Steven. 1991. *Labor Will Rule: Sidney Hillman and the Rise of American Labor.* Ithaca, NY: Cornell University Press.

Frisch, Morton, ed. 2007. *The Pacificus-Helvidius Debates of 1793–1794: Toward the Completion of the American Founding.* Indianapolis: Liberty Fund.

Gailmard, Sean, and John W. Patty. 2012. *Learning while Governing: Expertise and Accountability in the Executive Branch.* Chicago: University of Chicago.

Gary, Brett. 1999. *The Nervous Liberals: Propaganda Anxieties from World War I to the Cold War.* New York: Columbia University Press.

Gilligan, Thomas, and Keith Krehbiel. 1987. "Collective Decision-Making and Standing Committees: An Informational Rationale for Restrictive Amendment Procedures." *Journal of Law, Economics, and Organization* 3:287–335.

———. 1990. "The Organization of Informative Committees by a Rational Legislature." *American Journal of Political Science* 34:531–564.

Gilmour, John S. 2001. "The Powell Amendment Voting Cycle: An Obituary." *Legislative Studies Quarterly* 26:249–262.

Goodwin, Doris Kearns. 1976. *Lyndon Johnson and the American Dream.* New York: Harper and Row.

———. 1995. *No Ordinary Time: The Home Front in World War II.* New York: Simon & Schuster.

Grant, Philip A. 1979. "Catholic Congressmen, Cardinal Spellman, Eleanor Roosevelt and the 1949–1950 Federal Aid to Education Controversy." *American Catholic Historical Society of Philadelphia* 90:1–4.

Grofman, Bernard, Robert Griffin, and Gregory Berry. 1995. "House Members Who Become Senators: Learning from a 'Natural Experiment' in Representation." *Legislative Studies Quarterly* 20:513–529.

Grofman, Bernard, William Koetzle, and Anthony J. McGann. 2002. "Congressional Leadership 1965–96: A New Look at the Extremism versus Centrality Debate." *Legislative Studies Quarterly* 27:87–105.

Groseclose, Timothy, and Nolan McCarty. 2000. "The Politics of Blame: Bargaining before an Audience." *American Journal of Political Science* 45:100–119.

Gross, Emmanuel. 2003. "The Laws of War Waged between Democratic States and Terrorist Organizations: Real or Illusive?" *Florida Journal of International Law* 15:389–480.

Halberstam, David. 1972. *The Best and the Brightest.* New York: Random House.

Hammond, William. 1996. *Public Affairs: The Military and the Media, 1962–1968.* Washington, DC: United States Government Printing Office.

Harris, Mark, Franklin Mitchell, and Steven Schechter. 1984. *The Homefront: America during World War II.* New York: Putnam.

Helsing, Jeffrey W. 2000. *Johnson's War/Johnson's Great Society: The Guns and Butter Trap.* Westport, CT: Praeger.

Herrick, Rebekah, Michael Moore, and John Hibbing. 1994. "Unfastening the Electoral Connection: The Behavior of U.S. Representatives when Reelection Is No Longer a Factor." *Journal of Politics* 56:214–227.

Herring, George C. 2002. *America's Longest War.* 4th ed. New York: McGraw-Hill.

Hibbing, John R. 1986. "Ambition in the House: Behavioral Consequences of Higher Office Goals Among U.S. Representatives." *American Journal of Political Science* 30:651–665.

Hirsch, Alexander, and Kenneth Shotts. 2008. "Policy R&D and Legislative Organization." Technical report. Stanford, CA: Stanford University.

Howell, William G. 2003. *Power without Persuasion: The Politics of Direct Presidential Action.* Princeton, NJ: Princeton University Press.

———. 2011. "Presidential Power in War." *Annual Review of Political Science* 14:89–105.

Howell, William G., and Tana Johnson. 2009. "War's Contribution to Presidential Power." In *Oxford Handbook of the American Presidency,* edited by George C. Edwards III, and William G. Howell, pp. 724–748. New York: Oxford University Press.

Howell, William G., and David E. Lewis. 2002. "Agencies by Presidential Design." *Journal of Politics* 64:1095–1114.

Howell, William G., and Jon C. Pevehouse. 2007. *While Dangers Gather: Congressional Checks on Presidential War Powers.* Princeton, NJ: Princeton University Press.

Huber, John, and Charles Shipan. 2002. *Deliberate Discretion: The Institutional Foundations of Bureaucratic Autonomy.* New York: Cambridge.

Irons, Peter H. 2005. *War Powers: How the Imperial Presidency Hijacked the Constitution.* New York: Henry Holt.

Jackman, Simon. 2001. "Multidimensional Analysis of Roll Call Data via Bayesian Simulation: Identification, Estimation, Inference, and Model Checking." *Political Analysis* 9:227–241.

Javits, Jacob K. 1973. *Who Makes War: The President versus Congress.* New York: William Morrow.

Jenkins, Jeffrey A. 2000. "Examining the Robustness of Ideological Voting: Evidence from the Confederate House of Representatives." *American Journal of Political Science* 44:811–822.

Jessee, Stephen, and Neil Malhotra. 2010. "Are Congressional Leaders Middlepersons or Extremists? Yes." *Legislative Studies Quarterly* 35:361–392.

Johnson, Lyndon B. 1971. *The Vantage Point: Perspectives of the Presidency, 1963–1969.* New York: Holt, Rinehart, and Winston.

Josephson, Matthew. 1952. *Sidney Hillman, Statesman of American Labor.* Garden City, NY: Doubleday.

Kaiser, David E. 2000. *American Tragedy: Kennedy, Johnson, and the Origins of the Vietnam War.* Cambridge, MA: Harvard University Press.

Katznelson, Ira, Kim Geiger, and Daniel Kryder. 1993. "Limiting Liberalism: The Southern Veto in Congress, 1933–1950." *Political Science Quarterly* 108:283–306.

Kennedy, David. 2001. *Freedom from Fear: The American People in Depression and War, 1929–1945.* New York: Oxford University Press.

———. 2004. *Over Here: The First World War and American Society.* New York: Oxford University Press.

Kernell, Samuel. 2007. *Going Public: New Strategies of Presidential Leadership.* Washington, DC: Congressional Quarterly Press.

Kerr-Tener, Janet C. 1987. "Eisenhower and Federal Aid to Higher Education." *Presidential Studies Quarterly* 17:473–485.

Ketcham, Ralph, ed. 2003. *The Anti-Federalist Papers and the Constitutional Convention Debates.* New York: Signet Classic.

Kiewiet, D. Roderick, and Mathew D. McCubbins. 1985. "Congressional Appropriations and the Electoral Connection." *Journal of Politics* 47:59–82.

———. 1988. "Presidential Influence on Congressional Appropriations Decisions." *American Journal of Political Science* 32:713–736.

———. 1991. *The Logic of Delegation: Congressional Parties and the Appropriations Process.* Chicago: University of Chicago Press.

Koenig, Louis William. 1944. *The Presidency and the Crisis.* New York: King's Crown Press.

Kosterman, Rick, and Seymour Feshbach. 1989. "Toward a Measure of Patriotic and Nationalistic Attitudes." *Political Psychology* 10:257–274.

Kranich, Nancy. 2009. "The Impact of the USA PATRIOT Act: An Update." Free Expression Policy Project, http://www.fepproject.org/commentaries/patriotactup date.html.

Krebs, Ronald R. 2009. "The Citizen-Soldier Tradition in the United States: Has Its Demise Been Greatly Exaggerated?" *Armed Forces and Society* 36:153–174.

Krehbiel, Keith. 1992. *Information and Legislative Organization.* Ann Arbor: University of Michigan Press.

Krehbiel, Keith, Adam Meirowitz, and Jonathan Woon. 2005. "Testing Theories of Lawmaking." In *Social Choice and Strategic Decisions: Essays in Honor of Jeffrey S. Banks,* edited by David Austen-Smith and John Duggen, 249–268. New York: Springer.

Krehbiel, Keith, and Jonathan Woon. 2005. "Selection Criteria for Roll Call Votes." Paper presented at the annual meeting of the American Political Science Association, Washington, DC.

Kriner, Douglas. 2010. *After the Rubicon: Congress, Presidents, and the Politics of Waging War.* Chicago: University of Chicago Press.

Langguth, A. J. 2000. *Our Vietnam: The War 1954–1975.* New York: Simon & Schuster.

Lauderdale, Benjamin E. 2010. "Unpredictable Voters in Ideal Point Estimation." *Political Analysis* 18:151–171.

Leckie, Robert. 1996 [1962]. *Conflict: The History of the Korean War.* New York: Da Capo Press.

Leff, Mark H. 1991. "The Politics of Sacrifice on the American Home Front in World War II." *Journal of American History* 77:1296–1318.

Leonard, Arthur, ed. 1918. *War Addresses of Woodrow Wilson.* Boston: Ginn.

Leonard, Eugenie A. 1956. *Origins of Personnel Services in Higher Education.* Minneapolis: University of Minnesota Press.

Lewis, David E. 2003. *Presidents and the Politics of Agency Design.* Stanford, CA: Stanford University Press.

———. 2004. "The Adverse Consequences of the Politics of Agency Design for Presidential Management in the United States: The Relative Durability of Insulated Agencies." *British Journal of Political Science* 34:377–404.

Lewis, David E., and Terry M. Moe. 2010. "The Presidency and the Bureaucracy: The Levers of Presidential Control." In *The Presidency and the Political System,* 9th ed., edited by Michael Nelson, pp. 367–400. Washington, DC: Congressional Quarterly Press.

Lichtenstein, Nelson. 1977. "Ambiguous Legacy: The Union Security Problem during World War II." *Labor History* 18:214–238.

Lott, John. 1987. "Political Cheating." *Public Choice* 52:169–186.

———. 1990. "Attendance Rates, Political Shirking, and the Effect of Post-Elective Office Employment." *Economic Inquiry* 28:133–150.

Lott, John, and Stephen Bronars. 1993. "Time Series Evidence on Shirking in the U.S. House of Representatives." *Public Choice* 76:126–149.

Martin, Andrew, and Kevin Quinn. 2002. "Dynamic Ideal Point Estimation via Markov Chain Monte Carlo for the U.S. Supreme Court, 1953–1999." *Political Analysis* 10:134–153.

Martin, Waldo E. 1998. *Brown v. Board of Education: A Brief History with Documents.* Boston: Bedford/St. Martin's.

Matheson, Scott M. 2009. *Presidential Constitutionalism in Perilous Times.* Cambridge, MA: Harvard University Press.

May, Ernest. 1959. *The World War and American Isolationism, 1914–1917.* Cambridge, MA: Harvard University Press.

Mayhew, David R. 1974. *Congress: The Electoral Connection.* New Haven, CT: Yale University Press.

———. 1991. *Divided We Govern.* New Haven, CT: Yale University Press.

———. 2005. "Wars and American Politics." *Perspectives on Politics* 3:473–493.

McCarthy, Michael T. 2002. "Recent Developments: USA Patriot Act." *Harvard Journal on Legislation* 39:435–453.

McCarty, Nolan, Keith Poole, and Howard Rosenthal. 2001. "The Hunt for Party Discipline in Congress." *American Political Science Review* 95:673–687.

McCullough, David. 1992. *Truman.* New York: Simon & Schuster.

McMaster, H. R. 1997. *Dereliction of Duty: Johnson, McNamara, the Joint Chiefs of Staff, and the Lies That Led to Vietnam.* New York: HarperCollins.

Meernik, James. 1993. "Presidential Support in Congress: Conflict and Consensus on Foreign and Defense Policy." *Journal of Politics* 55:569–587.

Millis, Walter. 1935. *Road to War.* Boston: Houghton Mifflin.

Milner, Helen, and Dustin Tingley. 2010. "The Political Economy of U.S. Foreign Aid: American Legislators and the Domestic Politics of Aid." *Economics and Politics* 22:200–232.

———. 2011. "Who Supports Global Economic Engagement? The Sources of Preferences in American Foreign Economic Policy." *International Organization*, 65: 3768.

Moe, Terry, and William Howell. 1999. "The Presidential Power of Unilateral Action." *Journal of Law, Economics, and Organization* 15:132–179.

Morgan, Ruth P. 1970. *The President and Civil Rights: Policy Making by Executive Order.* New York: St. Martin's Press.

Morison, Samuel. 2002. *History of United States Naval Operations in World War II.* Champagne, IL. University of Illinois Press.

Mueller, John E. 1973. *War, Presidents and Public Opinion.* New York: Wiley.

———. 1994. *Policy and Opinion in the Gulf War.* Chicago: University of Chicago Press.

Munger, Frank, and Richard Fenno. 1962. *National Politics and Federal Aid to Education.* New York: John Wiley and Sons.

Nathan, Richard P. 1969. *Jobs and Civil Rights: The Role of the Federal Government in Promoting Equal Opportunity in Employment and Training.* Washington, DC: Government Printing Office.

Neustadt, Richard. 1954. "Presidency and Legislation: The Growth of Central Clearance." *American Political Science Review* 4:64–71.

Neustadt, Richard, and Ernest May. 1988. *Thinking in Time: The Uses of History for Decision Makers.* New York: The Free Press.

Nokken, Timothy. 2000. "Dynamics of Congressional Loyalty: Party Defection and Roll Call Behavior, 1947–1997." *Legislative Studies Quarterly* 25:417–444.

Nokken, Timothy, and Keith Poole. 2004. "Congressional Party Defection in American History." *Legislative Studies Quarterly* 29:545–568.

O'Donnell, Kenneth P., and David F. Powers. 1972. *Johnny, We Hardly Knew Ye: Memories of John Fitzgerald Kennedy.* New York: Little, Brown.

Oldfield, Duane, and Aaron Wildavsky. 1989. "Reconsidering the Two Presidencies." *Society* 26:5459.

Olson, Keith W. 1974. *The G.I. Bill, the Veterans and the Colleges.* Lexington: University Press of Kentucky.

Parmet, Herbert S. 1999 [1972]. *Eisenhower and the American Crusades.* New Brunswick, NJ: Transaction Publishers.

Patterson, James T. 1996. *Grand Expectations: The United States 1945–1974.* New York: Oxford University Press.

Peake, Jeffrey S. 2002. "Coalition Building and Overcoming Legislative Gridlock in Foreign Policy, 1947–98." *Presidential Studies Quarterly* 32:67–83.

Petersen, Mitchell. 2009. "Estimating Standard Errors in Finance Panel Data Sets: Comparing Approaches," *Review of Financial Studies* 22:435–480.

Polenberg, Richard. 1972. *War and Society: The United States, 1941–1945.* Philadelphia: Lippincott.

Poole, Keith T. 1981. "Dimensions of Interest Group Evaluation of the U.S. Senate, 1969–1978." *American Journal of Political Science* 25:49–67.

———. 2007. "Changing Minds, Not in Congress!" *Public Choice* 131:435–451.

Poole, Keith T., and Thomas Romer. 1993. "Ideology, Shirking, and Representation." *Public Choice* 131:435–451.

Poole, Keith T., and Howard Rosenthal. 1997. *Congress: A Political-Economic History of Roll Call Voting.* New York: Oxford University Press.

Posner, Eric, and Adrian Vermeule. 2007. *Terror in the Balance: Security, Liberty, and the Courts.* New York: Oxford University Press.

———. 2011. *The Executive Unbound: After the Madisonian Republic.* New York: Oxford University Press.

Posner, Richard A. 2006. *Not a Suicide Pact: The Constitution in a Time of National Emergency.* New York: Oxford University Press.

Prins, Brandon, and Bryan Marshall. 2001. "Congress Support of the President: A Comparison of Foreign, Defense, and Domestic Policy Decision Making during and after the Cold War." *Presidential Studies Quarterly* 31:660–678.

Pushaw, Robert J. 2004. "Defending Deference: A Response to Professors Epstein and Wells." *Missouri Law Review* 69:959–970.

Riker, William H. 1986. *The Art of Political Manipulation.* New Haven, CT: Yale University Press.

Robinson, Greg. 2001. *By Order of the President.* Cambridge, MA: Harvard University Press.

Roosevelt, Theodore. 1915. *America and the World War.* New York: Charles Scribner's Sons.

Rossiter, Clinton. 1956. *The American Presidency: The Powers and Practices, the Personalities and Problems of the Most Important Office on Earth.* Princeton, NJ: Princeton University Press.

———, ed. 1999 [1961]. *The Federalist Papers.* New York: Mentor Books.

———. 2005 [1948]. *Constitutional Dictatorship: Crisis Government in the Modern Democracies.* New York: Transaction Publishers.

Rothenberg, Lawrence, and Mitchell Sanders. 2000. "Severing the Electoral Connection: Shirking in the Contemporary Congress." *American Journal of Political Science* 44:316–325.

Rudalevige, Andrew. 2002. *Managing the President's Program: Presidential Leadership and Legislative Policy Formation.* Princeton, NJ: Princeton University Press.

Saldin, Richard. 2011. *War, the American State, and Politics since 1898.* New York: Cambridge University Press.

Sandler, Stanley. 1999. *The Korean War: No Victors, No Vanquished*. Lexington: University Press of Kentucky.

Savage, Charlie. 2007. *Takeover: The Return of the Imperial Presidency and the Subversion of American Democracy*. New York: Little, Brown.

Schick, Allen. 2000. *The Federal Budget: Politics, Policy, Process*. Rev. ed. Washington, DC: Brookings Institution Press.

———. 2007. *The Federal Budget: Politics, Policy, Process*. 3rd ed. Washington, DC: Brookings Institution Press.

Schickler, Eric. 2009. "Public Opinion, the Congressional Policy Agenda and the Limits of New Deal Liberalism, 1936–1945." Paper presented at the annual meeting of the American Political Science Association, Toronto, ON.

Schlesinger, Arthur. 1973. *The Imperial Presidency*. Boston: Houghton Mifflin.

———. 2004. *War and the American Presidency*. New York: W.W. Norton.

Schwarz, Frederick A. O., and Aziz Huq. 2007. *Unchecked and Unbalanced: Presidential Power in a Time of Terror*. New York: New Press.

Seidman, Joel. 1953. *American Labor from Defense to Reconversion*. Chicago: University of Chicago Press.

Shor, Boris, Nolan McCarty, and Christopher Berry. 2010. "A Bridge to Somewhere: Mapping State and Congressional Ideology on a Cross-Institutional Common Space." *Legislative Studies Quarterly* 35:417–448.

Skowronek, Stephen. 2008. *Presidential Leadership in Political Time: Reprise and Reappraisal*. Lawrence: University Press of Kansas.

———. 2009. "The Conservative Insurgency and Presidential Power: A Developmental Perspective on the Unitary Executive." *Harvard Law Review* 122:2071–2103.

Smith, Daniel. 1965. *The Great Departure*. New York: John Wiley.

Snyder, James M. 1992. "Artificial Extremism in Interest Group Ratings." *Legislative Studies Quarterly* 17:319–345.

Sparrow, Bartholomew H. 1996. *From the Outside In: World War II and the American State*. Princeton, NJ: Princeton University Press.

Sparrow, James. 2011. *Warfare State: World War II Americans and the Age of Big Government*. New York: Oxford University Press.

Staudt, Nancy. 2011. *The Judicial Power of the Purse: How Courts Fund National Defense in Times of Crisis*. Chicago: University of Chicago Press.

Stein, Herbert. 1984. *Presidential Economics: The Making of Economic Policy from Roosevelt to Reagan and Beyond*. New York: Simon & Schuster.

Stiglitz, Joseph, and Linda Bilmes. 2008. *The Three Trillion Dollar War: The True Cost of the Iraq Conflict*. New York: W.W. Norton.

Stimson, James A. 1999. *Public Opinion in America: Moods, Cycles, and Swings*. 2nd ed. Boulder, CO: Westview Press.

Stockdale, James B. 1995. *Thoughts of a Philosophical Fighter Pilot*. Stanford, CA: Hoover Institution Press.

Stone, Geoffrey. 2004. *Perilous Times: Free Speech in Wartime from the Sedition Act of 1798 to the War on Terrorism*. New York: W.W. Norton.

Storing, Herbert. 1981. *The Complete Anti-Federalist*. Chicago: University of Chicago Press.

Sullivan, Mark. 1933. *Our Times: The United States, 1900–1925*. New York: Charles Scribner's Sons.

Tilly, Charles, ed. 1975. *The Formation of National States in Western Europe.* Princeton, NJ: Princeton University Press.

——. 1992. "War in History." *Sociological Forum* 7:187–195.

Tocqueville, Alexis de. 1963 [1840]. *Democracy in America.* 2 vols. New York: Alfred A. Knopf.

Treier, Shawn. 2010. "Where Does the President Stand? Measuring Presidential Ideology." *Political Analysis* 18:124–136.

Truman, Harry S. 1956. *Memoirs.* Vol. 2. New York: Doubleday.

Tulis, Jeffrey. 1988. *The Rhetorical Presidency.* Princeton, NJ: Princeton University Press.

Vanbeek, James. 1991. "Does the Decision to Retire Increase the Amount of Political Shirking?" *Public Finance Review* 19:444–456.

VanDeMark, Brian. 1995. *Into the Quagmire: Lyndon Johnson and the Escalation of the Vietnam War.* New York: Oxford University Press.

Vatter, Harold G. 1985. *The U.S. Economy in World War II.* New York: Columbia University Press.

Vernon, J. R. 1994. "World War II Fiscal Policies and the End of the Great Depression." *Journal of Economic History* 54:850–868.

Volden, Craig, and Alan Wiseman. 2007. "Bargaining in Legislatures over Particularistic and Collective Goods." *American Political Science Review*, 101:79–92.

Wells, Christina. 2004. "Questioning Deference." *Missouri Law Review* 69:904–949.

Wildavsky, Aaron. 1966. "The Two Presidencies." *Trans-Action*, 4:714.

——. 1984. *The Politics of the Budgetary Process.* Boston: Little, Brown.

Wilson, Woodrow. 1901 [1884]. *Congressional Government: A Study in American Politics.* Boston: Houghton Mifflin.

——. 2002 [1908]. *Constitutional Government in the United States.* New Brunswick, NJ: Transaction Publishers.

Wittkopf, Eugene, and James McCormick. 1998. "Congress, the President, and the End of the Cold War." *Journal of Conflict Resolution* 42:440–466.

Wlezien, Christopher. 2005. "On the Salience of Political Issues: The Problem with 'Most Important Problem.'" *Electoral Studies* 24:555–579.

Wooldridge, Jeffrey. 2006. "Cluster-Sample Methods in Applied Econometrics: An Extended Analysis." Technical report, Michigan State University, http://econ .ucsb.edu/~doug/245a/Papers/Cluster Sample Methods in Applied Economet rics.pdf.

Workman, Andrew A. 2000. "Creating the National War Labor Board: Franklin Roosevelt and the Politics of State Building in the Early 1940s." *Journal of Policy History* 12:233–264.

——. 2002. "A Response to Bartholomew Sparrow." *Journal of Policy History* 14:204–213.

Yoo, John. 2010. *Crisis and Command: A History of Executive Power from George Washington to George W. Bush.* New York, NY: Kaplan Publishing.

Zentner, Scot. 1994. "Liberalism and Executive Power: Woodrow Wilson and the American Founders." *Polity* 26:579–599.

INDEX